A Transforming Journey...

From Common Ground to Holy Ground

~~Vicki Renee Bryant~~

"Without Biblical foundations we build our faith on perilous and shifting ground. The man of God must seek to lay the strong foundation of his belief in Jesus Christ on the Cornerstone of His teaching."

~Vicki Renee Bryant~

Email the Author:
hishouse2006@yahoo.com

Visit us on the Web:
www.hishouseowosso.com

A Transforming Journey...
by Vicki Renee Bryant

Printed in the United States of America

ISBN 9781615793761

Unless otherwise indicated, Bible quotations are taken from Life Application Study Bible, New American Standard Bible (NASB). Copyright © 2000 by Zondervan.

www.xulonpress.com

Author Acknowledgements...

T he book you are holding is not the work of one person. It is a collaborative effort and needs to be seen as such. *A Transforming Journey* is no different than my previous books, *For Such a Time as This...* and *About Face!*. My friend and sister in Christ, Esther Dodson, knows better than anyone else the amount of time and intensive labor that goes into each book, for she alone painstakingly edits my manuscripts by correcting my grammar, challenging my statements, and sometimes adding the 'fine touches' I often lack. Esther does this—often while suffering great pain from fibromyalgia—and while still working a full-time job. I dedicate *A Transforming Journey* to her. Words can never express my thankfulness for her attitude of service. This truly is her ministry.

As always, I wish to thank my husband Dan for his patience, support, positive attitude and help during the editing process. It isn't every man who would put up with my very expensive dreams. I thank my son and his family for their support and encouragement, and my parents for 'talking' the books wherever they go. None of us knew a few years ago what God had in store for me—and the twists and turns of my ministry have impacted my family's lives too.

I thank Tammy Randall for her countless volunteer hours at His House. Her reward may not be obvious here, but will surely be great in Heaven. Marta, Linda, Sarah, Cynthia, Debbie and Tammy... thanks to all of you for setting up at speaking engagements and minding the portable store. I could never do it alone—and frankly, I wouldn't even try it without your love and support. Some people are friend-rich, and I am surely one of those people.

Again I thank my Seekers class for their constant hunger for the Word of God and for their encouragement during the difficult journey of writing this book. Your support for Dan and me and for His House is such a blessing to us. Our only prayer is that in some small way we are able to pour into you as you so generously pour into us. To Deborah, Bonnie, Ed and Esther—thank you for your generosity. In a difficult year you have been a constant source of Christ-like love.

Thanks to my old friend Tom, who in God's perfect timing has become my new friend today! Your feedback on the first five entries was so encouraging. The laughter I have shared with former Owosso High School classmates has been good for my soul as I meandered down this path of a lifetime. God's timing in reuniting us has been perfect.

To the Reader: I thank you for taking the time to seek after the Word of God and to pursue a deeper walk with Jesus Christ. Your hunger is my joy! May the love of Christ reign in your hearts today, tomorrow and forever. Let me know how your *Journey* through these pages ends...

In the strong Name of my Lord Jesus,
Vicki Renee Bryant

Cover Photo: Alisa Slingerland
　　Images Forever Studio, Owosso, Michigan
Back Cover Photo: Alisa Slingerland

About this Transforming Journey...

†

On January 1, 2009, I awakened to a voice in my ears saying, *"From Common Ground to Holy Ground this year, Vicki."* I had no idea of the meaning of the words, but wrote them on a pad next to my office chair where I spend hours each morning poring over Scripture and preparing lessons. The phrase kept playing in my mind as I sought God's direction for the words' meaning. Those of you who have read my other books know this isn't the first time I heard a direct word from God. During prayer on that first crisp morning of the New Year, I asked the Lord to show me clearly what He was calling me to do.

Knowing the headstrong child He was talking to, the Lord revealed His plans in acceptable bits. First step: Change the teaching at my Seekers class from Acts to Exodus. I did so and then He urged me to keep teaching from there to the end of the book of Joshua. The Seekers were receptive—and I believe it is some of the best Bible study and application we have shared. God then told me to teach the same passages on my weekly television programming... again changing the Scripture portions I had already been using. We began to receive great feedback on the teaching from many people we had never met before. The *Common Ground to Holy Ground* challenge was next added to my public speaking appearances and was well received.

As God worked on me, I began to realize the original call was *"From Common Ground to Holy Ground this year, Vicki."* The call was to me, not just to those I would teach or speak to. My third book was nearly half finished when God showed me to stop working on it and write the devotional you now hold in your hands. This

vii

book, unlike my first devotional—*For Such a Time as This...*, is designed to be used in conjunction with a Bible. Little did I know the *Journey* would be as painful and transforming for me as it has been. He began to reveal that it was time for me to get the 'tabernacle' in shape—thus a thirty pound weight loss. Next He worked on my biting tongue and judgmental spirit—an ongoing process because the habits of a lifetime are difficult to change. Pride was next—and a failing Christian bookstore in a bad Michigan economy humbles even the hardest among us. He taught me that being kind is more important than being right and that having the last word is prideful, not Christ-like.

God took me to the woodshed as I poured my heart into these passages. I have been shaken, sifted, pruned, clipped, tried, tested and reshaped by the Potter. Did I like the process? Of course I didn't. Will you like the same process? I doubt it—but I believe that if you will stay the course and get yourself familiar with using the Bible in conjunction with this study, you too will come out stronger on the other end of the *Journey*. I pray these devotions will be as life-changing for you as they have been for me. You must be willing to be *Transformed* into the image of Jesus Christ. You will get out of this study equal to what you invest in it. You must hunger to learn how to climb from the *Common Ground* of this life to *Holy Ground* where you can truly feel the Presence of God.

As always, I would love to have your feedback on the entries. I have included the Steps to Salvation section in the back of the book for you to use personally, or as a witnessing tool. God bless you as you take the first step in this *Transforming Journey*.

Visit us on the WEB: www.hishouseowosso.com
Email the Author: hishouse2006@yahoo.com
For Public Speaking Events: (989) 723-8977

The Editor Says: I count it a privilege to have helped Vicki complete this book. I marvel at her passion for Biblical history and her ability to show how it is so very applicable to us today. Please study it *intently* to <u>hear</u> what God will say to you through it. He definitely spoke to me.

➤ Day 1: WALKING INTO BONDAGE
PASSAGE: **Exodus 1:1-7**
VERSE: **Exodus 1:1**

Now these are the names of the sons of Israel who came to Egypt with Jacob; they came each one with his household.

As we begin our year long journey out of bondage and into God's promised land of freedom and deliverance, we must first look at how we arrived in our position of bondage in the first place. The Hebrew people walked into Egypt willingly, happily, and without force. They were hungry; the food was there and the doors were opened wide for them to enter. Joseph, the beloved son of Jacob, was miraculously entrusted with great authority in this foreign land. Everything he did seemed to prosper, and Pharaoh—the King of Egypt—welcomed Joseph's family with open arms. After years of separation from his father (because of the betrayal of his older brothers), Joseph wanted his family near him so he could protect and provide for them. Nothing seemed contrary to the will of God; after all, He didn't stop Jacob's family from going into the land of Pharaoh. For many, many years all went well. Joseph forgave his brothers, everyone had plenty to eat during a time of terrible famine, and Pharaoh donated the land of Goshen for them to live in and graze their flocks. Maybe if they had remembered God's words to Abraham, *"Know for certain that your descendants will be strangers in a land that is not theirs, where they will be enslaved and oppressed four hundred years"* (Genesis 15:13), they wouldn't have so willingly gone. But then again, maybe they—like us—would have walked into bondage anyway.

COMMON GROUND: We have all heard that the grass is greener everywhere but where we live. In our flesh we are looking for the best and the easiest way to live our lives and provide for our loved ones. Neither Joseph nor Jacob could be faulted for wanting to be together and wanting to be where the abundance was. The problem was that they needed to seek God's hand, not follow flesh lusts.

9

HOLY GROUND: Before we jump into change or things which look too good to be true, we need to look closely and weigh all options against the Word of God. Things that look great to our eyes may be but illusions set before us by the enemy. God will never lead us into places where He will not be with us.

Father God, Help me to always seek to walk, stop, rest and lie down in places You lead me to. The enemy is seeking to direct my paths into ungodly territory where suffering and bondage await me. Please direct me to Your perfect places. Amen.

➤ Day 2: BONDAGE AND BLESSINGS
PASSAGE: **Exodus 1:8-14**
VERSE: **Exodus 1:12**

But the more they afflicted them, the more they multiplied and the more they spread out, so that they were in dread of the sons of Israel.

Everything was good for Jacob and his family until the new Pharaoh, who didn't know Joseph, was worried about the growing number of Hebrews in the land of Goshen. Jacob's initial seventy sojourners were now in great number and Pharaoh feared that they might ally themselves with his enemies and bring defeat upon his nation. The process of enslaving the Hebrews was probably slow and gradual... you know, so they didn't realize they were in bondage until it was too late to regain their freedom. Pharaoh appointed 'managers' over them who soon became taskmasters. The people God chose as His own were soon slaves in an enemy nation... just as He had spoken to Abraham hundreds and hundreds of years before. The enslaved people must have tried to remember when everything changed and likely blamed everyone but themselves for willingly walking into a bondage they could not escape from. God was still in control; and the more Pharaoh abused them... the more they multiplied and grew in number. Their number alone caused Pharaoh great fear and made him seek ways to stop their growth.

COMMON GROUND: Israel went from freedom to bondage without realizing what was happening. Bondage sneaks up on us and takes us by surprise. What starts as a 'few drinks' becomes an alcohol addiction. What starts as a 'glimpse at a girlie magazine' becomes a pornography addiction. Once Satan has us captured he is the one in control; the harder we fight, the tighter he holds on. **HOLY GROUND:** Walking in holiness and full fellowship with God helps us to escape the subtle snares of the Devil. If we don't take the first sip, we cannot get addicted. If we turn away after the first glimpse—and rebuke the fleshly lust—we will not become enslaved to sexual addictions. Watch your step!

Lord, I need you to keep me ever mindful that the enemy of my soul seeks to capture my body, mind and spirit and he will use my weakness to do just that. I cast off all forms of bondage... except for the bondage of devotion in my heart for You. Amen.

➤ Day 3: GOD-FEARING MIDWIVES
PASSAGE: **Exodus 1:15-22**
VERSE: **Exodus 1:17**

But the midwives feared God, and did not do as the king of Egypt had commanded them, but let the boys live.

Pharaoh had finally figured out how to stop the population explosion of the Hebrews. He commanded their midwives to kill all males at birth as they helped to deliver them. The midwives feared God and refused to commit these murders. When Pharaoh found that the male population continued to flourish he questioned the midwives, Shiphrah and Puah. They told him that Hebrew women were stronger than Egyptian ones, and that by the time the midwives answered the birthing calls the babies were already delivered! How funny is God? We will see time and again how He works in ways we would never imagine. Pharaoh commanded the Hebrew people to drown their male sons in the Nile River. Yeah, right! God showed favor to the obedient midwives and provided houses for them… and the Hebrews just kept on multiplying.

COMMON GROUND: Fear can make us do things we wouldn't normally think to do. The midwives could have obeyed Pharaoh's outrageous command, or they could entrust their lives and the lives of the Hebrew boys into God's hands. Common ground responses usually side with the world around us. **HOLY GROUND:** Obedience to God's ways in the face of personal peril is the right response. Let no man cause you to make immoral or ungodly decisions in the name of political correctness. The midwives would have murdered babies made in the very image of God. They chose life… and risked death! God rewarded faithfulness.

Father, I am often faced with choices and wrong decisions that could take me out of Your will. Help me to always weigh every decision against Your Word and to always remember that every child ever created was created in Your image and by Your hand. Amen.

➤ Day 4: A MOTHER'S DEEP FAITH
PASSAGE: **Exodus 2:1-4**
VERSE: **Exodus 2:3**

But when she could hide him no longer, she got him a wicker basket and covered it over with tar and pitch. Then she put the child into it and set it among the reeds by the bank of the Nile.

Knowing full well what the command of Pharaoh was, the Hebrew women continued to have children; after all, that is what God designed their bodies to do. A woman from the tribe of Levi gave birth to a healthy and beautiful son and hid him for three months from the prowling eyes of Pharaoh and his officers. Finally, when she could hide him no longer she made the most difficult decision a mother could make. She didn't drown him in the Nile, but she did make a bulrush basket, coat it with pitch inside and out, and then place her precious son within. She sent the basket down the river, hoping against hope that God would spare his life. Her daughter followed the basket on its journey so she could tell her mother what happened. That day a Levite mother entrusted her most prized possession—given to her by God—back into His hands. All she could do was pray for His mercy.

COMMON GROUND: What would you do in this situation? Many of us would continue to hide the child and live in fear every day that he would be discovered and killed. Terror would become our bondage and we would never be able to enjoy our days. **HOLY GROUND:** Sometimes God requires us to take our hands off that which we love the most and entrust it into His very capable hands. When we acknowledge that all gifts are from Him, all abilities are from Him, and the future belongs to Him, we really have no other choice but to trust Him with our loved ones.

Jesus, Letting go and letting You take control of my life and the lives of my loved ones is one of my hardest battles. Help me to remember that You gave these treasured gifts to me in the first place. Pry my fingers back and make me let go of anyone or anything I hold dearer than I do my faith in You. Amen.

➤ Day 5: ONLY GOD COULD PLAN THIS!
PASSAGE: **Exodus 2:5-10**
VERSE: **Exodus 2:7-8**

Then his sister said to Pharaoh's daughter, "Shall I go and call a nurse for you from the Hebrew women that she may nurse the child for you?" Pharaoh's daughter said to her, "Go ahead." So the girl went and called the child's mother.

I couldn't wait to write this entry. It should prove to all of you that God has a great sense of humor and loves to thumb His nose at those who deny Him or try to harm His children. As the baby floated in the basket, the daughter of Pharaoh heard the cries of the child and gathered the basket to her. Knowing full well this was a male Hebrew child and that her father had ordered the death of babies like him, she took him as her own. God orchestrated things so His chosen deliverer would live under the very roof of the one the Hebrews needed to be delivered from! Top that off with the fact that He provided Moses' birth mother to serve as his wet-nurse—and get paid to nurse her own son—and you have a perfect picture of His provision and protection for those He calls His own. After the baby was weaned his mother entrusted her beloved son into the hands of his adopted mother and learned to love him from afar.

COMMON GROUND: A natural reaction to having your child raised in a stranger's home—especially an enemy stranger—would likely be anger and resentment toward God for taking him from you in the first place. Most of us would throw a giant pity party and tell others of how unfaithful He was. **HOLY GROUND:** A God-centered response would be thankfulness that the child would not be a slave, would not live in poverty, and would be given great advantages. Our first thought should be for the best for our child; our second thought should be to praise God for every minute we held him, loved him and prayed over him.

Spirit of God, I confess that my selfish inclinations would make me resentful if the story above were my own. I would look at my loss and not my child's gain. Help me to trust that everything does indeed work together for the good of those who love You and are called according to Your purpose. Amen.

➤ Day 6: MOSES KNOWS WHO HE IS
PASSAGE: **Exodus 2:11-12**
VERSE: **Exodus 2:11**

Now it came about in those days, when Moses had grown up,
that he went out to his brethren and looked on their hard labors;
and he saw an Egyptian beating a Hebrew, one of his brethren.

Moses may have been raised in the palace of Pharaoh, but he knew exactly who he was. In the passage for today's entry Moses had come out among the laborers to see how they were being treated. He saw their suffering and their hard labor at the hands of his adopted grandfather and was likely trying to figure out a way to alleviate some of their burden. I doubt that this was the first time Moses had visited his Hebrew brothers. He likely had also kept in touch with the family God birthed him into; since we will see later that he had a relationship with his brother Aaron and his sister Miriam. Moses was a man torn between two peoples, but when he saw an Egyptian abusing one of his Hebrew brethren, his anger surged and he killed the Egyptian. Moses thought his deed had been hidden — that he has literally gotten away with murder. We are being given a glimpse here of a man who will one day be a great leader, but who also had a character flaw with his irrational anger.

COMMON GROUND: Our rash and impulsive behaviors can get us into a lot of trouble. When we fail to look at the consequences for our decisions we are walking headlong into future problems. No sin is really hidden anyway. Man may not see our actions, but God sees everything and He is the one we ultimately answer to. **HOLY GROUND:** Pausing to seek God's will before we act can save dealing with negative repercussions later. People who are intent on walking in God's presence must have the patience to think before they speak or act. We cannot take back unkind words or actions. They leave scars... scars on the hands and feet of our sweet Jesus.

Father God, I certainly need help in controlling my mouth and my hands from doing that which is contrary to what You call me to do. I know that You see all things and are very ashamed of some of what You have seen recently. Lord, I need Your mercy. Amen.

➤ Day 7: WHO DIED AND MADE YOU GOD?
PASSAGE: **Exodus 2:13-15**
VERSE: **Exodus 2:14**

But he said, "Who made you a prince or a judge over us? Are you intending to kill me as you killed the Egyptian?" Then Moses was afraid and said, "Surely the matter has become known."

Moses thought yesterday's murder was covered up, so he again went to walk among the Hebrew people. He saw two of them fighting and challenged their actions. The instigator of the fight looked in derision at Moses and asked him why he was trying to lord his authority over them. This man's reaction is easy to understand. He was a slave building cities for a king he despised. Moses had been pampered and sheltered in the palace of Pharaoh. His question struck a nerve when he asked Moses if he was going to kill him like he did the Egyptian the day before. Moses was devastated. He knew what was coming. No Hebrew dared to lay hands on an Egyptian... and no matter what; he was still a Hebrew in the eyes of Pharaoh. Regret about his actions settled in like an iron weight upon him. Moses knew that he must flee Egypt if he wanted to save his life. That meant leaving his home, his two families, and all else he held dear. The man who had never really fit into either of his lives was about to be excommunicated from both.

COMMON GROUND: Jealousy over the success of others can be a cancer which plagues us. I find it funny that we aren't jealous of Hollywood celebrities (or at least I'm not), but we are envious of others who have great talents/gifts, beauty, success or money. When we are jealous of what others have we can never be satisfied with what we have been blessed with. Our jealousy often comes out in the form of snide remarks like the Hebrew spoke to Moses. **HOLY GROUND:** Are you satisfied with what you have right at this moment? God tells us to give thanks in everything. The Bible says when I am grateful with little I will be blessed with more. Holy living requires us to keep our eyes at home, our hands to ourselves, and our thoughts centered on God's provision. If we were given all we are envious of... we still wouldn't be satisfied for *the eyes of a fool are never satisfied.*

Lord, How easy it is for me to be envious and jealous, and how hard it is to be grateful for that which You have given me. It must break Your heart when You give me enough and I want more. Today I will be more aware of my envy and will begin to rebuff it. Amen.

➤ Day 8: A NEW HOME AND A WIFE FOR MOSES
PASSAGE: Exodus 2:16-22
VERSE: Exodus 2:21-22

Moses was willing to dwell with the man, and he gave his daughter Zipporah to Moses. Then she gave birth to a son, and he named him Gershom, for he said, "I have been a sojourner in a foreign land."

Moses eventually settled in the land of Midian, a nation established by the descendants of Abraham. The priest of Midian was Reuel (Jethro) and he had seven daughters. These daughters had come to draw water at the public well in order to water their father's flocks. Area shepherds came and chased the girls away. Moses drove the shepherds off and helped Jethro's daughters get their water. When they told their father what had happened, he asked why they didn't bring the kind stranger home to meet him. After Moses was found and brought to Jethro's home, he felt welcome there and decided to make his home in Midian. Zipporah, the daughter of the priest, was given to Moses as his wife and bore him a son, Gershom. Moses was finally in a place where God could get his attention and show him the mission He had for him. Moses wouldn't have willingly moved to Midian, but God moved him to achieve His perfect purpose for Moses' life.

COMMON GROUND: Most of us like living in the status quo. We like to know what each day holds, where we will lay our heads at night, and how our needs will be met. I often ask people if they would be obedient if God told them to sell all they own and go into the mission field in a third-world country. In most cases the answer is an emphatic "No!" **HOLY GROUND:** Do you trust God to move you, direct your paths, and provide for your needs? Isn't that what faith is all about? Our response to His prodding and nudging will determine what He will do with our lives. Do you really believe what you say you believe? If so; you will allow Him to be Lord of your life and to move you to places where you can be used to fulfill His plans for you.

Father, Change often holds fear for me. I realize now that I will never understand how much You want to bless me if I never step out in faith and allow You to direct my paths. Making You Lord is going to be a new step for me. Thank You for patience. Amen.

➤ Day 9: CRIES OF PAIN AND PERSECUTION
PASSAGE: Exodus 2:23-25
VERSE: Exodus 2:23

Now it came about in the course of those many days that the king of Egypt died. And the sons of Israel sighed because of the bondage, and they cried out; and their cry for help because of their bondage rose up to God.

While Moses was being groomed for his encounter with God, the Hebrew people were still being mistreated and held in painful bondage. They cried out to God... and God heard their cries from Heaven. If we look back at the first entry and realize that God forewarned Abraham that his descendants would walk willingly into this bondage, we could lose compassion for them, but God never did. As the cries pulsed in His ears and as He looked down upon their suffering, His thoughts returned to a covenant promise He made approximately nine hundred years before to His friend Abraham. God's heart quickened as He realized that the time had come to liberate His children. He looked upon Abraham's descendants who believed He had abandoned them and began an amazing plan to bring them deliverance and freedom. God indeed heard their cries... and that should be a great comfort to all of us who call Him our Lord.

COMMON GROUND: How often have you cried out to God in prayer for an end to your suffering, only to be convinced that for some reason He is not hearing your voice? The pain, the financial hardship, and the family problems never stop; and the God you put your trust in has let you down. Your heart becomes hard and slowly you begin to walk away from faith in Him. **HOLY GROUND:** Are you a fair-weather prayer warrior? We are called to *pray without ceasing*. The Hebrews prayed for four-hundred years... and you think you have it bad! God answers prayers more than one way. I have heard there are 'Yes' answers, 'No' answers, and 'Not at this Time' answers. Have you ever wondered if God is testing your 'stick-to-it-iveness' quotient? Pray and trust on your journey to personal holiness this year.

Jesus, Patience is not one of my strong points. I want an answer;
I want it to be 'Yes' and I want it to be now. I must learn
that all things work together in Your time, not mine.
Lord, give me patience... and hurry! Amen.

➤ ## Day 10: OFF THE WELL-WORN PATH
PASSAGE: Exodus 3:1-3
VERSE: Exodus 3:3

*So Moses said, "I must turn aside now and see this
marvelous sight, why the bush is not burned up."*

Moses was just minding his own business and enjoying the quiet of the day with Jethro's flock when God grabbed his attention by displaying a miracle before his eyes. God wanted to talk to Moses and wanted him to step off the common path... the path of the sheep and their shepherds where everyone walked. He wanted Moses to take the road less traveled and to step out to see why the bush burned brightly but was not consumed by the fire. Moses had to make a decision... continue with his plans; or walk out of his way in order to see what God was doing. He had no idea that what he was seeing was a manifestation of God. All he knew was that his curiosity had to be satisfied—even if he had to climb over a few rocks, avoid a few brambles, and step into unfamiliar territory. God put the bush off at a distance to see how committed Moses would be to exploring new things. Why? God was going to send him into many other unfamiliar territories in the years to come.

COMMON GROUND: Are you too busy to step out of the grind of your everyday life and explore unfamiliar territory with God? Are your days so regimented that even the slightest interruption is a major inconvenience? Moses had to make a decision to walk off the path; and his willingness was rewarded. **HOLY GROUND:** Moses had no idea this was God's way of getting his attention. All he knew was that something 'different' was happening before his eyes, and that if he put forth some extra effort he could add a little spice to his life. God is waiting to show you amazing things, things you cannot even imagine, but first you need to step up, step out and step into His realm.

Spirit of God, I'd like to think I would leave the path, but I also confess that sometimes I am too busy to step aside and see what You are up to. Lord, give me a spirit of curiosity and adventure so I can run with You. Amen.

➤ Day 11: STANDING ON HOLY GROUND
PASSAGE: **Exodus 3:4-6**
VERSE: **Exodus 3:5**

Then He said, "Do not come near here; remove your sandals from your feet, for the place on which you are standing is holy ground."

God was watching Moses to see how he handled the burning bush. The moment he stepped off the well-worn path and began to approach the flames God spoke to him from within the fire. *"Moses. Moses,"* called God. *And he said, "Here I am."* Don't you find it strange that Moses didn't flee in fear when the voice boomed from the bush? Moses knew something wonderful was about to happen... and he didn't want to miss a single minute. God addressed Moses with the verse for this entry and the wandering shepherd without a home found his home on the holy ground of God. Moses' dirty sandals couldn't walk there. No, they had walked far too long on common ground. They had walked in anger, in sin, in hopelessness and in defeat. God wasn't willing to share His ground with those things. He then answered the unspoken questions of Moses' heart by telling him that He was the God of his forefathers. In reverence and fear Moses buried his face to shield his 'common' eyes from looking upon the holiness before him.

COMMON GROUND: God watched for Moses' reaction and then spoke directly to his heart. How long has it been since you stood on holy ground and heard the voice of God? As a believer, are you spending more time on common ground or holy ground? Common things deaden us to the wonder of holy things. We cannot walk automatically from one to the other. **HOLY GROUND:** Our God is everywhere... and so are sin, filth and evil. Only when we walk fully in the power and presence of the Lord will we be able to spend more time on holy ground than common ground. How is that done? Committed prayer, dedication to the application of His Word in our lives, and closing the doors of our hearts to the common things around us. Holy ground walking requires change; are you ready to take your sandals off?

Father God, Holy Ground sounds both wonderful and frightening to me. How can I ever be worthy to stand in Your presence like Moses did? The common has blinded and deafened me to Your truths. Today, I take off my sandals and walk with You. Amen.

➤ Day 12: I HEAR THEIR CRIES
PASSAGE: Exodus 3:7-9
VERSE: Exodus 3:7

The LORD said, "I have surely seen the affliction of My people who are in Egypt, and have given heed to their cry because of their taskmasters, for I am aware of their sufferings."

As we begin today's journey, we need to remember that Moses had witnessed the bondage of his people and tried to help them. He must have been reassured to hear God say that He heard their cries, saw their affliction and knew their sorrows. Imagine how relieved he was to hear that God had a plan to deliver them out of Egypt and to bring them into the land He had promised their ancestors... a land without bondage and hardship. Moses has seen so much in his lifetime. He knew that he was spared by God from certain death and was instead raised in the home of the King of Egypt. He knew he was blessed to find a home and family with Jethro. He had been given the opportunity to walk off the well-worn path and hear God talk to him from the bush. Moses had seen it all; and now he was being promised by his God that He would deliver

His people from bondage. With a grateful heart Moses praised his Lord and waited for Him to reveal His great plans.

COMMON GROUND: Moses was very grateful to hear that God heard the cries of his brethren. That assured him that God heard his own cries and cared about his personal needs. One common ground response might have been for Moses to ask God why He had let the people suffer so long. That doesn't sound like love, and many of us spend our days challenging God's ways. **HOLY GROUND:** Moses instead listened and was encouraged. He knew that he had clear examples of God's past faithfulness in his own story. Moses sat there at the bush, on holy ground, and waited with expectation to see God's amazing plan unfold. Holy ground walkers are willing to *be still and know He is God.*

> *Lord, Your ways are amazing to me; but they are sometimes difficult for my small human brain to process. Your promise to free the Hebrews from their bondage brings me great hope. Your hearing my cries and knowing my needs is a wonderful source of encouragement in my personal faith walk. Amen.*

➤ Day 13: I AM SENDING YOU!
PASSAGE: **Exodus 3:10-12**
VERSE: **Exodus 3:10**

"Therefore, come now, and I will send you to Pharaoh, so that you may bring My people, the sons of Israel, out of Egypt."

"Hey, wait just a minute here, God! You said You were going to bring them out. You never asked me if I was willing to be a part of this mission. This is too big of a challenge for me, God... and You really need to think about this some more!" Isn't it ironic that Moses was happy to have God deliver the Hebrews from bondage until effort was required on his part? Moses was likely ready to run back to common ground and forget the whole holy ground experience.

Moses probably figured he could negotiate the deal by reminding God that the leaders in Egypt wanted him dead for killing one of their citizens. God listened to him ramble on, and then gave him a prophetic word. *"Certainly I will be with you, and this shall be the sign to you that it is I who have sent you: when you have brought the people out of Egypt, you shall worship God at this mountain."* What did that mean? How could Moses worship God on Sinai again if Pharaoh killed him? Once again, Moses needs to make a decision… one which will influence his life from that day forward.

COMMON GROUND: This one scares you, doesn't it? What would your response be to this call on your life? Commoners like to serve God in their way and in the place <u>they</u> <u>think</u> they can do the most for Him. They want to show God how awesome they are and how grateful He should be for their service and faith. **HOLY GROUND:** Moses can oppose God—and be dragged kicking and screaming into service—or he can put his money where his mouth is and say, like the Prophet Isaiah, *"Here I am. Send me!"* I write these words from personal experience. When I was told to open our Christian bookstore I could have said I was too busy. When I was told to write *"For Such a Time as This…"* I could have said I hated to type. When the hundredth person asked me to write another devotional, I could have said I would run out of ideas. Instead, I did the *'send me'* thing… and look what you are reading!

Father, Your ways are perfect and are much higher than mine are.
Your plans take me down roads I never wanted to travel upon.
You have never, ever, ever let me down when I have been obedient.
Teach me to have a willing heart and a teachable spirit. Amen.

➤ Day 14: BECAUSE 'I AM' GOD
PASSAGE: **Exodus 3:13-15**
VERSE: **Exodus 3:13-14**

Then Moses said to God, "Behold, I am going to the sons of Israel, and I will say to them, 'The God of your fathers has sent me to you.' Now they may say to me, 'What is His name?' What shall I say to them?" God said to Moses, "I AM WHO I AM"; and He said, "Thus you shall say to the sons of Israel, 'I AM has sent me to you.'"

Moses was still trying to wiggle out of the mission God had set before him. He then brought a different argument forward. How could he go to the Hebrew slaves and tell them that their God had talked to him and sent him to them? Even more importantly, how could he answer their question if they wanted verification of exactly whose voice Moses had been hearing? They would never believe him; after all, they had been in bondage for four-hundred years! God, as usual, has a quick response. *"Tell them 'I AM' sent you, Moses."* What kind of answer was that? Moses didn't understand that God was telling him that since time began HE IS; in the current time HE IS; and forever and ever HE IS. God was, is, and always will be. He is *the same yesterday, today and forever.* "Moses, tell them I AM the God of their fathers Abraham, Isaac and Jacob, and I AM their God today. Now go. I AM sending you on a big adventure."

COMMON GROUND: How many times have people rejected your witness or your descriptions of God's past faithfulness? How did you react to their rejection? God sends us on these missions in spite of our doubts and fears. He wants to prove to us who He is, compared to everyone else in the world. Our wimpy attitudes don't change His plans. **HOLY GROUND:** Moses is thinking ahead of all the possible obstacles that might trip him up. That isn't wrong thinking if you still proceed in spite of the obstacles. Asking the hard questions pre-armed Moses with the answers for a later day and time. God will answer our questions if we are willing and obedient to His call on our lives.

Jesus, I toss and turn, doubt and fear, fill myself with anxiety, and allow it to paralyze me and make me ineffective in Your plans. It would seem sometimes that I have no faith at all! I know from Moses' story that You will always provide all I need for the ministries You send me into. Amen.

➤ Day 15: GATHER THE ELDERS
PASSAGE: **Exodus 3:16-18**
VERSE: **Exodus 3:16**

"Go and gather the elders of Israel together and say to them, 'The LORD, the God of your fathers, the God of Abraham, Isaac and Jacob, has appeared to me, saying, "I am indeed concerned about you and what has been done to you in Egypt."'"

Things were happening too fast for Moses. God was sending him back to Egypt (where people want him dead) to gather elders (who have no respect for him) and tell them that their God has heard their cries (yeah, right!). Moses was to give them God's promise that He had heard their cries and was going to liberate them from their bondage. Moses was to tell them God would send them into the land promised to their ancestor Abraham. Moses had some of his doubts silenced when God assured him that the elders of Israel would listen to his words and they would join him in confronting Pharaoh to talk to him. They were to tell the King that their God told them to go three days' journey into the desert to sacrifice to Him. It seemed that God had all the bases covered. He had the plan, had His man, and had enlisted the reinforcements. Moses was getting a little more receptive to what he was being told to do. But was God sure the elders would listen to him... and what about Pharaoh?

COMMON GROUND: Even when God begins to bring a plan's details together, we can allow our flesh to question the wisdom of following blindly after Him. Personal example: God gave me the vision for our store, provided the building, provided the fixtures, provided money for inventory, and provided volunteers to work when I couldn't. All was going well until I started to panic and cry! I doubted Him even after all He had already done... until a wise friend told me to 'grow up' and put some muscle behind my faith talk. **HOLY GROUND:** There is no doubt that having others to help us with a big project is a source of encouragement. Many hands do indeed make light work. However, those who want to walk fully in their faith must learn to step out without partners and co-workers. They must trust God alone to walk with them as they venture out on that Holy Ground journey.

Spirit of God, I confess that I tend to lean on others and trust in their help more than I do You. Every time I do that I cheapen what I call my faith. Help me to step boldly out and watch You work in, around and through my feeble hands. Amen.

➤ Day **16**: A CAPTURED SPOIL
PASSAGE: **Exodus 3:19-22**
VERSE: **Exodus 3:21**

"I will grant this people favor in the sight of the Egyptians; and it shall be that when you go, you will not go empty-handed."

Remember God's prophetic words to Abraham about the bondage his heirs would face for four-hundred years, as explained in a previous entry? Today we explore the second part of that prophecy which said, *"...and afterward shall they come out with great substance."* (Genesis 15:14 KJV). God, who witnessed His people being mistreated, was going to see to it that they were repaid for their suffering and would not leave Egypt empty handed. In order to provide for the needs of His children, God would cause the Egyptians to feel compassion or sympathy for them and to shower them with gold, silver, rich fabrics and gemstones. Later, these same 'spoiled' items would be used to create the furnishings, utensils, and priestly garments for His tabernacle. If you look ahead to Exodus 12:36 you will see that what God promised, He did. The Hebrews left the land of their bondage with great wealth because the Egyptians were 'very generous' with their possessions. God is so funny! He would spoil the taskmasters of His people and use the wealth to build a tabernacle where Israel could meet with Him in worship.

COMMON GROUND: Promises are cheap. In a world where vows are made and easily broken, where marriages are cast aside when they become uncomfortable, and where faith commitments fall by the wayside when the world starts to call… most of us take promises with a grain of salt. The common ground response to a promise is to assume it will be broken. **HOLY GROUND:** Man may break his promises, but *God is not a man that He should lie.* That means His promises will be kept, His word is true and He will never leave or forsake us like men will. When God told Abraham that his heirs would spoil their captors—it happened. When He tells you He will provide for your needs—it will happen. Choose to believe Him as you seek to walk in holiness.

Father God, I have been let down by many people and find it difficult to trust. If I take a little faith step into the trust area, please meet me there. I long to walk on holy ground, but must learn to stop doubting that Your promises are true. Amen.

➤ Day 17: SNAKES 'N' STAFFS
PASSAGE: **Exodus 4:1-9**
VERSE: **Exodus 4:3-4**

Then He said, "Throw it on the ground." So he threw it on the ground, and it became a serpent; and Moses fled from it. But the LORD said to Moses, "Stretch out your hand and grasp it by its tail." So he stretched out his hand and caught it, and it became a staff in his hand...

28

Moses was still having doubts about facing the Hebrew people and convincing them that He really had spoken with God. God was about to show Moses that this was no ordinary mission. God asked Moses a simple question, *"What is that in your hand?"* Moses looked down and remembered the common shepherd's staff he held clutched in his fist and wondered where God was going with this conversation. God told Moses to cast it down; then the staff became a serpent, which scared the daylights out of an already reluctant Moses. (Remember that 'enmity between the serpent and the seed of the woman' thing from the Garden of Eden!) Moses ran away from the snake, but God told him to reach out and pick it up by the tail. "What? Don't make me do that, God. I am afraid of snakes, especially snaky staffs! Please don't make me touch it!" God insists, Moses obeys, and the serpent becomes a staff again. "Hey, that was cool. Got any more neat tricks, God?" Moses asked. He was then directed to stick his hand in his tunic and the clean-fleshed hand came back out covered with leprosy. When Moses looked at it in horror, God told him to put it back in again and it came out with the flesh restored. Moses' confidence was growing. "Maybe I can do this," he thought. "Surely they will believe me when they see the snaky-staff trick and the leprosy thing. I mean, how could they doubt that God gave me these abilities?"

COMMON GROUND: Do you depend on miracles and signs to show people that you have been given directions by God? Are you someone who doesn't believe that God still works in miracles? Both are common reactions to inherent doubt about who God is. Satan loves to sow seeds of doubt in our hearts to cause us not to believe until we see amazing manifestations. **HOLY GROUND:** *Faith is the substance of things hoped for, the evidence of things not seen.* Walking with God in faith means that you believe in Him without seeing tricks. God still works in miracles, but He wants you to trust Him without them. *Without faith it is impossible to please God.* Sobering thought, isn't it?

Lord, I would love to have miracles like these to prove to people that I am walking in Your presence and doing Your bidding.

I understand from this entry that it is my testimony, not my tricks which will change hearts. May my telling what You have done in my life be enough of a 'miracle' for my witness to be heard. Amen.

➤ Day **18**: TONGUE-TIED
PASSAGE: **Exodus 4:10-11**
VERSE: **Exodus 4:10**

Then Moses said to the LORD, "Please, Lord, I have never been eloquent, neither recently nor in time past, nor since You have spoken to Your servant; for I am slow of speech and slow of tongue."

God certainly didn't pick a 'yes-man' when He chose Moses! Even after the miracles to show the people, and after God's words to reassure them, Moses was still trying to finagle his way out of going where God was sending him. Plan B included telling God how un-eloquent he was. After all, God wouldn't want to send a spokesperson who couldn't speak! He wouldn't want an incompetent, tongue-tied or stuttering deliverer for His people! Moses thought he was playing the big trump card until God responded to his flimsy excuses. *"Who has made man's mouth? Or who makes him mute or deaf, or seeing or blind? Is it not I, the LORD?"* Hey Moses, how do you respond to that one? "I am God. I made your mouth. I gave you words and speech. I know what you are capable of; and that is why you will go on this mission for Me!" I think God definitely won that round!

COMMON GROUND: Moses was playing the same game many of us play: "HERE I AM, SEND SOMEONE ELSE," and God was not amused. He isn't amused when you do it either. I guess passing the buck is common; after all, it started way back in the Garden of Eden. That does not make it right. Are you always looking for someone else to pass the mission off on? **HOLY GROUND:** Let me give you a bit of advice here. If He tells you to do it—do it. If

He tells you to go—go! If He tells you to speak—speak! Guess what happens when you walk in that kind of obedience? You will do, go and speak in ways and places you would never have imagined. He will always provide abundantly for those who are willing.

Father, You have given me clear missions in the past which I have ignored or passed on to others. I make every possible excuse because of fear... and laziness. Father, I don't want others to always have the blessing experiences... make me willing. Amen.

➤ Day 19: PROVOKING GOD
PASSAGE: Exodus 4:12-17
VERSE: Exodus 4:14

Then the anger of the LORD burned against Moses, and He said, "Is there not your brother Aaron the Levite? I know that he speaks fluently. And moreover, behold, he is coming out to meet you; when he sees you, he will be glad in his heart."

Making God mad isn't the smartest thing to do—especially when He causes bushes to erupt in spontaneous combustion! Moses was digging himself into a hole and needed to realize to whom he was talking. God understood the doubts and fears of the man He had selected to deliver His people. He had been with Moses as he struggled to find his identity and as he wandered as an alien far from his home. God understood because He knew the heart of the man He had chosen for this mission. Instead of punishing Moses for his doubts, God provided a companion—a sidekick—for him. Moses had to have felt a great relief when God spoke these words to him. *"You are to speak to him and put the words in his mouth; and I, even I, will be with your mouth and his mouth, and I will teach you what you are to do. Moreover, he shall speak for you to the people; and he will be as a mouth for you and you will be as God to him. You shall take in your hand this staff, with which you shall perform the signs."* God's plan for delivering the Hebrews was daunting and difficult. Moses could have done it with the help of God alone, but God cared enough about him to allow the burden to be shared. Aaron would speak whatever God said to Moses... as if the words were actually coming out of Moses' mouth. Then God painted a little prophetic picture by telling Moses that he *would use* the staff to perform signs in order to convince everyone that he indeed was sent on God's mission.

COMMON GROUND: In most cases doing work along with someone else is easier and more fun. The only problem with that is finding someone who is willing to help do the dirty jobs! Are you only willing to do kingdom work if God provides you with a side-kick or assistant? Maybe His plan is for you to step out and walk with Him alone. **HOLY GROUND:** Truly dedicated people will step up and step out, no matter how difficult the task seems. Moses risked God's wrath when he argued with Him because he could only see his own weaknesses and not his strengths. God already knows everything about us... and amazingly enough; He still wants to use us 'cracked pots' to achieve His purposes.

Jesus, Fear, weakness and doubt have kept me from stepping out in faith to accomplish Your purposes. I would rather do anything with an 'Aaron' to help carry the load. Help me to be willing to step out with You alone as my support. How else will I ever see the amazing things You want to do through my service? Amen.

➤ Day 20: HOMEWARD BOUND
PASSAGE: Exodus 4:18-23
VERSE: Exodus 4:18

Then Moses departed and returned to Jethro his father-in-law and said to him, "Please, let me go, that I may return to my brethren who are in Egypt, and see if they are still alive." And Jethro said to Moses, "Go in peace."

Moses was groomed and ready to return to Egypt and be used in the deliverance of the Hebrew people. Jethro offered his son-in-law his blessing and God sealed the deal when He told Moses the men in Egypt who had wanted to slay him were all dead. Moses must have thought everything was going to go smoothly, since these big obstacles were removed from his path. With his wife and sons in tow, Moses carried the staff of God in his hand and began his long journey home. As he strode purposefully back to the land of his youth, Moses must have pondering the words God spoke to him before he left. *"When you go back to Egypt see that you perform before Pharaoh all the wonders which I have put in your power; but I will harden his heart so that he will not let the people go." Then you shall say to Pharaoh, "Thus says the LORD, "Israel is My son, My firstborn.""* Moses must have wondered exactly how hard a heart could be hardened. What did God mean in His ominous statement, *"Let My son go that he may serve Me, but you have refused to let him go. Behold, I will kill your son, your firstborn."* Maybe things weren't going to flow along as smoothly as Moses thought!

COMMON GROUND: When Moses realized that the task ahead of him might hold great difficulties and challenges, he could have reneged on his promise to be used by God. All of us want an easy mission, but we grow more in God's grace in the Missions which seem Impossible. **HOLY GROUND:** There was a day when God's people loved a challenge. Think about the Pilgrims leaving England to break a new land where they could worship the Lord without the oppressive rules of the Church of England. How about those who have served in the mission field in foreign lands in order to share Christ with others? What about the old time circuit preachers who traveled from town to town on horseback to convict and convert lost souls? These examples show people who were willing to step off common ground, go through hardship and labor, in order to step onto holy ground territory. Holy service requires us to face challenges.

Spirit of God, If I had been in Moses' shoes, I may have decided the battle was too hard and the Hebrew people's freedom was not

worth my effort. How narrow my vision has been. I have assumed
You would do the saving and delivering through someone
else's labor. Lord, I confess my weakness. Amen.

➤ Day 21: BROKEN COVENANT
PASSAGE: **Exodus 4:24-26**
VERSE: **Exodus 4:25**

Then Zipporah took a flint and cut off her son's foreskin
and threw it at Moses' feet, and she said, "You are indeed a
bridegroom of blood to me."

Today's passage of Scripture is difficult to understand unless you know the history of God's covenant with the nation of Israel as set forth in the book of Genesis. We are told in verse twenty-four that God sought to kill Moses as he made his way back to Egypt to confront Pharaoh. Instead of these words causing us to fear God or reject Him all together, we need to dig deeper and find the reason for this sudden turn of events. Circumcision fulfilled a covenant relationship between God and His chosen people. Moses would have been circumcised in the home of his Hebrew mother, as commanded by God's law, before he went to be raised in Pharaoh's palace. His son Gershom, raised among the Midianites, would not have been circumcised. Moses could not enter God's service as long as the covenant was broken. Zipporah, not understanding the procedure—which she deemed bloody and unnecessary—was furious with Moses for requiring his son's foreskin to be removed. This rite may have caused a rift between Moses and his wife, but it healed a broken commitment between him and his God.

COMMON GROUND: Moses was forced to make a choice between being obedient to God and pleasing his wife. Common responses often lead us to please man rather than God—after all, we live with man. *Com*mon leads to *com*promise and spoils *com*munion with God. **HOLY GROUND:** Anything keeping us from complete obedience and fellowship with God needs to be removed before He can entrust us with the projects He has laid before us. Circumcision of the flesh was Moses' hindrance, but circumcision of the heart (removal of the outer self-defensive layer) is absolutely necessary. Our earnest desire must be to please God, not the people we live with every day.

Father God, I am a people-pleaser, and because of that have often not been a God-pleaser. Lord, my desire to be liked and accepted has led me to compromise. Circumcise my heart and remove anything hindering full obedience to You. Amen.

➤ Day 22: GOD HAS HEARD OUR CRIES!
PASSAGE: **Exodus 4:27-31**
VERSE: **Exodus 4:31**

So the people believed; and when they heard that the LORD was concerned about the sons of Israel and that He had seen their affliction, then they bowed low and worshiped.

Finally the day came for Moses to be reunited with his brother Aaron. The reunion was sweet because it was ordained of God. Moses related to his brother all that had happened and the call of God on both of their lives. Aaron, in full agreement and obedience, went with Moses to speak to the elders of the people of Israel. As God had planned, He spoke to Moses—Moses to Aaron—and Aaron to the people. Imagine the encouragement the people felt when they heard that God DID hear their cries, that He DID see their plight and that He HAD already begun to prepare a means of escape for them! Any doubts were removed when Moses showed them the snaky-staff and the leprosy signs. The people, who just hours before had been filled with hopelessness and despair; were humbled and grateful as they bowed to the ground and worshipped their God. Finally, freedom loomed on the horizon; their broken spirits were revived and their sore backs could feel the coming relief.

COMMON GROUND: Israel had lived in bondage for so many generations that those hearing this message didn't even know what freedom was! They could only imagine what not being slaves felt like. Of course they bowed down to thank God for this hope and His promise... all of us would have that common response. All their thoughts were of the good things to come—with no thought to possible requirements on their part. **HOLY GROUND:** Walking in faith and obedience doesn't mean that we are blind fools. Along with hope and promises comes the requirement to obey and remain faithful. Even if they were obedient, there were to be many rough roads ahead. Answered prayers are always something to be grateful for, but we must be willing to forge ahead—no matter what obstacles we encounter.

Lord, I love it when You answer my prayers. I confess that sometimes I have more shallow faith when they aren't being answered in my time frame. I want to be obedient, no matter how long the answers take to come, and to be willing to be honest and realize that even when they are answered, all things may not go as smoothly as I had hoped. Amen.

➤ Day 23: WHO IS GOD?
PASSAGE: **Exodus 5:1-9**
VERSE: **Exodus 5:2**

But Pharaoh said, "Who is the LORD that I should obey His voice to let Israel go? I do not know the LORD, and besides, I will not let Israel go."

Imagine how Pharaoh must have looked at Moses and Aaron with disdain when they came before him and requested that he allow the Hebrew slaves to travel three days into the wilderness to worship their God. Pharaoh wasn't being sarcastic here... he was merely stating fact. HE DID NOT KNOW THE GOD OF THE HEBREWS. Why would he lose the production of his slaves at the whim of two men who presumed to speak for their God? Here we get our first real glimpse of a hardened heart. Pharaoh was a practical man and Moses' request was anything but practical. Another thing to take into account is that Pharaoh may well have known of Moses' history—of his humble Hebrew birth and his years in the King's palace. He may have known that Moses killed an Egyptian man. Those things in themselves would have made the request 'sit wrong' with Pharaoh. One thing was absolutely certain... the King of Egypt would never willingly allow his slaves to leave their work to worship their God. What they did on their own time was their business, but on his time they would do as he commanded.

COMMON GROUND: Pharaoh's reaction to the request was pure common ground human response. Pharaoh looked at the bottom line: Lost time equaled lost work and money. He was honest in his statement that he didn't know their God. If you were an employer who had a request like this made by a Christian worker, how would you respond? Generally, human reactions are self-focused. **HOLY GROUND:** Let's look at the question in the Common Ground section: If you were an employer who had a request like this made by a Christian worker, how would you respond? Someone seeking to walk in God's ways and in full obedience to Him would realize that allowing the believer to go and tend to God's call would actually make him a better employee and a more willing servant. Worship should always make us better people in every part of our life. Those who would deny the request because 'they don't know your God' need to know who He is in your life.

Father, I have to admit that I have been Pharaoh-like in my responses to those who say God has told them to serve Him in some way other than that which seems 'normal' to me. I have doubted that You still talk to Your children. Forgive me and make my spirit hear Your Spirit for good discernment. Amen.

➤ Day 24: JUST WORK HARDER!
PASSAGE: **Exodus 5:10-23**
VERSE: **Exodus 5:17-18**

But he said, "You are lazy, very lazy; therefore you say, 'Let us go and sacrifice to the LORD.' So go now and work; for you will be given no straw, yet you must deliver the quota of bricks."

If you thought Pharaoh's response in the last entry was honest and hardhearted, you will really begin to see his character revealed in today's entry. Pharaoh concluded that the people had too much time on their hands—too much time to listen to Moses and Aaron as they stirred things up and caused dissatisfaction among the people. He scattered the Hebrews across the land to gather the straw that had before been supplied for them to make bricks. Their workload was increased and their daily quota was not decreased. The people who had grumbled for years at the unfairness of Pharaoh began to see someone new to blame their suffering on. Moses and Aaron were challenged and accused of causing Pharaoh to increase their labors. *"May the LORD look upon you and judge you, for you have made us odious in Pharaoh's sight and in the sight of his servants, to put a sword in their hand to kill us."* Isn't it funny how quickly Moses went from Hero to Zero? Moses was beginning to see what hardened hearts looked like and was distraught at the cutting words of those he was trying to help. *"O Lord, why have You brought harm to this people? Why did You ever send me? Ever since I came to Pharaoh to speak in Your name, he has done harm to this people, and You have not delivered Your people at all."* In this moment—as in many more to come—Moses is wondering why he ever stepped off the path to look at that burning bush!

COMMON GROUND: Even though we can fully understand the cries of the people against Moses, we need to see that our common ground instinct is to blame our suffering on someone... anyone! Often it is God who takes the blame for illness, poverty, suffering and pain. Funny, isn't it, that people who deny God's very existence blame Him for hard periods in their lives? **HOLY GROUND:** I said in an earlier entry that walking forth before God doesn't always mean a journey without hardships and obstacles. The people thought their journey out of Egypt would be a breeze... when God was planning to make it a whirlwind instead! Poor Moses! How like us to blame everything on the one who is trying to help us. Holiness requires us to walk in patience and faith—even in the midst of our suffering.

Jesus, I am quick to blame everything on others. Yes, I blame things on Your chosen leaders too. Help me to stop looking for someone to blame and to start looking for good in all situations and in all people. I grow in the obstacle courses—perhaps more than in the smooth paths of my life. Amen.

➤ Day 25: I WILL...
PASSAGE: Exodus 6:1-8
VERSE: Exodus 6:6

Say, therefore, to the sons of Israel, "I am the LORD, and I will bring you out from under the burdens of the Egyptians, and I will deliver you from their bondage. I will also redeem you with an outstretched arm and with great judgments."

God has a wonderful way of reassuring us that we are doing right when we are walking in obedience to His commands. Moses was frustrated with Pharaoh, with his own people, and with God who seemed to have sent him on a wild goose chase in Egypt. God very clearly reiterated to him that Pharaoh *would* let the people go, that he *would* actually force them out of his land, that the covenant He had made with Abraham, Isaac and Jacob *was* still in effect, and that He indeed *had* heard the cries of the people. He then told Moses to tell the people that He *would* bring them out of Egyptian bondage, that He *would* redeem them by His strength—not theirs—and that after it was all through, He *would* be their God and they *would* be His children... forever. Imagine the weight being lifted from Moses' shoulders as God poured forth His promises. *God is not a man that*

He should lie, so each promise would come to pass. As the leader of the people, Moses clung to the covenants and declarations of God as he realized that the burden wasn't on his shoulders alone. God was in control and would be victorious. God was going to walk before Moses and, even though the steps might not always be easy, they would lead Israel on the path He had ordained for them.

COMMON GROUND: Some days it is very difficult to cling to God's promises. Some days we do feel forsaken and alone. Some days we do feel like the upward climb is too steep and hard. Some days there is no end or even a glimmer of hope in sight. **HOLY GROUND:** In those days all we can do is turn to the promises of God's holy Word and claim them. When our eyes cannot see God's face before us, all we can do is look for His guiding hand on our lives in the past. When we come to that place in our journey we can know that we are surely stepping from common to holy ground and that He will reward the effort we put in that journey.

Spirit of God, I have often felt alone and without one person who understands my groaning. I praise God that when everyone else has abandoned me, You never have. Help me to find, claim and walk in Your Scriptural promises. You alone are my strength. Amen.

➤ Day 26: NO ONE IS LISTENING TO ME!
PASSAGE: Exodus 6:9-13, 30
VERSE: Exodus 6:12

But Moses spoke before the LORD, saying, "Behold, the sons of Israel have not listened to me; how then will Pharaoh listen to me, for I am unskilled in speech?"

Moses was facing a problem many leaders face... they can't get their followers to listen to them, let alone follow them. In this case it is easy to understand because these people had been enslaved for hundreds of years. Although Moses' message sounded good, they were looking at the reality of their lives. God was ready to grow Moses, so He sent him to Pharaoh to command that the people be released to go and worship Him in the desert. Moses was no one's fool and realized that if he couldn't get the people to listen there was no way under heaven that the King of Egypt would hear his words. Pharaoh was a proud man with an uncircumcised heart and body, and a man who in many ways thought he himself was God. Moses felt he had uncircumcised lips—those which would not be sufficient to do what God was commanding, and likely hoped that God would listen to his doubts and work this miracle by some other means. No, God had a plan and Moses—much to his chagrin—was an integral part of that plan. Imagine Moses' sense of frustration... because NO ONE WOULD LISTEN TO HIM!

COMMON GROUND: Frustration can be a paralyzing emotion which keeps us from accomplishing the will of God in our lives. This is a common response when no one listens to you or thinks your input is valuable. My husband worked in factories his entire adult life and was always frustrated that management refused to listen to the suggestions of the workers who knew about the daily performance of their jobs and knew what was necessary to improve productivity. That frustration often led to bad attitudes and low morale in the workplace. **HOLY GROUND:** How do we overcome the frustration in our lives in a Christ-like way? One of the keys is praying for patience. Yes, patience really is a virtue and it is a fruit of the spirit which changes our hearts, even if it doesn't change the people we are trying to get to listen to us. When frustration threatens your peace, simply pray and ask God to give you purity, patience and peace. Holy people must learn to handle their emotions in Christ-like ways... not in worldly ways.

Father God, Frustration, anger, defeat and fatigue are all very real emotions I am forced to deal with in my everyday life. I confess that I have handled them in wrong ways in the past. Please wash me in Your peace, give me a pure heart and bless me with patience. Make me more like You each day. Amen.

➤ Day 27: SENIOR BELIEVERS
PASSAGE: **Exodus 7:1-7**
VERSE: **Exodus 7:7**

*Moses was eighty years old and Aaron eighty-three,
when they spoke to Pharaoh.*

I have always heard that the Bible doesn't speak of a time of retirement for the saints of God. In this passage we see Moses and Aaron preparing to face Pharaoh for the first time in their early eighties... and you thought you were too old to teach Sunday School? God spoke amazing words as a command to Moses: *"See, I make you as God to Pharaoh, and your brother Aaron shall be your prophet. You shall speak all that I command you, and your brother Aaron shall speak to Pharaoh that he let the sons of Israel go out of his land."* Was the Lord proclaiming Moses was God? No, He was painting a picture for Moses to understand exactly how their communication with Pharaoh would happen. Just as God spoke His word to His prophets and had them proclaim that word to His people, Moses would speak to Aaron what God told him, and then Aaron would speak to the people as Moses' prophet. Unfortunately, for these 'senior citizens in training' God also revealed that He would harden Pharaoh's heart in order for the lay people of Egypt to see the hand of God through miracles and wonders. Without complaint about arthritis or bursitis, the two brothers prepared to do exactly as God commanded. Onward Senior Soldiers!

COMMON GROUND: Age is a great excuse to avoid ministry responsibilities. As our lives begin to wind down and our bodies begin to stiffen and ache, we often use those crutches to pass the baton on to the younger generation. Yes, that has to happen eventually, but think about the years of wisdom lost when the saints in our churches step aside. Unfortunately, senior citizens in our churches are usually put on a shelf or shoved off into an 'old folks' group when they still have so much to offer. **HOLY GROUND:** God proves in this passage that He can use anyone to accomplish His purpose. The elderly can still teach, lead and be God's voice in the church. Do you know wise elders who feel pushed out of ministry? Draw them in, include them in your activities, and watch how their white-haired wisdom pours forth.

Lord, We need more, not fewer, wise counselors in our churches today. I wouldn't like to be shelved because what I have to offer is felt to be unneeded. Sometimes—maybe at all times—our contemporary worship lacks depth and proven examples of Your amazing faithfulness. Give us a healthy balance of both. Amen.

➤ Day 28: SNAKE TRICKS
PASSAGE: Exodus 7:8-13
VERSE: Exodus 7:10

So Moses and Aaron came to Pharaoh, and thus they did just as the LORD had commanded; and Aaron threw his staff down before Pharaoh and his servants, and it became a serpent.

Finally the time had come for Moses and Aaron to confront Pharaoh and show the power of God through the miracles of their hands! God had equipped them for this mission with their snakey-staff and informed them that Pharaoh would command for them to *work a miracle.* Aaron cast down his staff and it quickly became a serpent. So far so good! Suddenly though, *the wise men and the sorcerers, and… the magicians of Egypt, did the same with their secret arts. For each one threw down his staff and they turned into serpents.* What in the world was going on? God had assured His messengers that He would convince the people of Egypt that He was the only God. How could that happen when magicians and sorcerers were able to counterfeit the signs He sent with them? Moses and Aaron were mortified until *Aaron's staff swallowed up their staffs.* Yeah! God *was* still in control! Pharaoh and his 'wise men' were left to wonder about their power against the God of the Hebrew people.

COMMON GROUND: Moses and Aaron wanted God to use their miracles to impress others. God had a better idea. He would let the enemy think he was equal in power, and then swallow him up in defeat when he wallowed in his pride. Maybe, just maybe, a touch of pride had crept into Moses' heart. That is quite common in the heart of those who are supernaturally equipped for ministry. **HOLY GROUND:** God works His miracles in His time, in His way, and for His glory—not ours! Ouch! Not only were Pharaoh's magicians humbled, but so were Moses and Aaron. Holy men seek to glorify God... never themselves. How is your humility level?

Father, Humbling hurts. I confess that I do things for my glory, and only when challenged do I deflect it over to You. Help my heart to be fully obedient to Your leading and to give You the glory for every gift, blessing and ability in my life... since they are all from You. Amen.

➤ Day 29: THAT BLOODY NILE
PASSAGE: **Exodus 7:14-25**
VERSE: **Exodus 7:20**

So Moses and Aaron did even as the LORD had commanded. And he lifted up the staff and struck the water that was in the Nile, in the sight of Pharaoh and in the sight of his servants, and all the water that was in the Nile was turned to blood.

Pharaoh's heart was hard following the failure of his wise men to defeat the work of Moses the day before. God sent Moses and Aaron to rub more salt in the stinging wound of defeat. They were told to go to him in the morning and tell him, *"Let My people go, that they may serve Me in the wilderness. But behold, you have not listened until now."* God knew Pharaoh wouldn't listen to their words, so Moses was to instruct Aaron to stretch his staff over the Nile River and watch as the waters turned to blood. The Nile was the main source of water for cooking, cleaning, bathing and irrigation in Egypt—a land with very little annual rainfall. Turning the river to blood would eliminate drinking water, kill all fish and life within its banks, and would cause the stench of blood to fill the land. Pharaoh refused to listen and soften his heart toward God's people. His own Egyptians were forced to dig deep into the ground for drinkable water. Yet, for seven days the King of Egypt refused to summon Moses to intercede with God for relief for his nation.

COMMON GROUND: Moses and Aaron could have let God's commands take a back seat to their compassion for the Egyptian people. God gave them a clear mission—as He often does us. Far too many of us allow our hearts to overrule our brains. If God wanted Pharaoh and his people to see His hand, who would Moses be to soften the message or refuse to perform the task at hand? **HOLY GROUND:** Often, speaking the hard Biblical truth of required holiness is compromised in order for us not to offend others. We are called to walk in obedience to God's commands and not to allow our hearts to trump those commands. Moses and Aaron had to be completely dedicated to achieving God's purpose, even though the innocent people of Egypt would be affected by turning the Nile into blood.

Jesus, People need to come into a place of holy perfection before You, and they will never do that if I refuse to speak Your hard words in love to them. Help me to seek to please You and not the people around me. Truth is truth—and sometimes it hurts. Amen.

➤ Day 30: HOPPIN' MAD
PASSAGE: **Exodus 8:1-15**
VERSE: **Exodus 8:6-7**

So Aaron stretched out his hand over the waters of Egypt, and the frogs came up and covered the land of Egypt. The magicians did the same with their secret arts, making frogs come up on the land of Egypt.

Today we look at the second of God's ten plagues which were sent upon Pharaoh and his nation. Again God told the prophets to tell the king to let His people go, and he was told that if he didn't do so *...the Nile will swarm with frogs, which will come up and go into your house and into your bedroom and on your bed, and into the houses of your servants and on your people, and into your ovens and into your kneading bowls.* Let me say here that this would be the worst plague for me! I hate frogs, toads, crickets, grasshoppers, and anything else that has the ability to hop on me! These frogs would be so plentiful that they would even be found in the upper level bedrooms of the Egyptian homes! YUCK! Again, Pharaoh refused to humble his heart and Aaron stretched out his staff over the waters and frogs came and covered the land. Notice here that Pharaoh's wise men and magicians were again able to replicate the work of Aaron and bring forth frogs. Maybe Pharaoh felt like I do about these little green hopping monsters... because he summoned Moses and said, *"Entreat the LORD that He remove the frogs from me and from my people; and I will let the people go, that they may sacrifice to the LORD."* Moses interceded and the frogs died. Everywhere were piles of dead, stinky, heat fried frogs... and when Pharaoh saw the plague had ended, he reneged on his word and refused to let the Hebrews go to worship their God.

COMMON GROUND: Let's find today's application in the fact that in spite of a clear warning of the consequences, Pharaoh refuses to walk in obedience to God—even when he has already seen several manifestations of His presence in Egypt. Why do we, in our common ground responses to God's warnings, think we are smarter than He is? Why do we think adultery is only wrong for other people, or that stealing is only stealing if it is a major theft? Why do we believe that making money illegally will be acceptable to God as long as we tithe on the increase? **HOLY GROUND:** Holy people will always respond to the commands and warnings in the Bible as God's correction for their lives. Adultery, theft, lying, blasphemy, and worshipping other gods will only hurt us and separate us from the God who created and loves us. Humble yourself to the commands, or humble yourself in the painful consequences... the choice is yours.

Spirit of God, Pharaoh isn't the only one who has refused to listen the first time... thus having to face difficult consequences for his actions. I have done the same. Lord, I need a spirit of obedience which will keep me from having to pay dearly for my sins. Amen.

➤ Day 31: HEAD ITCHIN' MAD
PASSAGE: **Exodus 8:16-19**
VERSE: **Exodus 8:17**

And they did so; for Aaron stretched out his hand with his rod, and smote the dust of the earth, and it became lice in man, and in beast; all the dust of the land became lice throughout all the land of Egypt. (KJV)

The NASB version of the above verse says this third plague was gnats, but my sick little mind preferred the King James Version of lice! Imagine all the dust of the very dusty nation of Egypt becoming lice and covering the flesh of man and mammal. Makes you want to scratch yourself doesn't it? After Aaron sent the lice to cover the land Pharaoh paged the magicians and sorcerers to perform a wonder which would prove their ability to compete with the work of God's emissaries. Full of themselves after their frog-making efforts, the magicians came to create lice... or better yet, to stop the lice from multiplying... and thus dilute God's power. I had to giggle as I wrote this entry and pictured the magicians trying to conjure up lice of their own as they scratched their heads and picked lice off their bodies. They, like everyone else, were desperate for relief. But the relief didn't come. For the first time, they were completely unable to copy or stop the plague. *Then the magicians said to Pharaoh, "This is the finger of God." But Pharaoh's heart was hardened, and he did not listen to them, as the LORD had said.* The magicians were getting it... but Pharaoh's heart remained hardened.

COMMON GROUND: How many people see the work of God in the lives of His children, yet they refuse to acknowledge His provision? The magicians were like that at first because they were employed by Pharaoh and challenging him could cause them death. Common ground responses will lead us to be too proud to admit that we are wrong. That keeps us walking outside of the will of God. **HOLY GROUND:** The Magicians have the right response here. They openly proclaim to Pharaoh that God's hand alone could bring all these horrible plagues upon the nation of Egypt. Admitting that they were wrong and were impotent to fight against God's power was a holy ground response to the situation.

Father God, When I am wrong, help me to admit it and get back into right standing with You. I have been a denier in the past like the magicians were, but Your proven history calls me to look at who You really are. You are God of gods and Lord of Lords. Amen.

➤ Day 32: SWATTIN' MAD
PASSAGE: **Exodus 8:20-32**
VERSE: **Exodus 8:24**

Then the LORD did so. And there came great swarms of flies into the house of Pharaoh and the houses of his servants and the land was laid waste because of the swarms of flies in all the land of Egypt.

Disgusting is the thought of filthy flies covering everyone and everything in the land, but that is what God's next plague was because Pharaoh continued to harden his heart against God and the Hebrew people. One thing made this plague glaringly different from the others the Egyptians had witnessed. This time, God pulled the plague back from the land of Goshen where the Hebrews lived. *"I will put a division between My people and your people. Tomorrow this sign will occur."* Even more powerful than the seemingly out of control plagues would be that they could be controlled by the hand of God and He could dictate where the flies swarmed. If God was trying to get the attention of the Egyptian population, that was a perfect way to do it. Pharaoh—in order to stop the plague on his people—tried to concoct a compromise with Moses. He told the brothers they could go worship their God within the land of Egypt. Moses wasn't buying into the compromise because that was not God's command. *"We must go a three days' journey into the wilderness and sacrifice to the LORD our God as He commands us." Pharaoh said, "I will let you go, that you may sacrifice to the LORD your God in the wilderness; only you shall not go very far away. Make supplication for me."* Do you think Pharaoh is in any way humbled at this point? He had better get a big flyswatter! Don't fall for kind words and empty platitudes.

COMMON GROUND: Far too often we remove the protective hedge God has granted to us and assume that our 'righteousness' brings our blessings. God is our Provider and part of that provision is protection. When we believe good things come to us because of who we are, we are failing to acknowledge what He is doing in our lives. After a while, He will simply pull the hedge back and leave us to our own devices. **HOLY GROUND:** The child of God is commanded to give thanks in *all* things. If God is our Stronghold, our Defender, our Strength and our Provider, then we need to give Him the glory for being those things in our lives. As the Hebrews watched the horrible plague of flies and saw that none of them crossed the hedge God had set, how could they help but give thanks to Him?

Lord, I thank You for the hedge of protection around me, my home, my family and all the children of God. I am grateful that every good and perfect gift—including protection—comes from Your loving hand in my life. Give me an attitude of gratitude. Amen.

➤ Day 33: "MOO"VE OVER PHARAOH
PASSAGE: **Exodus 9:1-7**
VERSE: **Exodus 9:6**

So the LORD did this thing on the next day, and all the livestock of Egypt died; but of the livestock of the sons of Israel, not one died.

Plague five would cause great suffering on the people of Egypt. The previous plagues were upon their flesh and in their homes, but the plague affecting the livestock would have great consequences. We are told in verse three that the plague would be upon *the horses, on the donkeys, on the camels, on the herds, and on the flocks.* That affected transportation, food, milk, wool products, and the investment of all the families of the land. Pharaoh was warned very specifically that this plague would come upon the *livestock which are in the field.* Once again, the hard heart of the leader would bring suffering upon his people. Knowing that the plague was to come on the animals in the field, Pharaoh could have made the effort to get them to shelter. Instead, all the fielded livestock of Egypt died. Once again, the plague was stayed from touching the livestock of the Hebrew people. You have to wonder about the number who still remained faithful to the King as the plagues intensified.

COMMON GROUND: Pharaoh ignored a clear warning and refused to take action to prevent disaster for the people he reigned over. How many times have you had a clear word or warning from God to not follow a certain path, only to ignore the caution and walk headlong into your own 'self-inflicted' plague? The common response to God's warnings is to temper our hearts against Him and do things our own way. **HOLY GROUND:** The warnings, laws, statutes and cautions of Scripture are put within its pages to keep us from walking headlong into trouble. A man desiring to walk in holiness will read and heed these words and prevent problems and plagues from stealing the blessings of the day.

Father, Your Word is full of cautions, warnings and alerts to things which will draw me away from being fully in Your will. May Your Spirit speak loudly enough to overcome all the platitudes of my enemy who longs to have me walk out of Your will and into his. I want to serve You in all my ways and for all my days. Amen.

➤ Day 34: BOILIN' MAD
PASSAGE: **Exodus 9:8-12**
VERSE: **Exodus 9:10**

So they took soot from a kiln, and stood before Pharaoh; and Moses threw it toward the sky, and it became boils breaking out with sores on man and beast.

I know that you are sick of the plagues... imagine how the Egyptian people felt! In this sixth plague God was going to send painful boils upon the people and animals of Pharaoh's kingdom. The King had been warned as he watched Moses throw furnace ashes into the air and it fell like a fine dust over the land. I don't know if you have ever had boils—I haven't, but I watched Dan suffer horribly with them from a blood disease he contracted while serving in Vietnam. We haven't heard from the magicians since they told Pharaoh that he was fighting against the very hand of God. In this plague they couldn't try to replicate the trick if they wanted to; *because of the boils, for the boils were on the magicians as well as on all the Egyptians.* Pharaoh's heart remained hard—just as the Lord had predicted. God was patiently breaking down the walls of loyalty between the King and his subjects. If everyone was suffering and Pharaoh had the power to stop the plagues by simply letting the Hebrews go, then the people must have been growing distrustful of his ability to lead in a rational way.

COMMON GROUND: Following inept and unqualified leaders is a problem for the child of God. When we get on a bandwagon because someone is a great speaker or a charismatic leader, we are failing to look deeper at the condition of their heart. Pharaoh was losing the respect of his subjects, his servants, and probably his own family. He had a serious 'heart condition' which kept him from caring about anyone but himself. **HOLY GROUND:** As believers, we are to weigh all things against the Bible and form our judgments and opinions based on Scripture. Following the 'popular' teachings of those in leadership isn't good for government, and certainly isn't good for the church. Do you form your opinions based on emotion and popular culture... or on the Word of God? Serious question; answer honestly.

Jesus, I need to remember that pretty words and handsome faces are not reflections of godly hearts. May I learn to look deeper and seek all direction from Scripture, so that I am not led astray by false prophets and foolish leaders? Amen.

➤ ## Day 35: WARNINGS IGNORED
PASSAGE: Exodus 9:13-21
VERSE: Exodus 9:20-21

The one among the servants of Pharaoh who feared the word of the LORD made his servants and his livestock flee into the houses; but he who paid no regard to the word of the LORD left his servants and his livestock in the field.

God was speaking a hard word of truth to Pharaoh. He told him to let the people go to worship Him, or He would send more debilitating plagues upon the people and land of Egypt until everyone knew that there was none like Him in all the earth! God warned the king that if it was His will, He could stretch out His mighty hand and eradicate Egypt from the earth. The crusher came when God told Pharaoh, *"...for this reason I have **allowed you to remain**, in order to show you My power and in order to proclaim My name through all the earth."* Pharaoh must have been absolutely furious—yet he refused to concede. Finally though, we have a glimpse showing that the plagues were getting through to some of the Egyptian people. God warned that He was about to send a plague of hail unlike any the land of Egypt had ever seen. He warned that every man and beast left in the field would be destroyed by the stoning of the hail upon their flesh. As we look at the verse above, some of Pharaoh's people listened this time and brought the servants and livestock into shelter. Yet, there were some who paid no regard to the warning and left their servants and livestock unprotected in the fields.

COMMON GROUND: As I struggled to come up with the application for this entry, I was led to think about how many people who refuse to humble themselves before God are reduced to a heaping pile of shame before they come to the end of themselves. God allows the free will of man to reign... until he has painted himself into an inescapable corner. Others watch as God sits by and patiently waits for that man to fall in defeat. **HOLY GROUND:** Once we have exhausted all other possibilities, many of us finally release our lives to God in submission. Wouldn't it be easier to avoid the 'plagues' and submit in the first place... rather than have to go back and try to repair the damage our choices have wrought? Pharaoh could have released the people from bondage for approximately two weeks and lost their production—but then had them back to serve him. Instead, he chose to blatantly disobey God and pay horrendous prices for his choices. He will lose everything because of his unwillingness to submit.

Spirit of God, I don't wish to be the bad example for others to see how not to walk with God! Change my heart to submit and obey so I am not like Pharaoh who had to lose everything before he would bow to Your authority. Amen.

➤ Day 36: HOLY HAILSTONES, MOSES!
PASSAGE: **Exodus 9:22-35**
VERSE: **Exodus 9:24-25**

*So there was hail, and fire flashing continually in the midst of the
hail, very severe, such as had not been in all the land of Egypt
since it became a nation. The hail struck all that was in the field
through all the land of Egypt, both man and beast; the hail also
struck every plant of the field and shattered every tree of the field.*

Those who listened to Moses' warning in the last entry must have
been abundantly grateful that they had done so when the seventh
plague began to manifest itself throughout Egypt. Thunder, lightning and hail battered the country like never before. The animals
and people in the fields were killed. Every plant was struck down
and every tree destroyed. Pounding, beating, unending hail fell
over every inch of Egypt... except for Goshen where the Hebrews
lived. God's wrath poured out in such a way that people must have
hidden in absolute terror from the fury they saw unleashed before
them. Water to blood, frogs, lice, flies, livestock disease, boils, and
now hail... what else could God have planned as judgments against
Pharaoh? The King called Aaron and Moses and told them, *"I have
sinned this time; the LORD is the righteous one, and I and my people
are the wicked ones. Make supplication to the LORD, for there has
been enough of God's thunder and hail; and I will let you go, and
you shall stay no longer."* Moses went to intercede for Egypt, but
not before he told Pharaoh he knew his heart had not changed and
that he had not yet come to the place of acknowledging that the
Almighty, not Pharaoh himself, was God.

COMMON GROUND: Mere lip service does no good when we
stand before God and attempt to placate Him with rash promises
and unsupported confession. It is easy to 'promise and pray' when
we are in a hard time. Unfortunately for us, God knows our hearts
and knows when the promises (and the prayers for that matter) are
from a sincere heart. Pharaoh might have fooled some people when
he professed God as righteous and himself as a sinner, but his fruit

production didn't match his flowery words. **HOLY GROUND:** A Christian's word should be as sure as his faith in Christ. Our shallow commitment to keeping promises blackens His righteous eye and reflects poorly on our Christian brothers. Holy men will give their word and then follow through as promised. That may be more Bible than some people will ever read... so how good are you at keeping your word?

Father God, Covenants and promises seem to be dispensable in today's world. Help me to be a promise-keeper so others will see how You have begun a good work in my heart and are carrying it through to completion. Amen.

➤ Day 37: WE ARE DESTROYED!
PASSAGE: **Exodus 10:1-7**
VERSE: **Exodus 10:7**

Pharaoh's servants said to him, "How long will this man be a snare to us? Let the men go, that they may serve the LORD their God. Do you not realize that Egypt is destroyed?"

God told Moses that He had hardened Pharaoh's heart in order to make a mockery of his pride and self-worship and to show once and for all that He was God. *Moses and Aaron went to Pharaoh and said to him, "Thus says the LORD, the God of the Hebrews, "How long will you refuse to humble yourself before Me? Let My people go, that they may serve Me."* Pharaoh was riddled with pride—so much so that he was willing to lose everything because of his own stubbornness. Today we see the anger and disappointment of the people around the King. *"How long will this man be a snare to us? Let the men go, that they may serve the LORD..."* The people are asking their king, "Do all of us have to die in order for you to be right? Our crops, fields, trees, livestock and homes are destroyed... don't you care? What are you holding out for... the end of the land of Egypt?" We can see the frustration and the attempt by his close advisors to get Pharaoh to see reason. They—like the magicians—had come to the realization that the Hebrew God was the real God. They had witnessed His protection of Israel in the midst of the fury of these plagues. And now, His spokesmen have prophesied yet another plague... locusts!

COMMON GROUND: The common and holy responses to this entry are much alike. When we see the obvious before our eyes and need to convince someone of what is happening righteous anger is justifiable. These men had remained faithful to Pharaoh through everything, but now they see him leading their nation into destruction. **HOLY GROUND:** My one caveat here is that we need to speak in both love and Biblical wisdom. In order for us to convince others that the things we see happening in our world today are all the signs of the end of the age as Jesus spoke them, we must be well grounded in the Bible and well studied in exactly what it says. That Word must be hidden in our heart in order for us to convince others of our sincerity.

Lord, My real need today is for You to help me to understand Your Word and to hide it in my heart, so that I can be Your witness to others who aren't aware of the implications of what is going on in our world. Give me the foundation and the boldness to speak out about Biblical prophesies unfolding before our very eyes. Amen.

➤ Day 38: MUNCHIN' MAD
PASSAGE: Exodus 10:8-20
VERSE: Exodus 10:15

For they covered the surface of the whole land, so that the land was darkened; and they ate every plant of the land and all the fruit of the trees that the hail had left. Thus nothing green was left on tree or plant of the field through all the land of Egypt.

Pharaoh had a compromise ready for Moses and Aaron. He told them the Hebrew men could go and worship their God, leaving their women and children behind in his care! Sounds reasonable, as long as you are willing compromise on God's commands! Moses put a stop to that idea, *"We shall go with our young and our old; with our sons and our daughters, with our flocks and our herds we shall go, for we must hold a feast to the LORD."* The King refused, telling them their hearts were set on evil (if that isn't the pot calling the kettle black!) and he would not allow them to take their families—because once away, they would never return. No deal—here come the locusts. *The locusts came up over all the land of Egypt and settled in all the territory of Egypt; they were very numerous. There had never been so many locusts, nor would there be so many again. For they covered the surface of the whole land, so that the land was darkened; and they ate every plant of the land and all the fruit of the trees that the hail had left. Thus nothing green was left on tree or plant of the field through all the land of Egypt.* This ninth plague wasn't the one to permanently change Pharaoh's heart. God listened to Moses and sent a very strong west wind to drive the locusts into the Red Sea. Everything was destroyed... everything except Pharaoh's pride.

COMMON GROUND: Moses could have made a common decision and compromised with Pharaoh. He could have led the Hebrew men into the wilderness to worship God. Surely, God would be happy with that much... right? Compromise of our Christian values is NEVER right. God will not wink at sin or disobedience; and neither should we. **HOLY GROUND:** Moses' response to Pharaoh's compromise was the right one. He held onto holy ground by refusing to allow common ground responses to sneak in. In his fatigue and frustration he could have bent the rules, but then he would have had to answer for that. He chose holy!

Father, As I look around me the world—and yes even the church—compromise is the norm. Christian values are mocked and made fun of while secular progressive ideals are lauded through the media, the entertainment industry, and in academia. God help our nation as we draw further and further away from Your truths. Amen.

➤ Day 39: OVERWHELMING DARKNESS
PASSAGE: Exodus 10:21-29
VERSE: Exodus 10:22-23

So Moses stretched out his hand toward the sky, and there was thick darkness in all the land of Egypt for three days. They did not see one another, nor did anyone rise from his place for three days, but all the sons of Israel had light in their dwellings.

Have you ever been in darkness so heavy that you could actually feel it in your spirit? Our human nature is to draw toward the light for a sense of well-being. Many people fight serious emotional battles when they are deprived of light for long periods of time. Imagine then this tenth plague which consisted of three days of absolute darkness in Egypt. The people couldn't see one another, couldn't light lamps, and could see no glimmer of hope from the continuing wrath of God upon the Egyptian nation. Only in the land of Goshen was there light. Again, God was making a distinction between those who walked in obedience with Him and those who rejected and opposed His commands. Pharaoh had had enough. *"Go, serve the LORD; only let your flocks and your herds be detained Even your little ones may go with you."* What a dolt! Hasn't he learned that God's servant Moses will not bow to his compromises? No, the Hebrews will not leave their herds and flocks behind! It was quick thinking on Moses' part when he responded, *"You must also let us have sacrifices and burnt offerings, that we may sacrifice them to the LORD our God. Therefore, our livestock too shall go with us; not a hoof shall be left behind, for we shall take some of them to serve the LORD our God. And until we arrive there, we ourselves do not know with what we shall serve the LORD."* Moses is right. How would they know what God will require from them in the worship when they did finally get before Him without Pharaoh's control? Pharaoh made a painful but true prophetic statement in his anger. *"Get away from me! Beware, do not see my face again, for in the day you see my face you shall die!"* Moses said, *"You are right; I shall never see your face again!"* Pharaoh had no idea of the destruction which lay ahead.

COMMON GROUND: Moses had no real idea what worshipping the Lord in the wilderness would entail. He did know that animal sacrifice was part of their worship. He could have agreed with Pharaoh and gone unprepared into communion with God, thinking He would be satisfied with Moses for just getting the people out of Egypt... even if not the livestock. **HOLY GROUND:** Moses realized that true worship required preparation. That doesn't mean spontaneous worship cannot happen—it surely can, and is often more powerful than rehearsed programming. Moses looked at what he knew, at what God had told him, and at the importance of the situation... and refused to enter the presence of God without being prepared.

Jesus, Worship is something I have struggled with in the past. I never know how passionate or reverent I need to be. My concern has left me empty. Jesus, I want to revere You in every way, but I also want You to know how passionately I love You. Show me through Your Spirit how to worship as it pleases You. Amen.

➤ ## Day 40: HEDGE OF PROTECTION
PASSAGE: **Exodus 11:1-10**
VERSE: **Exodus 11:7**

But against any of the sons of Israel a dog will not even bark, whether against man or beast, that you may understand how the LORD makes a distinction between Egypt and Israel.

God was finished with Pharaoh's stubborn ways. He was about to bring the final plague, the final judgment against Egypt. This one would be so serious that Pharaoh would actually <u>force</u> the Hebrews out of his land. First, God advised Moses to tell the Hebrews to spoil their captors (as we first read about in entry 16), in order that they would leave with great wealth. The spoil came easy because *the LORD gave the people favor in the sight of the Egyptians. Furthermore, the man Moses himself was greatly esteemed in the land of Egypt, both in the sight of Pharaoh's servants and in the sight of the people.* How interesting it is that the Egyptian people esteemed (or respected) Moses, rather than hating him for the suffering they had endured at the hand of him and his God. That is a clear indication that they were aware that Pharaoh, not Moses, was the reason for their suffering. Moses very solemnly informed Pharaoh that the firstborn of all of Egypt (both man and beast) would die in the plague of the firstborn. *Moreover, there shall be a great cry in all the land of Egypt, such as there has not been before and such as shall never be again. But against any of the sons of Israel a dog will not even bark, whether against man or beast that you may understand how the LORD makes a distinction between Egypt and Israel.* Moses left that meeting burning with anger at the waste Pharaoh was about to bring upon his land... the land of Moses' birth. Pharaoh refused to listen and God prepared for His protection of the Hebrew population in the midst of horrible death and destruction.

COMMON GROUND: The Egyptian people could have blamed Moses for all the destruction throughout their land. It is always easy to blame the man who comes in and seems to bring trouble with him. That would have been the common response... blame someone—anyone—for the hardship you face in your life. **HOLY GROUND:** The people were not blind and realized that their own King and his officials refused to obey the Hebrew God—clearly more than a stone idol—and brought the horror and destruction upon them. Their respect for Moses probably included admiring his continued bravery in confronting Pharaoh at the risk of his own life. Moses had earned their respect because he never backed down from the authority of Egypt.

Spirit of God, Help me to see clearly what is going on before my eyes before I make false accusations and judgments. Give me God-colored-glasses to look through, not the eyes of this world. Amen.

➤ Day 41: BLOOD OF PERFECT LAMB
PASSAGE: **Exodus 12:1-7**
VERSE: **Exodus 12:5**

Your lamb shall be an unblemished male a year old;
you may take it from the sheep or from the goats.

Today we begin our study of the preparation for the escape of the Hebrews from their bondage in Egypt. God commanded Moses and Aaron to give very specific instructions to the Hebrew congregation... instructions, which if disobeyed, could cost them their lives. Each home was to take a spotless, unblemished and perfect lamb on the tenth of Nisan and set it apart from the other members of the flock. The perfect little lamb was to be sequestered until the fourteenth day of Nisan, which God ordained as the first month of the Hebrew calendar (our March-April). As we see in the text for today, if any home was too poor or too small to afford a lamb, one could be shared with a neighbor. At twilight on the evening of the fourteenth everyone was to kill their lamb and smear his blood on the top and sides of the doorpost of his home. That blood—if you were to draw an imaginary line from the top center of the doorpost down and from the right side to the left—formed the shape of a cross. How amazing that thousands of years before Jesus was ever born the people of Israel were using the shed blood of an innocent lamb to paint a cross on the door of their home in order to be delivered from the angel of death!

COMMON GROUND: God's commands were very specific and in great detail because He knew what the next few days would mean in the lives of the Egyptians, as well as the Hebrew slaves. How common it is to try to cut corners or give partial effort to the things God commands us to do. We gloss over His words and think He will wink and look the other way. In these Passover passages we will see how vital complete obedience was. **HOLY GROUND:** Explicit instructions are made to be followed explicitly. Do you want lazy workers assembling your next home appliance or your future automobile? Do you want a physician who does surgery the right way or the fast way? Do you want a God who only protects you when it is convenient for Him? Holiness requires complete obedience... down to the smallest detail.

Father God, No, I do not want only part of Your commitment to me. I long to walk in full, uncompromised obedience, but I haven't always taken all Your commands as seriously as I should have. Today is a new start. Amen.

➤ Day 42: BE PREPARED!
PASSAGE: **Exodus 12:8-13**
VERSE: **Exodus 12:11**

Now you shall eat it in this manner: with your loins girded, your sandals on your feet, and your staff in your hand; and you shall eat it in haste—it is the LORD'S Passover.

In this second session regarding God's Passover we see the urgency of Moses' commands pick up. The people were given specific commands in the preparation of the lamb for eating. They were to roast it with fire (not boil it), eat it with bitter herbs and unleavened bread, and not leave any of it to eat the next day. Again, God was being very precise because compromise could cost them their lives. The most interesting part in these instructions was how God told them to eat the meal. They were to be fully clothed, fully shod and ready to move at a moment's notice. Why would God tell them to eat Passover as if they were going to be heading out at any moment? He knew that in just a matter of hours they would indeed be heading out, and this was the dress rehearsal! If we look ahead thousands of years from this Exodus event, we see the urgency for us to partake in Christ before we find ourselves at the end of our earthly life. We are to 'partake' of ALL He has to offer us and not leave for tomorrow what He calls us to do today. The Hebrews had no idea what the next few hours held, but when the cries of death began to sound they were completely grateful to have been spared the horror the Egyptians faced.

COMMON GROUND: Unfortunately, the modern Christian church feels no sense of urgency to tell people about Christ. The church itself is not unlike society as a whole which believes the world will never end, and even if it did, God would welcome everyone into heaven because He is a 'loving' God. Thus, a common response to this passage is that time is not of the essence. As a result, we are not evangelizing as we should. **HOLY GROUND:** Do you feel an urgency to tell others about your faith? Imagine how you would feel if you failed to witness to a lost family member when God gave you the opportunity... and that person died before you had another chance. Imagine standing before God and having Him remind you of that missed opportunity which prevented your loved one from gaining heaven. Are you getting a better picture of urgency? The Hebrew people ate with urgency and eagerly awaited God's direction. Holy men today will do the same.

Lord, Urgency has been seriously lacking in my witness to others. Moses' specific commands brought protection on God's chosen people. My witness to lost souls can do exactly the same thing today. Teach me, Holy Spirit, how to share my faith in love. Amen.

➤ Day 43: BLOOD PREVENTS DEATH
PASSAGE: Exodus 12:14-28
VERSE: Exodus 12:23

For the LORD will pass through to smite the Egyptians; and when He sees the blood on the lintel and on the two doorposts, the LORD will pass over the door and will not allow the destroyer to come in to your houses to smite you.

Today let's look at the significance of the Lamb's blood for the nation of Israel and the significance of Jesus' blood in the life of the Christian. It is vital for you to understand that nothing but the blood on the doorposts of the homes in Goshen could prevent the Death Angel from killing the firstborn of the Hebrew people. It didn't matter how kind they were, how good their work ethic was, or how generous their hearts were... nothing but the blood of that lamb would protect them. God told them when the Death Angel passed over and spied the blood on the doorway of their homes he would *Pass Over* that dwelling and move on to ones which were not protected. Readers, this is a clear-cut picture of what Christ does for the believer. He is the innocent Lamb who shed His blood — blood which somehow amazingly washes us clean. When our lives come to an end on this earth, we step into our new eternal life and never face death or its horror again. We are redeemed by His blood, just as the Hebrew people were redeemed from the Death Angel. Being a 'good' person wasn't enough for the Hebrews — and it isn't enough for us today. We MUST be washed clean by the blood of Jesus Christ.

COMMON GROUND: It is common in many 'enlightened congregations' to no longer talk about the blood of Christ. That 'blood' word seems to make our sensitive society squeamish. Let me ask you this question: If the blood alone protects us from the Death Angel, and we are not talking about the blood, how will people ever come to realize their need for His atoning blood? **HOLY GROUND:** We should be proclaiming the cleansing blood of Christ from our rooftops! Without that blood, every man will face judgment unprotected and alone. With that blood, every man will face judgment, be deemed righteous before God, and will enter into heavenly rest to live forever with the Perfect Lamb of God. When is the last time you claimed that blood over your home, your family, your marriage, your job and your nation? Holiness can never be achieved without the shedding of innocent blood for our sins.

Father, I understand now the significance of the Passover Lamb and the blood on the doorposts of the Hebrew homes. I claim that same blood over my marriage, my family, my home, my finances, my faith walk and my prayer life. Make me holy as I gladly acknowledge Your mercy and grace. Amen.

➤ Day **44**: GET OUT OF HERE!
PASSAGE: **Exodus 12:29-41**
VERSE: **Exodus 12:31**

Then he (Pharaoh) called for Moses and Aaron at night and said,
"Rise up, get out from among my people, both you and the sons of
Israel; and go, worship the LORD, as you have said."

At midnight, the obedience of the Hebrews was rewarded as the Death Angel began to kill the firstborn of the animals, the prisoners, the Egyptians and the house of Pharaoh. Not one house in all of Egypt was spared death. Not one house of the Hebrews felt death. As the cries of his subjects fell upon the ears of the King, he finally broke and conceded that God had won. He sent for Moses and Aaron and told them to *rise up and get out* of his decimated land. The Egyptian people—who had long ago tried to get Pharaoh to concede—urged the Hebrews to hasten their departure before their God destroyed every last one of them. The Hebrews took their spoil, their unleavened bread, and the clothes on their backs and walked into the first freedom they had felt in over four-hundred years! The passage today tells us that six-hundred-thousand men left that day along with their wives, children and livestock. What an amazing feat! If you figure a very conservative four members per family, that would mean that a minimum of two million, four hundred thousand people walked out of Egypt! Pharaoh was a broken man; Egypt was a broken nation; and the bondage that Israel had willingly walked into was broken from their backs.

COMMON GROUND: Have you tried to witness to others who have openly or angrily rejected your talk of Christ? If so, the common response is to wash your hands of the situation and walk away. Our flesh tells us that we tried and they rejected, so now their blood is upon their heads. Pharaoh was given ten warnings and ten plagues in order to change his heart. Only God could determine when the last chance to listen would be. We are not to stop trying to share our faith with others. **HOLY GROUND:** The Prophet Ezekiel was told to be a Watchman to the nation of Israel. He was to define their sin, tell them how to repent of it, and lead those who would listen back to God. The Watchman was to do that and bear no sin if he obeyed God's directive. However, if the Watchman refused to speak the difficult words—and the people died in their sins—their blood would be on his head. Our witness is vital in order for us to fulfill the commission of evangelizing the world. We are God's Watchmen.

Jesus, I have certainly been frustrated when people have rejected my witness. Yes, I have stopped trying to evangelize them. My job as a Watchman is to do what You tell me, when You tell me to do it, and for as long as You tell me to do it. Help me to bathe my witness in prayer in order that my heart doesn't become hardened to their need for You. Amen.

➤ Day 45: NEVER FORGET
PASSAGE: **Exodus 13:1-10**
VERSE: **Exodus 13:8**

You shall tell your son on that day, saying, "It is because of what the LORD did for me when I came out of Egypt."

Now that the Hebrews had their freedom, God gave them specific instructions to keep the Passover festival each year so they would never forget how His hand had delivered them from their bondage. Isn't it funny how God knows our character? He knows that we tend to forget His blessings and provisions. He knows we start to believe in our own power and not in His. He knows we will begin to forget His faithful healings and deliverance and give credit to others for the miracles in our lives. Some things never change, and there truly is nothing new under the sun! God told them to keep the festival, honor it with reverence and remembrance, and to teach it to their children. Then He gave a strange command to the people. They were to from that day forward devote their firstborn offspring (man and beast) to God in exchange for His protection of their firstborn when the Death Angel visited Egypt. The nation of Israel was to never forget that without God they would have remained in Egyptian bondage for many, many more years—even centuries.

COMMON GROUND: How quickly we forget the provision of God! He heals us... and we credit medicine. He provides for our financial needs... and we credit our good work. He gives us a loving family and marriage... and we think it is because we are 'good' people. It would almost be better for us if time didn't heal all wounds, so that we would continually be aware of His past provisions. America is a great example of this truth. How quickly we have forgotten that our freedoms are from God—not from government or man. **HOLY GROUND:** Holy men must walk with an 'attitude of gratitude' and 'tanks full of thanks' in order for us to remind ourselves and our children of God's constant care and protection. How else will we teach our children to be grateful for what they have and to be obedient to the God of their fathers?

Spirit of God, Your provision and protection is amazing and unending... yet I confess that I have failed to remember to thank You in the past. Here is one big "Thank You, Lord" for all the past blessings; and beginning today, I will teach my children how to have grateful hearts. I will begin today to devote myself and my children to service in Your kingdom. Amen.

➤ Day 46: AVOIDING PITFALLS
PASSAGE: **Exodus 13:11-22**
VERSE: **Exodus 13:17**

Now when Pharaoh had let the people go, God did not lead them by the way of the land of the Philistines, even though it was near; for God said, "The people might change their minds when they see war, and return to Egypt."

In yesterday's entry we talked about God knowing the hearts of those He has created. This means He knows our strengths, as well as our weaknesses. We pick up our story with God leading the liberated Hebrew slaves out of Egypt on their journey to the land He promised their forefathers. Knowing their tendency to find fault with their leaders, God took them the long way to their eventual goal—via the Red Sea. The path through Philistine territory was shorter, but He knew their hearts were not ready for battle and that the fierce Philistine warriors would scare them—maybe enough for them to walk back into Egyptian bondage. Instead, God brought them around the Philistine land and through the wilderness. If you already know this story, you might be thinking He was giving them a preview of what walking in the wilderness might feel like! As the Lord led them by a cloud during the day and a pillar of fire by night, He was their constant companion. The nation of Israel, led by their God, could have walked on holy ground much sooner if only they had been willing to trust Him and believe that He would never lead them into defeat. God knew their hearts, so that made the journey much longer!

COMMON GROUND: Let's admit the truth—that we are often like the people of Israel who would rather take the long journey than to walk headlong into a spiritual battle with God in the lead. Let's also admit that He knows our weaknesses and knows how quickly we can be diverted from our original purpose. Our common ground response it to avoid challenge or trouble at all costs; and that costs us precious moments of watching Him work in amazing ways through our lives. **HOLY GROUND:** If we know that God will never leave or forsake us, and that every battle we face brings Him near to fight for us, why are we so afraid to face the unknown? A holy response in the above story would be for us to tell God we would walk into Philistine territory because we would not be walking in alone. How many times does God have to dumb-down what He wants to do through us because of our fearful hearts and status-quo minds?

Father God, I admit that fear has held me in the past.
The people of Israel didn't even know they were going the long
way around because of their past weaknesses. I hate to think of
how many times You have had to do this—send me on a holy detour
because of my fear and trepidation. Make my heart fearless
as I walk each day in Your perfect will. Amen.

➤ Day 47: HARD HEART CHANGE
PASSAGE: **Exodus 14:1-9**
VERSE: **Exodus 14:4**

"Thus I will harden Pharaoh's heart, and he will chase after them; and I will be honored through Pharaoh and all his army, and the Egyptians will know that I am the LORD."

Just when you thought the Hebrew people were free and walking with ease into the land of promise... here is another rub! Pharaoh—when he comes back into his right mind—realizes that he has just released hundreds of thousands of slaves to their freedom! Who will build the cities? Who will make the bricks? Who will serve in the fields, in the pastures, and in the Egyptian homes? What had he done? Surely it hadn't been a reasonable decision. The only choice he had was to chase them down, round them up, and walk them back into bondage. He chose his top military officers and his best chariots, decided he needed all the power he could muster, and then got all the chariots in Egypt to pursue the Hebrews. God seemed to have lost all reason when He arranged for the freed people to have their backs to the Red Sea—in a way that would leave them no means of escape when the Egyptian army overtook them. That 'back against the wall' feeling has crippled more than one child of God. Is there a time in your life when you were in a tough position and there seemed to be no way out? Remember the gut-wrenching fear? Now you know how Israel felt... face the enemies or drown!

COMMON GROUND: It would be very easy for me to say that the common response to the 'back against the wall' situation is to give up, and that the holy response is to stand strong in the faith. I will not say that here. I too have had my back against the wall and felt the very real terror of defeat. Our bodies are made to react in certain ways when threatened, and fear is an obvious manifestation of that. **HOLY GROUND:** One difference here is that God had sent Moses to tell the people that He had heard their cries. He had warned Pharaoh, brought the plagues, provided the Lamb's blood, kept the Angel of Death from their homes, spoiled their captors, led them out with Pharaoh's permission, and delivered them by cloud and fire to where they were now. Maybe—just maybe—He was still in control. Holy ground requires us to remember God's past faithful provision and to trust in His continued protection—no matter what our eyes see.

Lord, Just reading this causes me to react—like Israel—in fear.
I have to admit that irrational fears sometimes plague me and hinder me from being as faith-filled as I should be. Help me to look at Your proven past provision before I fold in a heap of fear. Amen.

➤ Day 48: BONDAGE WAS BETTER
PASSAGE: **Exodus 14:10-12**
VERSE: **Exodus 14:12**

"Is this not the word that we spoke to you in Egypt, saying, 'Leave us alone that we may serve the Egyptians'? For it would have been better for us to serve the Egyptians than to die in the wilderness."

Today's entry is the first of many where the people Moses had delivered from bondage began to grumble against him. When the Hebrews looked at the Red Sea behind their back and the rapidly approaching army of Pharaoh in front of them, they reminded Moses of how they had told him in Egypt to leave them alone and let them stay like they were before he came in and caused Pharaoh to begin to abuse them. They remembered how they were forced to make bricks without the straw being provided for them—due to the King feeling like they had too much idle time to ponder insurrection. As the people watched Pharaoh's army near, they asked Moses: *"Is it because there were no graves in Egypt that you have taken us away to die in the wilderness? Why have you dealt with us in this way, bringing us out of Egypt?"* In a moment like this, we long for a strong leader to talk sense into our terrorized hearts. Moses was also the likely target for their anger, *because he is the one who forced them to leave Egypt!* How ironic that they would look at their bondage with fond longing after they had cried out to God for hundreds of years for deliverance. How quickly they forgot the whips of the taskmasters and the lack of freedom. Suddenly, bondage sounded good to them... much better than death!

COMMON GROUND: In our lives we are always looking for someone to blame... and within the church this is no different. How easy it is to whine and complain about those in authority. You see, the fault belonged to Pharaoh, not Moses. This man who had risked his life for these people was their whipping post... a common status of those in places of authority. **HOLY GROUND:** How often do we fault the first face we see—other than the one we see in the mirror? The people were wasting their energy, and possibly their last moments, accusing Moses—instead of praying for God's intervention. Their accusations served no purpose other than to hurt this godly leader and make him wonder why he had come to their rescue in the first place. Fortunately, Moses remembered that he was born for this purpose.

Father, Instead of blaming others and finding fault with those in authority, help me to come alongside them, encourage them and let them know I appreciate their service. If I hate the back against the wall feeling, how much more must those who lead large groups hate the sense of defeat? Amen.

➤ Day 49: STAND STILL AND WATCH
PASSAGE: **Exodus 14:13-18**
VERSE: **Exodus 14:13**

But Moses said to the people, "Do not fear! Stand by and see the salvation of the LORD which He will accomplish for you today; for the Egyptians whom you have seen today, you will never see them again forever."

Moses' response wasn't petty or even rude. He spoke in the confidence which comes from seeing God's proven history of selection, direction and protection. Moses saw the army and felt the gut-busting fear. Somehow though, in the midst of all that he knew God was up to something big. Notice his exact choice of words... *"Do not fear! Stand by and see! You will never see them again..."* and then finally, *"The LORD will fight for you while you keep silent."* In Vicki language that means, "Buck up, stand up, watch up and shut up—while you watch the mighty hand of God destroy your enemies!" God then gave Moses the most unusual of all the commands He had ever given (and in Moses' life that is a strong statement). *"As for you, lift up your staff and stretch out your hand over the sea and divide it, and the sons of Israel shall go through the midst of the sea on dry land. As for Me, behold, I will harden the hearts of the Egyptians so that they will go in after them...then the Egyptians will know that I am the LORD, when I am honored through Pharaoh, through his chariots and his horsemen."* What could God mean? How can they pass through the depths of the sea? A lesser man would doubt. A weaker man would crumble under the pressure. Moses was ready. He was born for this moment and wasn't about to let it pass, no matter what the situation before him looked like!

COMMON GROUND: Most of us common folk would doubt that God was in control. Some of us would prepare to fight—and some would prepare to die. What would your response be? Would you believe the leader who said your *eyes were about to see the salvation of the Lord,* when all you could see was death staring you in the face? **HOLY GROUND:** Don't give a quick answer. I think God is truly asking you this question: "Do you believe what He promises, or what your eyes see?" Each one of us will face death at one point. Does death still hold a fear over you? Do you really believe what you say you believe? If you believe your last breath here is followed by your next breath in the presence of Jesus, why do you still fear dying? Give it some thought.

Jesus, Preparing for death is a very sobering thought, yet it is one all of us need to ponder. I am sure You often thought of Your impending crucifixion and the agonizing death You would face.

What kept You strong? Show me how to not allow death to have its fearful stronghold over my life. I do believe that I will be with You when I draw my last earthly breath. Amen.

➤ Day **50**: WHO'S IN CONTROL HERE?
PASSAGE: **Exodus 14:19-22**
VERSE: **Exodus 14:21**

Then Moses stretched out his hand over the sea; and the LORD swept the sea back by a strong east wind all night and turned the sea into dry land, so the waters were divided.

Several times in Scripture we see God's hand change the regular time cycles in order to accomplish His purpose. We will see an example of this in the book of Joshua when He makes the daylight last longer in order for a battle to come to complete victory. Today we see Him move a cloud—actually the cloud of His presence—between the Hebrew people and the Egyptian army—which put the army in complete darkness. While the Egyptians were wondering what was happening, Israel was watching God part the Red Sea by a strong east wind and open it up for them as a dry highway in the seabed. Imagine their thoughts and their fears as Moses directed them to walk across with their families, their belongings and their livestock. I wonder who the first brave soul to step onto the ground was. What were they thinking as they gingerly stepped and fearfully watched the piled up water beside them? Were they completely in awe as we are when we read this account today, or were they too concerned about God moving the cloud and the army of Pharaoh pursuing them? All we can know for certain is when there was no possible way out of their dire predicament, God made a way... a way wide enough for at least 2.4 million souls to cross safely on dry ground without a loss of life. He is surely an amazing God!

COMMON GROUND: In my own life my common response has usually manifested itself in questioning God to death! "Will the water flow back in? How can the seabed really be dry? Can't you simply turn the enemy back and let us find an easier way around the sea? What if we get in there and they charge ahead in spite of the dark cloud?" Have you ever been there and done that? In my situation it is usually a stall tactic to keep me from stepping into fearful or unknown territory. **HOLY GROUND:** Those first steps of faith are the hardest ones to take. Thank God that each step gets easier as we build a pathway paved with God's faithful provisions. The Hebrews will come to find that God's patience can only be stretched out for so long. Holiness requires obedience without questions. We are called to obey in spite of our questions.

Spirit of God, I question and question, in order to get all the answers before I step out in faith. That isn't faith at all! I confess that I have tried to hinder Your progress by seeking to know all the answers before I move. Please direct me and give me a double dose of obedient faith. Amen.

➤ Day 51: GOD IS FIGHTING FOR US!
PASSAGE: **Exodus 14:23-31**
VERSE: **Exodus 14:25**

He caused their chariot wheels to swerve, and He made them drive with difficulty; so the Egyptians said, "Let us flee from Israel, for the LORD is fighting for them against the Egyptians."

For the Egyptian army chaos reigned. The cloud moved and they charged headlong into the place where the Red Sea had parted for Israel. Suddenly that chaos erupted full force. Wheels fell off chariots and they began to swerve out of control. The army of Pharaoh realized that these were not mere accidents, but that the God of the Hebrews was fighting against them! What a frightening fact that would be if you were an Egyptian soldier wondering what else God had up His sleeve to use against you! By the time they decided to turn back and leave the seabed, God had commanded

Moses to stretch out his staff over the sea, so the waters would return and drown the Egyptian army. *The waters returned and covered the chariots and the horsemen, even Pharaoh's entire army that had gone into the sea after them; not even one of them remained.* The Lord showed His power that day to not only His people, but to everyone who witnessed the destruction of the entire mighty Egyptian army. We see in these passages that the winds and the seas truly do obey God's commands. Israel walked the same path the Egyptians tried to use... but with God on their side the dry seabed became holy ground!

COMMON GROUND: Today we will find our application in the efforts of Pharaoh to stop the evacuation of Israel from his land. He might have had the biggest army, the mightiest horses and the sturdiest chariots, but he didn't have God on his side fighting for him. Pharaoh made the common mistake of trusting in himself and the authority he commanded... thinking that was enough. Pride led to the destruction of his entire military. **HOLY GROUND:** A man who realizes that God is his source, his provision, his shield and his strength will never depend on himself or his own abilities to fight the difficult battles of life. Do you feel like you are fighting battles on your own and getting nowhere? Remember that God will go to battle for you, but He is waiting for you to ask for His intervention. He is a gentleman and will never force Himself on you.

Father God, I need You as my partner in every part of my life. Far too many times in the past I have trusted in my own abilities and failed to call upon You when I faced battles. As of today, I am asking You to walk with me every step of my walk on my journey from Common ground to Holy ground. Amen.

➤ Day 52: WHO IS LIKE OUR GOD?
PASSAGE: **Exodus 15:1-15**
VERSE: **Exodus 15:11**

Who is like You among the gods, O LORD? Who is like You,
majestic in holiness, awesome in praises, working wonders?

When Moses watched the waters pour back in upon the army of Pharaoh and looked around him at the congregation of Israel — dry and unhurt — he couldn't help but erupt into a song of praise to his God. In Biblical times songs were often used to relate historic events in order to remind future generations of God's past faithfulness. Moses watched as the miracles of God played out before his eyes like a movie... and his heart was filled to overflowing. Moses sang songs of God being his strength and the One who put a song on his lips. He called God a warrior with a right hand which shattered His enemies. Moses recalled that a mere breath from God's nostrils piled the waters up and then released them at the perfect time to drown the approaching enemy. He then talked about who God was to the nation of Israel. *"In Your lovingkindness You have led the people whom You have redeemed; in Your strength You have guided them to Your holy habitation."* Notice that the humble Moses didn't take credit for leading the people, redeeming them from the hand of Pharaoh, or being a source of strength for them. He gave God all the credit in a true picture of submission and subservience. How tragic it is that those 'sub' words are so distasteful to us today. Had Moses refused to submit to God's perfect will and implement His perfect plan, none of these miracles would have happened. Moses is the kind of leader we all need to shepherd us. His first loyalty… and his first worship... went to God alone.

COMMON GROUND: In our 'modern and enlightened' society we look at submission as a dirty word. The picture we paint of the submissive wife is one of a doormat being trodden upon by her authoritative husband. Common folk will balk at submission on all levels and in all parts of their lives. Submission is actually a great blessing. Look at Moses' life. His submission to God led him to adventures he would never have been part of if he were hardened or unwilling to subject himself to God's plan. **HOLY GROUND:** I would encourage you to look through the Gospel accounts and see how Jesus handled the art of submission to the Father. Though they were co-equal in all things, Jesus was fully willing to submit to His Father's authority. That should be a picture for all of us to follow. In our walk toward holiness, submission to God's ultimate authority must be one of our first steps.

Lord, I have been taught that submission is a dirty word and that I will be walked all over if I yield to others. Now I see that it is not a true picture of what submitting to Your authority means. Help me, Father, to be willing to take my commands from You and to walk in the ways You lead me. Help me walk in complete obedience. I will need help, for this is all new to me. Amen.

➤ Day **53**: THIRSTY MULTITUDE
PASSAGE: **Exodus 15:16-27**
VERSE: **Exodus 15:24**

So the people grumbled at Moses, saying, "What shall we drink?"

After Moses sang and praised God for His awesome provision, his sister, Miriam, grabbed a timbrel and she and the other women sang and danced saying, *"Sing to the LORD, for He is highly exalted; the horse and his rider He has hurled into the sea."* What a time of celebration as everyone thanked Moses and praised God. Unfortunately, the celebration was short lived. For the next three days they traveled in the wilderness of Shur… and found no water to drink. Finally they came to the waters at Marah and were so excited to be able to soothe their dry and scratchy throats with water. Imagine their horror when they found the waters were bitter and undrinkable! The thirst turned to anger and Moses was the closest target for them to unleash upon. "Why did you bring us here? There is nothing to drink—are you trying to kill us out here in the wilderness?" Moses cried out to God who showed him a tree and commanded him to throw it into the waters. Before the eyes of the parched congregation God turned the water sweet and they drank their full. God had their attention and made a new covenant with them there in Marah. *"If you will give earnest heed to the voice of the LORD your God, and do what is right in His sight, and give ear to His commandments, and keep all His statutes, I will put none of the diseases on you which I have put on the Egyptians; for I, the LORD, am your healer."* Great promise isn't it? Listen to God, faithfully obey His commands and remain disease free… how hard can that be?

COMMON GROUND: We will talk several times throughout this book on rash promises and quick agreements given without real thought. The congregation likely thought they could/would easily obey God's commands and keep His laws. When God provides for our needs and all our thirsts are satisfied it is easy to pledge obedience and faithfulness. **HOLY GROUND:** God's call to obedience is never to be taken lightly or without careful thought. God was making a promise to place an amazing hedge of protection around the nation of Israel. That same promise is ours today. I am not saying sickness will never come—or family problems or financial difficulty—but God will hedge us, protect us and walk with us through the storms. Sounds good… but obedience and holiness are still required!

Father, Help me to take Your promises as the Gospel truth and not to make rash promises I cannot keep. I want an open and transparent relationship with You. Lord, how grateful I am for Your amazing hedge of protection surrounding my life. Amen.

➤ Day **54**: BREAD FROM HEAVEN
PASSAGE: **Exodus 16:1-7**
VERSE: **Exodus 16:4**

Then the LORD said to Moses, "Behold, I will rain bread from heaven for you; and the people shall go out and gather a day's portion every day, that I may test them, whether or not they will walk in My instruction."

Israel had been out of bondage for two months when the complaining began in earnest. The people were crying out because of their hunger. Again, they were fondly reminiscing about how great life had been in Egypt and were challenging Moses about all he had taken them away from. Now, don't get me wrong. I understand thirst and hunger, and that the body has very real needs, but they made a career out of whining and harping on Moses... who could do nothing but intercede with the Lord on their behalf. God responded with the verse for today's entry. Certainly the people had to be thrilled to know that food was on the way. I wonder if they thought the Wonder Bread truck was going to pull up and drop off wrapped and sliced loaves. After all, what does heavenly bread look like? Notice the rest of the verse. God said He was going to use the bread as a character test for Israel. The test was: 1. The people were to gather their own bread. 2. They were to take only what was needed for each day's use. 3. On the sixth day they were to gather enough for the Sabbath also. 4. Obey number three because no bread will come on the seventh day. The test sounded easy enough and Moses and Aaron told the people to watch, because again they would see the provision of the Lord. Let's hope it works, because Moses and Aaron must have been tired of being used as Israel's punching bags.

COMMON GROUND: Let's address God using manna (heavenly bread) to test the faithfulness of the people of Israel. Why would He need to perform such a test? He had dealt with this bunch before! A common response would be to think it is wrong for God to test His children, as that doesn't seem very loving or trusting. The common truth is that most of us fail God's tests every day of our lives. We bend the rules and rationalize doing so. That is no different than the bread test in today's passage. **HOLY GROUND:** Holiness seekers should welcome tests like this because it gives them a chance to be victorious in their obedience. I personally think we should review our day just before we close our eyes at night and ponder the victories and defeats of the past twenty-four hours. Obedient people need not fear the daily exams of God.

*Jesus, I stink at tests! No, I'll rephrase that. I used to stink at tests,
but from this day forward I am going to review and assess
my day, confess my failures, thank You for my successes,
and prepare for tomorrow's tests. Amen.*

➤ Day 55: YOU WILL EAT QUAIL!
PASSAGE: **Exodus 16:8-13**
VERSE: **Exodus 16:8**

*Moses said, "This will happen when the LORD gives you meat
to eat in the evening, and bread to the full in the morning; for the
LORD hears your grumblings which you grumble against Him...
Your grumblings are not against us but against the LORD."*

If you have already read the passage for today's entry, I would like
you to turn to Numbers 11 and read what I find to be some of the
funniest Scriptures in the Bible. God was fed up with the grumbling
and whining of the people. Nothing Moses or God did could please
them. As we read in this chapter, the Hebrew people were reminiscing about the fish, cucumbers and melons they used to eat in
Egypt. They were sick of manna and wanted something they could
really sink their teeth into. Besides that, the manna was a fine seed
that fell from heaven and had to be gathered, ground and baked. No
Wonder Bread after all! Moses, in absolute frustration, asked God
why he was saddled with this whining and ungrateful people. He
reminded God that he didn't ask for the job or give birth to them,
and he was tired of playing 'Daddy' to them. God told Moses to
proclaim these words. *"Tomorrow...you shall eat meat; for you have
wept in the ears of the LORD... Therefore the LORD will give you
meat and you shall eat. You shall eat, not one day, nor two days, nor
five days, nor ten days, nor twenty days, but a whole month, until it
comes out of your nostrils and becomes loathsome to you..."* Think
God is seriously fed up here? I love it! They will eat it until it comes
out of their nostrils! It makes me think about my son who used to
ungratefully whine for pizza every night when I had cooked nutri-

tious homemade meals. I would have loved to see the pizza come out his nostrils... but I digress. God sent the quail as promised—maybe that would fill the bellies and silence the whiners.

COMMON GROUND: Has there been a time in your life when your ingratitude would have provoked God like this situation did? When He sends 'bread,' do you long for 'meat?' When He sends peace, do you long for excitement? When He sends smiles, do you long for belly laughs? When He sends enough, do you whine for more? Commoners will never be satisfied and God will never be enough for them. **HOLY GROUND:** When we thank God for the small things... bread, peace, smiles... He reads our hearts and sends... meat, excitement, belly laughs. God wanted to bless the people He delivered from bondage, but how could He do that when the freed soul can rarely be satisfied? Is this a hard word to listen to? Think about why it is.

Spirit of God, It goes without saying that I have been ungrateful and as unpleasant as I find the nation of Israel in this passage. Lord, I do not want to be the recipient of Your wrath... thus I will learn gratitude and contentment in whatever situation I find myself. Amen.

➤ Day 56: MANNA MANNERS
PASSAGE: **Exodus 16:14-36**
VERSE: **Exodus 16:18**

When they measured it with an omer, he who had gathered much had no excess, and he who had gathered little had no lack; every man gathered as much as he should eat.

As we read in the last two entries, God was sending the manna to satisfy their hunger, as well as to test the obedience of the people who proclaimed to serve Him. Today we see more detailed 'Manna Manners' and how specific God was in His call for that obedience. *"This is what the LORD has commanded, 'Gather of it every man as much as he should eat; you shall take an omer apiece according to the number of persons each of you has in his tent.'"* That seems easy enough to obey. Notice that those who had fewer people in their tent weren't required to gather as much because the command was to gather only as much as was necessary to feed each mouth. When they measured it with an omer, he who had gathered much had no excess, and he who had gathered little had no lack. That is amazing—no one gathered more than the exact amount he needed! It was like God's spirit stopped them from gathering too little or too much. *"Let no man leave any of it until morning."* That was a pretty clear-cut command, but they did not listen to Moses and some left part of it until morning... and it bred worms and became foul. There is always someone who thinks they are smarter than God! Then the people were told *"...on the Sabbath to the LORD... you will not find it in the field. Six days you shall gather it, but on the seventh day, the Sabbath, there will be none."* It came about on the seventh day that *some of the people went out to gather, but they found none.* On day six they were to gather two days worth of manna seed. Sounds to me like the same rocket scientists who tried to store it overnight hadn't learned their lessons. As with all tests—some pass and some fail.

COMMON GROUND: As I looked for the application in this story I kept coming back to the trust issue. If Israel had truly trusted that God would provide for their daily needs—their 'Daily Bread', they wouldn't have tried to hoard and save the uneaten manna overnight. Real trust in God's provision is a precious and rare commodity even in the Christian church. Far too many of us take the common road which leads to self-reliance instead of the holy road leading to God-reliance. **HOLY GROUND:** God made this promise to us in Psalms 37:25 *"Yet I have not seen the righteous forsaken or his descendants begging bread."* Why then do we continue to fear for His provision? Why do we spend so much time working and storing up for future needs while we ignore the more urgent needs of relationships, families and spiritual growth? Saving is wise and necessary, but focus on that should never blur our need for time with our Provider. Surely if God would send manna to the whining nation of Israel, He will keep His promise and provide for those who seek to walk in holiness.

Father God, I can clearly state that You have never withheld Your provision from me. I have food, shelter, family, friends and a living Savior who directs my paths. Help me to not dwell on the unknown tomorrow but to fully focus on the unfolding today. Amen.

➤ Day 57: AMALEKITE VICTORY
PASSAGE: **Exodus 17:1-16**
VERSE: **Exodus 17:11**

So it came about when Moses held his hand up, that Israel prevailed, and when he let his hand down, Amalek prevailed.

After another whining session because of their thirst, the people of Israel seemed quite content to dwell in the Wilderness of Sin (the Bible's title for it—not mine), even after Moses struck a rock and fresh, clean water poured forth. Just when things were looking up for the leaders and the congregation… the blasted Amalekites came to attack Israel. Moses commanded his protégé Joshua to gather an army and to prepare for battle the next day. *"Choose men for us and go out, fight against Amalek. Tomorrow I will station myself on the top of the hill with the staff of God in my hand."* Joshua was being groomed for a leadership role and Moses was watching over the battlefield with the staff of God in his hands. As long as Moses kept the staff raised and pointed up toward heaven—Joshua's army was winning the battle. As we all know, holding anything (even an empty hand) over our head for a long period of time is difficult. Moses was a warrior for God, but he was still human and fatigue kept causing his arm to falter. Each time that happened, the battle turned in favor of to Amalekites. God, in His infinite wisdom and provision, sent Aaron and Hur up the hill with Moses. They placed a large rock under him for a seat and one stood on each side of their leader, holding his arms toward the sky. Finally, at sunset the battle was won. Joshua had defeated the enemy with power and might… and a little good old-fashioned teamwork!

COMMON GROUND: How much of a team player are you? Ever heard the old adage that many hands make light work? Think about preparing for a banquet, potluck or funeral dinner at your church. Isn't it easier and more fun to divide the work and enjoy fellowship with others than to do it all yourself? Why then are so few people willing to chip in and give a hand? Common responses will always lead us to believe that there is enough help and ours is not needed. Nothing could be further from the truth. God needs all hands on deck if the church is to impact our world. **HOLY GROUND:** Moses could have told Aaron and Hur that he didn't need their help. If he had done that, Joshua may well have lost the battle and Israel would have been defeated. God sent three men up the hill because one couldn't do the job alone. When He sends others to help you, thank Him for the provision; and then get busy doing the work He has delegated for you to do.

Lord, Make me a team player, a fellow encourager
and a 'body-builder' in Your kingdom. Amen.

➤ Day 58: JETHRO'S VISIT
PASSAGE: **Exodus 18:1-12**
VERSE: **Exodus 18:9**

Jethro rejoiced over all the goodness which the LORD had
done to Israel, in delivering them from the hand of the Egyptians.

Good news travels fast. Jethro, the father-in-law of Moses, heard of all that had happened through Moses' work for God and prepared to visit him. Moses' wife and sons were in Midian and were to be reunited with him. Jethro approached Moses' camp near the Mountain of God (Sinai) and was brought up to date as *Moses told his father-in-law all that the LORD had done to Pharaoh and to the Egyptians for Israel's sake, all the hardship that had befallen them on the journey, and how the LORD had delivered them.* Jethro—even though he did not serve the same God as his daughter's husband—rejoiced at all the Lord had done through Moses. No one can fully reject God when they see His amazing provision; Jethro was no exception. *So Jethro said, "Blessed be the LORD who delivered you from the hand of the Egyptians and from the hand of Pharaoh, and who delivered the people from under the hand of the Egyptians. Now I know that the LORD is greater than all the gods; indeed, it was proven when they dealt proudly against the people."* Moses was sharing his faith simply by relating what God had done in his personal situation... and his audience was listening!

COMMON GROUND: There are times when our personal testimony of God's faithfulness in our lives will be the only real witness others will hear. I personally get frustrated when I hear people say, "My faith is a personal thing and I keep it to myself." As far as I am concerned, that is selfish! We are called to go into *all nations* and proclaim the good news of Jesus Christ. *All nations* include our local sphere of influence. How are you 'going' and 'proclaiming' in your sphere? **HOLY GROUND:** Part of our stepping up this year to personal growth will be stepping up our personal witness. You aren't the only one God wants on holy ground this year! He wants you to bring friends, neighbors, family and strangers along on the journey... go and tell others what great things the Father has done in your life.

Father, My witness has been weak, but I have a personal story about how You have worked and are working in my life. Embolden me to tell others so they—like Jethro—will be persuaded to serve the true God. Amen.

➤ Day 59: A TEACHABLE SPIRIT
PASSAGE: Exodus 18:13-27
VERSE: Exodus 18:23-24

"If you do this thing and God so commands you, then you will be able to endure, and all these people also will go to

their place in peace." So Moses listened to his father-in-law and did all that he had said.

Moses was excited to share with Jethro all that God was doing, and the next morning brought him along to watch what a day's work consisted of in Moses' life. From morning until evening the people came to Moses, who served as a judge in all their disputes and in their inquiries of God. Jethro was concerned: *"What is this thing that you are doing for the people? Why do you alone sit as judge and all the people stand about you from morning until evening?"* Moses replied, *"Because the people come to me to inquire of God. When they have a dispute, it comes to me, and I judge between a man and his neighbor and make known the statutes of God and His laws."* Jethro explained to Moses that he could not possibly be all things to all people. He advised him to *be the people's representative before God... teach them the statutes and the laws, and make known to them the way in which they are to walk and the work they are to do... select out of all the people able men who fear God... place these over them as leaders of thousands, of hundreds, of fifties and of tens... let them judge the people at all times... let it be that every major dispute they will bring to you... and they will bear the burden with you.* Moses never thought to delegate duties because he felt a personal responsibility to tend the flock God had given him charge over. He appointed judges and set up a court system (much like the American judicial system) and, other than very difficult disputes, they heard the needs of the people.

COMMON GROUND: What we see from today's passage of Scripture is that Moses had a decision to make. Was he going to hold onto the reins, reject Jethro's teaching and have total control over the people? Or, was he going to have a 'teachable spirit' that would listen to reason and delegate some of the duties? Fortunately for Moses, he listened to sound advice. A common response to 'friendly advice' is to take it as criticism, rather than as assistance. **HOLY GROUND:** How good are you at taking advice or godly criticism? I confess that I am quick to get defensive, even when I know that the person speaking to me is giving sound Biblical counsel. I will work on that this year... do you need to do the same? God will send wise counselors only if we will hear them.

Jesus, I confess that I have reacted wrongly or been offended by some You have sent to give me wise counsel. Help me to get over thinking that I have to always be right and to develop a teachable spirit like Moses had. Pride is an issue—break it in me. Amen.

➤ Day 60: A PECULIAR TREASURE
PASSAGE: **Exodus 19:1-8**
VERSE: **Exodus 19:5-6**

"Now then, if you will indeed obey My voice and keep My covenant, then you shall be My own possession among all the peoples, for all the earth is Mine; and you shall be to Me a kingdom of priests and a holy nation."

Today I will address one of my favorite Scriptures in the entire Bible. God is telling the nation of Israel—and us as grafted-in believers—exactly what is expected of us. Let's look closely at the specifics He lays out before us. We are to *obey His voice, keep His covenant, be His* possession, *be a kingdom of priests* and *be a holy nation.* I love the King James Version which reads we are to be *a peculiar treasure* of the Lord's. We have already discussed obedience several times, so let's look at the other things God expects of us. In order to be 'peculiar' we must dare to be different. Peculiar people don't blend in with the crowd or compromise to be like the rest of the world. They are to bear the mark of Christ and stand out in the crowd. We Christians are called to be *in the world but not of the world,* which means we are to walk, talk, act and think differently than society around us. We are also called to be a *kingdom of priests* in a very secular world. We are blessed to have full access to the words, laws, commands and throne of God just as the Old Testament priests had. As believers we are to use those things in our own lives, as well as to show others how to walk with Christ.

Finally, we are expected to be *a holy nation*. Does that one really warrant additional teaching? A holy nation reflects God's love and His own holiness.

COMMON GROUND: Here we see a very real problem: The modern Christian church is walking on very common and worldly ground today. We are compromising the message, so as to not look peculiar in society. We are ignorant of the commands and words of the Bible and have lost communication with Jesus, our High Priest. Most of us would rather hide from God than step into His presence. Finally, our common living has made our nation—and the church body itself—anything but holy. Sin has seeped into the camp and is slowly taking full control. **HOLY GROUND:** The holy ground solutions are really quite simple. Be different! Be bold! Be strong! Be Word taught! Be in the presence of God! Be holy. Nothing more is necessary for this application.

Spirit of God, I don't even know where to begin. Lord, this journey is harder than I thought it would be. Hear the cry of my heart, "I want to be holy as You are holy." Amen.

➤ Day **61**: WORSHIP PREPARATION
PASSAGE: **Exodus 19:9-15**
VERSE: **Exodus 19:14**

So Moses went down from the mountain to the people and consecrated the people, and they washed their garments.

After God had given the commands for how His children were to walk before Him, they all agreed to be *peculiar, royal and holy priests* as He said. The Father then told Moses to prepare the people for an encounter with Him three days later when He would come down the mountain in a cloud and speak to Moses within their hearing. God's plan was that, once they heard Him interact with Moses, they would be obedient and respectful to their leader. Moses gave strict commands on how they were to prepare themselves for this encounter with their God. They were to wash their bodies and garments (outward cleanliness) and prepare their hearts for God to speak to them (inward cleanliness). Moses knew from personal experience that being in the Presence of Creator God was a reverential and awe inspiring thing. He wanted his people to experience this form of worship for themselves and to realize just how amazing God's blessings had been. He knew that genuine worship required preparation—some physical, some emotional, and some spiritual. As he directed, the people did.

COMMON GROUND: Can you think of a time when you have really (and I do mean really) prepared for an encounter with God? Have you cleaned yourself from the inside out in order to come into His Presence? Do you sometimes hurry in and hurry out—if you even seek His Presence at all? A common attitude might be that God needs to meet us on our level and at our convenience. Here is a revolutionary thought: *Your worship experience will reflect the amount of effort you put into preparation for it.* **HOLY GROUND:** How do you prepare? Seek Him in a quiet place with no external distractions. Remember who it is your want an encounter with. Often we spend hours preparing for a date or dinner party and can't give God the time it takes to thank Him for our Corn Flakes. Read from Scripture, and then talk to Him about what you have read, and seek His guidance—after acknowledging that His guidance is all you need. Remember that you cannot be in the world for weeks on end and not have its influences penetrate your spirit. You need His renewal in order to hear His voice and feel His hand upon you.

Father God, Sometimes I feel like I don't even know how to pray, let alone come into Your presence. I long to worship You as You so deserve to be worshipped. The world has desensitized me to how very evil it is. Please remove its residue so I can come before You in purity and honor. Amen.

➤ Day 62: REVERE HIS PRESENCE
PASSAGE: **Exodus 19:16-25**
VERSE: **Exodus 19:16**

*So it came about on the third day, when it was morning, that
there were thunder and lightning flashes and a thick cloud upon
the mountain and a very loud trumpet sound, so that all the
people who were in the camp trembled.*

On the third day Moses brought the consecrated and cleansed congregation to the mountain to meet with their God. When the thunder began to clap and the lightning to flash, the people grew afraid and trembled before the amazing power of the God who knew each of them by name, knew their hearts, and even knew the number of hairs on their heads. Suddenly the ram's horn shofar blew a long blast and God and Moses talked to one another. God called His obedient servant to come up the mountain. *Then the LORD said to him, "Go down and come up again, you and Aaron with you; but do not let the priests and the people break through to come up to the LORD, or He will break forth upon them."* Moses didn't understand why he must tell them again, but God was adamant. The mountain was to be set apart as holy; anyone trying to break forth up the side of it would surely die. Sounds to me like this will not be like any other encounter Moses has had with God!

COMMON GROUND: This passage of Scripture makes me think of a song whose refrain says, *"I am a friend of God. I am a friend of God. I am a friend of God. He calls me Friend!"* The song is great and technically true, but the reverent fear and awe of who God is should never be taken away in our worship. Moses and Abraham were friends of God, but they never failed to fall on their face before Him in reverence and respect. Maybe the common folk had mistakenly thought a genuine encounter with God would be like an encounter with any other friend, but He brought them back to reality with the first flash and clap of His power. **HOLY GROUND:** Where has the church's reverence for God gone? It left along with the strict Biblical teachings, the definition of sin, the truth that change is required in the life of the believer, and the teaching of Jesus' blood shed for the remission of sins. It left with all talk of hell—and with the arrival of the false belief that heaven is the place all 'good' people will spend eternity. Holy people must fight to get sound Biblical doctrines reinstated in their churches. God will not be mocked!

Lord, The ear-tickling messages in churches today turn my stomach. How many of Your children are being led astray by not being told to revere and fear the Name of the Lord? Father, is there any hope for us? Yes, we must humble ourselves and pray, turn from our sins and seek Your face. Amen.

➤ Day **63**: NO OTHER GODS
PASSAGE: **Exodus 20:1-3**
VERSE: **Exodus 20:3**

You shall have no other gods before Me.

As Moses waited upon God on the mountain, He began to speak some of the most important words in all of Scripture. He spoke to Moses what Moses was to speak to the people as God's mouthpiece. God was defining sin for Moses. The first four of the commandments address how we are to respect, honor, serve and revere God. That is fully appropriate because we can never treat our fellow man with dignity and respect if we first don't learn to respect his Creator. Later, when the laws are written on stone tablets, the first tablet will contain the four commandments relating to our worship of God. *"I am the LORD your God, who brought you out of the land of Egypt, out of the house of slavery. You shall have no other gods before Me."* God sums up in one sentence why the nation of Israel should obey Him... He delivered them from their bondage in Egypt! What does He mean when He states that Israel shall have no other gods before Him? Is God insecure? No, but He is *El Qanna*—a jealous God. He refuses to take leftovers after we worship on the other altars of our lives. Our god is whatever comes first in our life... money, fame, pride, physical beauty... self. God simply wants to be first in our life. When we are obedient in that, He will bless us in all other areas of our lives. God is asking you today... is He first in your life? If not, what god needs to be removed from your heart?

COMMON GROUND: Common people—even many in the church—will tell you because you live under the New Covenant of Jesus' grace that you never again need to look back at these commandments because you are free of their bondage. I say "Garbage!" I raised a child and know that, even though I was a gracious and loving mother, my son still needed to have a set of 'House Rules' to live by! How can we ever define sin and show people what they need to turn from without these moral laws? **HOLY GROUND:** Holy people will use the commandments of God as the guideposts for their lives. Yes, Jesus' blood washes our sins white as snow, but that doesn't mean adultery, theft, murder and coveting are okay in the life of the believer. He is a jealous God because He wants nothing to come between you and Him and the covenant relationship you have! That should encourage—not discourage—you.

Father, Please reveal to me anything... anything at all that I have allowed to come between You and me. I determine today to make You my God in every single area of my life. Amen.

➤ Day 64: NO GRAVEN IMAGES
PASSAGE: Exodus 20:4-6
VERSE: Exodus 20:4

You shall not make for yourself an idol, or any likeness of what is in heaven above or on the earth beneath or in the water under the earth.

Y ou might read this Scripture and think you are okay because you don't have any little carved idols sitting around your house as the centers of your worship. Idols can be things that don't look like carved gods to us... cars, houses, jewelry, material possessions and fame. It is time for a real life example for this entry. For the last thirty years I have had two addictions. One is potato chips—and God is working with me in that area as I write today. The other addiction (or idol) in my life is purses! Yep, purses! For years I couldn't shop without buying a purse. I could smell a leather store from ten miles away! I would even send Dan to buy me a purse and then complain if he picked one out I didn't like. (Yes, the man is indeed a saint!) For some crazy reason I thought a purse would take away my pain, calm my broken heart, or cheer me up when I was blue. Guess what? After a day or two—the purse was just a purse; it didn't change the circumstances of my life. Purses were my idols—the things I trusted to 'fix' the broken parts of my life. Little did I know that Jesus alone could fix my internal brokenness. Let me ask you an important question. What are the idols in your life? What things do you think you couldn't live without? One day you will live without them, either in heaven with Jesus or in hell with an eternity of regret.

COMMON GROUND: When Exodus was written there were serious concerns because all of the nations around Israel worshipped pagan gods. God was surely talking about those idols, but He was also addressing the things I talked about in the teaching section. One other thought... people will make idols of the sun, moon, stars, angels and themselves. No matter what your idol is, God knows the truth. **HOLY GROUND:** As people called to holiness, we must remember that images or pictures we see of God or His Son Jesus are merely man's interpretation of what they would look like. Though they are pleasing to the eye and comforting to the spirit, they are never to be looked at as absolute depictions. God is spirit; no man living today knows what Jesus looked like, and the Holy Spirit is cautioning you to not look for idols in order to worship.

Jesus, There is so much I need to learn about Your commands and Your Word. Help me each day to keep my eyes on You as

I long to see Your face. For now, picturing Your nail-pierced wrists is enough for me. Amen.

➤ Day 65: NAME IN VAIN
PASSAGE: **Exodus 20:7**
VERSE: **Exodus 20:7**

You shall not take the name of the LORD your God in vain, for the LORD will not leave him unpunished who takes His name in vain.

As we look at this third commandment of God for the nation of Israel, I will tell you this is one of my favorites to teach on. Taking God's name in vain can involve a lot of different aspects. Let's look at some: 1. We take God's name in vain when we profess faith and live a life contrary to that profession, thus bringing the claim of 'hypocrisy' upon ourselves and the entire body of Christ. 2. We take it in vain when we make a covenant (a promise of 'so help me God') and then break that covenant. This would also apply to breaking the vows taken at marriage… Ouch! 3. When we want to add emphasis to our words and say, "I swear to God…" and then dishonor Him by not keeping our word… we have taken His Name in vain. 4. Cussing or swearing using the Name of the Lord is another way we break this commandment. 5. Finally, my personal belief is that profession of faith in Jesus Christ gives us full authority to use His Name to rebuke, challenge and witness in that name. When we fail to use the Name we are given—we were given that right in vain. I will explain this later in the application section. The commandment has a very clear warning at the end… *the LORD will not leave him unpunished who takes His name in vain.* Remember, God will not be mocked!

COMMON GROUND: Many times I have had the opportunity to witness to someone about the difference Christ has made in my life. When I fail to do so, I am always convicted. One time, in order to get rid of my conviction, I sat down and wrote a letter to the people

I failed to proclaim Christ to and hurriedly stuck it in the mail. I felt really good about myself until the letter came back to me because I had addressed it wrong! Against my fleshly desires, I re-addressed and re-mailed the letter. God is so funny! **HOLY GROUND:** For most of my life I didn't walk with Christ. I cussed and swore like a drunken sailor and used the Lord's Name to punctuate my profanity. One day someone at a nearby restaurant table challenged my use of Jesus' Name. She said, "Please don't take the Name of my Lord in vain. It breaks my heart to hear it." I was offended... she was right... and today I understand just what she meant. His Name is holy and must roll off holy lips.

Spirit of God, May I never use Your Name to make a promise I do not intend to keep. May I never fail to use Your Name when I have the opportunity to witness to others? Lord, I have failed miserably and need so much help. Amen.

➤ Day 66: KEEP THE SABBATH
PASSAGE: **Exodus 20:8-11**
VERSE: **Exodus 20:8**

Remember the Sabbath day, to keep it holy.

Here we come to that age-old debate on what exactly keeping the Sabbath means. I think that in order to understand this commandment we must first look at the intention for which it was given. God created the entire world in six days—no simple feat! He then took the seventh day to look at all He had created, to enjoy the work of His hands, and to rest His spirit from the work of the past six days. God rested on the Sabbath—and was renewed by that rest. If that is the case, the command to honor (celebrate) the Sabbath is a gift—a sabbatical—from our labors. God wasn't being dictatorial in this command; instead, He was giving us a much needed day for reflection (on God and His creation), a day to enjoy the works of our hands (and His), and a day to reflect on who He is in our lives.

You see, God knew the stuff of the world would cause us to take our eyes off of Him—and He was right, wasn't He? Picture a nation where everyone rested, spent time with their families, attended church and gloried in the blessings of God one day each week. Imagine how that would change our character all the other days of the week. Do you think God is pleased with a nation which treats the Sabbath like every other day? He knew that our free will would lead us to lives without any rest.

COMMON GROUND: I know what you are thinking. "I work all week and need Sunday to catch up, shop, do the laundry, and decorate the house..." That is the common response—even among Christians—in our nation. Is it possible that with better time management those things could be done during the rest of the week in order for you to enjoy the 'gift' of rest on the Sabbath? Imagine coming to that day knowing you were going to rest and seek God... not dirty socks. Sounds good, doesn't it? **HOLY GROUND:** One thing I would ask you to consider is that in order for us to eat out, buy groceries, place phone orders, and get tech support on Sunday... others have to work on their Sabbath, too. If America stopped being super consumers on Sundays, others wouldn't have to work to serve our needs. Our nation was much more focused and holy when we honored the Sabbath.

Father God, I am just beginning to realize that the Sabbath rest is a gift, not a restriction. Help me to better use my time during the week so that I might relax and enjoy Your abundance on the day You have set aside for us. Amen.

➤ Day 67: HONOR YOUR PARENTS
PASSAGE: **Exodus 20:12**
VERSE: **Exodus 20:12**

Honor your father and your mother, that your days may be prolonged in the land which the LORD your God gives you.

This entry is all about the building of strong families, which are the backbone of any strong nation. Oh, how we need to pay attention to this command as we look at a society where the elderly are ignored, fathers are not in the homes, and working mothers are left to raise their children alone. God's command to honor the mother and father was given because the parents were the ones to teach the things of God to their children. Each of God's precious children is entrusted to earthly parents who are to nurture, feed, love and teach God's truths to them. When that job is done correctly the children naturally treat their parents with the respect the parental rank deserves. Just as military personnel are required to 'salute the rank' of their superior officers, so must children grow up understanding that their parents are the authority in their household. This is the first command with a promise attached... *that your days may be prolonged in the land.* Those who honor their parents will learn to honor all authority and will be better workers, leaders and parents themselves.

COMMON GROUND: Many people would respond to this entry by saying that their parents didn't 'deserve or earn' respect because of their lifestyles and actions. I understand that completely, but we are taught by the Word of God to honor them anyway and to look for the things they did right and honor those things. This kind of respect has to be taught; and in our permissive society we have failed to teach our young people the common art of respecting others. **HOLY GROUND:** No matter how bad your parents were, God loaned you to them for a time. If you are reading this, likely you are a born-again Christian with a hunger for God's truths. Look deep into your heart. Learn to forgive. Be grateful for the blessings of the past and step forward that you may be a better parent or example to the young people you come in contact with. Holy people seek to be holy in all areas of their lives.

Lord, Help me to speak with honor and respect of my own parents. Make me a better Mother, Father, Grandparent, that I may deserve the honor shown to my rank. Father God, I honor You. Amen.

➤ Day 68: DON'T KILL
PASSAGE: Exodus 20:13
VERSE: Exodus 20:13

You shall not murder.

Well, that commandment sounds clear enough! Whenever I witness to people about faith and attempt to define sin, they always think they have kept this sixth commandment, which makes them good people, and because of it they are assured of going to heaven. As you will see in future entries, God makes clear distinctions between accidental murder (manslaughter) and planned (premeditated) murder. Unfortunately for some of us, Jesus expanded on this command in a way that leaves few of us unscathed. Read this Scripture from the Sermon on the Mount found in Matthew chapter five. *"You have heard that the ancients were told, 'YOU SHALL NOT COMMIT MURDER' and 'Whoever commits murder shall be liable to the court.' But I say to you that everyone who is angry with his brother shall be guilty before the court; and whoever says to his brother, 'You good-for-nothing,' shall be guilty before the supreme court; and whoever says, 'You fool,' shall be guilty enough to go into the fiery hell."* Jesus put much higher requirements on being guilty of murder than God's commandment seemed to hold. He said hating someone, being angry with them, calling them a good-for-nothing, or even calling them a fool is grounds for judgment, death, and even hell! So much for thinking you hadn't broken this one, huh?

COMMON GROUND: Why would Jesus say that simply hating someone or calling them a fool was murder? Murder can be a physical act, and it can also be a spiritual act of killing someone's soul. When we speak that way to someone, we are telling them that God made a flawed product and they are of no value. Our deepest identity is our identity of what God made us to be. If we destroy that identity, we are surely killing the spirit. **HOLY GROUND:** I pray that you will never be the victim of a physical murder or a spiritual murder. I also pray you will take these words to heart and watch what you say to others that could cause them such emotional harm. Holy people must look at every person God created and seek to see the potential God wrapped into them. Only when we speak godly words about God's highest creation will we hear these words: *"Well done, thou good and faithful servant; now enter into your rest."*

Father, My words have been unkind and hateful. I have looked at the human beings You created and judged that some were 'fools' and 'good for nothings.' Those were my assessments and they were wrong. Father, change my heart that I may hear those words of acceptance when I stand before Your throne. Amen.

➤ Day 69: NO ADULTERY
PASSAGE: Exodus 20:14
VERSE: Exodus 20:14

You shall not commit adultery.

Which part of that commandment don't you understand? This is another command that on the surface seems to exonerate those of us who have never had a physical adulterous affair outside our marriage. Again, Jesus added to the definition when He said in the Sermon on the Mount, *"... but I say to you that everyone who looks at a woman with lust for her has already committed adultery with her in his heart."* Ladies, don't get too smug. The same applies to us! Adultery is divided loyalty. Adultery wants something that doesn't belong to you. Adultery is lusting after something which makes what you already have appear not to measure up! (Reread them!) Over the years I have listened to all the lines used to advance inappropriate relationships: "My wife/husband doesn't understand me—I have fallen out of love with my spouse—God must have wanted us together, or we wouldn't have ended up working at the same job." No matter what the excuses... sin is still sin. You can roll it in sugar and pour chocolate over the top... it is still sin! Let me address one other issue here. Pornography, erotic movies, smutty romance novels and flirting are all adultery. All of them serve to blur our vision of marital love and make us long for something more exciting. With the internet making pornography readily accessible, we are growing a generation of young men who will never be satisfied with a 'normal' sexual relationship in marriage. We are also rearing a generation of young women who fantasize about being swept off their feet by swashbuckling men... or even by vampires, as portrayed in a new book and movie series.

COMMON GROUND: When we are walking on common ground we will be bombarded by the things I wrote about in this lesson. I tell both men and women that the first look is free. You cannot help it if someone walks in front of you wearing inappropriate clothes, or someone who is handsome or beautiful. It is the second look and all subsequent looks that are adulterous. This is why the pornography business is flourishing. Taking those subsequent looks is ruining the moral fiber of our nation. Fantasy with no responsibility always sounds better. **HOLY GROUND:** Keep your eyes to yourself! Holiness may require you to remove anything which can be a source of weakness for you. It is better to live without a computer (or soap operas) than to die with an adulterous heart. One other thought... adultery can be both physical and spiritual. When we begin to make other things our gods, or to worship the god-of-self, we are committing adultery against the One who died for our sins.

Jesus, I have looked at others in an inappropriate way. I have lusted after those I am not married to. I am even guilty of some spiritual adultery in my life. Lord, help me to be strong in the face of temptation... all forms of temptation. Amen.

➤ Day 70: DON'T STEAL
PASSAGE: **Exodus 20:15**
VERSE: **Exodus 20:15**

You shall not steal.

I pray that you are learning more each day about how to walk in holiness before God. Many would say because we live under grace that we are no longer held by these laws. I agree with the grace, but feel that the modern church has failed to define sin. Without that definition, sin has crept into our churches like it has into society as a whole. We are not making disciples of new believers and showing them that God does indeed require us to walk in holiness. Without sin being defined, the individuals in the church body must determine their own moral standards. Stealing is a great example of that truth. Most people would say they never stole anything that belonged to another person. When we begin to remove the surface soil and expose the deeper ground of the heart, we find that people have stolen, but their rationales change. Here are some challenges to the theft question: Have you stolen anything from work—even a pencil or a paperclip? Have you cheated on your taxes? Do you do personal work or surf the internet on company time? Have you withheld your tithes from the church? Have you copied someone else's work? Stealing is taking anything that doesn't belong to you. That hits closer to home, doesn't it? I told someone recently that I didn't see "You shall not steal anything over $5," when I read the commandment. Thinking the company can afford it, or that the IRS already takes too much of your money, will not hold up in God's holy standard of judgment.

COMMON GROUND: Isn't it funny how our society judges thieves to different degrees? We watch looting during a disaster and think it is okay because people are poor. We watch Wall Street workers steal billions of dollars and think they aren't as bad because they are stealing from the rich. We steal hours of work from our employers each week and think it is okay. Stealing was wrong in Moses' day and it is still wrong in ours. **HOLY GROUND:** What you borrow, return. What you have stolen, give back. What God has blessed you with, be grateful. One other thing... do you steal the minutes and hours of each day by wasting them and not seeking to know God more? That is the most tragic of all kinds of stealing. We can never get back those lost minutes.

Spirit of God, Reveal to me any ways that I am stealing. I am guilty of some of what was said in this entry. I long to stand before the throne without these things hanging over my head. Give me new awareness of areas which require change. Amen.

➤ Day 71: DON'T LIE
PASSAGE: **Exodus 20:16**
VERSE: **Exodus 20:16**

You shall not bear false witness against your neighbor.

Today's commandment has several different facets. Let's look first at the damage which can be done by lying and gossiping. I imagine if this commandment read, "You shall not gossip about your neighbor," that most of us—if not all of us—would be convicted by it. Gossip is so easy, isn't it? Proverbs 18:21 tells us, *Death and life are in the power of the tongue, and those who love it will eat its fruit.* Our tongues—our words—have the power to bring life and encouragement, or death and discouragement. Gossip in most every case brings the latter. We must learn to curb our tongues and avoid this tearing down. We need also to look at how lying in a court of law can do harm to our neighbor. God knew—as did the founders of our great nation—that a nation could not survive unless its system of justice was incorruptible. Later in the Bible God would say that a man couldn't be convicted on the witness of only one man—and that two or more witnesses were required. Why would He say that? False testimony for reasons of jealousy, anger, revenge or personal gain would destroy the system of true justice. Finally, lying for the sake of lying would corrupt the heart of the liar. Deceit in any form was wrong in the days of the written law of God... and still is today.

COMMON GROUND: How common is gossip in your circle of friends or in your church body? Gossip will destroy the unity of hearts who worship together. Lying, exaggerating, and giving any kind of false testimony does the same. **HOLY GROUND:** Here is a thought: Don't bring gasoline to the gossip fire; bring water to douse it instead. You cannot be a holy ground walker and still indulge in gossip, backbiting, sniping, lying and tearing God's people down. As I write this, I am as convicted as I hope you are.

Father God, I may not have given false testimony in court, but I surely am guilty of lying and gossiping about others. Lord, I am ashamed. In my own flesh I am incapable of putting out these fires, but with You all things are possible. If You need to sew my lips shut, do so to silence me. Amen.

➤ Day 72: DON'T BE JEALOUS
PASSAGE: **Exodus 20:17**
VERSE: **Exodus 20:17**

You shall not covet your neighbor's house; you shall not covet your neighbor's wife or his male servant or his female servant or his ox or his donkey or anything that belongs to your neighbor.

I'll bet you thought we would never get to the end of these studies on the Ten Commandments. My concern is that this very basic foundational teaching has been removed from the church and has been replaced with ear-tickling messages which make people feel good, rather than bringing change through convicted spirits. Are you the jealous or covetous type? Do you look around you and see what everyone else possesses and want it? Are you unsatisfied with what God has given you? The problem with coveting or being jealous is that we are telling God He hasn't done right by us. Look at these examples: "I want beautiful clothes like she has, instead of the ones I wear every day—Her hair is so much nicer than mine—I wish I had more room in my house like my best friend has—She is thin; I wish I could be more like her—She is a great singer; why don't I have any talent?" God's response to these statements might be: *"I clothed her for modesty, gave her hair to warm her head, provided shelter for her and her family, gave her a healthy body, and gave her special gifts and disciplines... but none of what I provided was enough. Maybe I should simply stop sending blessings to this ungrateful child."* Coveting and jealousy can never lead to good in our lives—for we will always find someone who has more, bigger and better things than we do.

COMMON GROUND: The week I wrote this entry I had been catching up with high school classmates on Facebook. One was talking about a northern Michigan home in a nice area. Another talked about a trip to Europe. Yet another one talked about her artwork and gallery. Needless to say, my very common response was to compare that to my home in the 'galvanized ghetto,' which I call our manufactured home community! Suddenly I was convicted that my house—which provides shelter, warmth, and a haven for Dan and me, wasn't enough. I was jealous of the travel, convinced that I had no artistic ability, and felt like a consummate failure. Needless to say, the Holy Spirit was at work in my jealous heart. **HOLY GROUND:** Sin causes us to be self-centered instead of God-centered. The essence of being saved by Christ is to shift that focus back onto God and His abundant blessings. Holy people are grateful and content... period.

Lord, I can fool myself into thinking I am not jealous or envious of other people... but I cannot fool You. Teach me to be content and grateful for all I have. I am sorry, Lord. Amen.

➤ Day 73: NO FANCY ALTARS
PASSAGE: **Exodus 20:18-26**
VERSE: **Exodus 20:25**

If you make an altar of stone for Me, you shall not build it of cut stones, for if you wield your tool on it, you will profane it.

After the Commandments of God were given in order for the people to understand what sin was and why God despised it, they stood at the mountain and trembled before Him. They were so fearful that they asked Moses to be the middle-man between them and God. Moses tried to calm their fears and told them God was setting the laws in order to test their obedience and to keep them from sinning. God told Moses to tell them not to make or worship other gods and to make an earthen altar in order to offer burnt offerings and sacrifices on it. The altar was a place to honor Him and to thank Him. He then gave the command at the top of this entry. Why would God tell them not to use cut stones to build this altar? We must understand that God was instating for the first time the official religious traditions for His children Israel. He was specific and methodical—because He was looking for obedience. Remember, the idols and gods of the nations around them were cut of stone or wood. God would have no part in that sort of worship. Building a big fancy or ornate altar could be a source of pride for the people. No, God wanted a humble people to worship Him on a humble altar, using the materials He created, and in the form He created them.

COMMON GROUND: God knew the instincts of the people would be to build a place of worship and then worship <u>it</u> instead of Him! Don't we do that today? God never asked for ornate churches or places of worship. He instead commanded us to see His face in the world He created. **HOLY GROUND:** You need to get yourself ready to meet with God, share private moments in worship, and hear of His plans for your life. This does not have to happen in a church building. Walk with your eyes wide open and enjoy His created world. Look around you, smell His air, listen for His still small voice, and let His Spirit touch your soul.

*Father, No church building can house You because You created the
materials those buildings are made from. I need only to
walk outside, look at the amazing works of Your hands,
and allow my spirit to commune with Yours. Amen.*

➤ Day 74: SERVANT'S LAWS
PASSAGE: **Exodus 21:1-11**
VERSE: **Exodus 21:2**

*If you buy a Hebrew slave, he shall serve for six years;
but on the seventh he shall go out as a free man without payment.*

Slavery is a distasteful institution. God never condoned slavery, but His people—even though they were delivered out of that bondage—still had slaves among them. Many people became slaves because of debt, poverty or crime; some sold themselves as indentured slaves—working a specific number of years for their freedom. Though God didn't sanction the slavery, He did lay down foundational laws for how slaves and servants were to be treated. As we see in the verse above, no Hebrew man was to be a slave for more than seven years. As you read the passage for today's lesson, did you catch the words in verse five saying that some servants loved their masters and didn't wish to be freed in that seventh year! We wonder why that would be, but having a roof over our heads, food on our tables, and clothes on our backs in exchange for work is what we do in our own lives today. Don't most of us work five or six days each week for those very same things? We also see that a male slave who came alone and then was married could leave, taking his wife with him. If, however, they had children, the wife and children had to stay with the master. Few men would leave their families like that and would prefer to stay. Yes, there were—and always will be those who abuse their slaves and servants, but most were fair and cared well for those who served them in obedience.

COMMON GROUND: The thought of one man owning another is not popular in our society, but most of the years of our nation men worked their entire lives—often for the same employer. Benefits and wages were paid for a fair week's labor... and it was a satisfactory system for all involved. Those days are history because employees come and go in today's workplace with little loyalty on the part of employers or employees. **HOLY GROUND:** As I sought an application for holiness, the thing which kept coming back to my mind was that our work ethic should be to do everything we do for the glory of God. Respect is earned by how we conduct ourselves in the workplace.

*Jesus, Help me to be the best representative of Your love that
I can be in the workplace, the church and the marketplace.
I must never forget that shoddy work habits reflect on You,
for I bear Your name before men. Amen.*

➤ Day 75: MURDER LAWS
PASSAGE: **Exodus 21:12-22**
VERSE: **Exodus 21:12**

He who strikes a man so that he dies shall surely be put to death.

The laws in this section of Scripture may seem outdated or even without application in our world today. The laws are timeless and still apply to the things of our day. The American system of justice and our code of laws are based directly upon the laws we will talk about in the next few entries. Anyone who says our laws are not Biblically based is lying to you. How do we determine right and wrong if not from Biblical truths? How—without the Bible—do we know adultery, murder, theft or perjury is wrong? Today we will look at laws pertaining to murder. Look and see if you catch glimpses of America's criminal laws within these Old Testament truths. God makes delineation between two kinds of murder in these verses. *He who strikes a man so that he dies shall surely be put to death. But if he did not lie in wait for him, but God let him fall into his hand, then I will appoint you a place to which he may flee.* There is a huge difference in accidental death and premeditated murder. God knew they needed to be punished in different manners. The man who killed intentionally (with premeditation) was to be killed for taking a life God created. The man who committed manslaughter (killing without intention) was to have a sanctuary city he could flee to and be kept safe until he could be tried for the killing. Take notice of the other crimes God felt were serious enough to warrant the death sentence: Striking the mother or father and kidnapping. The death penalty was instituted to prevent sin from reigning in Israel… and in America. Unfortunately for us, the death penalty is no longer a deterrent because the trial lawyers have taken over the system and the appeals process has distorted justice.

COMMON GROUND: Recently I taught a class and talked about the death penalty. The common response was one of thinking with the heart instead of the brain. Our media has made a practice of telling us that innocent people are being killed by using the death penalty. There are of course instances of that; however, common sense would tell us that this is a rare occurrence. Funny, but the same people changed their minds when I asked what if the murder victim was their child or their spouse. What then was the response? "Hang them!" **HOLY GROUND:** God's system of justice was laid out for a holy people. It was laid out to be administered by honest men of integrity and would be ruined if run by anyone else. God's laws for kidnapping, premeditated murder and manslaughter form the foundation of criminal justice in our nation.

Spirit of God, Help me understand the reason for Your laws. You are a God of order—not chaos. If men are left to their own devices, evil will indeed prevail. I need to think with my brain and not be misled by my soft heart. Amen.

➤ Day 76: INJURY LAWS
PASSAGE: **Exodus 21:23-36**
VERSE: **Exodus 21:24-25**

*...eye for eye, tooth for tooth, hand for hand, foot for foot,
burn for burn, wound for wound, bruise for bruise.*

During a recent Bible study class we were discussing today's passage. One lady responded to this teaching, "What about turn the other cheek?" She is right, Jesus told us in Matthew 5:39, *"... whoever slaps you on your right cheek, turn the other to him also."* These teachings would appear to contradict each other. How can God say that evil is to be repaid eye for eye and tooth for tooth when Jesus said if someone slaps your face you are to turn the other cheek so he can slap that one too? We are looking at two different things entirely. As Christians we are called to forgive... and yes, turn that cheek. This teaching is to prevent our resorting to revenge on every action taken against us. The justice system still has the responsibility to carry out a trial and pronounce a penalty for the sin. God was instituting a set of rules where the punishment fit the crime, instead of the barbaric practices in many ancient countries. God's system of justice would prevent sentences of death for the loss of an eye or a hand.

COMMON GROUND: Again, it is easy to call these laws barbaric in the light of our sensitive predispositions. Would it surprise you to know that today there are these same types of judgments, except that we assign a dollar value to the eye, tooth or hand, and award the victim that amount of money? **HOLY GROUND:** Yes, yes, yes we are called to forgive others. I have a friend who had to sit at the sentencing of a young man who killed her son in a drunken driving accident. She forgave him, but there were still consequences for his actions. Laws are written to prevent chaos and anarchy in society.

*Father God, Help me to forgive those who inflict pain and
suffering on my life. If Jesus could pray for the forgiveness of those
who crucified Him, I can surely do the same for those who hurt me.
Amen.*

➤ Day 77: THEFT LAWS
PASSAGE: **Exodus 22:1-15**
VERSE: **Exodus 22:14**

If a man borrows anything from his neighbor, and it is injured or dies while its owner is not with it, he shall make full restitution.

As we move onward through these laws, you will be glad to know that the end is coming. I hope though that you are getting a clear picture of how our system of justice—and that of many other nations—is based upon God's given laws for the nation of Israel. Today we look at theft laws. I remember years ago hearing my parents talk about what they would do if someone broke into our home. My mother said she would shoot the robber and drag him into the house until the police could get there. As a typical Type-A first-born child, I was terrified that it would happen. I heard a news report recently about a man who was shot in a house he was robbing and the homeowner was the one arrested! The police officer being interviewed said the homeowner should have shouted a warning before shooting! How God must cringe after He gave such clear-cut laws for theft. *If the thief is caught while breaking in and is struck so that he dies, there will be no blood guiltiness on his account.* The entire passage for this entry delineates the restitution God instated for those who lost possessions at the hand of others.

COMMON GROUND: Many in our society feel they are entitled to that which others work hard to earn. We have become a welfare society and made it acceptable to 'steal' from the rich and give to the poor. That was never God's intention and is never mentioned in Scripture. Theft is theft, no matter how you whitewash it. **HOLY GROUND:** Each of us has abilities, and the responsibility to earn a living and take care of our own. None of us is entitled to that which belongs to others. Restitution brings reconciliation... and yes, the laws on theft are still used in our judicial system. Our founding fathers must have been intent on holy living.

Lord, I have learned from these entries that Your truths and commands are timeless and that Your children are called to follow them, no matter how unpopular they may seem. Amen.

➤ Day 78: MORALITY LAWS
PASSAGE: **Exodus 22:16-31**
VERSE: **Exodus 22:22-23**

You shall not afflict any widow or orphan. If you afflict him at all, and if he does cry out to Me, I will surely hear his cry...

Can you recall the era when morals mattered and our society was based on a foundation of those same morals? When I am teaching I use this analogy: In fifty years we have gone from "Leave it to Beaver" to "Desperate Housewives", and we are foolish enough to believe we are better for it! Think about it. The family as God created it is becoming passé. Keeping the marriage bed pure is looked at as old-fashioned and prudish. As we begin to read today's passage we realize that virginity was once held in high esteem; witchcraft and sorcery were condemned; and widows and orphans were to be cared for by the body of Christ—not the government. Members of God's congregation were not to lend to one another and charge interest or retain possession of something given as collateral for a loan. God's name wasn't to be blasphemed; the rulers of the people were not to be cursed; and the people were called to be holy. Most of these laws are no longer applied in America. Maybe if they were... no, certainly if they were... we would be a better people.

COMMON GROUND: Today, half of all marriages end in divorce; the birthrate of children born outside of marriage flourishes; the unborn are sacrificed daily on the altar of self-preference; and families are scattered with their ties broken. All of that is the result of common living instead of holy living. How God must grieve when He looks at us. **HOLY GROUND:** Many Christians fail to speak out on these topics because they do not wish to be called narrow-minded or religious. Not defining sin is the same as condoning it. Does that make sense to you? We are called to use the Bible as our guidepost and measuring stick, then to speak out for truth. Any questions?

Father, I see my nation self-destructing from within. Are we without hope; or can we be turned once again to be the people You made us to be? Our identity must lie in what You command us to be... not in what our flesh longs to be. Give me the boldness to call sin by its real name. Amen.

➤ Day 79: SLANDER LAWS
PASSAGE: **Exodus 23:1-7**
VERSE: **Exodus 23:1**

You shall not bear a false report; do not join your hand with a wicked man to be a malicious witness.

In order for God's people to walk in godliness and justice, we must keep our system of justice unsullied and fair. In a nation where those who are accused are also given a trial where evidence and witnesses are presented, this need for integrity is vital. We see in today's entry that false or lying witnesses who seek to subvert justice can cause great havoc. Look at some of the rules. 1. Do not ally yourself to a corrupt man to further his cause. 2. Do not be a malicious witness intent on causing harm to others. 3. Do not side with a poor man over a rich man—or a rich man over a poor one. 4. Do not give a false witness or lie during testimony. Each of these rules, when followed, will keep the system of justice working as it was designed. Why would God concern Himself and warn against these things? He knew a corrupted legal system would corrupt a land and turn it from Him. We see examples of this in the news today as judges overturn the verdicts of juries to further their own political and moral agendas. God will not be mocked in this area either.

COMMON GROUND: Think about the horror of someone giving false testimony against you in a court of law—or just spreading lies about you in any other situation. Most of us dearly value our good reputation and would be devastated if this happened to us. Why then are perjury (spoken lies under oath), libel (written lies against another person) and slander (spoken lies to defame someone's character) so common in our society today? **HOLY GROUND:** Holy people are called to speak truth—even when truth hurts. We are also called to *love our neighbor as we love ourselves,* and we surely don't want someone to libel or slander our name.

Jesus, The thought of lying under oath terrifies me; so why doesn't lying under other circumstances do the same? Help me to always, always, always speak truth. I certainly do want to walk in complete holiness. Amen.

➤ Day 80: BRIBERY LAWS
PASSAGE: Exodus 23:8-9
VERSE: Exodus 23:8

You shall not take a bribe, for a bribe blinds the clear-sighted and subverts the cause of the just.

On the morning of writing this entry I was watching the news and thinking about the corruption in our nation's capital, in our financial district (Wall Street), and in America's major banking and manufacturing industries... basically in all powerful portions of our society. What leads well-intentioned people onto a path of corruption and greed? In many cases it is a bribe—money or any other valuable consideration given or promised with the intent to corrupt the behavior of a person. Bribery has a direct impact on money makers, law makers, athletes and others in positions of influence. Likely it all starts out quite harmlessly—you know... a little payoff for a favor, a vote, a bonus. Obviously, bribery is not a new concern because God advised Moses about it thousands of years ago. Wherever man loves something more than God, bribery is a very real possibility. So many will sell their souls to 'dance with the Devil,' then wonder how their lives have fallen apart. Ephesians 6:24 sums it up like this... *Grace be with all those who love our Lord Jesus Christ with **incorruptible** love.* Only when we are incorruptible in our walk with Christ can we overcome temptation and not be susceptible to bribery.

COMMON GROUND: Many, even those who profess to love Christ wholeheartedly, are vulnerable to temptation. The enemy of your soul knows your every weakness because you have revealed it to him in past failings. You must move yourself up from the level of the common man. **HOLY GROUND:** Once we have rejected the temptation to sin, we must build upon that success by rejecting it again. The foundation of a strong and incorruptible faith comes from a proven history of rejecting the bribes of Satan. Declare to the heavens that you cannot be bought, bribed or tempted outside the holy will of God!

Spirit of God, The thought of being bribed has never occurred to me before. Yes, the enemy wants to use my weaknesses to bribe me out of Your will. I claim Your Name, Your strength, Your authority and Your hedge of protection around my heart. Amen.

➤ Day **81**: SABBATH YEARS
PASSAGE: **Exodus 23:10-13**
VERSE: **Exodus 23:10-11**

*You shall sow your land for six years and gather in its yield,
but on the seventh year you shall let it rest and lie fallow,
so that the needy of your people may eat...*

God's command to sow and reap a harvest six years and allow the land to lie fallow on the seventh likely served multiple purposes. Not only did the fallow year allow the earths nutrients to replenish themselves, but the people learned the discipline of storing up for that non-productive year. Instead of using all they produced—even when it seemed logical to do so—they saved a portion to be used later. God was teaching a great Biblical principle in the area of farming which should translate into all other areas of our lives. Instead of using all our means, or even living beyond our means, we need to save for a future day when the money, food and energy will be in less abundance. When we learn the principle of saving for the Sabbath (day or year) we will better use our time and resources. Notice also in today's passage that the poor and the animals were allowed to eat of whatever did grow and sprout in that Sabbath year. God's provision was needed because the poor would not have had surplus to store up in the other six years of the calendar.

COMMON GROUND: Most of you are not farmers and know about as much as I do about fallow fields. I called a local farmer and he said that instead of fallow fields most farmers rotate crops in their fields. Each crop draws different nutrients from the soil and rotating keeps the soil balanced. On to the application: Saving for the future seems to be a lost art in our world today. America is the richest nation on earth and has a horrible rate of saving. Why? We tend to think the abundance will always be with us and that saving is a passé practice. We need to apply this principle of God—all of us. Believe me; I have walked for years on the common ground of not preparing for the future, just like much of our nation. **HOLY GROUND:** If we would tithe ten percent and save ten percent of all we receive, we would be in God's will. He gives us this promise in Malachi 3:10. *"Bring the whole tithe into the storehouse, so that there may be food in My house, and **test** Me now in this,"* says the LORD of hosts, *"if I will not open for you the windows of heaven and pour out for you a blessing until it overflows."* God is asking us to test Him in this. Shouldn't a holy people, who claim to believe in Him and His promises, do that testing through obedience?

Father God, I confess that I have not been saving from my abundance for the lean times. I have counted on You to provide in those days—forgetting that You have provided in all the others in my past. Father, teach me to put aside a 'fallow' ten percent of all I make and offer back to You the portion You deserve. Amen.

➤ Day **82**: FESTIVAL COMMANDS
PASSAGE: **Exodus 23:14-19**
VERSE: **Exodus 23:14**

Three times a year you shall celebrate a feast to Me.

Today we look at God's reasoning for setting the holy day (holiday) feasts in Israel. Why would God command people to come to the tabernacle—and later the temple—with *the choice first fruits of your soil* and offer of them to Him? The answer is really quite simple; God wanted His people to never forget His past provisions for them and the fact that all they had came from His hands. *The Feast of Unleavened Bread* was to remember the Passover event when He spared the Hebrews' lives from the hand of the death angel. That celebration was in the spring. *The Feast of the Harvest* (Pentecost) was to honor the year's coming crop abundance and was held in the summer. *The Feast of the Ingathering* (Feast of Tabernacles) was in the fall and was to thank God for the production mercies of their fields. Their offering back to Him during these festivals showed their dependence on Him for the next planting, growing and harvesting seasons. Three times each year the men were required to travel to the place God designated to pay homage to him. They were not to come to the place empty-handed, for that would show that God had not provided amply for them.

COMMON GROUND: How tragic it is that so few people come before God in reverence or thankfulness for all they have been given. Look at how common our reactions have become to the Sabbath, Christmas, Easter and Thanksgiving. These holy days were given as reminders for us, yet we ignore their meanings altogether, or we look at them as burdens. It surely must break His heart. **HOLY GROUND:** In Bible times the people were to come before God three times a year to show their gratitude and thanksgiving. How long has it been since you sat in His Presence and thanked Him for your home, family, friends, jobs, health, freedom and faith? Holy people must acknowledge who God is in their lives. That will mean changes in our schedules in order to set aside time to simply praise His Name and thank Him for all our blessings.

Lord, My 'thank-You' has been sorely lacking. I seem to come before You in prayer with a long laundry list of needs and very few praises on that list. I promise to set aside time (more often than three times a year) to come before You in gratitude. Amen

➤ Day 83: REMOVE FALSE GODS
PASSAGE: **Exodus 23:20-26**
VERSE: **Exodus 23:22**

But if you truly obey his voice and do all that I say, then I will be an enemy to your enemies and an adversary to your adversaries.

This passage of Scripture is a clear-cut picture of what the life of one who follows and obeys God looks like, in comparison to the one who walks in his own wisdom and direction. God was promising the nation of Israel that He would send an Angel (likely Jesus) ahead of them to lead them into the Promised Land. They were to obey His every command and not rebel or sin against Him. The verse above is His awesome provision in exchange for obedience. The ones who walk in His pathways will have God on their side to fight their enemies! The promise also has a caveat attached to it... *You shall not worship their gods, nor serve them, nor do according to their deeds; but you shall utterly overthrow them and break their sacred pillars in pieces.* Israel was to serve God alone and destroy every trace of the foreign gods they would encounter when they did come into the Promised Land. The amazing promise to Israel for their obedience was that God would bless their bread and their water; and would will remove sickness from their midst. He also promised there would be no one miscarrying or barrenness in the land; and He would fulfill the number of their days. What reward obedience brings with it!

COMMON GROUND: Let's apply the portion of Scripture calling for the breaking down and removing of any trace of foreign gods from the midst of God's people. The contemporary church has failed miserably in this area. The biggest god we have failed to remove from our midst is the god of self! We want to be entertained, made comfortable, and patronized when we walk into our houses of worship. Most have forgotten why they are going to church... not for how it makes them feel, but to worship the One who died to forgive their grievous sins—even self-worship!

HOLY GROUND: Where is the awe and reverence for God in the house of God? When did we begin to go to church for entertainment, rather than to learn to walk in holiness? When is the last time you were challenged and convicted by a message from the pulpit? I won't dwell on this, other than to say that if you don't have your toes stepped on by a message from the Shepherd, then the Shepherd isn't leading the flock by demanding them to walk in holiness. How can the flock then be transformed by the renewing of their minds?

Father, I want to know anything I am doing which is displeasing to You. I need that conviction in order for me to begin to walk on Holy Ground this year. I want truth. I hunger for Your Presence. I do not want to be entertained. Open my eyes to all truth through Biblical messages. Amen.

➤ Day 84: NO COMPROMISES!
PASSAGE: **Exodus 23:27-33**
VERSE: **Exodus 23:32-33**

You shall make no covenant with them or with their gods. They shall not live in your land, because they will make you sin against Me; for if you serve their gods, it will surely be a snare to you.

What an awesome passage we will be looking at today. God was telling His children that He would stir terror in the hearts

118

of their enemies! He would go before them, causing their mighty enemies to flee before Israel's smaller army. God would give the lands to the nation of Israel... only if they would walk before Him without compromise. God—knowing full well that Israel couldn't manage the entire Promised Land until they multiplied in number— promised to give it to them in fits and starts as they could manage it. God was ready to bless Israel... if only they would keep their eyes on Him and not on the distractions around them. Imagine Israel keeping that promise and never walking into Babylonian, Assyrian, Persian or Roman bondage. Imagine Israel not weakening their loyalty to their Creator and thus never suffering for having done so. Turn your thoughts to our current times. Imagine God placing godly fear in the hearts of those who hate Jews and Christians today. Instead of atheists spreading their beliefs throughout the public forum, they would have a supernatural fear keeping them from speaking their lies. Those who are working so hard to remove all signs and symbols of Christian beliefs from the marketplace would stop their campaigns because of fear of God's wrath. This all sounds great, except that compromise always rears its ugly head within the body of Christ.

COMMON GROUND: Why did I emphasize compromise in this entry? Compromise is a subtle tool of the enemy who knows if he can get you to waiver just a bit from your personal beliefs, then he can get you walking back on common ground in no time. Here are a few areas susceptible to compromise in the life of a believer: Church attendance, personal Bible study, prayer commitment and Kingdom service. If we allow our passion for any of them to cool, we can easily be led astray. Remember, compromise is a subtle movement—not usually a drastic action. **HOLY GROUND:** Here is a revolutionary thought: We need church for fellowship and feeding; we need personal Bible study for growth; we need a committed prayer life for intercession; and we need to be the hands and feet of Jesus Christ in service to be effective in our Christian witness. Holiness requires sacrifice and commitment. It isn't achieved overnight and it demands work and change in the life of the believer.

*Jesus, In hindsight I can see the places where compromise
has subtly crept into my personal walk with You. My prayer
commitment and personal Bible study are both lacking and are
hindering me from walking where You call me to be.
Starting today, I take my direction from You—not from my weak
flesh. Jesus, make me holy as You are holy. Amen.*

➤ Day 85: RASH PROMISES
PASSAGE: Exodus 24:1-8
VERSE: Exodus 24:3

*Then Moses came and recounted to the people all the words
of the LORD and all the ordinances; and all the people
answered with one voice and said, "All the words which
the LORD has spoken we will do!"*

How easy it is to make a quick promise or a lightly-taken commit-ment without giving deep thought to the impact of our words. I believe Israel fully intended to keep that promise to obey God's every command. I also believe that most people who come into a personal relationship with Jesus Christ believe they will be able to walk in holiness all their days. If that is the case, why did Israel so quickly fall away... and why do ninety percent of Christian converts also fall away from their initial promise of godly obedience? I think the answer to this is revealed in Moses' story. He alone was willing to stand before the terrifying presence of the living God. Moses laid his soul bare for God to examine and test with fire. *Then He said to Moses, "Come up to the LORD, you and Aaron, Nadab and Abihu and seventy of the elders of Israel, and you shall worship at a distance. Moses alone, however, shall come near to the Lord..."* Because of a proven history of obedience, Moses alone was allowed to come up the mountain for a face-to-face encounter with the Lord.

COMMON GROUND: In order for us to have a proven history of obedience, we must at some point begin to obey! Moses' promises to God weren't rash and impulsive. He made commitments and kept them—often at great personal cost. It is very common to make promises lightly and break them when the going gets rough. Common is definitely not what God is looking for. **HOLY GROUND:** When God looked at the heart of His servant Moses, He saw it truly was a servant's heart. He knew that anything He entrusted to Moses would be in good hands, and even though things would get rough Moses would have the dedication to see the mission through to completion.

Spirit of God, May I never rashly promise You my obedience.
I do not want to do that which is unpleasing or foreign to
Your plans for me. Give me a Moses-like heart—one which
is true to You—period. Amen.

➤ Day 86: UP THE MOUNTAIN
PASSAGE: Exodus 24:9-18
VERSE: Exodus 24:12

Now the LORD said to Moses, "Come up to Me on the mountain and remain there, and I will give you the stone tablets with the law and the commandment which I have written for their instruction."

Moses and the elders climbed the mountain as God had commanded. Before the elders could turn aside and Moses could proceed on, they saw the glory of God before them. The elders must have been terrified, for they had been warned that Moses alone could stand before God. Think of their awe as they gazed upon God's *Shekinah* glory before them standing upon a sapphire-like pavement. God gave them a glimpse of His presence so they would understand better the impact of Moses' mission on their behalf. After a brief period of time Moses was called to come higher up the mountain alone. Taking his protégé Joshua with him, he told the elders to bring any legal matters for the nation to Aaron and Hur. Moses climbed toward the crest of the mountain as God's cloud came down and obscured him from the view of those below. For seven days Moses waited patiently on Mount Sinai for God to speak to him. Finally, the voice of the God of all creation spoke and called Moses into His presence... out of the sight of the elders and the people. There Moses remained for forty days and forty nights.

COMMON GROUND: If patience is truly a virtue, then Moses deserves the Congressional Medal of Honor for patiently waiting for the call of God to come up to a higher place. How patient are you with your requests before the throne of your Lord? The common response to waiting for an answer to prayer is to lose patience if it isn't answered within the first ten minutes. Moses humbled himself on God's mountain, waiting seven days to be called into His presence. Make you feel a little sheepish? **HOLY GROUND:** God answers prayers in His timing, not ours. Moses was so hungry to walk on Holy Ground that time meant nothing to him. He would have waited much longer if the call hadn't come when it did. Why? Whatever God had to say to Moses was worth the wait! Nothing down below could compare to what was about to happen up on the mountain. Holy people are desperate to hear from their Lord; are you listening for His voice?

Father God, I need to tune out the noise of this world and tune in to You by whatever means You use to communicate with me. Whether it be by prayer, Bible study, sermons, or Your still small voice... speak to me, Lord. Amen.

➤ Day **87**: FREE-WILL OFFERING
PASSAGE: **Exodus 25:1-9**
VERSE: **Exodus 25:8**

Let them construct a sanctuary for Me, that I may dwell among them.

In the days ahead we will be looking at the commands God gave to Moses for the furnishings and utensils to be placed within the tabernacle he was to erect as God's earthly dwelling place. God's first command was for Moses to ask for free-will offerings from the people. Notice that this was not a mandatory offering required by God. He desired the people to willingly sacrifice for the tabernacle from the generosity and love in their hearts. Look at the needed materials: Gold, silver, bronze, fine fabrics, animal skins, oil, acacia wood and spices. All these supplies would serve as the tabernacle's frames and coverings—the furnishings and the items needed for ordered worship within its walls. Also, precious stones were needed for the priestly garments. God was preparing to show Moses a vision with every detail of the work that lay ahead. He then told Moses, *"Let them construct a sanctuary for Me, that I may dwell among them. According to all that I am going to show you, as the pattern of the tabernacle and the pattern of all its furniture, just so you shall construct it."* Notice these things: The sanctuary was for God—not to please those who would enter it. God would dwell among the people once the tabernacle was erected, and it was to be completed exactly as He commanded.

COMMON GROUND: Let's apply the concept of a free-will offering, or sacrifice, to God. Commonly, most people wish to give the bare minimum—only that which is necessary to meet God's demanding requirements! We count our pennies to see if we are giving exactly ten percent. We debate whether to tithe on gross or take-home pay. We withhold our hours and minutes of service, thinking our 'generous' financial tithe is enough. **HOLY GROUND:** God is looking for willing and generous hearts who long to serve and give back to Him because they realize all they have comes from His hand and His provision in the first place. Imagine if we tithed or gave additional gifts out of gratitude rather than obligation. Imagine if we tithed also from our twenty-four hours each day and gave that 'time tithe' to Kingdom service. Holy people willingly offer with an attitude of gratitude, not obligation.

Lord, I have certainly withheld in my generosity to Your Kingdom. I have counted and rationed in giving You what is left after

I have done all I deem necessary with my time and finances.
Give me that 'attitude of gratitude'. Make me a cheerful giver
from all You have given me. Amen.

➤ Day 88: THE ARK OF GOD
PASSAGE: **Exodus 25:10-16**
VERSE: **Exodus 25:10**

They shall construct an ark of acacia wood two and a
half cubits long, and one and a half cubits wide,
and one and a half cubits high.

The first and most important piece of furniture for the tabernacle is the Ark of the Covenant. This long, narrow, carefully ornamented, gold-covered box was to be the special symbol of God's presence amongst the people. The ark itself was revered, but the items to later be put inside it for storage reveal an exact representation of a coming Messiah—our Jesus who would bring Himself to earth to dwell among His people. God's commands for the ark include these words: *"You shall put into the ark the testimony which I shall give you."* Moses had no idea what God's purpose for putting the specified items into the ornate box was when He spoke those words, but today we have the complete Bible to examine. In Hebrews 9:4 we find the list of the arks contents ...*a golden jar holding the manna, and Aaron's rod which budded, and the tables of the covenant.* How do these three items represent a coming Messiah? Jesus is *the bread of Heaven*; He is the miracle-working rod and scepter of the Father—and He is also the perfect fulfillment of Mosaic Law. The ark of God's covenant with the Hebrews—and with us through a grafting promise—is the perfect picture of Jesus, painted thousands of years before His coming to the earth to dwell among us.

COMMON GROUND: Ignoring truths of Scripture is common in most segments of society—unfortunately, even within some portions of the church! I love digging and mining the hidden (obscure) truths of the Bible. Did lights come on when you read about the ark's contents representing Jesus? Don't allow what is common in society to become common in your life. Commit to dig, mine and pocket the golden nuggets of God's Word. **HOLY GROUND:** The ark was to be placed in the holiest portion of God's tabernacle—the place where only the High Priest could enter once each year. Today we can come into the very presence of our Holy God because Jesus perfectly fulfilled the contents of that ark. Are you excited about that? You have access to the Holy of Holies—praises to our Lord and Savior, Jesus Christ!

Father, I am learning that Old Testament Bible truths are proven out in the New Testament teachings of Jesus Christ. How grateful I am to be able to walk boldly into Your presence, Father God. I need no middle-man or intercessor... Your throne is a prayer away! Amen.

➤ Day 89: MERCY SEAT
PASSAGE: **Exodus 25:17-22**
VERSE: **Exodus 25:17**

You shall make a mercy seat of pure gold,
two and a half cubits long and one and a half cubits wide.

If you were to choose a specific place to have an encounter with God, what would your ideal meeting place look like? God, in His infinite wisdom, designed a place with great attention to detail—a place for His glory to rest among the people He loved. Atop the Ark of the Covenant there was to be a mercy seat—a covering for the ark, fashioned of pure gold. Upon that cover were to be two cherubim (angels) with their wings spread wide to cover and protect the precious contents within. These angelic representations are a picture for us of the sheltering wings of God's angelic messengers who serve His purpose and shelter His children. As I wrote this entry I thought about the various meanings of the word 'mercy' as related to this tabernacle furnishing. Mercy is compassion, pity, or benevolence shown to someone who has offended us and does not deserve that compassion. In the online dictionary mercy is defined as "the discretionary power of a judge to pardon someone or to mitigate punishment." There in that tabernacle God would watch over His children, see their sins and shortfalls, and once each year have the blood of a spotless sacrificed lamb placed upon the corners of the mercy seat to pardon and atone for the sins of Israel. And that, my friend, is a wonderful picture of what Jesus did for you and me on a lonely wooden cross thousands of years later. Our sins merit death, not mercy… but Jesus shed His innocent blood to give us life instead of what we deserve.

COMMON GROUND: My prayer is that you are reading these entries carefully and learning from them. Each tabernacle furnishing represents Christ in the tabernacle of the believer's heart. Mercy! Just think about what being forgiven when you don't deserve to be feels like. It is common to think we are all 'good people' and God should be glad to have us worship His Name. We need to look at the true nature of sin as defined in Exodus 20… and come before the mercy seat with grateful hearts. **HOLY GROUND:** Holy people are convinced that without Christ's shed blood they would be headed for an eternity of suffering… because they realize the depth of their sin nature. Have you taken His mercy for granted? It is time for a new awareness of the Easter message.

Jesus, It is easy to forget that I deserve eternal death for my sins.
Instead, I am walking from this life of temptation toward an
eternity without suffering or sin. May I never again take
Your mercy and grace for granted. Amen.

➤ Day **90**: TABLE OF SHOWBREAD
PASSAGE: **Exodus 25:23-30**
VERSE: **Exodus 25:30**

You shall set the bread of the Presence on the table
before Me at all times.

John 6:33 reads: *For the bread of God is that which comes down out of heaven, and gives life to the world.* Jesus is that *Bread* sent from Heaven and bringing life to a lost world. Even in the days of Moses we were given a glimpse of the coming Messiah. The next tabernacle furnishing is the table of showbread fashioned from acacia wood, covered with pure gold, and ornamented with rings on its sides, so that it could be moved with the other furnishings when God so instructed the Hebrew people. In order to get a better picture of the purpose for this table we must look forward to the 24th chapter of Leviticus: *Then you shall take fine flour and bake twelve cakes with it; two-tenths of an ephah shall be in each cake. You shall set them in two rows, six to a row, on the pure gold table before the LORD.* These loaves were to represent the twelve tribes of Israel being continually present before the Lord in His dwelling place. When the priest looked at them he remembered that he was repre-senting all the children of Israel. Notice that this table was not in the holiest area of the tabernacle, but was instead outside the veil sepa-rating the Ark of the Covenant from the rest of the furnishings. The bread on this table was meant to show God's presence among the tribes. Today, the *Bread of Life* lives within the hearts of Christians in the form of the Holy Spirit.

COMMON GROUND: Jesus defined Himself as both the *Bread of Life* and *the Living Water*, giving sustenance to all who would call upon His Name in pure faith. Isn't it funny how 'common folk' think they don't need His bread or water in order to survive? They have replaced them with other 'bread' and <u>un</u>holy 'water'… and unfor-tunately, they think they are going to spend eternity in the presence of our Holy God. **HOLY GROUND:** We need to tell others about the sustaining grace of our Jesus. Recently I heard a pastor ask when the last time was that we wept and pleaded for someone to come to know Jesus Christ. He said, "You need to sincerely tell them they are just one breath away from realizing their absolute worst nightmare!" Powerful truth, isn't it? Share your *Bread* and *Water*! Don't hoard it for yourself.

Spirit of God, I have been lazy in my witness and my zeal for saving the lost souls of this world. I confess that my attitude toward some is that they deserve what they are going to get after they die here. Your Word tells us it is Your will that not one should perish. Help me to share Your life-giving sustenance with everyone I encounter. Amen.

➤ Day 91: THE LAMPSTAND
PASSAGE: **Exodus 25:31-40**
VERSE: **Exodus 25:31**

Then you shall make a lampstand of pure gold. The lampstand and its base and its shaft are to be made of hammered work; its cups, its bulbs and its flowers shall be of one piece with it.

With the tabernacle to be covered with curtains and animal skins, and no windows to allow natural light to enter, it would be a very dark place. Within those holy walls we find the next custom furnishing God ordained Moses to have made. The lampstand—today known as a menorah—was the sole source of light within the temporary house of God. Fashioned of pure solid gold, the lampstand was to have seven branches with three on each side of the single central arm. God was very specific in how it was to be made of one piece and how the cups (bowls) at the top of each arm would hold pure olive oil used to shed light within the walls. The priests were to trim and keep the lampstand burning, and all utensils used with it were to be made of solid gold. This lampstand is a precursor to Jesus Christ—*the Light of the World.* One obvious difference between the lampstand and Jesus is that He was not hidden behind curtains or a veil. Instead, He walked boldly upon the earth, shining His light for all to see. The light the lamp-stand shed can also represent the light the church is to shed within a dark and lost world.

COMMON GROUND: When light shines upon that which is common, flaws become much more obvious. Jesus' light does that same thing by showing us how to go from ordinary and common to extraordinary and holy. One problem: sin despises light shining upon its darkness. Isn't it funny how in some cases we long for light and in others we absolutely dread it? **HOLY GROUND:** The lamp-stand shone light in the darkness of the tabernacle. Remember that darkness is not a real or tangible property… it is merely the absence of light. We are surely not shining as we should, as evidenced by the society the modern church dwells in. Look around you and see where you can shed the light of Christ in your sphere of influence. The lost are like moths drawn to a flame, but we must light the flame to draw them. Holy people shine in darkness.

Father God, Make me like the polished gold tabernacle lampstand shining in the darkness around it. Jesus is the Light of the World, and as His disciple I am called to be the same. Light me, trim me and fill me to overflowing with the oil of Your joy and holiness. Amen.

➤ Day 92: HOLY OF HOLIES
PASSAGE: **Exodus 26:31-34**
VERSE: **Exodus 26:33**

You shall hang up the veil under the clasps, and shall bring in the ark of the testimony there within the veil; and the veil shall serve for you as a partition between the holy place and the holy of holies.

Within the confines of the tabernacle was a place set apart for the Ark of the Covenant, as we talked about in a recent entry.

The area partitioned off was called the Holy of Holies and was to be set apart from the common priestly area where the lampstand, table of showbread and incense altar were kept. In addition, there was to be an outer courtyard where the Levites worked with the priests in animal offerings made upon the burnt offering altar. The Holy of Holies is our focus today. Only one time each year was the inner sanctum to be entered. On that day the High Priest approached the veil separating the holiest place in order to make atonement for the nation of Israel on their Day of Atonement. This was a terrifying prospect for the priest who had bells and pomegranates sewn around the hem of his tunic. The tinkling bells served two purposes: First, they would let the priests in the outer area hear the movements of the High Priest as he placed blood on the corners of the ark and mercy seat. Secondly, they were believed to warn God with their tinkling that the priest was in there... so that God would not come into the holy place. The fear of the priest was that if he came face-to-face with God, he would immediately die.

COMMON GROUND: Recently I asked a class if they would want to come into the presence of God—to stand in the holy place in His presence. Initially most said they would. I then reminded them of how the mountain shook, the lightning cracked, and the thunder rolled when Moses went up the mountain. As evidenced by the expressions on many faces, they began to have second thoughts about it. Being in God's presence will never be a common experience... even after ten thousand years in heaven. **HOLY GROUND:** The High Priest held a degree of respect and authority with the people. He also carried a great deal of responsibility on their behalf. The blood he carried into the holiest place was shed for all the sins of Israel for the past year. That is a heavy burden to carry, no wonder he was afraid to enter that place with sin-tainted blood. No wonder the other priests listened with intensity for the continued ringing of those bells.

Lord, I shudder to imagine how terrified the High Priest was to enter into Your dwelling place carrying the sins of Israel. I need to shudder the same way as I picture my own sins and how they nailed You to Calvary's cross. Thank You, Jesus, that Your death destroyed the veil separating us from You. Today I come boldly before the throne of grace to confess my sins. Amen.

➤ Day 93: OFFERING ALTAR
PASSAGE: **Exodus 27:1-8**
VERSE: **Exodus 27:1**

And you shall make the altar of acacia wood,
five cubits long and five cubits wide; the altar shall be square,
and its height shall be three cubits.

In the Garden of Eden God instituted a system of offering innocent animals for the sins of His highest creation—man. Adam and Eve attempted to cover their sinful flesh with fig leaves, but man-made religious practices will never bring absolution of sin. Thousands of years later God became flesh and offered Himself for the final sacrifice for all sin for all time. Jesus became the sin of man in order for us to be reconciled to the Father. Between Eden and the cross were millenniums during which animals were used to shed innocent blood—blood offered upon God's altar—in order for sins to be covered and man to be restored to his Creator. The burnt offering altar of the tabernacle was to be used for this specific purpose. It was to be set in the courtyard, outside of the curtains to the holy place where the incense altar, the table of showbread and the lampstand stood. Upon that altar animals would be burned and blood would be poured, sending a pleasing aroma into heaven where it would eradicate the stench of sin from the nostrils of God. The command to shed blood for the atonement of sin should show us how seriously God looks upon our transgressions.

COMMON GROUND: I have talked to many people who find the idea of animal sacrifice absolutely distasteful. That response is quite common until we comprehend the seriousness of sin and realize how sin ruins our perfect fellowship with the Father. For all the people who offered lambs, rams and oxen for their sins, the option of offering their own flesh instead would be even more distasteful. **HOLY GROUND:** Thank God for our Savior whose death brought reconciliation and restoration for all men who will believe and receive His grace. One perfect spotless Lamb was sacrificed for every sin ever committed in the past, for every sin being committed as He died, and for every sin which will ever be committed in the future. Indeed—Holy, Holy, Holy is the Lamb of God.

Jesus, I now understand that the tabernacle sacrifices were temporary bandages for our sin wounds. Only a man could understand the sin nature of our hearts and make atonement for us. No animal ever walked willingly to the slaughter; but You, my Jesus, did that for me. Thank you. Amen.

> ## ➤ Day **94**: GARMENTS OF HONOR
> ### PASSAGE: **Exodus 28:1-5**
> ### VERSE: **Exodus 28:2**

You shall make holy garments for Aaron your brother, for glory and for beauty.

Recently in a Seekers Bible Study discussion we talked about a friend of mine who visited a different church and was taken aback at the pastor wearing jeans and a casual shirt to give the sermon. She was uncomfortable. During the class we talked about the fact that God looks at the heart and not the clothes; however, most of us are led to dress our best to come into the house of the Lord. We do that in order to show reverence and respect. The priests in our reading for today were to dress in specific clothing, which clearly served to set them apart from the others who would come to worship the Lord at the tabernacle. We see in the above verse that Aaron and his sons were to have garments for glory and beauty. God's command to Moses was, *"You shall speak to all the skillful persons whom I have endowed with the spirit of wisdom, that they make Aaron's garments to consecrate him, that he may minister as priest to Me. These are*

*the garments which they shall make: a breastpiece and an ephod
and a robe and a tunic of checkered work, a turban and a sash, and
they shall make holy garments for Aaron your brother and his sons,
that he may minister as priest to Me. They shall take the gold and the
blue and the purple and the scarlet material and the fine linen.*" God
was specific about priestly garments. How do you think He would
feel about the casual attire in the contemporary church?

COMMON GROUND: During the same class discussion mentioned
above, one woman stated that we had gotten lazy in all aspects of
our lives—marriages, parenting, jobs, physical appearance, friendships, religion. She is right. I don't believe that God judges us by
our clothes, but He surely will judge our heart's commitment and
sincerity. **HOLY GROUND:** How are you approaching God? Is your
heart properly 'attired'? Is your prayer life 'clothed in humility' as
you come before Him? The garments didn't make the priests holy—
they merely reflected the committed hearts beneath them. Likewise,
a new suit or dress will never fool God by hiding a hardened heart
underneath.

*Jesus, Please reveal to me the perfect balance between good
grooming and obsession about appearance. I do want to dress
nicely for You, but I would willingly come in rags if that is what it
takes to remove my pride and give me a humble attitude. Amen.*

➤ Day 95: PRIEST'S EPHOD
PASSAGE: Exodus 28:6-14
VERSE: Exodus 28:11

*As a jeweler engraves a signet, you shall engrave the
two stones according to the names of the sons of Israel;
you shall set them in filigree settings of gold.*

Do you remember earlier entries referring to how Israel 'spoiled'
the Egyptian people before their Exodus out of their land? It

would seem that God had future plans for the fine fabrics, pieces of gold and precious gems gathered there. Today we look at the ephod—one of the most striking portions of the priestly garments. The ephod was to be worn only by the high priest and was a short coat without sleeves, held closely to his body with gold chains attaching it to the breastpiece underneath. It was to be made of fine gold, purple, blue and red fabrics and fine linen. Golden sockets were to be made on the shoulders to hold two onyx stones with the names of the twelve tribes of Israel in birth order—six on each shoulder. The priest would thus carry with him the responsibility for the twelve tribes during the tabernacle service. There would never be a time when he didn't realize the awesome burden he carried as the intercessor between God and his Hebrew brothers and sisters.

COMMON GROUND: Imagine knowing that intercession between God and His children was your responsibility. In some denominations the priest still serves as the intercessor that hears the confessions of his people and pleads their case before God. There is nothing common about that sort of obligation—and it is never to be taken lightly. **HOLY GROUND:** At the moment of Jesus' death, the temple curtain was torn in two from top to bottom by Divine Hands, which was a sign to us that we now have full access to the throne of God and don't need an earthly priest to give us that access. Jesus is our High Priest who sits at the right hand of God making intercession for His children—with our names engraved on His heart instead of on ephod stones.

Spirit of God, How blessed I am to have direct access to the throne of God's grace where I can confess and repent of my sins, find Your grace and feel the restoration I so long for. You are my High Priest and my burden bearer; I am so grateful. Amen.

➤ Day 96: BREASTPLATE
PASSAGE: **Exodus 28:15-30**
VERSE: **Exodus 28:29**

Aaron shall carry the names of the sons of Israel in the breastpiece of judgment over his heart when he enters the holy place, for a memorial before the LORD continually.

Underneath the ephod, and covering the heart of the high priest, was to be a special garment called the breastpiece. It was to be fashioned of the same materials and craftsmanship as the ephod, and was to be adorned with four rows of precious gems. Each stone represented one of the twelve tribes in the order of their birth. Many of the stones are familiar to us today: Ruby, topaz, emerald, turquoise, sapphire, diamond, amethyst and onyx. There are also stones less recognized like beryl, jacinth, agate and jasper. The stones were a constant reminder—as were the engraved ones on the shoulder of the ephod—that the priest represented all twelve tribes of Israel, and not merely the tribe of Levi from which he hailed. The breastpiece had gold chains attached which affixed it to the ephod, keeping both firmly in place as the priest ministered in the tabernacle. Inside two pockets on the front of the breastpiece were two stones called the urim and thummin which the priest used to determine God's will for His people.

COMMON GROUND: When the Israelites needed direction from God the priest would consult the urim and thummin, determine (or translate) God's direction, and relate that to the people. It sounds unusual, but God is the One who established this procedure as a way of keeping His people aware of their need for His guidance. It is common practice for us today to consult our flesh, our emotions, or other people for choices we face in our lives. **HOLY GROUND:** We must remember that the people of Moses' day did not have the written 'instruction book' we have today. The Bibles which sit in most homes—at least in America—contain the same directions, cautions, warnings and advice the priests sought for their people. A holy person must seek God's plans through prayer and personal

135

Bible study. Written on the pages of the Bible we find everything we need to live lives of holiness.

Father God, Thank you for the specific details of the breastpiece. These directions prove to me that You are a God of detail and that You care about all Your children. I may not be a direct member of one of the twelve tribes, but I am a direct member of the family of God and thus seek Your will for my life. Amen.

➤ ## Day 97: CHECKPOINT #1
PASSAGE: **Proverbs 4:1-6**
VERSE: **Proverbs 4:2**

For I give you sound teaching; do not abandon my instruction.

You have been very patient and diligent with all of the Exodus teaching. My prayer is that you are learning new truths, new history, and how to apply Scripture to your life situations. How are you doing in your journey from Common to Holy Ground? These entries are not designed to be read and then cast aside. Every journey requires steps taken toward an eventual goal. The goal here is holiness and intimate fellowship with the God of all creation. Are you looking at the responses in the applications and seeking to apply these truths in your life? I am proud of you because this is a more difficult devotional than my last one. Working through it requires a commitment to learn… and as the verse above states, we are not to abandon God's instruction. Every minute you dedicate to learning His truths will be rewarded as diligence to know Him more.

COMMON GROUND: Common people are looking for a 'god,' but few really want the God of the Bible. They want the benefits of knowing He is near without wanting Him to change their lives. God demands to have all of us. He demands that our commitment be wholehearted and unwavering. **HOLY GROUND:** Hungry people seek to know more every day about the God they serve. They invest precious minutes in fellowship, worship, learning and seeking His direction through prayer and study. You must be very hungry... and He is waiting to feed you with the pure sweet truth of His Word.

Lord, I have come this far in the study of Exodus and am glad for the hours spent. Continue to teach me Your ways and reveal to me the steps I need to take in order to make this life-changing journey. I am at Your feet... waiting for each morsel. Amen.

➤ Day 98: ANOINT THE PRIESTS
PASSAGE: Exodus 29:1-9
VERSE: Exodus 29:5-7

You shall take the garments, and put on Aaron the tunic and the robe of the ephod and the ephod and the breastpiece, and gird him with the skillfully woven band of the ephod; and you shall set the turban on his head and put the holy crown on the turban. Then you shall take the anointing oil and pour it on his head and anoint him.

Before the tabernacle could become the sanctioned house of worship in the midst of the nation of Israel, the priests who would oversee its ministries had to be anointed (consecrated or made sacred) through a ceremony that usually involved the applying of oil to dedicate him for service to God. Aaron's anointing ceremony included the sacrifice of a bull and two rams to God, a physical cleansing of his body (as well as that of his sons), and the eventual donning of the priestly garments. Aaron, as the high priest, was to wear the ephod, the breastpiece, and the turban bearing a solid gold nameplate reading *Holy to the Lord*. Once all of the holy garments were in place, Moses was directed to anoint his brother with oil by pouring it upon his head. Aaron's sons were dressed in priestly garments and anointed alongside their father in the process God ordained for those who would serve in His tabernacle. The animals were to be offered on the bronze altar and their blood daubed upon the priests' right earlobes, right thumbs and right big toes. Once the anointing ceremony was complete, the priests were ready to take their place in oversight and ministry of the tabernacle of God.

COMMON GROUND: This process may seem laborious and unnecessary to those of us who seek to take shortcuts in our approach to worship. We must note that outward grooming was only part of the anointing process. God was looking for inward holiness, inward cleansing, and heart-deep obedience to His every word. **HOLY GROUND:** It is imperative that we come to God in holiness. That doesn't have a single thing to do with our clothes or outward appearance, but does have to do with taking time to prepare to enter His presence. Remember, we are called to be a *royal priesthood*, and that means serving Him, ministering to His people and interceding on their behalf. Do you prepare to enter the throne-room of grace, or do you walk in without preparing your heart?

My Jesus, I may not understand the blood on the ears, thumbs and toes, but I fully understand Your shed blood washing me clean on Calvary's cross. Teach me to prepare for worship—to anoint my heart for time in Your presence. I long to be a royal priest in every sense of the word. Amen.

➤ Day 99: PRIEST OFFERING
PASSAGE: **Exodus 29:10-28**
VERSE: **Exodus 29:18**

You shall offer up in smoke the whole ram on the altar; it is a burnt offering to the LORD: it is a soothing aroma, an offering by fire to the LORD.

When we discussed the offering of the animals as part of the priestly anointing process in yesterday's entry, we were talking specifics given by God to Moses for the anointing to be complete. Let's look today at why those animals needed to be offered. Each sacrifice will later be replicated when Jesus becomes the ultimate

Sacrificial Lamb and our once and forever High Priest. The bull represents an offering to God for the atonement of sins as the priests took upon themselves the sins of the nation as a whole. We see this same sin exchange at Calvary where Jesus became sin as we read in 2 Corinthians 5:21, *He made Him who knew no sin to **be sin** on our behalf, so that we might become the righteousness of God in Him.* The first of two rams was to be offered as a burnt offering to honor God and to represent the dedication of the priests, as well as the nation to God's service—that Israel would be a living sacrifice to the God who delivered them from bondage. Again, Christ fulfilled this portion of the priestly anointing service and we are commanded to follow His example in Romans 12:1: *Therefore I urge you, brethren, by the mercies of God, to present your bodies a **living** and holy **sacrifice**, acceptable to God, which is your spiritual service of worship.* The third sacrifice was the ram of ordination which was offered as a mutual covenant between God, the priests, and Israel, His chosen nation. Jesus Christ is *the mediator of a **new covenant*** through His shed blood. Three innocent animals were offered at the anointing ceremony of Aaron the priest—only One needed to be offered at the anointing ceremony of the saints.

COMMON GROUND: Briefly... it is very hard for common men to offer themselves as living sacrifices for anyone—laying their lives down in service—let alone for an unseen God. **HOLY GROUND:** Holiness will require sacrifice of time, pride, money, service and love. Our goal should be to become Christlike. How hard are you working to achieve that goal?

Jesus, You are the perfect, ultimate sacrifice for the sins of this world today, yesterday and forever. Aaron and his sons could never bring about eternal reconciliation with God. How grateful I am for Your willingness to suffer on my behalf. I love You, Jesus. Amen.

➤ Day **100**: MY GLORY SANCTIFIES
PASSAGE: **Exodus 29:35-46**
VERSE: **Exodus 29:43**

*I will meet there with the sons of Israel, and it
shall be consecrated by My glory.*

Part of the preparation of the tabernacle was for it and its furnishings to also be anointed for service and holiness to God. The altars—places of prayer and offerings—were to be consecrated for seven days. They were to be made holy, even though unholy sin offerings would be placed upon them. Along with the people's offerings, which would be brought to the tabernacle daily, two yearling lambs were to be offered each morning and evening as a sign that God would meet there with His people. Look at His promise: *"I will meet there with the sons of Israel, and it shall be consecrated by My glory. I will consecrate the tent of meeting and the altar; I will also consecrate Aaron and his sons to minister as priests to Me. I will dwell among the sons of Israel and will be their God. They shall know that I am the LORD their God who brought them out of the land of Egypt, that I might dwell among them; I am the LORD their God."* Notice the number of *wills* and *shalls* in the passage. Those words are covenants (promises) that God was giving to Israel and to the modern church today. He will meet us, consecrate us, dwell among us and be our God. His presence sanctifies His people... not our man-made attempts at religion or holiness.

COMMON GROUND: Aaron and his sons could have easily thought that their ordination as priests made them holy. They could have proclaimed and held their authority over the people—and sometimes people in ministry do just that. We can never mix worldly flesh with God's righteousness— which is a common practice in today's 'Seeker friendly' churches. **HOLY GROUND:** Let me say here that God takes holiness very seriously. Look at the commands He gave for His earthly home! If we are to be His *peculiar treasure, royal*

priesthood and holy nation, then our personal holiness must never be taken lightly. We cannot be a little worldly and a little holy!

Spirit of God, Reveal to me anything which keeps You from taking up residence in my spirit. Live in me. Live with me. Walk with me. Talk with me. Make me uncommon in every way possible. Amen.

➤ Day 101: ALTAR OF INCENSE
PASSAGE: **Exodus 30:1-10**
VERSE: **Exodus 30:7**

Aaron shall burn fragrant incense on it;
he shall burn it every morning when he trims the lamps.

Today we revisit the tabernacle furnishings as we look at the altar of incense. Upon this altar special incense would be burned and the incense represented the prayers of the people as they were lifted up to God's throne. This altar was to be made of acacia wood and overlaid with pure gold. Only a specific formula of incense was to be burned upon it. If we look ahead to verses 34-38 of the same chapter, we find the specific ingredients: *"Take for yourself spices, stacte and onycha and galbanum, spices with pure frankincense; there shall be an equal part of each. With it you shall make incense, a perfume, the work of a perfumer, salted, pure, and holy."* After God gave the recipe He gave this caution: *"The incense which you shall make, you shall not make in the same proportions for yourselves; it shall be holy to you for the LORD. Whoever shall make any like it, to use as perfume, shall be cut off from his people."* Notice that this specific formulation was to be used to worship God alone and was never to be replicated for other uses.

COMMON GROUND: The incense altar was a place where the priest would burn the incense as a picture of the prayers of Israel being lifted to God. As the fragrance arose from the small flat censer dishes, the sweet smell was pleasing to God and showed reverence for who He was. One side benefit of the burning incense was that it took away the smell of the animal flesh which had been offered the previous day on the bronze altar. **HOLY GROUND:** The fragrance of Christ should be upon all His children and is part of our being *peculiar* in this world. Think about your life for the last week—are there stinky or smelly sins not confessed which keep your fragrance from being pleasing? Today, we do not need incense to cover them. Instead we need only to confess them, accept the cleansing from them, and walk forth in sweet-smelling holiness.

Father God, All I can offer is my heart, my faith and my prayers. May they be fragrant and pleasing to You, as was the incense burned in the tabernacle of old. I long to walk in holiness. Amen.

➤ Day 102: ATONEMENT MONEY
PASSAGE: Exodus 30:11-16
VERSE: Exodus 30:14

Everyone who is numbered, from twenty years old and over, shall give the contribution to the LORD.

What do you think your life is worth to God? Is it worth the ten-percent you tithe? Is it worth more than that? Looking ahead to the sacrifice of Jesus Christ to redeem us from Satan's bondage, I would say we are very valuable in the eyes of our Creator. Today we look at the levy (tax) Moses was instructed to collect as he took a census of Israel's population. The instruction was to collect a half-shekel from every male over twenty. The exact same amount was levied against every man, showing that no one is higher or lower in God's estimation and that He shows no partiality or favoritism. In other offerings men were to give to their ability, but this tax was to be used for the service, maintenance and supplies needed in the tabernacle. God was showing that all who benefit from the use of the tabernacle had an equal responsibility to help to meet its expenses. Some Biblical scholars believe this was an annual levy and insist that Jesus was paying His fair share when He sent Peter to catch a fish, take money from its mouth and pay their tax (Matthew 17:27).

COMMON GROUND: How willing are you to pay your fair share and to offer your share of service in order for your church to function as a house of worship and to fulfill the great commission to go into the entire world telling others of the saving grace of Jesus Christ? That fair share might require giving above and beyond normal tithes and offerings. It is so common for us to believe someone else will cover the expenses or do the work. In this case God made sure the expenses were covered by making the tax mandatory and fair. **HOLY GROUND:** Imagine a church where no one served and no one offered extra according to their ability. How long would that church be effective in the community and its own body? Now, imagine a church where everyone was tripping over each another to give for special needs, where people were excited to serve in all areas of ministry, and where they couldn't be silenced from sharing the gospel with the lost! That is the church God is calling us to be—holy and committed to serve. He already offered His Best for us—and we must in turn offer ours to Him.

Lord, I have withheld time and money from my local house of worship. When I do that, I am shortchanging You and the work needing done in Your kingdom. Lord, give me a generous, serving heart. Amen.

➤ Day 103: BRONZE LAVER
PASSAGE: **Exodus 30:17-21**
VERSE: **Exodus 30:20**

...when they enter the tent of meeting, they shall wash with water, so that they will not die; or when they approach the altar to minister, by offering up in smoke a fire sacrifice to the LORD.

The bronze laver—the final piece of furniture for the tabernacle—was to be used for the external cleansing of Aaron and the priests as they served within the holy place. Notice the impact of the words in today's verse... *they shall wash with water, so that they will not die.* Why would God say that approaching him in an unclean state could lead to death? To understand this statement we need to look all the way back to the Garden of Eden and the fall of man. When sin entered the world it divided man (the Created) from God (the Creator), causing a separation between the holy and pure God and His soiled children. God cannot look upon evil (nor will He sanction it in any form) and the only hope of reconciliation was for Him to somehow cleanse man's sins. In Exodus we read of an external cleansing at the bronze laver. At Golgotha we learn of a one-time-for-all-time internal cleansing by the shed blood of Jesus. Approaching God in any state but clean is an affront to His holiness and results in spiritual death.

COMMON GROUND: Let me urge you to never enter the house of God in the same manner that you enter the doors of your local department store. The cleansing process at the entrance of the tabernacle was a daily reminder that the House of God was different and was in no way common. **HOLY GROUND:** The bronze laver paints a picture for us of preparing and cleansing ourselves before we enter into God's holy Presence. Those of us who know Jesus and are cleansed by His shed blood need only to confess our daily sins—intentional and unintentional—to be welcomed before His throne. In a quest for personal holiness we must recognize the House of God as He sees it... a piece of holy ground set aside for worshipping Him.

My Jesus, Far too often my church is a place for fellowship, gathering together and encouragement. None of those are bad, but I see it must first be a place of absolute unfettered worship. We can gather and be encouraged at a local restaurant, but genuine worship requires much more. Amen.

➤ ## Day 104: OIL & INCENSE
PASSAGE: **Exodus 30:22-33**
VERSE: **Exodus 30:32**

It shall not be poured on anyone's body, nor shall you make any like it in the same proportions ...and it shall be holy to you.

Just like the incense we studied a few entries ago; the holy anointing oil used in tabernacle service was to be made of a specific and exclusive recipe. *"Take also for yourself the finest of spices: of flowing myrrh five hundred shekels, and of fragrant cinnamon half as much, two hundred and fifty, and of fragrant cane two hundred and fifty, and of cassia five hundred, according to the shekel of the sanctuary, and of olive oil a hin. You shall make of these a holy anointing oil."* I don't know if you have ever smelled myrrh or cassia—wonderful earthy Middle Eastern spices, but they were to make up the biggest share of the fragrance for the oil. The anointing process served several purposes, but the main one was to dedicate the tabernacle furnishings for service. All the items used, from furniture to utensils, were to be consecrated and set apart for the specific purpose of priestly use in the Tent of Meeting. *"This shall be a holy anointing oil to Me throughout your generations. It shall not be poured on anyone's body, nor shall you make any like it in the same proportions; it is holy, and it shall be holy to you. Whoever shall mix any like it or whoever puts any of it on a layman shall be cut off from his people."*

COMMON GROUND: Why do we have such a difficult time understanding that God is holy, His commands are absolute, and His reasons may not make sense to us at all? Think about how we have made the ritual of honoring Him convenient for ourselves and often indifferent to His divinity. When we look at these truths, the impact of anointing oil and incense used exclusively for service to the Lord is awesome. **HOLY GROUND:** It is time for us to look very closely at how we enter into God's presence. Is your personal devotion or worship time holy and precious to you? Are you offering yourself completely to Him as a 'fragrantly anointed' servant? Ponder this truth: You are just as unique and precious to Him as every other person He has created. Do you need to rethink your approach to worship?

Jesus, My attitude toward You and our Father has been irreverent in many ways. I long to be that 'fragrantly anointed' servant. May today be a new beginning in my worship and devotional time as I examine more closely the condition of my heart? Amen.

➤ Day 105: GOD'S GIFTINGS
PASSAGE: **Exodus 31:1-11**
VERSE: **Exodus 31:3**

I have filled him with the Spirit of God in wisdom, in understanding, in knowledge, and in all kinds of craftsmanship...

After describing in careful detail all of the tabernacle furnishings and utensils, God told Moses He had gifted two men, Bezalel of Judah and Oholiab of Dan, with the talents necessary to craft each item to God's exact specifications. *"...and in the hearts of all who are skillful I have put skill, that they may make all that I have commanded you."* That verse should certainly strip away the pride of our personal accomplishments! Every gift and ability is given by God at His discretion. Have you ever listened to someone with a wonderful singing voice and wished you were able to sing like that? God didn't give you (or me) that same talent. As Bezalel and Oholiab began the construction of the furnishings, using the best materials available to them, the plans of God unfolded before their eyes. These two men and all who worked alongside them were born for this very purpose, at that specific time and in their unique circumstances. None of it was by accident.

COMMON GROUND: Moses could have responded to God's choosing of these talented men in a negative way: "Hey! I am the one who led these people, listened to their whining and faced their wrath. Why does someone else get to do the fine work?" Isn't that the common reaction to seeing someone else be successful in business or ministry? God didn't gift Moses as a craftsman because He needed him to be a leader instead. **HOLY GROUND:** Bezalel and Oholiab were gifted and obviously took very seriously every detail Moses gave to them and were fully aware of the importance of the work they were assigned. In Exodus 39 we see these words paraphrased ten times: *...the work of the tabernacle was done just as the Lord commanded Moses.*

Spirit of God, May I use the unique gifts You have given me
to do all things... just as You have commanded. Give me
a grateful and obedient heart to serve You. Amen.

➤ Day 106: STONE TABLETS
PASSAGE: Exodus 31:18
VERSE: Exodus 31:18

When He had finished speaking with him upon Mount Sinai,
He gave Moses the two tablets of the testimony, tablets of stone,
written by the finger of God.

Let's pretend that you are Moses and have been in the presence of God for forty days and nights. You have heard His voice and listened intently as He delineated every detail about the tabernacle and its furnishings. You have heard how seriously He takes obedience and reverence for His law. God Himself has painted a picture of perfect, unfettered worship with priests to intercede on behalf of your people. Finally, He has written on stone tablets the basic ten laws detailing how we are to love Him and love our neighbors. Now, you pick up the heavy tablets and hold them near to your heart. "Dear God, I am holding the precious writing of Your holy hand. How do I merit being in this amazing position? Do I really have to return down to the camp? Do I really have to leave Your mountain?" Reluctantly, you turn and begin your journey from God's holy ground—walking back toward the common ground of the world.

COMMON GROUND: Could you picture yourself in Moses' shoes? Could you feel the pain of separation as you left the holiness of the Creator to walk back to the ungodliness of the creation? When is the last time you pictured yourself actually in the presence of the Creator of the world? If it has been a while—you need to get back on the holy ground pathway. **HOLY GROUND:** I often hear believers say that they don't feel the presence of God or His Spirit in their times of devotion and prayer. Usually I ask if the things of the world are distracting their focus—pulling it away from Him. God longs for our unfettered, unhindered, uninterrupted and unhurried fellowship. Only then can He get us back on that pathway.

*Father God, You haven't changed, but my attention level has.
I could almost feel myself in Moses' shoes with Your glory
around me. Today I will seek that sort of encounter with
You during my own devotions. Amen.*

➤ Day 107: QUICK TO FORGET
PASSAGE: **Exodus 32:1**
VERSE: **Exodus 32:1**

*Now when the people saw that Moses delayed to come down
from the mountain, the people assembled about Aaron and said
to him, "Come, make us a god who will go before us; as for this
Moses, the man who brought us up from the land of Egypt,
we do not know what has become of him."*

One of the most difficult passages for me to study in all of Scripture is Exodus 32. We will break the events down in deeper detail over the next few entries. I ask that you look closely at the actions of Israel in this chapter and the parallels I will make to the contemporary Christian church. Moses had been on the mountain with God for nearly forty days—and the people had a very short attention span. They turned to Aaron, who obviously didn't handle leadership responsibilities well, and asked him to fashion an idol for them. They wanted another 'god' to go before them into the Promised Land—a replacement for Moses, who they thought may well have died while on the mountaintop. All of God's provisions and Moses' hard work were forgotten. What a blatant spit in God's face!

COMMON GROUND: The Christian church of the twenty-first century is not much different from the Hebrew people at the base of Mt. Sinai. We have forgotten the hard work and suffering of those who established—and often died for—the Bible and tools of the faith we have access to today. God has been abundantly faithful, but we commit spiritual adultery as we establish other gods and idols to focus our worship upon. Without strong Moses-like leadership we have diverted our attention, compromised our messages and forsaken holiness. **HOLY GROUND:** To redirect your spiritual footsteps this year you will need to intentionally commit time to learning of God's past faithfulness by studying the Bible history books and looking back at His faithful provisions for you in days gone by. Israel forgot far too quickly how God had provided for their every need—not their every want, but their every need. We do not want to repeat their failure.

Lord, I do not want to fail You by forgetting Your mercy in my life.
Open my eyes to anything I am placing too much emphasis on or
putting too much faith in. You alone are my Lord and Savior. Amen.

➤ Day **108**: SPOILED SPOILS
PASSAGE: **Exodus 32:2-4**
VERSE: **Exodus 32:2**

Aaron said to them, "Tear off the gold rings which are
in the ears of your wives, your sons, and your daughters,
and bring {them} to me."

In earlier entries I taught about God softening the hearts of the Egyptian people in order for Israel to leave their bondage there and step into freedom with riches and wealth gleaned from the hands of their masters. Today we see how the precious, priceless treasure God provided was used in a way to provoke His anger. How can we possibly understand how Aaron (of all people!) could involve himself in the creation of a man-made idol in order to appease the Israelites? Aaron knew first-hand of God's amazing miracles and provisions. He had walked beside his brother Moses every day in this long exodus to freedom. We may not understand it, but we see from the verse for this entry that he encouraged the people to bring their fine golden jewelry to him. Aaron may have been trying to diffuse the impatience of the people, but his disobedience in fashioning the golden calf idol was a direct and very public display of rebellion against God.

COMMON GROUND: Compromise—no matter the reason for it—is wrong and damages our unique personal relationship with our Creator. Aaron's disobedience is a clear example of allowing the opinions and words of others to lead the believer's feet from Holy to Common Ground. It is a move backward—a spiritual setback—when we are called to press forward toward the ideal goal God has set for us. **HOLY GROUND:** In your pursuit of personal holiness be ever mindful of distractions, disruptions and detours. They may seem harmless, but be assured that one compromise will lead to another... and another... and another. Avoid compromise and PRESS ON!

My Jesus, Now I understand how deadly serious compromise
is in our relationship. May Your Spirit give me a new
alertness to the subtle works of the enemy which lead to
huge sins like Aaron's? Amen.

➤ Day **109**: DIVIDED WORSHIP
PASSAGE: **Exodus 32:5-6**
VERSE: **Exodus 32:6**

*So the next day they rose early and offered burnt offerings,
and brought peace offerings; and the people sat down to eat
and to drink, and rose up to play.*

Watch how easily believers can be led into the false belief that they can worship more than one god. After Aaron fashioned the golden idol the people proclaimed, *"This is your god, O Israel, who brought you up from the land of Egypt."* Remember, all this was happening just forty days after Moses climbed the mountain to meet with God on their behalf. In those forty days all the miracles and wonders their eyes had witnessed were cast aside, and a golden calf—fashioned before their very eyes—became the 'god' who brought them out of bondage! Unbelievable, isn't it? God is *El Qanna* (a Jealous God) and will not share worship with any other. When the Hebrews offered offerings to God and the idol, they forgot everything God had said about having NO other gods before Him. The same still applies today; we cannot serve God and money, God and fame, nor God and self.

COMMON GROUND: We can judge the Hebrew people for their blatant disobedience and Aaron for his compromised leadership, but then we have to look in the mirror! Is God—the God of all Creation—the only god in your life? Have you allowed any other thing to come between you and unfettered fellowship with Him—kids, career, money, popularity, acceptance, political correctness, busyness, fun or entertainment? **HOLY GROUND:** If you have a personal relationship with Jesus Christ, then you are in a covenant (promise) with Him. He has every right to be jealous when anything tries to separate the two of you. He will use every tool at His disposal to restore your relationship. Just like a wife—in a covenant relationship with her husband—should fight against anything which tries to ruin her marriage, Jesus should fight for those He redeemed.

Jesus, I hadn't thought about You being jealous over me and my divided loyalties. It is amazing to me that You care so much... even when I break our covenant. Thank You for coming after me. Amen.

➤ Day 110: AN ALL-SEEING GOD
PASSAGE: Exodus 32:7-8
VERSE: Exodus 32:7

Then the LORD spoke to Moses, "Go down at once, for your people, whom you brought up from the land of Egypt, have corrupted themselves."

Moses—with a mixture of sadness and purpose—is ready to return to the people when God says to him, *"They have quickly turned aside from the way which I commanded them. They have made for themselves a molten calf, and have worshiped it and have sacrificed to it and said, 'This is your god, O Israel, who brought you up from the land of Egypt!'"* Imagine the betrayal Moses felt at hearing those words. Imagine the gut-wrenching frustration and anger he must have felt. It is a good thing Moses was not like me, for I expect I would have said, "God, let's start over and You make a new, smarter and more obedient batch!" Moses had a decision to make: Walk down the mountain and try to restore order in the camp, or remain on Mount Sinai on Holy Ground with God.

COMMON GROUND: How do you respond to those who claim to walk with the Lord and continue to fall back into the habits of the past and compromise that faith profession? Are you sometimes ready to give up on them... leave them to their own resources... and doubt that they will ever truly change? In our own flesh that is the very common response. **HOLY GROUND:** It is God's will that none should perish, that none should be aligned with the enemy, and that none should spend eternity separated from Him. If that is His ultimate will, do we have the right to stop being His hands and feet and His heart and soul to those who are lost or captured in bondage? Holiness requires commitment to seeking, finding, and discipling the lost.

Spirit of God, Giving up in frustration is more my style than standing beside someone who seems bent on personal destruction. I needed this reminder that I was once there—bonded to the enemy of my soul—until you set me free and redeemed my soul. Amen.

➤ Day 111: GOD'S TEMPTATION
PASSAGE: **Exodus 32:9-10**
VERSE: **Exodus 32:10**

"Now then let Me alone, that My anger may burn against them and that I may destroy them; and I will make of you a great nation."

One common thread throughout the books we are studying in these daily devotionals are the times when God was fed up with the Hebrews, His chosen people, and was ready to wipe them out and start over. This entry talks about that very thing. Imagine this: You have two children and have provided for their every need since they were born into your family. They have never gone without food, clothing, shelter or love. As those adorable toddlers become adolescents and those trying adolescents become teens, you wonder if their ungrateful little hearts could get any worse. Nothing you do can please them, yet you continue to try. Their clothes aren't as expensive as those of their friends; the reliable used car isn't the shiny new sports car they wanted; and they long to go away to a distant school, rather than to commute to the local community college. Have you ever thought (or said), "I brought you into this world and I can take you out of it"? Now you know how Father God, felt in the face of the Hebrews' rejection.

COMMON GROUND: How do you react to ungrateful children in your life? Can you understand why God would be tempted to start over with a new nation from the seed of Moses? God was seeing a common trait among His highest creation... an attitude of ingratitude. **HOLY GROUND:** Funny, isn't it, how we think we are 'good people' compared to all the other sinners God created? We compare ourselves to Ted Bundy or Jeffery Dahmer and fancy ourselves quite righteous. Remember, God sees the heart... the part of you no one else can see. He sees ingratitude. He knows the sting of rejection at the hand of those He gives life itself to. Let us develop an attitude of thanksgiving for all He has done for us.

Father God, If not ungrateful, I have at least been lacking in sending You thanks for every blessing in my life.
Help me to not judge others—even the Hebrews—when I honestly examine my own heart. Amen.

➤ Day 112: GOD'S REPUTATION
PASSAGE: **Exodus 32:11-14**
VERSE: **Exodus 32:12**

"Why should the Egyptians speak, saying, 'With evil intent He brought them out to kill them in the mountains and to destroy them from the face of the earth'? Turn from Your burning anger and change Your mind about doing harm to Your people."

Notice how Moses referred to the Hebrews as God's own people and subtly reminded Him of the covenant He made with Abraham. Moses was as angry as God, but mostly he was worried about God's reputation being tarnished. Setting anger and frustration aside—not for the sake of the people who did not deserve God's mercy—Moses told God that all He has done on behalf of His chosen people would be of no value if the nations around saw them destroyed. Moses was concerned that God, who delivered the Hebrews from their horrible bondage in Egypt, would become the laughingstock of the Egyptian people. If that was the case, all who watched His miracles and may have been influenced by them would no longer be drawn to what He represented. God was angry. Moses was angry, but wisdom reigned when God was persuaded to give the Hebrews one last chance.

COMMON GROUND: The Christian walk is not always an easy walk. It is very easy for us to allow our actions and choices to blacken the eyes of Jesus when we act in less than holy ways. When we do that our witness is compromised and we make all Christians look like the 'hypocrites' we are believed to be by the secular world. **HOLY GROUND:** How have your words and actions this week reflected on Jesus? I ask my grandson if he would misbehave if Jesus were sitting on a stool in the corner of the room where he was being naughty. He always says he wouldn't, and I tell him Jesus is always with him. Sobering thought, isn't it? Rethink the answer to the question I asked before. Would you say, think and do the same things you did this week... if Jesus was standing next to you?

Lord, I hadn't thought about how my words, thoughts and deeds reflect on Your holiness. I need to be more aware of anything I do that reflects negatively on Your precious Name. Amen.

➤ Day 113: BROKEN COMMANDMENTS
PASSAGE: **Exodus 32:15-19**
VERSE: **Exodus 32:19**

It came about, as soon as Moses came near the camp, that he saw the calf and the dancing; and Moses' anger burned, and he threw the tablets from his hands and shattered them at the foot of the mountain.

As Moses descended the mountain and returned from his holy ground encounter with God, he heard the revelry and singing from below. Joshua, his aide, said he heard the sound of war in the camp. In utter disgust Moses said to him, *"It is not the sound of the cry of triumph, nor is it the sound of the cry of defeat; but the sound of singing I hear."* Moses' anger burned hotter and hotter as each step drew him closer to common ground and common men. When his eyes actually witnessed the debauchery before him he was sickened. But, when he watched the worship of the golden calf idol, rage washed common sense away and he threw the stone tablets engraved with the Ten Commandments to the ground. There they lay shattered, just like the relationship between Moses and the people he had begged God to save.

COMMON GROUND: Compromise in holiness always leads to compromise in other parts of our lives. As the Hebrews cavorted, drank and acted on all the lusts of their flesh, they inched farther away from all they had promised God they would be. Compromise is a funny thing, in that each compromise makes the next one easier... until we wake up in a cesspool of sin, wondering how we got there. Who could blame Moses for his angry reaction to the people he had worked so hard to deliver from bondage? **HOLY GROUND:** God's commandments were being thrown to the ground and trampled as the people worshipped other gods, adored a graven image, dishonored His Name, and more than likely committed offenses against one another too. I have to believe that God's heart was as broken as the stone tablets. How could holiness ever be restored? Only sincere repentance brings that kind of restoration.

My Jesus, I confess that there are times in my life when I run roughshod over Your teachings in order to act on my own flesh lusts. Forgive my sincerely repentant heart and restore me in Your grace and mercy. Amen.

➤ Day 114: PASSING THE BUCK
PASSAGE: **Exodus 32:20-24**
VERSE: **Exodus 32:24**

*"I said to them, 'Whoever has any gold, let them tear it off.'
So they gave it to me, and I threw it into the fire,
and out came this calf."*

After casting the stone tablets to the ground, Moses took the golden calf idol and burned it in the fire. He ground the gold to powder, scattered it upon the water and made the people drink it. Moses wasn't finished yet though. He turned to Aaron and said, *"What did this people do to you, that you have brought such great sin upon them?"* Notice that Moses didn't shift blame from his brother. Aaron then tried the oldest trick in the book—passing the buck: *"...you know the people yourself, that they are prone to evil. For they said to me, 'Make a god for us who will go before us; for this Moses, the man who brought us up from the land of Egypt, we do not know what has become of him.'"* Aaron passed the blame to the 'naughty Hebrews' who must have tied him up and tortured him into going along with them! In one of the most foolish statements in all the Bible Aaron said to Moses, *"I said to them, 'Whoever has any gold, let them tear it off.' So they gave it to me, and I threw it into the fire, and out came this calf."* If Aaron's sin wasn't so tragic, his idiocy would be laughable. Would Moses (or God, for that matter) really believe the gold earrings and bracelets morphed themselves into a golden calf? In this case—as in most cases—passing the buck was used to shift blame and shirk responsibility. How disillusioned Moses must have felt! How furious God must have been.

COMMON GROUND: How tragic! The gold that God spoiled from Egypt—which was priceless—had been destroyed and wasted and had become worthless. Priceless treasure became worthless junk because of disobedience to God's command to not worship idols. **HOLY GROUND:** Aaron's flesh failure to accept personal responsibility for his actions is a common response. How do you handle situations when you are accused (rightly) for your sins? A step toward holy ground might be a commitment to acknowledge failure with honesty, confess the sin and turn from it in true repentance. Don't pass the buck. Step up and be responsible.

Jesus, In the past I have shirked responsibility and tried to shift blame to others that clearly should have fallen on my head. Help me on this journey to walk in holiness this year. Amen.

➤ Day 115: WHO'S WITH GOD?
PASSAGE: **Exodus 32:25-29**
VERSE: **Exodus 32:27**

He said to them, "Thus says the LORD, the God of Israel,
'Every man of you put his sword upon his thigh, and go back and
forth from gate to gate in the camp, and kill every man his brother,
and every man his friend, and every man his neighbor.'"

*N**ow when Moses saw that the people were out of control—for Aaron had let them get out of control to be a derision among their enemies—then Moses stood in the gate of the camp, and said, "Whoever is for the LORD, come to me!" And all the sons of Levi gathered together to him.* Moses had surely had enough. It was time for Israel's ordained leader to take control of his people. It was also time to sift the wheat from the chaff and to get rid of the wasteful chaff that hinders the wheat from being suitable for use. Notice that the Levites joined Moses, which makes sense because Moses and Aaron are from the Levite tribe. Imagine the emotional struggle as Moses tells them to take their swords, go throughout the camp and kill those who did not cross to the side of the Lord. Their commitment to God had to be greater than their compassion for their sinning Hebrew brothers.

COMMON GROUND: Would you choose God's side or the world's side if forced to make that decision? You may feel God was too harsh in His judgment against the idol makers. Maybe you think He should have given them a second chance. Could a holy God allow sin to reign in the Hebrew camp... even for a short time?
HOLY GROUND: *"You have been set apart to the Lord today, for you were against your own sons and brothers, and he has blessed you this day."*(NIV) Their decision to obey the difficult command set them apart, made them different, made them peculiar, made their commitment sure, proved they were wheat and not chaff, and was reckoned to them as righteousness!

Spirit of God, It is easy to say I would choose You in this same situation, but I acknowledge that I haven't been so tested as of this time. Strengthen me to be willing to always choose right and fight against wrong. Amen.

➤ Day 116: WILL YOU FORGIVE THEM?
PASSAGE: **Exodus 32:30-32**
VERSE: **Exodus 32:32**

"But now, if You will, forgive their sin—and if not, please blot me out from Your book which You have written!"

Moses very bluntly condemned the actions of the people, making no excuses for their blatant disregard of God's command to holiness. *"You yourselves have committed a great sin; and now I am going up to the LORD, perhaps I can make atonement for your sin."* Moses will again go to God and intercede on behalf of his people. This trip into God's presence was different than all the previous ones because Moses was willing to sacrifice his own life on behalf of an undeserving people. (Does that sound familiar to you at all?) *"But now, if You will, forgive their sin—and if not, please blot me out from Your book which You have written!"* A portrait of true selfless leadership is being painted for us in this passage. Moses is saying, "Forgive them <u>if</u> it is Your will, Lord; but if You will not do that, take my life—erase it from history—and let me not be remembered as the failed leader of Your children." Moses would rather be forgotten forever than be remembered for his inability to control the nation he was charged to lead.

COMMON GROUND: In a day when political and often church leaders are worried more about their own personal needs than their constituency, Moses stands out in the crowd. He didn't try to gloss over the sins of Israel hoping God would take sin lightly. Instead, he acknowledged the sin and was so mortified by it that he would rather have never existed than to have been a failure. **HOLY GROUND:**

Moses didn't ignore the 'sin in the camp' or try to justify the actions of his people. He was seeking full atonement from God. Big request—Big Man—Big God!

Father God, Moses is the true portrait of what You call leaders to be. Whether in the workplace, the public arena or the church, leaders are to stand tall and take responsibility for their flocks. Lord, we need Moses-like leaders in our world today. Amen.

➤ Day 117: WITH CONSEQUENCES
PASSAGE: **Exodus 32:33-35**
VERSE: **Exodus 32:34**

"But go now, lead the people where I told you. Behold, My angel shall go before you; nevertheless in the day when I punish, I will punish them for their sin."

Here is a revolutionary statement: Sin has consequences! Isn't it funny how people think a simple "I'm sorry" can remove the sin, as well as the consequences? God told Moses, *"Whoever has sinned against Me, I will blot him out of My book."* Moses would not be held accountable for Israel's sin; each sinner would himself be responsible for his own choices. What a reassurance to a man who had literally laid down his life for his friends. Moses would not be remembered as a failed leader, but his followers would be remembered for their failure to follow his example. Each sinful choice would reap repercussions—some of which would not be assessed until a much later date. God said that on the day He punishes they would receive their punishment. Lest they take the momentary reprieve too lightly, He smote them with a plague to remind them of their failure.

COMMON GROUND: In our flesh we would like our wrong choices to have no consequences. The reality is that without them we would never learn to avoid the pain they bring in our lives.

Consequences should serve as deterrents to keep us from repeating the same sin again and again. Do you think the Hebrew people learned their lesson here and would walk wholly holy before God? **HOLY GROUND:** Correction, discipline, rebuke and pruning are never pleasant experiences. God loves us too much to leave us in the flesh-driven state we were born in. Only when we let His Spirit reign in us to direct and correct us will we walk in holiness. Our personal sinful choices bring unpleasant consequences and we must learn from them to avoid repeating them in the future.

Lord, I reluctantly give You permission to reveal wrong, correct it, and bring the necessary consequences in order for You to teach me to walk in holiness before You all of my days. Amen.

➤ Day 118: YOU'RE ON YOUR OWN
PASSAGE: **Exodus 33:1-6**
VERSE: **Exodus 33:3**

"Go up to a land flowing with milk and honey; for I will not go up in your midst, because you are an obstinate people and I might destroy you on the way."

Big, big consequence! God told Israel to go ahead and go into the land He promised them… the land of abundance… the land flowing with milk and honey… but they would walk into that land alone. God would not go with them, saying He would be tempted to destroy them along the way. Sounds harsh, doesn't it? How *harsh* do you think the noise of their worship of the golden calf sounded in God's ears? The other verses for today's entry say the people responded with acts of mourning as they thought about going up against the inhabitants of the land without God fighting on their behalf. Finally God was getting their attention. *"You are an obstinate people; should I go up in your midst for one moment, I would destroy you. Now therefore, put off your ornaments from you, that I may know what I shall do with you."* God commanded them to remove their jewelry as a means of showing outwardly their inward repentance. Israel was slowly having their pride stripped away and their hearts humbled.

COMMON GROUND: Imagine God telling you He would allow you to walk wherever you wanted to walk, but that you would walk that path alone... without His direction and without His hedge of protection. Does it scare you? Common men walk that way every single day... living their lives without His input and reaping dire consequences. **HOLY GROUND:** The terror of walking without God should paralyze the heart of any true believer. It is like walking in blindness without a cane or a seeing-eye dog. It is like driving in a foreign metropolis without a map or GPS server. It is like jumping from an airplane without learning how to release a parachute. I don't know about you, but I <u>never</u> again want to find out what walking without His guidance feels like. Been there, done that, and hated every minute of it.

My Jesus, Knowing that walking in Your will keeps You walking beside me is enough to keep me on the right path. No matter where I go I want You walking beside me, directing my steps, slowing my pace in dangerous terrain, and speeding it up in smooth places. You are in the driver's seat... and I feel safe with things that way.
Amen.

➤ Day 119: FRIEND OF GOD
PASSAGE: **Exodus 33:7-11**
VERSE: **Exodus 33:11**

Thus the LORD used to speak to Moses face to face, just as a man speaks to his friend. When Moses returned to the camp, his servant Joshua, the son of Nun, a young man, would not depart from the tent.

Moses spent time with God like we spend time with a friend. What more could any child of God desire? How do friends communicate? One talks, one listens; one pours out, the other receives; one cries, the other wipes away the tears; one confides, the other keeps the words confidential. In the tent of meeting, the temporary tabernacle of God, Moses sought guidance, confessed doubts, relayed fears and received direction. The people were in awe of Moses' relationship with God and *when all the people saw the pillar of cloud standing at the entrance of the tent, all the people would arise and worship, each at the entrance of his tent.* Moses' worship became their worship. After all, the guidance he received was for their benefit. Joshua, fearing someone unworthy might enter and defile the tabernacle, remained at watch... guarding the door in between Moses' visits.

COMMON GROUND: It is common in today's society to believe God is just one of the guys and to forget the reverence and awe Moses gave to Him. Notice, Moses went to the tent and *the LORD used to speak to Moses face to face, just as a man speaks to his friend.* God initiated the friend to friend relationship, and I doubt that Moses ever spoke to Him in less than a reverent way. It is okay to seek the friendship of God, but it is never okay to irreverently approach His throne of grace. **HOLY GROUND:** Holy people will never take being in the presence of God lightly. They will still themselves, seek His will, listen for His answers, and come away from the encounter forever changed. How are you doing on this part of your journey? Work on preparing your heart to enter into His gates with praise!

Jesus, I have often prayed to You in hurried and irreverent ways.
I confess that I sometimes forget who I am talking to.
Forgive me and teach me how to remain ever mindful of Your
glory and the respect You so deserve. Amen.

➤ Day 120: TEACH ME YOUR WAYS
PASSAGE: **Exodus 33:12-14**
VERSE: **Exodus 33:13**

"Now therefore, I pray You, if I have found favor in Your sight,
let me know Your ways that I may know You, so that
I may find favor in Your sight. Consider too,
that this nation is Your people."

Moses had some serious questions to ask God. He wanted clearer directions and increased assurance that he was chosen specifically to finish the mission before him. Can you relate to that? Have you ever asked God to make Himself more real to you—to reveal His plans in a clearer way? The God we serve is big enough to handle your questions. He is waiting for that cry of your heart. Look at the verses for today's lesson. *And He said, "My presence shall go with you, and I will give you rest."* Moses finally had his answer. God's presence would be with him in the journey ahead... and at the end of that journey Moses would find peace!

COMMON GROUND: Would God's promise of His constant presence be enough to please you? All of us can think of things we would like to receive... money, fame, skinny bodies, health, beauty... but what is it that you most desire? What one thing means more to you than these earthly desires? Is God's presence—with the promise of peace at the end of the journey—enough? That may be the only promise you get. **HOLY GROUND:** Look closely at yourself at this point in your journey. Write down the things you seek from God. What does your list show about your priorities? Are the desires worldly or godly? Are they physical or spiritual? Are they common or holy? There is nothing wrong with money, health or beauty, but we must remember that we can take none of them with us when we leave this life. Money will never hold your hand on your death bed, but God will. And then... rest.

*Spirit of God, This seeking Your presence is new to me.
I long for that, but I honestly do not know how to 'seek' on a
deeper level. You are my Teacher, my Guide, my Comforter and
my Companion. I will follow Your lead. Teach me. Amen.*

➤ Day 121: I KNOW YOU BY NAME
PASSAGE: **Exodus 33:15-17**
VERSE: **Exodus 33:17**

*The LORD said to Moses, "I will also do this thing of
which you have spoken; for you have found favor in My sight
and I have known you by name."*

One last appeal to God for His hand to be with Moses and the Hebrew people as they journeyed onward toward the Promised Land: *"If Your presence does not go with us, do not lead us up from here. For how then can it be known that I have found favor in Your sight, I and Your people?"* Moses wanted to walk nowhere without the power of God walking with him. His words were a soft plea to God that if He would not—for any reason—be with them, then they did not want to move forward until the separation was healed and the chasm was bridged. Then Moses got to the real heart of the matter... *"Is it not by Your going with us, so that we, I and Your people, may be distinguished from all the other people who are upon the face of the earth?"* Moses realized that the only thing distinguishing Israel from every other nation in the world was the presence of God, the provision of God, and the protection of God. He found the reassurance he needed in the words at the beginning of this entry... God was showing him favor... and He knew Moses by name!

COMMON GROUND: God knew Moses by name—and He knows you by name too! Why is that so important? Why is it a life-changing truth? You are not just a Social Security number to God. You are loved, you are created for a special reason, and your life has value. You have a name... and the God of all creation knows you by that name. More importantly though is the fact that He knows your heart. **HOLY GROUND:** God knows your name, but He will not shout over the din of the world to get your attention. Moses sought after God and listened for His replies. Moses hungered to know God more every time they came together in fellowship. Moses would never settle for lukewarm; he wanted a burning hot (burning-bush hot) relationship with his Lord. After all: God knew his NAME!

Father God, How humbling it is to know that You, the Creator of the Universe, know my name! May I never forget that truth, and may I never take one step outside of Your hedge of love. Amen.

➤ Day 122: HE HIDETH MY SOUL
PASSAGE: Exodus 33:18-23
VERSE: Exodus 33:21-22

Then the LORD said, "Behold, there is a place by Me, and you shall stand there on the rock; and it will come about, while My glory is passing by, that I will put you in the cleft of the rock and cover you with My hand until I have passed by."

"Father God, can I just see Your face? I long to see the face of my Creator... the glory of my Lord," was Moses' heart cry. Have you ever thought that if you could just see Jesus' face you could focus better in prayer or worship better? I have asked the same question Moses did... and have yet to see the face of my Savior. I see His heart instead as I read the passages of Scripture where we are given glimpses of how He lived and walked on this earth. Moses wanted to see God's face, but was told he could not do so and live. Instead, God placed Moses in the cleft (crevice/indentation) of a rock and passed by him, allowing His servant to see Him from the back. Today, we celebrate this story with the great Fanny Crosby hymn, "He Hideth My Soul." Here is an excerpt:

A wonderful Savior is Jesus my Lord,
A wonderful Savior to me; He hideth my soul in the cleft
of the rock, Where rivers of pleasure I see.

Refrain: He hideth my soul in the cleft of the rock that shadows a
dry, thirsty land; He hideth my life in the depths of His love, And
covers me there with His hand, And covers me there with His hand.

COMMON GROUND: The interesting twist on Fanny's hymn is that she was completely blind and couldn't see Jesus' face, even if He were standing right in front of her. Like Moses, seeing God was the desire of her heart. **HOLY GROUND:** Will you allow the words of "He Hideth My Soul" to become the cry of your heart? Here are more:

A wonderful Savior is Jesus my Lord, He taketh my
burden away; He holdeth me up, and I shall not be moved,
He giveth me strength as my day. (Refrain)

With numberless blessings each moment He crowns, And filled
with His fullness divine, I sing in my rapture, oh, glory to God,
for such a Redeemer as mine! (Refrain)

When clothed in His brightness, transported I rise,
To meet Him in clouds of the sky, His perfect salvation,
His wonderful love, I'll shout with the millions on high. (Refrain)

Lord, There is nothing else I can say to top these words. Amen.

➤ Day **123**: SECOND CHANCES
PASSAGE: **Exodus 34:1-4**
VERSE: **Exodus 34:1**

Now the LORD said to Moses, "Cut out for yourself two stone tablets like the former ones, and I will write on the tablets the words that were on the former tablets which you shattered."

Moses and God had some unfinished business to take care of. Remember those stone tablets he threw down and smashed in anger? God wanted that moral law written down and physically present with His children as a reminder of how He wanted them to live their lives. He told Moses to hew new tablets and bring them up the mountain the next morning. No one else was to be on Mt. Sinai—just God and His chosen leader. I have to wonder what Moses was thinking as he prepared the tablets and set off on his early morning journey up the mountain. Was he remembering the last time he was up there? Was he angry at the people because he had to make this follow-up trip? Did he question why God didn't just give the commandments without the trip? No! Moses was being given another chance to stand on Holy Ground in the presence of his Lord. He wouldn't have wanted it any other way. Imagine the anticipation as each step brought him closer to the place where he and God could talk face to face and friend to friend.

COMMON GROUND: Moses never tired of being before God and having unique encounters with Him. Isn't if funny how we get tired of people? You know how, we ignore their phone calls, dodge around grocery store corners to avoid them, and even hide when they knock on the door. Believers should never get tired of seeking the presence of God. **HOLY GROUND:** We claim we want to be in God's presence all the time! Do you really want to stand in the presence of a Holy God? Are you like Moses—jumping at every opportunity to spend uninterrupted time alone with Him? Holy ground walking will require holy encounters with our Lord... a soul-baring kind of encounter. Are you up to the challenge? If so, put on those hiking shoes—you may need to walk on some uncommon ground to get there!

My Jesus, Today I want to walk somewhere new with You.
Take me to a higher level of faith over rough and rocky trails
and around high mountains to a place of solitude,
fellowship and growth. Amen.

➤ Day 124: CHARACTER OF GOD
PASSAGE: **Exodus 34:5-7**
VERSE: **Exodus 34:6-7a**

Then the LORD passed by in front of him and proclaimed,
"The LORD, the LORD God, compassionate and gracious, slow
to anger, and abounding in lovingkindness and truth; who keeps
lovingkindness for thousands, who forgives iniquity,
transgression and sin..."

Imagine this picture: Moses arrived at the God-arranged spot for their encounter and *the LORD descended in the cloud and stood there with him as he called upon the name of the LORD.* Moses was standing on the mountain, calling upon the Name of the LORD, praying for his people and seeking the face of God... while God was standing next to him in a pillar of cloud. Moses worshipped Him by telling of His awesome attributes. God is *compassionate and gracious* (showing mercy to those who do not deserve mercy); *slow to anger* (even when provoked by His stubborn children); *and abounding in lovingkindness and truth* (speaking truth whether the listener wants to hear it or not); *who keeps lovingkindness for thousands, who forgives iniquity, transgression and sin* (forgiving, even though the wages of sin is death).

COMMON GROUND: Most of us think worship is merely singing songs in a church service. Sincere worship is honoring our LORD for who He is, what He does and what He has done for us. Moses knew how to worship. What would you say about God if He was standing next to you while you identified His character? **HOLY GROUND:** Maybe one of your steps on this journey is to better relate to who

God is in your life. Take some identifying characteristics of God from the Bible and meditate upon their meanings. Here are a few to get you started: Holy, righteous, omnipotent (all powerful), omniscient (all knowing), omnipresent (all places), jealous, merciful, patient and loving.

Jesus, You were obedient, kind, compassionate, patient, tolerant, wise and discerning on this earth. Teach me the meaning of these characteristics so I can strive to be more like You. Amen.

➤ Day 125: GO WITH US, LORD!
PASSAGE: Exodus 34:8-9
VERSE: Exodus 34:9

He said, "If now I have found favor in Your sight, O LORD, I pray, let the LORD go along in our midst, even though the people are so obstinate, and pardon our iniquity and our sin, and take us as Your own possession."

"Father God, I know the people are stubborn. I know they are hard-headed. Yes, they are obstinate and sinful. Please come with us anyway!" Moses is my kind of leader. He makes no excuses for his people. Actually, he reminds God of just how bad they are—before asking Him to not abandon them in their quest for the Promised Land. Moses humbled himself before God and pled on behalf of Israel, knowing full well they didn't deserve the mercy God had promised them. Why did Moses continue to intercede for people who had proven they were unfaithful and disobedient? He was given a job to do and he had no intention of stopping until the mission was accomplished. Moses was willing to lay down his personal welfare for undeserving and foolish people. Sounds a little like Jesus, doesn't it? *Father forgive them... they don't know what they are doing.*

COMMON GROUND: Aren't you glad you aren't God? I know some people think they are—but seriously! Aren't you glad you aren't Moses—constantly having to risk your own life for the sake of people who whine at you, complain about you and thumb their nose at the God you serve? Leadership can be the most thankless job in the world. How are you treating the leaders you know? **HOLY GROUND:** Notice here that Moses isn't any more perfect than the people he is commissioned to lead... and he would have been the first one to state that openly. The leaders in your home, workplace, church, community and nation are all fallible human beings. They still need your prayers and support. Moses, no matter what the past held, was still willing to pour out his soul for his people. One last question: if you are a leader, are you like Moses?

Spirit of God, In my life I am both a leader and a follower. Help me do both to the best of my ability and to put forth great effort because my character reflects Your Name. Give me a sincere Moses-like heart for the lost and downtrodden. Amen.

➤ Day 126: WATCH ME WORK!
PASSAGE: **Exodus 34:10**
VERSE: **Exodus 34:10**

Then God said, "Behold, I am going to make a covenant. Before all your people I will perform miracles which have not been produced in all the earth nor among any of the nations; and all the people among whom you live will see the working of the LORD, for it is a fearful thing that I am going to perform with you."

Wow! The promise Scripture above is wonderful to behold. God was telling Moses He will perform miracles—a never-seen-before type of miracles—so that all the people in all the nations around Israel would see them and know their God was indeed God. Notice that He said *it is a fearful thing that I am going to perform with you.* Does that mean God was setting out to cause fear in hearts?

No. In this text the word fear means awesome or amazing. Imagine venturing out into uncommon territory with a promise like that paving the way before you. These words are like God saying to you, "Go ahead. Step out into that new adventure. Walk on those new and unfamiliar roads. No matter where you walk I will be beside you. Dare to dream—for I am going to make great things happen through your hands. Others will see your success and will be drawn to dream big too! Let nothing hold you back… this is My promise to you."

COMMON GROUND: Isn't it sad that we dream so small—yet God wants to bless us so big? When we opened our Bible store I figured we would need at least $300 per week in sales to keep the doors open… and that is what I told God. For the first twelve weeks of business we had sales between $290 and $310 each week. I was quite proud of myself until someone told me I was binding up God's generous spirit. **HOLY GROUND:** Once my eyes were opened to that truth, I simply said, "Father God, you know the needs. Please send whatever You wish and we will receive it with grateful hearts." In a rough Michigan economy when many chain stores are closing, His House is holding its own. Our bills are paid and we are able to sow into other ministries. God has never failed us… because we strive daily to make His House a holy ground place.

Father God, I think I dream small in order to not be disappointed.
Help me to see through Your generous eyes all You have ordained
for me and for my family. Whatever You send is exactly enough.
Amen.

➤ Day 127: WATCH FOR SNARES
PASSAGE: **Exodus 34:11-13**
VERSE: **Exodus 34:12**

"Watch yourself that you make no covenant with the
inhabitants of the land into which you are going, or it
will become a snare in your midst."

Read the verse for today very carefully. Note that <u>no</u> *covenant* is to be made with those in the lands the Hebrew people were preparing to take… because *it <u>will</u> become a snare.* Why would God say it was wrong to make peace treaties, non-aggression pacts or any other contract with the nations surrounding Israel? He knew one very real truth… divided loyalties always interfere with deep faith commitments. How could God be so sure that was the case? Past history! Adam and Eve ignored God's command and negotiated with the serpent. Cain contracted with jealousy and killed his brother. Solomon intermarried with women from the nations around Israel, and the children those wives bore to him diluted his commitment to the God who had so richly blessed his kingdom. Unholy alliances may seem harmless at first—even a blessing—but they will always come between us and the God we claim to serve.

COMMON GROUND: Compromise is a way of life in American society today. We sanction sin in our midst and condone thievery and lying in order to get ahead, and we fail to keep our promises and commitments. Compromise is common and has made even the church lukewarm in its stand for righteousness. **HOLY GROUND:** As unpleasant as speaking truth may be to us, it is still a requirement of Scripture. *Be on your guard! If your brother sins, rebuke him; and if he repents, forgive him.* (Luke 17:3) If we do not confront the sin we see in our midst, it may well become the trap we ourselves fall into. Holiness is a command—never an option!

LORD, Give me the temerity and boldness to take a stand for what Your Word says is right and to take an equally bold stand against everything else. The call to personal holiness may well cost me dearly… but it's a price I am increasingly ready to pay. Amen.

➤ Day 128: A JEALOUS GOD
PASSAGE: **Exodus 34:14-17**
VERSE: **Exodus 34:14**

...for you shall not worship any other god, for the LORD,
whose name is Jealous, is a jealous God...

Please don't skip the step of reading today's passage with emphasis on verse 14 as read above. I've mentioned before that God is a jealous God, and it certainly bears mentioning again. *El Qanna* is the name for our Jealous God—and the fact that He is jealous over His children should be a great blessing to each of us. Once we make a promise to honor God and to serve Him alone we enter a covenant relationship with Him. Think about it this way: Marriage is a covenant relationship between a man and a woman. Anything which seeks to divide or destroy that relationship becomes a threat, and the parties to the marriage have the right to fight jealously to preserve the union. God has that same authority in our covenant relationship with Him; in jealousy He will fight for us, fight to keep our hearts, and fight to keep us focused on what He has called us to do. Just as an outsider can try to break up a marriage, the Outsider (Satan) can and will try to break up our coalition with God.

COMMON GROUND: Jealousy for wrong reasons is never a good thing and has caused much suffering in our world. Jealousy to preserve a commitment is another thing altogether. I don't know about you, but I am very grateful that God cares enough to fight for me. This is a picture of His love—a love deep enough that He was willing to die in order for me to spend eternity with Him. **HOLY GROUND:** Love on the part of your Creator means that He will fight against anything—especially sin—which tries to divide your loyalty to Him. Many, many people have tried to run and hide (ever hear of a foolish man named Jonah?) from the presence of the LORD, only to relent and fall back into His arms of grace. His seeking after the lost is all about love for His creation... aren't you glad?

My Jesus, If I ever seek to turn from You and turn toward anything or anyone who seeks to destroy our relationship, You have my permission to hunt me down and bring me back to Your fold. I am grateful that You are El Qanna—my Jealous Redeemer. Amen.

➤ Day 129: ENLARGED BORDERS
PASSAGE: **Exodus 34:23-25**
VERSE: **Exodus 34:24**

"For I will drive out nations before you and enlarge your borders, and no man shall covet your land when you go up three times a year to appear before the LORD your God."

How would you like to have the borders of your service to God enlarged? If God asked you the same question about your physical property, you would probably agree. If He said He could give you a larger home with more room, it might sound good to you. In both cases the expansion would be beneficial to the recipient (you). In the passage for today's entry God was talking about Israel expanding their land holdings and not having a viable threat from neighbors who desired their land. What was required on the part of the people was to worship three times each year at the temple in the Holy Land. Look at the bigger picture here... what if God said, "I will give you more outreach, more ministry opportunities, more chances to witness, and will keep the Enemy from stopping you. In exchange, you are to worship Me and Me alone, keep yourself pure and never forsake Me as your God." Would you take Him up on the proposal?

COMMON GROUND: Very often we want the border (ministry) expansion without expanding our commitment to serve the LORD. It is common to want more recognition and more glory jobs within the church. It is not common to be excited when the expansion requires hard work or sacrifice. **HOLY GROUND:** God's blessings always require that we remember who He is and worship Him with gratitude. I am someone who is willing to say, "Here I am, send me"; and because of that willingness God continues to expand my ministry horizons. Are you a willing and obedient servant, or a 'Here I am, send someone else' kind of worshipper?

Jesus, I do want my ministry borders expanded... but am reluctant to offer more of myself. Help me, LORD, to be willing and obedient—committed and dedicated to do all You place before me. In return, I will worship You in the temple of my grateful heart. Amen.

➤ Day 130: FORTY DAYS WITH GOD
PASSAGE: Exodus 34:27-28
VERSE: Exodus 34:28

So he was there with the LORD forty days and forty nights; he did not eat bread or drink water. And he wrote on the tablets the words of the covenant, the Ten Commandments.

Moses spent the next forty days and nights fasting, listening to God and worshipping on Mount Sinai. During that time *Adonai* (the Great LORD) reiterated the words of the law to him and rewrote them on a second set of stone tablets. Let's look today at another name of God. I often use the Complete Jewish Bible in my teaching, as well as during my personal study. Look at how verse 28 reads in that version: *Moshe was there with Adonai forty days and forty nights, during which time he neither ate food nor drank water. (Adonai) wrote on the tablets the words of the covenant, the Ten Words.* The use of the name *Adonai* signified the honor given to God by the Hebrew people as they confessed Him to be their majestic LORD and acknowledged His total authority. Learning the names of God will add a depth to your personal prayer life. Thank Him for being *El Qanna*—your jealous God. Worship Him as *Adonai*—your great LORD. Honor Him as El Shaddai—your Almighty God. Acknowledge Him as *El Roi*—the God who sees all.

COMMON GROUND: I have always put extra effort into remembering people's names. For years as I worked with the public, I built relationships with my customers by using their names. In a very impersonal day and age the use of another's name can be very personal and endearing, making them feel special. **HOLY GROUND:** Sometimes our prayer life gets routine and we need something to reignite the fire of the past. Using the Names of God the Father and Jesus Christ the Messiah will bring those prayers to life as you recognize Him for His characteristics. Using His titles should result in a more intimate connection with Him. In later lessons we will discover more about these names and begin to learn them. Grow your prayer life and see how much closer you will feel to the LORD.

El Elyon, You truly are God Most High. How I love learning Your names. I revere Your name, but confess that saying 'God' has stopped being personal and intimate for me. As I acknowledge who You are... hear my love and awe, Father God. Amen.

➤ Day 131: A HOLY COUNTENANCE
PASSAGE: Exodus 34:29
VERSE: Exodus 34:29

It came about when Moses was coming down from Mount Sinai (and the two tablets of the testimony were in Moses' hand as he was coming down from the mountain), that Moses did not know that the skin of his face shone because of his speaking with Him.

As Moses descended Mount Sinai with the two new stone tablets of the law, his face gleamed with the glory of God's presence. Moses didn't realize that his outward appearance was changed — he was too busy thinking about the inward change of his heart. Moses had been with God and would never be the same again. His thoughts, his words, his actions, his love-walk, his faithfulness, his obedience, his worship, his commitment and his service would never again be lukewarm. Standing in the presence of God, hearing

His voice, beholding His glory would have changed anyone. Man's flattering words would never again satisfy, for Moses heard the only words that mattered to him: "Moses, you alone are to come up the mountain for I consider you My friend." That encounter would be impossible to forget, for it would forever alter how Moses looked at himself... a chosen friend of the God of Israel.

COMMON GROUND: When I ask my students if they want to stand in the presence of God they automatically respond to the affirmative. After all, what Christian wouldn't want to feel God next to him or see Jesus standing before him? I remind them that God cannot look upon sin or evil; He sees the heart and knows everything... and then I ask them again if they still want to stand in His presence. **HOLY GROUND:** In our pursuit of holiness we must honestly assess the condition of our heart and allow the Holy Spirit to make necessary changes. Only when we are pure on the inside can we stand in the presence of God and have our countenance changed. I know several people who 'glow' with the joy of the LORD... He shines through them into this dark world.

Father God, I long to be in Your presence like Moses was,
but I confess that the condition of my heart is not blameless. Please
work in me so that I am that worthy, that holy and that welcome.
I bare my soul to You for full assessment. Amen.

➤ Day 132: BARED BEFORE GOD
PASSAGE: Exodus 34:30-35
VERSE: Exodus 34:34-35

But whenever Moses went in before the LORD to speak with
Him, he would take off the veil until he came out; and whenever
he came out and spoke to the sons of Israel what he had been
commanded, the sons of Israel would see the face of Moses,
that the skin of Moses' face shone. So Moses would replace
the veil over his face until he went in to speak with Him.

We learned in the last entry about the physical and spiritual change for the man who has stood in the presence of God. Let's look today at how the people reacted to Moses' new appearance. *So when Aaron and all the sons of Israel saw Moses, behold, the skin of his face shone, and they were afraid to come near him.* Before we judge the people for being afraid of Moses' shining face we must honestly assess how we look at people who have had a genuine encounter with the living God of all Creation. Do we look at them in distrust? Aren't we a little afraid their passion might be contagious? Do we think they have gone over the top in their worship? All of these questions are legitimate, but we are to weigh all things against the Bible... and the story of Moses' transformation before God is within its pages. Moses, out of compassion for his people, covered his changed countenance with a veil when he walked among them. But notice this one thing... he never stopped seeking God because of what others thought. He boldly approached the throne, removed the veil and spoke to the One in whose image he had been formed.

COMMON GROUND: Our common response to those who disapprove of our openness about our faith is to squelch our passion when we are around them. Moses never did that. He covered his face—not to hide his shame at its appearance, but to show others that he respected their concerns. We must be willing to be bold for Christ, but to not be offensive. We will never convert hearts by hitting people over the head with a Bible! **HOLY GROUND:** A holy response says, "I will not now or ever compromise or bend my beliefs to suit you, but I do respect your right to believe what you do." In the sixth chapter of the book of Daniel we find him praying openly *in his house*—as he had made a habit of doing—in spite of a warning not to pray to anyone other than the Babylonian King. Daniel was arrested for his prayers, but he would rather have faced imprisonment than compromise his worship of his God.

LORD, Define for me the fine line between compromise of my faith and being offensive in my thought, word or deed. I want others to know You like I do, but realize it is possible to turn them off with criticism, negativity, and being judgmental. Amen.

➤ ## Day 133: A WILLING OFFERING
PASSAGE: Exodus 35:5-9
VERSE: Exodus 35:5

*Take from among you a contribution to the LORD;
whoever is of a willing heart, let him bring it as the LORD'S
contribution: gold, silver, and bronze...*

God was ready for Israel to set up the temporary tabernacle we talked about in earlier lessons. The call was put out for the materials, labor and financial support to be raised from the voluntary offerings of His people. Now all the explicit plans for the tabernacle, its furnishings, the priestly garments and the Levite service would finally be carried out. In those prior lessons we studied all of the items to be used in tabernacle service, and now we see the fulfillment of the commands. These are freewill—not mandatory—offerings and the people could give as little or as much as they chose. God wanted only that which His people offered willingly above their normal tithe. Why would He make this offering voluntary rather than mandatory? The same reason He wants us to willingly run to Him for cleansing, hope and salvation. God could have reached down and dropped all the materials needed before the people. Instead, He allowed them to be a part of the process... to have a sense of ownership, for this would be the focal point of the camp... the place where He would dwell among His people.

COMMON GROUND: How generous are you with money to be used in service to the LORD? How generous are you with your time and your gifts? I would confess here that I am good at tithing, but bad at giving financially above that level. In my own defense, I tithe many hours each week in preparation for teaching Bible studies, writing books and counseling with those who find their way to my door. I do okay, but I could always be more generous. **HOLY GROUND:** What keeps believers from being generous to kingdom work? When we realize that every single thing we have comes from the loving hand of our God, doesn't it seem right to give cheerfully back to Him? Is it that we feel we don't have extra? Because if that is so, we are proclaiming that God hasn't provided enough. Look at your heart here... examine your motives. I know what is Biblically required, but I'm talking about giving above and beyond the requirement.

My Jesus, Generosity isn't a problem in other areas of my life. Only You, LORD, can teach me to be generous and cheerful in my generosity. I realize that I could never out give You. You gave Your best on Calvary's cross. Amen.

➤ Day 134: WILLING HEARTS
PASSAGE: **Exodus 35:21-29**
VERSE: **Exodus 35:21**

Everyone whose heart stirred him and everyone whose spirit moved him came and brought the LORD'S contribution for the work of the tent of meeting and for all its service and for the holy garments.

Watch how the offering worked as each person brought what they had... *Then all whose hearts moved them, both men and women, came and brought brooches and earrings and signet rings and bracelets, all articles of gold... so did every man who presented an offering of gold to the LORD. Every man, who had in his possession blue and purple and scarlet material and fine linen and goats' hair and rams' skins dyed red and porpoise skins, brought them. Everyone who could make a contribution of silver and bronze brought the LORD'S contribution; and every man who had in his possession acacia wood for any work of the service brought it. All the skilled women spun with their hands, and brought what they had spun, in blue and purple and scarlet material and in fine linen. All the women whose heart stirred with a skill spun the goats' hair. The rulers brought the onyx stones and the stones for setting for the ephod and for the breastpiece; and the spice and the oil for the light and for the anointing oil and for the fragrant incense. The Israelites, all the men and women, whose heart moved them to bring material for all the work, which the LORD had commanded through Moses to be done, brought a freewill offering to the LORD.*

COMMON GROUND: Notice one thing about the above passage— each person brought what he had to the offering. The man who had gold brought gold; he wasn't expected to bring the fine linen or the onyx stones. On the other hand, the woman with the ability to spin fine fabric wasn't looked down upon because she didn't bring acacia wood. Each man brought that which God had already amply provided for him. **HOLY GROUND:** I have heard people say they cannot afford to go to church because they have nothing to put in the offering plate as it is passed. I have tried to explain that their service, loyalty and faithfulness are what God is really looking for. Yes, it does take money to run a church and support missions, but you must understand the money will come from the obedient servants God has given it to. Your tithe is a form of worship.

Jesus, I may not have a lot of money—or gold or silver or fine linen—to bring to You, but I bring a willing heart to serve in whatever capacity You need me in. Now I understand the 'church flowerbed' is scattered with a variety of 'seeders,' and each man's 'seed' blends together with the rest to make a perfect bouquet.
Amen.

➤ Day 135: TEACHING OTHERS
PASSAGE: **Exodus 35:30-35**
VERSE: **Exodus 35:34**

He also has put in his (Bezalel's) heart to <u>teach</u>, both he and Oholiab, the son of Ahisamach, of the tribe of Dan.

The tabernacle materials were gathered but still needed to be assembled and constructed into the perfect place of worship God deemed it to be. *See, the LORD has called by name Bezalel the son of Uri, the son of Hur, of the tribe of Judah. And He has filled him with the Spirit of God, in wisdom, in understanding and in knowledge and in all craftsmanship...* God designated several skilled craftsmen to perform the service, and then gave them patient hearts to teach others to work alongside them. Bezalel and Oholiab couldn't possibly do all the embroidery, weaving, engraving and construction themselves, so God sent able assistants—willing students to sit under excellent tutoring and share the workload. The two gifted artisans could have insisted on doing all the work in order to get all the praise. They could have been stingy with their knowledge. Instead, for the glory of God, they passed the baton to hungry students.

COMMON GROUND: Have you ever watched someone who wouldn't share a cherished family recipe, teach someone else a skill, or equip another to follow in their shoes... for fear of being replaced? It is common to want to shine or excel in a skill—you know, something you alone are known for—and keep the knowledge a secret, but how can the next generation carry the torch if they aren't taught the skill? How else can they become a working part in the machine of service? **HOLY GROUND:** Several years ago, in preparation for a community Thanksgiving dinner, the 'senior women' in our congregation taught the 'teen ladies' how to make homemade pies with crusts from scratch and fresh fillings. I don't know who was more blessed—the teachers, the learners or the eaters! Pie making would be a lost art if someone didn't take the time to teach that special skill to the next generation... and isn't that how the LORD would want us to pass the baton in the relay race of life?

Spirit of God, Show me where the gifts and abilities You have blessed me with can be used to enhance the skills of others. I want to share what I know—to pass the cloak like Elijah did to Elisha— so that kingdom service will not die at my hands. Amen.

➤ Day 136: POURED OUT BLESSINGS
PASSAGE: **Exodus 36:2-3**
VERSE: **Exodus 36:3**

*They received from Moses all the contributions which the
sons of Israel had brought to perform the work in the construction
of the sanctuary. And they still continued bringing to him
freewill offerings every morning.*

Generosity is contagious! As the people watched the donated materials begin to accumulate, they grew increasingly more excited about the tabernacle which would soon stand among them. I can see how these events unfolded as one man brought some animal hides and another remembered that he had some he could offer. As one woman shared finely woven fabric another would say, "I have some gold thread which would look beautiful embroidered on that." The tabernacle treasury was filling up, as were the hearts of the people who brought of their wares to fill it. God works that way because you cannot out-give Him. If you give Him your last dime, He will pour out blessings for your faithfulness and generosity. If you serve others, then in your moment of need He will reimburse you in abundance. If you praise His precious Name with your last breath He will usher you into the place of eternal plenty. Each item delivered to the treasury carried the goodwill of the people toward the God who had delivered them from bondage and promised to walk with them into their new home.

COMMON GROUND: Do you believe you cannot out-give God? If you do, can you recall times in your life when that principle proved itself to be true? So few will ever come face to face with that reality because they hold stingily to all they have, always fearing someone will steal it from them. They don't give because they are afraid the receiver might come back for more. They are under the mistaken impression they can take their wealth with them after their life here is finished. **HOLY GROUND:** In our hunger for holiness we must realize that every single thing we have—from our next breath to our last dollar—comes from the God who created us and supplies all our needs. Are we foolish enough to doubt He will keep supplying those needs so we can keep giving them away and being a blessing to His children? Think about it!

Father God, Generosity has not been one of my strengths. This makes me realize that I have doubted Your ability to always give me enough for my own needs and extra to supply the needs of others. Give me an open hand and a generous heart. Amen.

➤ Day 137: OVERFLOWING!
PASSAGE: Exodus 36:4-7
VERSE: Exodus 36:6-7

So Moses issued a command, and a proclamation was circulated throughout the camp, saying, "Let no man or woman any longer perform work for the contributions of the sanctuary." Thus the people were restrained from bringing any more. For the material they had was sufficient and more than enough for all the work, to perform it.

What a problem to have! There were more than enough materials needed for the tabernacle. There was more than enough embroidered fabric, hammered gold and overlaid wood. There was so much skilled workmanship that Moses had to *restrain* the outpouring of generosity and service. Have you ever been in a situation like that? The closest I can recall was following the death of my younger brother when the people from our church, our small-group friends, and my Seekers' class began to fill my house and the funeral home lounge with food. My refrigerator couldn't hold any more; the counters and appliance tops were covered and the cupboards were jammed full. The outpouring was overwhelming and was a great witness to my non-Christian relatives who kept asking, "Where is all this food coming from?" I smiled and told them this is what the church—the body of Christ—is really all about! Imagine having to restrain generosity... indeed, what a problem to have!

COMMON GROUND: The story above is far from common. Actually, it is quite a rare event in today's impersonal society. We send emails, rather than visit face to face (friend to friend). We throw money at needs, rather than rolling up our sleeves and digging in to help. We lock our doors to keep others out, rather than opening them wide to invite them in. The tabernacle would never have been built and furnished for the good of everyone if selfish people withheld their labor and love. **HOLY GROUND:** The truths in the two accounts above need no more teaching. They simply need to be applied to our outreach ministries and our neighbors' needs. Give until it hurts and then give some more.

LORD, Imagine having too many workers for the harvest, too many soul-winners in the field, and too much generosity to contain it all. LORD, that should be the condition of Your church today. It is time for us to unclench our hands, step out of our doors and get busy! Amen.

➤ Day 138: JUST AS GOD SAID
PASSAGE: **Exodus 37:1-39 & 43**
VERSE: **Exodus 39:43**

And Moses examined all the work and behold, they had done it; just as the LORD had commanded, this they had done. So Moses blessed them.

The passage for today was rather lengthy, but can be summed up in these few words... *all the work* was done *just as the LORD had commanded.* As I thought about the implications of this portion of Scripture I was led to realize how often we cut corners, or try to do things our way or an easier way than how God directs us. What if Moses decided he didn't like the way God ordained the tabernacle furnishings to be placed? What if the Levites felt the hangings were too labor-intensive, or that pure gold shouldn't be wasted on the shovels and utensils for worship? What if the priests didn't want bells on the hems of their garments to ring when they served in the house of God? If everything had to be done exactly as God revealed to Moses on Mount Sinai, why do we think the other revelations given to him there aren't applicable in our lives today? Why do we excuse abortion and not consider it 'murder?' Why do we allow adultery and fornication in the house of God? Why do we fail to write the words of God's laws on our doorposts and in our hearts? Somehow, at some time and some place we turned from doing things His way to doing things our way—always a more convenient way which requires much less effort. The condition of the modern church reflects the lack of emphasis on holiness.

COMMON GROUND: While writing this I was replying to an entry on Facebook by my friend Tom Z. He wrote, *"I find my delight in being a pawn in the hand of God and to be moved about at His slightest whim."* In response I wrote, *Imagine when we stand before Him and hear, 'Well done, My good and faithful servant. Check Mate—Game Over—You Win!' Is that what you are waiting to hear?* **HOLY GROUND:** How are you doing at being His willing and obedient pawn? At the end of your journey will you say like Moses, "I did it His way," or like Sinatra, "I did it MY way?" Great food for thought as you travel this one day of your holiness journey.

My Jesus, I want to do it Your way—every day—in every way—no matter what price I must pay. Amen.

➤ Day 139: SET IT-SANCTIFY IT!
PASSAGE: **Exodus 40:1-11**
VERSE: **Exodus 40:2**

On the first day of the first month you shall set up the tabernacle of the tent of meeting.

Finally, the work was completed and the tabernacle was ready for the furnishings to be placed. They would be brought in order of importance, thus the Ark of the Covenant was carried in and placed in the holiest portion of the tabernacle. The veil dividing the Holy of Holies from the rest of the space was hung and the rest of the furniture was located where God had commanded. The command to *take the anointing oil and anoint the tabernacle and all that is in it... and consecrate it and all its furnishings* was strictly followed. The anointing and consecration rituals were used to set the tabernacle items apart for holy service to God. They were never to be used in ways contrary to that which He deemed them to be used. Every command was followed to the letter. Why would anyone take a shortcut or disobey a direct command at this late date? God was preparing His earthly resting place among the Israelite people and they were compelled to honor His directions in every way.

COMMON GROUND: There was nothing common about the work being done at the house of God. Other nations carved their idols (gods) from wood or stone. The tabernacle would have nothing so common. Only the finest woven fabrics, the strongest pieces of wood, the purest precious metals and the most perfect gemstones would be used for service there. After all, the people would be worshipping the God who created the stones and wood which other nations called their gods. **HOLY GROUND:** Are you bringing God only your best—or are you grudgingly giving him some of the rest? This is a serious question to honestly evaluate your spiritual growth. You are now more than one-third of the way through these devotionals. Are you growing and hungering to give your best to Him? He doesn't want leftovers or hand-me-downs. Give Him the first part of everything and He will honor the offering.

Jesus, My most common offering can be made extraordinary when You use it for Kingdom work. I am an ordinary believer who serves an extraordinary God. May I always bring the best I have to offer? Amen.

➤ Day 140: EVERLASTING PREISTHOOD
PASSAGE: **Exodus 40:12-16** and **30-32**
VERSE: **Exodus 40:15**

...and you shall anoint them even as you have anointed their father, that they may minister as priests to Me; and their anointing will qualify them for a perpetual priesthood throughout their generations.

Walls up... check. Ark in place... check. Furnishings and utensils anointed... check. Moses was nearing the end of the tabernacle work God had delineated for him on Sinai. Next was the preparation of Aaron and his sons for service as priests in the house of God. The priests were to be washed at the door of the tent, be dressed in their holy garments, and then be anointed with oil. All steps needed to be carefully obeyed in order to *qualify them for a perpetual priesthood*. What a thrilling yet humbling experience this must have been. I still find it amazing that following the golden calf incident God would allow Aaron to be the high priest over His congregation. God uses cracked pots and flawed vessels to achieve His ultimate purposes. From that day forward the priests would stop and wash at the bronze laver each time they entered the tabernacle, which was a God-ordained reminder that purity, cleanliness and holiness are required for each of us to serve Him. After all... we are called to be a *royal priesthood*.

COMMON GROUND: Are you a cracked pot or a flawed vessel? God wants you. Are you a fallen sinner or a believer who has drifted away? God wants you. Are you thinking you have nothing to offer Him? Let Him take your 'nothing' and work miracles with it. **HOLY GROUND:** All you need to be anointed into God's *royal priesthood* is a *willing spirit and a broken and contrite heart*. If Aaron could be consecrated as holy, surely you can too. Cry out to Him for that anointing and make Him the LORD of you life. (If you don't yet have a personal relationship with Jesus Christ; or if you can't state with 100% certainty that you are 'saved' by His blood; please turn to the Steps to Salvation section in the back of this book and read the pages carefully).

Spirit of God, You alone can mend my broken places, bandage my hurts and strengthen me for service. I will clean up the outside and patiently allow You to clean up the rest. Work in me, LORD. Amen.

➤ Day 141: FILLED WITH GOD'S GLORY
PASSAGE: Exodus 40:33-35
VERSE: Exodus 40:35

Moses was not able to enter the tent of meeting because the cloud had settled on it and the glory of the LORD filled the tabernacle.

Once the work was completed and the priests were ready for service, the glory of God came and filled the tabernacle so fully that Moses couldn't even fit inside to worship Him. Imagine the amazement of the people as the cloud which had led them by day came down and covered the tabernacle. They knew it was the place where God would reside among them, but having His presence so close must have been an overwhelming feeling. Moses was finally seeing God's promise to dwell among His people fulfilled. All he had worked for on behalf of Israel was now rewarded. All he wanted to do was to enter the tabernacle, fall at the feet of his God and worship Him. Do you think he was disappointed because he couldn't get inside... or thrilled that God so filled His tabernacle that there was no room for anyone else? A hint to that question might be found in Isaiah 6... why don't you go read that chapter and see what happens when a humble man has an encounter with the glory of the living God.

COMMON GROUND: Where has the glory of God gone? Why isn't His presence as strong in today's houses of worship? What fills our churches in place of the Presence of God? How many of us want God to take over His worship services and have total reign there? Have we grown too accustomed to man-centered worship rather than God centered encounters? **HOLY GROUND:** These are serious questions for you to ponder. God longs to be the center of attention when His children gather for worship. He wants to be the only reason we go to church—(what a revolutionary thought!)—and He wants to fill our receptive hearts with His love. Until our programs and choreographed services are set aside, there is no room for the LORD to fully occupy His houses of worship.

Father God, I cannot imagine the wonder of You being such a strong presence among Your people—because I have never felt that before. Come LORD, fill my temple as I lay aside my personal agenda and allow You full reign in my heart. Amen.

➤ Day 142: LED BY HIS GLORY
PASSAGE: Exodus 40:36-38
VERSE: Exodus 40:38

For throughout all their journeys, the cloud of the LORD was on the tabernacle by day, and there was fire in it by night, in the sight of all the house of Israel.

Wouldn't it be awesome to be so certain about where God wanted to lead you that you could look up, see the cloud, and simply walk in the direction it led? Israel had it made! They never needed to take an incorrect turn or walk down a wrong road. If they followed the cloud by day and the pillar of fire by night, they would never, <u>ever</u> be out of God's perfect will! We do not have the cloud to follow today, so how do we discern the will of God in our lives? I have the answer to that question. It comes from the Old Testament book of Proverbs and reads: *Trust in the LORD with all your heart and do not lean on your own understanding. In all your ways acknowledge Him, and He will make your paths straight. Do not be wise in your own eyes; fear the LORD and turn away from evil.* (Proverbs 3:5-7) Seeking God's will in prayer, waiting for His clear direction, and being willing to walk wherever He sends you are the keys.

COMMON GROUND: It is common for men to walk down the paths they deem to be right and then ask God to bless the journey. I have found myself doing that many times… and I feel forsaken when my schemes fail. **HOLY GROUND:** God will always provide what is needed for the missions He ordains, but He is in no way obligated to pour out blessings when we step out on our own. Holy men will seek God's approval before venturing into any area He hasn't clearly placed in front of them.

LORD, I confess my impatience in waiting for Your approval for my missions. Help me to not take one step without seeking Your will, calling for Your direction and being willing to obey Your direct commands. Amen.

➤ Day **143**: SALT SEASONING
PASSAGE: **Leviticus 2:13**
VERSE: **Leviticus 2:13**

Every grain offering of yours, moreover, you shall season with salt, so that the salt of the covenant of your God shall not be lacking from your grain offering; with all your offerings you shall offer salt.

The Bible contains dozens of references to salt—even calling on Christians to be 'salt and light' in a salt-less and very dark world. What does salt have to do with our faith and what is a salt-covenant? In Old Testament Bible times men carried a pouch of salt on their belt. The salt was used as a seasoning, as a preservative for meat, and to seal a covenant or promise with another party. When two men came into agreement—for example, on the price of an animal purchase—they would each reach into his salt pouch, take a pinch out and drop it into the other man's bag. The pouch would be gently tossed back and forth between the owner's hands until the grains were mixed with his own. At that point one man's salt couldn't be separated from the other man's... and the deal couldn't be taken back.

COMMON GROUND: The reason for offering salt with the grain and meat offerings in today's passage is the same. God was painting a picture of an irrevocable covenant promise between Him and His people. They were His people and He was their God—forever. **HOLY GROUND:** How faithful have you been to the salt-covenant God made with you when He sacrificed His Son on Calvary's cross? Have you gone back on the promises you made to honor and obey Him? Maybe it is time to renew and recommit to the covenant and begin a new walk in holiness!

My Jesus, A renewed covenant with You means that I will never be able to be separated from Your love, and that I will never wish to walk in my own counsel. Yes, today I long to renew our covenant. Amen.

➤ Day 144: PRIESTLY PROVISION
PASSAGE: **Leviticus 7:29-35**
VERSE: **Leviticus 7:34**

For I have taken the breast of the wave offering and the thigh of the contribution from the sons of Israel from the sacrifices of their peace offerings, and have given them to Aaron the priest and to his sons as their due forever from the sons of Israel.

God's provision is for all of His people, including and especially for those who serve Him in full-time ministry. Aaron and his sons would not be able to work regular jobs, but would completely dedicate their service to God's tabernacle. Remember that those who worked in His house also had families to feed and needed to provide housing for them, as well as for themselves. Aaron and his sons were provided for from the offerings brought by the people to the house of God. A share of the tithes belonged to them and, as we see in today's passage, a share of the offerings was their food provision. As the people were obedient in their tithes and offerings the priests and Levites would have food and shelter for their families. The same holds true today. When we give our tithes, then our pastors, church staff and supported missionaries are provided for... a small reward for all they do on behalf of the kingdom of God.

COMMON GROUND: Yep, here is that "How are you doing on your tithes?" talk! Many people foolishly believe that ministry is isolated to a couple of hours on Sunday morning, and that therefore pastors earn way too much for the minimal work they do. Little regard is given for sermon and teaching preparation, counseling, outreach, visitation and community involvement—all of which are part of the pastor's ministry. **HOLY GROUND:** Just one thought for this section: If your pastor is to live off your generosity and obedience, how is his standard of living while he serves the kingdom of God? You get compensated for your labors... and he is entitled to the same provision.

Jesus, I have to admit that I have been a 'reluctant giver' in the past and have not given full recognition to the labor of Your servants. May I begin today to grow in godly generosity? Amen.

➤ Day 145: GOD IS NOT MOCKED
PASSAGE: **Leviticus 10:1-5**
VERSE: **Leviticus 10:1**

Now Nadab and Abihu, the sons of Aaron, took their respective firepans, and after putting fire in them, placed incense on it and offered strange fire before the LORD, which He had not commanded them.

Nadab and Abihu grew up watching their obedient (well, sometimes obedient) father, Aaron. What would lead them to compromise God's absolute commands for burning incense and do it their own way? These two chosen priests—two of Aaron's four sons—died for offering incense other than that which God had commissioned them to offer. It doesn't seem like a sin deserving of death, does it? First Peter 4:17 reads, *"...it is time for judgment to begin with the household of God; and if it begins with us first, what will be the outcome for those who do not obey the gospel of God?"* If God had allowed sin to go unchecked, it would have become an epidemic. Abihu and Nadab would have gotten away with this first mockery of God's rules and would have used that as a foundation for future compromises. Judgment, beginning at the house of God, means the church's leaders will be on the front line at judgment... answering for their every action. They will have to give an accounting of how their sins led others astray.

COMMON GROUND: What made Abihu and Nadab think they could mock (challenge) God's ultimate authority? What makes us do the same thing under different circumstances? Jesus calls sin 'leavening' and says a little of it will pollute the whole church. **HOLY GROUND:** When does compromise prove acceptable in the eyes of our Creator? If the answer is **never**... then why has compromise of the holiness message become so acceptable within todays Christian churches?

> *Spirit of God, This passage shows me how a little compromise can easily lead me astray in my walk with You and in my journey toward holiness. I understand better why the evil needed to be addressed—it was a reminder of how seriously You will fight against sin—especially in Your church. Amen.*

➤ Day 146: YOU MUST BE DIFFERENT
PASSAGE: Leviticus 10:6-11
VERSE: Leviticus 10:10-11

...and so as to make a distinction between the holy and the profane, and between the unclean and the clean, and so as to teach the sons of Israel all the statutes which the LORD has spoken to them through Moses.

We have discussed before the call for the people of God to be different—peculiar—set apart or unworldly. Why is this call so vital in our personal faith walk? We find the answer in today's verse ...*to make a distinction between the holy and the profane, and between the unclean and the clean.* There must be a distinction between God's people and those who do not belong to Him. Here is the rub—you cannot serve both God and the devil. You cannot be a little holy. You cannot worship the world and Jesus at the same time. Hard words, aren't they? In our Leviticus study the difference was apparent in the external clothing of the priests and Levites and in the fact that they were not to drink strong drink. They were to be holy in every single way because their example would *teach the sons of Israel all the statutes which the LORD has spoken.* Those who served God were to be an example of obedience, so others would see their actions and follow their lead.

COMMON GROUND: Here is the hard part... how are we to be different than the worldly people we associate with every day? What shows us to be unique, *peculiar*, and completely His? The clothing of the priest showed that he was set apart for a different purpose than those around him. Our unique characteristics aren't usually shown in what we wear, but in how we conduct our lives. **HOLY GROUND:** Here are a few clues: Modesty, temperance, self-control, compassion, kindness, gentleness, consistency, love and humility. Do unbelievers know they are in the presence of a 'Child of the King of Kings' when they are around you?

*Father God, Manifest such a change in my heart that it can be seen
from the outside... that others may know beyond a shadow of a
doubt that I belong to You and have been forever changed by
Your love, mercy, compassion and forgiveness. Amen.*

➤ Day 147: SCAPEGOATS
PASSAGE: **Leviticus 16:1-34**
VERSE: **Leviticus 16:9-10**

*Then Aaron shall offer the goat on which the lot for the LORD fell,
and make it a sin offering. But the goat on which the lot for the
scapegoat fell shall be presented alive before the LORD, to make
atonement upon it, to send it into the wilderness as the scapegoat.*

Aaron was instructed to take two male goats for a sin offering
annually on the Day of Atonement and present them before
the LORD at the doorway of the tent of meeting (tabernacle). There
he was to cast lots between them, with one being the sacrifice for
Israel's sin, and the other being the scapegoat. The one chosen as the
offering would be killed and offered, as per God's rules, upon the
altar of the tabernacle. This sacrifice represented how God would
forgive the sins of the people. The second goat was held still while
Aaron confessed the sins of the people over its head. It was then
given into the care of a man chosen for the job of releasing the goat
into the wilderness... thus representing God's removal of the sin
from within the camp itself. That scapegoat carried Israel's iniquities to a lonely and solitary land—never to return.

COMMON GROUND: This practice is unnecessary in the Christian
church because Jesus completed the Atonement Day rituals by dying
on Calvary's cross. He is the forgiveness for every sin ever committed
since time began... and like the scapegoat, He carried our sin on His
head. Jesus became our sin, and in that moment He was cast out of
God's presence to a solitary land away from His Father for three days
until He arose to new life. **HOLY GROUND:** The scapegoat was

innocent and blameless—as was our Jesus. Both assumed the iniquity of men who deserved to die. Have you realized how grateful you need to be for the substitutionary death of Jesus for your sins?

LORD, Thank You my LORD, my Redeemer, my Savior.
I am renewed in my often ungrateful heart that You were willing
and obedient to assume my sin, hang it on Your cross and
resurrect me to newness of life. Amen.

➤ Day 148: YES, YOU CAN BE HOLY
PASSAGE: Leviticus 18:1-5
VERSE: Leviticus 18:4

You are to perform My judgments and keep My statutes, to live
in accord with them; I am the LORD your God.

I have chosen specific teachings from Leviticus because many of its verses are reiterations of previous teachings from Exodus. Once the sacrificial system was firmly established for the people of God, basic applications on how to live a holy life were affirmed through Moses' teaching. Today's passage and its commands sound quite simple on the surface, but the application is much more difficult to live than the promise is to make. God told Israel, *"You shall not do what is done in the land of Egypt where you lived, nor are you to do what is done in the land of Canaan where I am bringing you..."* In a nutshell, God was telling them (and is thus telling us), "Don't live like you lived before you served Me and don't be influenced by others to live the way they do." Hmmm... I told you the promise would be harder to keep than it was to make!

COMMON GROUND: According to this portion of Scripture we *can* overcome where we have been and the influences our pasts have had on our current situations. We *can* also withstand the influences of the world and still walk in holiness—Hallelujah! **HOLY GROUND:** This victorious entry should be an encouragement to you. You do have the power and capability to walk in godliness, overcome worldly influences, and present yourself in righteousness before the God who is holy and calls us to be holy. You *can* do this!

My Jesus, In You alone can I overcome my past, live victorious in my present, and walk unhindered into my forever. I praise Your empowering love for this feeble servant! Amen.

➤ Day 149: SEXUAL PURITY
PASSAGE: **Leviticus 18:6-24**
VERSE: **Leviticus 18:24**

Do not defile yourselves by any of these things; for by all these the nations which I am casting out before you have become defiled.

Part of the purity and holiness which believers are called to live includes sexual purity. The verses in today's passage give specific statutes and moral laws for sexual purity by defining those things which are abominable to God in this area of the believer's life. God realized that the immoral acts which were openly practiced in the lands that Israel was preparing to enter could be stumbling blocks for His people. Sexual immorality has negative influences on any society. We may think the pollution from blatant immoral sex practices is something new, but these verses written literally thousands of years ago prove this to be a wrong assumption. The marriage bed was a gift given by God to man for communion, procreation and pleasure, but it has been defiled by our disregard for His call to fidelity. Homosexuality is addressed in this passage, as it is in many other portions of Scripture... and is considered an abomination. Enough said.

COMMON GROUND: Immoral sexual practices lead to disease, divorce, broken families and even death. God created intimacy between a man and his wife as a bond between them which was never meant to be shared with anyone else. Look at this teaching with logic and not emotion. The sexual perversion on television, in movies, in books and on our streets has destroyed all regard for marital faithfulness... and our society is worse off for it. **HOLY GROUND:** All sexual relations outside the bonds of marriage between one woman and one man are wrong... period. This includes pornography, adultery, and sex outside of marriage. The call to holiness includes purity in all aspects of our lives... not just in our public lives.

Jesus, Make me pure in this part of my life. I can see how sexual perversions have affected society and cheapened the sanctity of marriage. May I weigh all things against Your call for holiness. Amen.

➤ Day 150: NO TURNING ASIDE
PASSAGE: Leviticus 19:1-4
VERSE: Leviticus 19:4

Do not turn to idols or make for yourselves molten gods; I am the LORD your God.

*S*peak to all the congregation of the sons of Israel and say to them, 'You shall be holy, for I the LORD your God am holy.' Well, here is the command to end all commands. Pastors are commanded by God to tell their flocks that holiness is required in the body of Christ. Why would God demand holiness? The answer is really quite simple... holiness reflects the *peculiarity* which sets the people of God apart from all the rest of the people in this world. If God's people are created in His image and if He is holy... then the logical conclusion is that those who profess faith in Him are called to this high standard. Nothing short of complete holiness will satisfy our LORD. No compromise. No shortcut. No fooling God. No more fooling other people. No watered down holiness. No hidden sin. No serving other gods. The hard truth in this lesson is that we turn to idols... those other gods we fashion to please ourselves... gods designed to suit our specific needs. We want gods who wink at our sins, look away and excuse our iniquities, and who require no change in our hearts. Unfortunately, few pastors are preaching holiness from the pulpits.

COMMON GROUND: What happens when the hard holiness message is not proclaimed? The church ends up weak, ineffectual, ill-equipped for kingdom work, smug and self-absorbed, willing to compromise, and politically correct. It may be growing in numbers, but it's not growing in godliness. In other words, the church is common—just like the rest of society! **HOLY GROUND:** A true holiness message with accountability and discipleship will grow strong believers, bold believers, peculiar believers, and effective believers who will make a difference in the world they live in.

Spirit of God, The call to holiness requires change on my part.
I am finally at the point where I am willing for You to mold me,
shape me, and create of me the man/woman You meant
for me to be. Amen.

➤ Day 151: LEAVE A GLEANING
PASSAGE: **Leviticus 19:9-10**
VERSE: **Leviticus 19:10**

Nor shall you glean your vineyard, nor shall you gather the fallen
fruit of your vineyard; you shall leave them for the needy
and for the stranger. I am the LORD your God.

Without an established welfare system the poor people of Israel would have had no way to feed their families. God instituted a plan for them to be fed in a way which would allow them to keep their dignity. When a farmer harvested his field he would leave the corners untouched and would not go back and pick up what was passed over in the initial harvest. The needy could go and glean (harvest) the corners without being attacked or insulted. The Old

Testament book of Ruth paints a great picture of gleaning as Ruth followed the harvesters of Boaz, working hard and taking of the leftovers to feed Naomi, her mother in law, and herself. At the end of each day Ruth was tired from hard work, but could look at the grain she took home in the pride of a job well done.

COMMON GROUND: Modern state-sponsored and taxpayer funded welfare removes the pride aspect of providing for the poor. Human nature leads us to not value or be grateful for that which we do no work to obtain. Giving someone a check and requiring no service on their part invites them to live a lazy and uninvolved lifestyle. **HOLY GROUND:** Jesus said the poor would always be with us. He understood that a helping *hand-up* was not the same thing as a mandated *hand-out*. Charity begins at home in the generous hearts of God's people. As a holy people we are to serve the needs we see, care for our brothers and provide for the poor. Doing so with dignity will make poverty a short-lived state… not a lifelong habit.

Father God, Show me how to wisely discern needs and to reach out in love to help others, but to never enable them to remain in their poverty state forever. Amen.

➤ ## Day 152: BUSYBODIES
PASSAGE: Leviticus 19:16-18
VERSE: Leviticus 19:16

You shall not go about as a slanderer among your people, and you are not to act against the life of your neighbor; I am the LORD.

No gossip allowed! Tie that tongue and stop speaking against others—as per the commandment of God. If you cannot say something nice, say nothing at all. Zip that lip! Why would God feel it so important to not slander or gossip within the body of His people? The answer is really quite obvious. Gossip, slander and 'sharing confidences' divide us. Gossip is a symptom of a deeper problem. In most cases we gossip about others to destroy them or to make ourselves look better. Do you remember the earlier story of Aaron and Miriam complaining and carping against Moses? They said they were doing it to get back at him for marrying a foreign wife, but in reality they were jealous of his special relationship with God and the call He put upon Moses' life. We need to look at our motives and make certain that the words we speak are words we would speak if Jesus were standing next to us.

COMMON GROUND: Our words cut like a knife, cannot be taken back, cause great destruction and wound spirits. Families are destroyed, churches divided, and friendships severed because of words which should never have been spoken. **HOLY GROUND:** *Have mercy on me, O God, according to your unfailing love; according to your great compassion blot out my transgressions. Wash away all my iniquity and cleanse me from my sin. For I know my transgressions, and my sin is always before me.* (Psalms 51:1-3 NIV) All I would add here is, "And seal my lips to keep them from evil."

LORD, I speak before I think, and the motives of my heart are not always pure. LORD, silence me from speaking cutting and hate-filled words meant to cause pain for others. Amen.

➤ Day 153: DELAYED GRATIFICATION
PASSAGE: **Leviticus 19:23-25**
VERSE: **Leviticus 19:25**

In the fifth year you are to eat of its fruit, that its yield may increase for you; I am the LORD your God.

I love the Scriptural basis for today's lesson. God was teaching delayed gratification... you know, good old-fashioned patience, to His people. Here is the text in its entirety: *When you enter the land and plant all kinds of trees for food, then you shall count their fruit as forbidden. Three years it shall be forbidden to you; it shall not be eaten. But in the fourth year all its fruit shall be holy, an offering of praise to the LORD. In the fifth year you are to eat of its fruit, that its yield may increase for you; I am the LORD your God.* Just imagine—you plant the apple tree, watch it grow, and it produces fruit for three years (and you know you can taste in your mind how good that juicy, delicious, crispy, crunchy, sweet, tart, bright red apple would taste). Yet, you are forbidden to eat of it. Year four comes along with an even bigger and more luscious crop... and you are commanded to pick the fruit and offer it up to the LORD. When you feel like all hope is lost you can finally take the first bite when the fifth year's harvest is ready. Do you think it was worth the wait? Do you understand why God would delay your apple-gratification?

COMMON GROUND: With this law God was trying to prevent '<u>I</u> Disease.' You know... "I want it. I want it all. I want it now. I want it without heed to the laws. I want it so bad I will do anything to get it." If patience is a virtue, we are raising a virtue-deficient generation of impatient children. **HOLY GROUND:** Think about this. While the people watched the fruit grow, fall to the ground and rot for three years... and while they watched it be offered to God in the fourth year... He was still providing all they needed to live. He was teaching them the law of provision—different than what they wanted, but provision nevertheless.

My Jesus, My patience and delayed gratification levels are very low. I want it, want it all, and want it now. Please teach me the fruit tree principle so I can apply it to my life and learn to live it daily. Amen.

➤ Day 154: SEEKING SPIRITS
PASSAGE: **Leviticus 19:26-20:6**
VERSE: **Leviticus 20:6**

As for the person who turns to mediums and to spiritists, to play the harlot after them, I will also set My face against that person and will cut him off from among his people.

As unpopular as this entry will be, I will do my best to make you understand how seriously God takes sorcery, witchcraft, psychic practices, the occult, astrology and spiritualism. I encourage you to read the entire passage for this entry—not because it all pertains to these topics, but because it is a great roster of rules for godly living. Do you see any 'buts' or 'exceptions' in the verse above? Do you see gray areas or places where God would tolerate these practices? Try here: *Do not turn to mediums or spiritists; do not seek them out to be defiled by them.* It looks pretty straight-forward to me. Anyone practicing these things is defiled, and that which is defiled can never be considered holy before our LORD. Believers have absolutely no business involving themselves in sorcery (Harry Potter), witchcraft (Wicca or white witchcraft), astrology, visiting psychics, or taking part in spiritualist activities (fortune telling, reading auras, tarot card readings)... period! You cannot 'dabble' in darkness and walk in the light!

COMMON GROUND: We have talked about this topic before... and God found it important enough to address dozens of times in His Word. Play with the occult and you are opening the front door and inviting demons into your life, your family and your home. **HOLY GROUND:** One of the least popular jobs assigned to us as Christ's disciples is that of speaking out against these things in a society riddled with references to them and glorification of them. *God will not be mocked...* and we will be held accountable for not speaking out against evil.

*Jesus, The occult is everywhere around us on television,
on the internet, in movies, in books... even in spiritualist churches.
Raise my awareness level and open my mouth to
address this permeating evil. Amen.*

➤ Day 155: MY WAY OR THE HIGHWAY!
PASSAGE: **Leviticus 20:22-26**
VERSE: **Leviticus 20:24**

*Hence I have said to you, "You are to possess their land,
and I Myself will give it to you to possess it, a land flowing
with milk and honey. I am the LORD your God,
who has separated you from the peoples."*

Whew! After yesterday's difficult lesson I cannot wait to talk to you about being set apart as children of light... chosen of God and destined for a special purpose. This is a good news/bad news kind of entry. The good news for Israel was that God was sending them into a fruitful and abundant land. The bad news is that God gave an ultimatum along with the promise: *You are therefore to keep all My statutes and all My ordinances and do them, so that the land to which I am bringing you to live will not spew you out.* Hmmm... obedience would bring blessings and disobedience would result in a land which would spit them out of its boundaries. Why does God continually counter blessings with warnings? Why doesn't He ever back off the command to obey and just let us live our lives the way we want to? Why does He have to be so blasted strict? Again, the answer is obvious. We are set apart to serve Him—and His holiness requires our holiness.

COMMON GROUND: Our relationship with God is not a democracy; it is instead a benevolent monarchy with Him as the monarch—the one in control. Don't like that? Tell Him to keep His blessings to Himself and His hands off your life, but don't come whining when the wind goes out of your sails, the sun stops shining, and the hedge of protection He affords is gone. **HOLY GROUND:** Here is a painful statement: Most of us want the benefits of God without obedience to Him or acknowledgement of Him as part of it. We want His Essence without His requirements. He doesn't work that way. He will not change, so you will have to!

Spirit of God, Change hurts. I am reluctant to loosen my hold and relinquish control to You. Only the Spirit can help me to find peace in abandoning control and trusting in You. Amen.

➤ ## Day 156: PRICE OF BLASHPHEMY
PASSAGE: Leviticus 24:11-16
VERSE: Leviticus 24:16

Moreover, the one who blasphemes the name of the LORD shall surely be put to death; all the congregation shall certainly stone him. The alien as well as the native, when he blasphemes the Name, shall be put to death.

Blasphemy is a serious breaking of God's moral law. It is the crime of ascribing to oneself the rights or qualities of God, or acting out in irreverence toward anything held sacred. Jesus was often accused of blasphemy for making Himself out to be the fulfillment of Old Testament Messianic prophecies. In today's passage we find a man from the tribe of Dan blaspheming God's holy name. He was arrested until God could be consulted as to proper punishment for his crime. The sentence of being stoned to death surely sounds quite harsh to our sensitive hearts, but God knew that unpunished blasphemy would spread and grow out of control into a national problem. Sin could not be tolerated in the camp. (Now where have you heard that one before?) *If anyone curses his God, then he will bear his sin.* I can hardly imagine how the blasphemers in our world today will pay for their sin.

COMMON GROUND: As I prepared this entry I thought about how Jesus, God and the Christian religion are mocked in our society and in our institutions of higher education. My heart breaks for those who choose to deny the God who created them. What they call their 'truth' had better be real truth because they are setting themselves up for their eternal destination. I wouldn't want to be in their shoes come judgment day. **HOLY GROUND:** As a follower of Christ your responsibility is not only to keep yourself from blasphemy, but to address it when you hear it spoken within your hearing. As surely as they will answer for their sin, we will answer for our passivity and our unwillingness to defend the Name of our LORD.

Father God, Yes, the sentence of stoning sounds harsh,
but I am increasingly growing to understand how serious and
pervasive sin can be. Give me boldness to address blasphemy when
I hear it. It won't make me popular with man—but then,
man cannot save my soul. Amen.

➤ Day 157: JUBILEE!
PASSAGE: **Leviticus 25:8-16**
VERSE: **Leviticus 25:10**

You shall thus consecrate the fiftieth year and proclaim a
release through the land to all its inhabitants. It shall be a jubilee
for you, and each of you shall return to his own property,
and each of you shall return to his family.

What a great idea God has for His people. Every fifty years Israel was to celebrate a year of Jubilee. Beginning on Atonement Day in the fiftieth year a trumpet would sound and a holy celebration was to begin. Each man was to return to his own home. He was to take back the land assigned to him according to his tribal heritage and was to pay the one who purchased it from him, according to the number of years left in their contract. In that year they were not to sow or reap new crops, but were to live off that which the land bore on its own. Jubilee meant a new start—a 'do-over' for the nation of Israel. In that year the land always returned to the Biblical plan God had for its division. He took His specific land allotments very seriously... and in obedience the people showed their reverence for His wishes that Israel never be sold to strangers, nor even transferred between tribes.

COMMON GROUND: Most of us live with lots of regrets. Imagine a year of restoration... a year of recommitment... a year of coming home and knowing that is where God wanted you to be. Would you like to start over? Maybe I should ask; do you need to start over? **HOLY GROUND:** Proclaim this year your year of Jubilee. Live leaner, trust God to provide, return what you don't need, come home, and recommit to the ways of God. A year of restoration is exactly what you need.

LORD, I have so many regrets. Help me to see where You can
restore that which the locusts have destroyed.
I would love to unload some of my baggage... and a year
of Jubilee is just what I need. Amen.

➤ Day 158: DON'T SELL MY LAND
PASSAGE: **Leviticus 25:23-28**
VERSE: **Leviticus 25:23**

The land, moreover, shall not be sold permanently, for the
land is Mine; for you are but aliens and sojourners with Me.

Yesterday I talked about purchasing back the land sold to others in the nation of Israel. At the time God was giving these laws they must have seemed rather foolish. The Hebrew people hadn't even seen the land, let alone divided it and had time to sell it to others. God took His ownership of the physical land of Israel so seriously that He began creating provisions for it years before His people even took possession. One of the ways it was to be kept in ownership by specific tribes was for a kinsman-redeemer (sort of a next of kin) to step in and purchase the land of a man who fell into poverty or even died. The kinsman-redeemer had to be of his tribe, clan, and distinct family, and had to agree that if the seller ever regained enough to buy it back he could do so at a fair and honest price. One good news law stated that in the year of Jubilee the land reverted to the rightful owner as long as he was still alive.

COMMON GROUND: Let me paint a picture for you. Let's say each of the 50 states of our nation belonged to a specific group of people. For example, Georgia belonged to the descendants of George... and God had commanded that no one other than George's ancestors was to ever own that land. One of George's great, great grandsons fell on hard times and sold the property to one of his cousins. Once he had the money he could repurchase the Georgian property of his lineage; or in the Jubilee it would be returned to him. In that way the sons of Tenn (Tennessee) or Floria (Florida) could never permanently own George's rightfully assigned land. **HOLY GROUND:** God took the ownership of Israel very seriously—still does—and we are treading on thin, thin ice when nations try to force Israel to divide her God-given land for a false peace with the nations around her who want her destroyed. Have you ever considered why that little strip of land is the cause of such hatred and animosity? It is rich, lush and beautiful... but many hints throughout Scripture talk about what lies beneath its surface. Maybe natural gas reserves, maybe precious minerals or gems, maybe oil... maybe the fights aren't just for the Promised Land...

My Jesus, Your Word tells me to pray for the peace of Jerusalem. LORD, I don't pray for pseudo or false peace... but that they would instead know the Prince of Peace. You are their forever peace. Amen.

➤ Day 159: OBEDIENCE BLESSINGS
PASSAGE: **Leviticus 26:1-6**
VERSE: **Leviticus 26:6**

*I shall also grant peace in the land, so that you may lie down with
no one making you tremble. I shall also eliminate harmful beasts
from the land, and no sword will pass through your land.*

In Leviticus 26 we find God delineating specific blessings He would
pour out upon Israel—as long as they obeyed His commands, did
not worship other gods, reverenced His tabernacle and observed
the rest of the Sabbath. Today we will look at the blessing of rain.
Now, I know some of you do not think rain is a blessing... that is
because you are not farmers, foresters, vine-keepers or grocers. God
promised Israel *...rains in their season, so that the land will yield
its produce and the trees of the field will bear their fruit.* Without
rain there would be no olives for oil, grapes for drink, wheat for
bread, water to drink, water for animals, and water for bathing. Are
you getting a picture of just how important rain in its season was?
God said the rain would fall during each season, leading to abundant
harvest. If your livelihood depended on rain you would be a lot more
excited about this promise!

COMMON GROUND: In addition to rain God promised peace,
security, lack of fear and control of wild beasts... all in exchange
for something as simple as obedience. It is so common for us to
take freedom, peace and security for granted. We have forgotten
that all those things are blessings ordained by our Creator. **HOLY
GROUND:** Holy people realize that God pours out His mercy and
blessings upon the obedient. What has God provided—something
you have taken for granted—that you need to thank Him for today.
It is time to develop a holy attitude of gratitude.

*Jesus, Obedience to Your ways seems a small price to pay for
the blessings I receive from Your hands. Rain Your blessing
showers upon me as I walk in obedience and recognition
of my dependence on Your provision. Amen.*

➤ Day 160: MORE BLESSINGS
PASSAGE: Leviticus 26:7-13
VERSE: Leviticus 26:9

So I will turn toward you and make you fruitful and multiply you, and I will confirm My covenant with you.

Today we will look at more blessings for obedience promised to the nation of Israel. We look at them because they are promises that you as a child of God are also entitled to. *You will chase your enemies and they will fall before you by the sword; a hundred of you will chase ten thousand, and your enemies will fall before you by the sword.* That promises you victory in battles! *I will turn toward you and make you fruitful and multiply you, and I will confirm My covenant with you.* This promises you abundance! *You will eat the old supply and clear out the old because of the new.* Each year will provide all you need as you finish the previous year's provision! *I will make My dwelling among you, and My soul will not reject you.* He will live with you and never forsake you! *I will also walk among you and be your God, and you shall be My people.* He will walk around each bend in life's road beside you! *I am the LORD your God, who brought you out of the land of Egypt so that you would not be their slaves, and I broke the bars of your yoke and made you walk erect.* He will deliver you from bondage, bring you into a place of freedom, and allow you to walk upright and unfettered!

COMMON GROUND: It would be common to read the previous passage lightly. Please go back, read the promises, pray for the Holy Spirit to encourage your heart, and apply these truths in your life. **HOLY GROUND:** Are the blessings of God as spoken above worth complete obedience? You alone must make that decision.

Spirit of God, I am overwhelmed by these promises.
Help me to remember them, apply them and walk in them every day. Nothing my flesh desires compares to Your provision. Amen.

➤ Day 161: DISOBEDIENCE CURSES
PASSAGE: **Leviticus 26:14-20**
VERSE: **Leviticus 26:14-15**

*But if you do not obey Me and do not carry out all these
commandments, if, instead, you reject My statutes, and if your
soul abhors My ordinances so as not to carry out all
My commandments, and so break My covenant...*

When you are finished with this entry and the next one you will be more grateful for the two prior ones containing God's blessings for obedience. Now we look at the other side of the coin, the side revealing curses for disobedience to God's moral and civil laws. Here are a few of the consequences... *I will appoint over you a sudden terror* (fear), *consumption* (plagues) *and fever* (disease) *that will waste away the eyes and cause the soul to pine away* (grief and mourning); *also, you will sow your seed uselessly, for your enemies will eat it up* (hunger and loss). *I will set My face against you* (abandonment) *so that you will be struck down before your enemies* (defeat); *and those who hate you will rule over you* (bondage, servitude), *and you will flee when no one is pursuing you. I will also break down your pride of power* (weakness); *I will also make your sky like iron* (drought) *and your earth like bronze* (unproductive ground). *Your strength will be spent uselessly, for your land will not yield its produce and the trees of the land will not yield their fruit* (famine).

COMMON GROUND: Give some thought to this. Most people would blame God for bringing these curses upon the land, with little or no regard to their own actions leading to them. It is common to blame God when things go wrong and to completely ignore Him at all other times. **HOLY GROUND:** Are you convinced yet as to why the call for holiness is one that simply cannot be ignored? Look at these curses and the ones in tomorrow's lesson in the light of our nation today. Surely we are bringing our suffering upon ourselves.

Father God, The curses are almost more than my soul can bear to think about, but I do see them manifested in America today. Indeed, we will pay a dear price for our national rejection of Your commands. LORD, turn the hearts of America to Your truths. Amen.

➤ Day 162: MORE CURSES!
PASSAGE: Leviticus 26:21-35
VERSE: Leviticus 26:27-28

Yet if in spite of this you do not obey Me, but act with hostility against Me, then I will act with wrathful hostility against you, and I, even I, will punish you seven times for your sins.

Bet you can't wait to continue with this curse list! Why am I using so many pages to emphasize these painful truths? My job isn't to tickle your ears, but to give you the hard messages of God's truth. And... if you don't like the teaching... take that up with Him; He wrote it! *I will let loose among you the beasts of the field, which will bereave you of your children and destroy your cattle and reduce your number* (ravaging wild beasts)...*I will also bring upon you a sword* (war)... *I will send pestilence* (epidemic illness) *among you, so that you shall be delivered into enemy hands. Ten women will bake your bread in one oven, and they will bring back your bread in rationed amounts* (food rationing), *so that you will eat and not be satisfied* (starvation). *I then will destroy your high places, and cut down your incense altars, and heap your remains on the remains of your idols* (destruction of what you worship), *for My soul shall abhor you. I will lay waste your cities... I will make the land desolate* (broken empty cities) *so that your enemies who settle in it will be appalled over it* (national humiliation).

COMMON GROUND: Have you had enough bad news? Okay, here is the good news: Walk in His ways, obey His commands, be willing to carry Jesus' cross, and avoid the curses. It doesn't mean bad things never happen to Christians. It means God carries us through those testing times. **HOLY GROUND:** It is always easier to do right in the first place than to face the consequences of having done wrong. Believe me—I have been there, done that and bought the T-shirt. It is easier to not need to apologize or repent.

LORD, May holiness begin in my heart, move into my home, on into my family, out into my community, and on into this lost world. Nothing my flesh desires is worth facing these curses. Amen.

➤ Day 163: IF THEY REPENT
PASSAGE: **Leviticus 26:36-46**
VERSE: **Leviticus 26:42**

...then I will remember My covenant with Jacob, and I will remember also My covenant with Isaac, and My covenant with Abraham as well, and I will remember the land.

Aren't you glad God shows both the blessings and the curses to us? How can a parent discipline a child for misbehaving if they have never taught them how to behave... and what the consequences for disobedience are? It would be patently unfair, wouldn't it? Even after clearly stating the curses for disobedience, God gives us one more glimpse of His loving and merciful heart. Look at these verses from today's passage. *If they confess their iniquity and the iniquity of their forefathers, in their unfaithfulness which they committed against Me, and also in their acting with hostility against Me...then I will remember My covenant with Jacob, and I will remember also My covenant with Isaac, and My covenant with Abraham as well, and I will remember the land... But I will remember for them the covenant with their ancestors, whom I brought out of the land of Egypt in the sight of the nations, that I might be their God. I am the LORD.* I find it amazing that no matter how God is rejected, He never forgets who He is and what His promises of the past have been.

COMMON GROUND: Recall the child mentioned in the teaching section. Once that child knows the blessings of obedience and the curses of disobedience, he has the free will to obey or to suffer the consequences of his actions. He can also seek restoration when he has a truly repentant heart. You and I am just like that child. **HOLY GROUND:** Obedience is a choice. Repentance is an act of contrition. Holiness is a goal to pursue. Each requires willingness to change.

My Jesus, Please reveal anything, anything at all, that keeps me from complete communion with You. How grateful I am for Your abundant grace—grace I in no way deserve—grace I can never earn—grace, grace, God's grace! Amen.

➤ Day 164: TITHES
PASSAGE: **Leviticus 27:30-34**
VERSE: **Leviticus 27:30**

Thus all the tithe of the land, of the seed of the land or of the fruit of the tree, is the LORD'S; it is holy to the LORD.

Let's move on to a happier subject today. Let's talk about tithes. This should shake you out of your lethargic state! We have talked before about tithing, so let's look at it from a different perspective. The process of handing over the tithe is both physical and spiritual. Carrying a goat or lamb, or walking an ox to the tabernacle required effort... as did lugging the grain or wine for their offerings. More important than the physical part of handing something over to God is the motive for it, the struggle with it, and the condition of the heart which gives. The entire tithe and offering system was established as a test—a way for God to see the true motive of the heart. Was the offering given to impress God or someone else who might be watching? Was it sacrificed in order to receive back from God... you know what I mean... were you giving to get something in return? Was it given in blind obedience, or as a form of worship and acknowledgement of who God is? God could watch the action, read the heart, observe the reluctant release of a grasp and know who loved Him.

COMMON GROUND: Do you have a reluctant release on that tithe check? Do you serve in the kingdom for His glory or yours? Are your Christ-like words genuine... or rehearsed so others will think you are holy? Second Corinthians 9:7 tells us: *Each one must do just as he has purposed in his heart, not grudgingly or under compulsion, for God loves a cheerful giver.* **HOLY GROUND:** Here is an exercise for you to test your heart. As you write out your next tithe check, write on a sheet of paper all God has given to you and sign and date it. Do the same with the next one, or with any offering (additional money sown into the kingdom above the tithe). Begin to see how much He gives and how insignificant ten-percent is to give back. You will soon learn the truth that you cannot out-give God.

Jesus, Psalm 37:25 says, "I have been young and now I am old, yet I have not seen the righteous forsaken or his descendants begging bread." I do have enough—more than enough—to sow into Your kingdom and into the lives of those who serve within it. Amen.

➤ Day 165: LEVITE LABORS
PASSAGE: **Numbers 1:47-53**
VERSE: **Numbers 1:50**

But you shall appoint the Levites over the tabernacle of the testimony, and over all its furnishings and over all that belongs to it. They shall carry the tabernacle and all its furnishings, and they shall take care of it; they shall also camp around the tabernacle.

It is important to realize that Moses authored four of the five books covered in this devotional. He wrote the laws and commands, historical records, census counts, and the actions of the people and the faithfulness of God for future generations. You may think Israel's history is boring and that it has no application to the modern

Christian church... you are wrong. We are grafted into the family of Israel—adopted sons because of our faith in their Messiah. Look at the passage for today's entry and see how specific God was about the work He ordained for the Levites, the tribe Moses and Aaron were born from. The sons of Levi should be *over the tabernacle of the testimony, and over all its furnishings and over all that belongs to it. They shall carry the tabernacle and all its furnishings, and they shall take care of it; they shall also camp around the tabernacle so that there will be no wrath on the congregation of the sons of Israel. So the Levites shall keep charge of the tabernacle of the testimony.*

COMMON GROUND: As Israel wandered forty years in the wilderness, the job of the Levites never changed. They were in charge of keeping, maintaining, moving and resetting the tabernacle. They were to serve the priests, strictly obey God's commands for their labor, and do all of it with a grateful heart. No glamour—No glory—No outpouring of gratitude from the people. The Levites were called to be servants in every sense of the word. **HOLY GROUND:** Do you get bored with your assigned service in the church? Would you like a more glamorous job where others would acknowledge and thank you for your work? I'd bet the Levites felt the same way... wash the dishes, clean the grates, skin the offerings, dismantle the tent... set up the tent, place the dishes, skin the lambs... Service— any service—is holy when done for right motives.

Spirit of God, Help me to realize that my job isn't to work for my glory but for Your purpose. May I be satisfied with Your "Well done, thou good and faithful servant" and not need the accolades of man. Amen.

➤ Day 166: CAMP CROSS-ING
PASSAGE: **Numbers 2:1-34**
VERSE: **Numbers 2:2**

The sons of Israel shall camp, each by his own standard,
with the banners of their fathers' households;
they shall camp around the tent of meeting at a distance.

I haven't taken the time in prior entries to really talk about the twelve tribes of Israel and explain their significance in the nation of Israel. Jacob, one of the great characters of Genesis, was the father of twelve sons—each one representing a tribe of people who would eventually inherit the Promised Land. I love history and get all excited to study Genesis and the rich historical record written there. Today we see God giving instructions as to how the camp (Israel in tents on their journey into the land of Canaan) is to be set. Very deliberate plans were made for how the camp was to be organized... with the Tabernacle in the very center. On the eastern side were the tribes of Judah, Issachar and Zebulun, with a total army of 186,400 soldiers. On the south would be Reuben, Simeon and Gad, with an army of 151,450 men of military age. Westward would be Ephraim, Manasseh and Benjamin consisting of 108,100 men of fighting age. Lastly, to the north would be Dan, Asher and Naphtali with a census of 157,600. When the camp was completely set, someone with a high vantage point would have looked down and seen the <u>perfect shape of a cross</u>... with the house of God in its center. How awesome is God's foresight and planning? Wow!

COMMON GROUND: Every time the camp was dismantled it was later reset in this same exact pattern. As God looked down from heaven, He saw the cross and knew His ultimate plan would one day culminate on another cross where His Son would pay the price for the sins of all men for all time. **HOLY GROUND:** Are you realizing how deliberate and exacting our God is? Are you humbled by being chosen by Him and adopted into His family? Tell Him.

*Father God, I am reminded of my lack of wisdom and insight when
I look back and see Your provision from the beginning of time.
Thank You, LORD, for allowing me to call You Father. Amen.*

➤ Day 167: LEVITE SPECIFICS
PASSAGE: **Numbers 3:11-39**
VERSE: **Numbers 3:14-15**

*Then the LORD spoke to Moses in the wilderness of Sinai,
saying, "Number the sons of Levi by their fathers' households,
by their families; every male from a month old
and upward you shall number."*

Yesterday I showed you the shape of the cross that was formed by the Hebrew camp which was set up in a specific pattern. If you could look closer toward the center of the cross, you would see the families of the Levites camped between the tabernacle itself and the tribes on its sides. Levi had three sons, Gershon, Merari and Kohath. As God gave responsibilities to each of those families, He also said where they were to camp when the tabernacle was stationary. The 7,500 Gershonites were to camp westward and were to perform all the services relating to the curtains, coverings, hangings, cords, and the tent itself. The 8,600 Kohatites camped on the south and were in charge of the tabernacle furnishings including the incense altar, the offering altar, the bronze laver, the Ark of the Covenant, the lamp stand an all their utensils. Lastly, the Merari with 6,200 men from one month old and up were to camp on the north side of the tabernacle and were in charge of all the frames, bars, pillars, sockets and tools for erecting the temporary house of God. Moses, Aaron, the priests and their families camped on the east... the sunrise side of the tabernacle.

COMMON GROUND: We have talked before about specific duties for the kingdom of God and the fact that they didn't necessarily bring glory or honor. Each Levite man had an assigned task that seemed somewhat inconsequential. When all their labors were put together, the tabernacle was erected, furnished and ready for God to dwell among His children. Many hands made light work. One man couldn't possibly do it all himself. **HOLY GROUND:** In your holy walk you will have duties that seem inconsequential to you. Remember that we are all parts of the same body, the body of Christ. Only when we each do our part will the world be changed. I will do my part and you do yours—together we will enjoy the fruits of our labors.

LORD, My offering along with the offerings of all your other children will work together to achieve Your ultimate purpose. LORD, I am willing to be whatever part of the body You need me to be. Amen.

➤ Day 168: NAZIRITE SEPARATION
PASSAGE: **Numbers 6:1-12**
VERSE: **Numbers 6:2**

*Speak to the sons of Israel and say to them,
'When a man or woman makes a special vow, the vow of a
Nazirite, to dedicate himself to the LORD...'*

Have you ever given thought to someone dedicating their life to God's service and forsaking worldly pleasures in order to keep that dedication pure and powerful? In Biblical times this vow was called a Nazirite vow and it required strict adherence to a set of rules ordained by God. *He shall abstain from wine and strong drink... nor shall he drink any grape juice nor eat fresh or dried grapes... All the days of his vow of separation no razor shall pass over his head. He shall be holy until the days are fulfilled for which he separated himself to the LORD; he shall let the locks of hair on his head grow long... All the days of his separation to the LORD he shall not go near to a dead person. He shall not make himself unclean for his father or for his mother, for his brother or for his sister, when they die, because his separation to God is on his head.* As you can see, the vow required obedience and great personal sacrifice from the one making it. Samson, Samuel and John the Baptist are all Biblical characters who took the Nazirite vow of separation.

COMMON GROUND: Why would God put seemingly ridiculous restrictions on the lives of those who simply wished to serve Him? What do grapes, haircuts and mourning dead loved ones have to do with obedience or worship? God knew that anyone unable to control themselves in these areas would be unable to serve Him in total discipline and self control. **HOLY GROUND:** Our faith walk should be one of obedience, self-sacrifice and focus. If that focus is on things outside of Christ Himself, we will never be willing to carry His cross. Total commitment to God was the measure of a true Nazirite and is the measure of a true believer today.

My Jesus, Commitment, obedience, discipline, sacrifice and dedication are words whose meanings are changing daily as I grow in my relationship with You... and I am growing. Praise God! Amen.

➤ Day **169**: PRIESTLY BENEDICTION
PASSAGE: **Numbers 6:13-27**
VERSE: **Numbers 6:24-26**

The LORD bless you, and keep you; The LORD make His face shine on you, and be gracious to you; The LORD lift up His countenance on you, and give you peace.

The Nazirite vow we talked about yesterday was taken by the priests who were to serve God in the tabernacle. After the vow was completed, then for a specified number of days burnt offerings and sin offerings were made on behalf of the priests. Lastly, a benediction or blessing pronounced by God was spoken through Moses over those dedicated to the LORD'S service. *The LORD bless thee, and keep thee: the LORD make his face shine upon thee, and be* gracious unto thee: the LORD lift up his countenance upon thee, and give thee peace. *(KJV)* Does that sound familiar to you? This same benediction, or invocation, is often pronounced by pastors over their congregations in today's churches. There is a reason for that as we see in verse 27: *So they shall invoke My name on the sons of Israel, and I then will bless them.* God was telling the priests to pronounce the benediction blessing over his flock—and in return for that obedience He would bless them.

UN-COMMON GROUND: Imagine your pastor standing before you with his hand on your head saying: "LORD, bless this child and keep him in Your hands; LORD make Your face shine upon him, and be gracious and merciful unto him; LORD lift up Your face to look upon him, and give him peace." This action and these words would be anything but common. What a rare and precious encounter it would be. **HOLY GROUND:** Today I pray that benediction over you. Wherever you are, whatever your age, no matter which denomination you call your own... I ask the LORD'S blessing upon you, today and every day of your life.

Jesus, Thank You. Amen.

➤ Day 170: *SHEKINAH* GLORY CLOUD
PASSAGE: **Numbers 9:15-23**
VERSE: **Numbers 9:15**

Now on the day that the tabernacle was erected the cloud covered the tabernacle, the tent of the testimony, and in the evening it was like the appearance of fire over the tabernacle, until morning.

When the *Shekinah* glory cloud of God's presence covered the tabernacle the people did not move. We read in verse 22: *Whether it was two days or a month or a year that the cloud lingered over the tabernacle, staying above it, the sons of Israel remained camped and did not set out; but when it was lifted, they did set out.* Talk about patience in waiting for direction from God! Can you imagine remaining stationary for a full year—not moving onward toward your ultimate destination of the Promised Land—as you watched the cloud rest upon the tabernacle? On the other hand, can you imagine the work of packing up the tents and supplies of the nation of Israel, the tabernacle, all its utensils and furnishings and being led to a new location—sometimes several days in a row? Here is what I can imagine: When the *Shekinah* glory of God is before your eyes and you know He is the One doing all the leading... how can you <u>not</u> feel His power and be amazed by His presence?

COMMON GROUND: Patience had to have been tested as Israel waited for the cloud to move. After all, these people were on a journey to the land promised their Fathers centuries before. They had to have been desperate for permanent housing, the ability to plant and harvest and to own their own property. **HOLY GROUND:** Admit it... we hate waiting for God to open doors, close doors, direct paths, answer prayers, or give us His permission. We hate it because we forget who He is. He is the omnipotent, all-powerful God who will direct our paths... in His perfect timing. P-A-T-I-E-N-C-E is most certainly a virtue!

Spirit of God, I have paid lip-service in professing my willingness to follow You in obedience. Promises are easy to speak, hard to keep, and are often stumbling blocks after they are spoken. Holy Spirit, help me to be patient and sincere before You. Amen.

➤ Day 171: TRUMPETING VICTORY
PASSAGE: **Numbers 10:9-10**
VERSE: **Numbers 10:9**

When you go to war in your land against the adversary who attacks you, then you shall sound an alarm with the trumpets, that you may be remembered before the LORD your God, and be saved from your enemies.

Israel was commanded to use the blast of the trumpet to call their people to worship, to sound alarm for impending danger, in celebration of their feasts and festivals, and to summon them to war. Note in the verse for today's entry that the sounding of the trumpet for war against the adversary was done so the people would *be remembered before the LORD.* The trumpet was not the polished and shiny musical instrument we think of today but was a ram's horn called a shofar. The people were always on alert for the blast of that horn. In the modern Christian church the horn isn't blown because the battle is rarely an attacking enemy nation. Instead, today's battles are spiritual in nature and the enemy is often unseen. How do we get God's attention and remind Him that we belong to Him and need to be saved from that invisible enemy? We proclaim Scripture. We shout out the Name of Jesus Christ. We begin an earnest prayer of protection and seek God's help in the battle before us.

COMMON GROUND: When the ancient shofar was sounded the people became one united body ready to worship together, celebrate the goodness of God together, and fight together. How uncommon that unity is today. Actually, the sounding of proclaimed Scripture needs to be heard much more frequently from the mouths of His children. **HOLY GROUND:** On holy ground God's people will all speak one language—the language of the Holy Word of God. His promises, His provisions, His warnings and His prophesies will be proclaimed forever by those redeemed by the blood of Jesus—the One who fought the greatest battle ever fought—the eternal battle between good and evil.

Father God, May I begin today—and continue for every day
of my life—to sound the shofar of Scripture in joy and in rebuking
the evil plans of the enemy of my soul! Teach me the words
I need to carry with me into all battles. Amen.

➤ Day 172: ARK OF HIS PROTECTION
PASSAGE: **Numbers 10:33-36**
VERSE: **Numbers 10:35**

*Then it came about when the ark set out that Moses said,
"Rise up, O LORD! And let Your enemies be scattered,
and let those who hate You flee before You."*

We learned in previous entries how the cloud of God's presence covered the door of the tabernacle and remained there until in His perfect timing the nation was moved. Today we look at the movement of the people when the cloud lifted and served as a guiding compass before them. Whenever the Ark of the Covenant was moved by the Levites, Moses would proclaim, *"Rise up, O LORD! And let Your enemies be scattered, and let those who hate You flee before You."* His proclamation served the same purpose as the declaration of Scripture I talked about in yesterday's entry. Moses was claiming God's hedge of protection around those who served Him and fought alongside Him for the preservation of the Hebrew people. That call was for God to rise up against those who despised His Name. The ark represented the presence of God among His people. *When it came to rest, he said, "Return, O LORD, to the myriad thousands of Israel."* Notice that the first proclamation was against God's enemies and the second was to solicit His protection around His children.

COMMON GROUND: Do you pray for God's protection of your house, life, family and health? Doing so is proof of your belief that He is able to—and desires to—protect that which is important to you. Moses wasn't foolish enough to think Israel no longer needed God's hedge once they had escaped Egyptian bondage. He was wise enough to realize there were additional battles ahead. **HOLY GROUND:** Thank God for His past faithfulness, request His strength for you to get through today and pray for His continued protection in all your tomorrows. Carry His ark within your heart.

LORD, You have never failed me in the past—thank You. Please walk through this day with me—thank You. May I gladly have You as my constant traveling companion in all the days of my tomorrows. Again, thank You for Your faithfulness. Amen.

➤ Day 173: THEY ARE YOURS—NOT MINE
PASSAGE: Numbers 11:1-15
VERSE: Numbers 11:11

So Moses said to the LORD, "Why have You been so hard on Your servant? And why have I not found favor in Your sight, that You have laid the burden of all this people on me?"

W ell, we haven't talked about whining for a while, so let's look again at the ingratitude of the Hebrew nation. Notice that in the first few verses of today's Scripture passage that God got fed up with the whining and complaining of the people—people He couldn't satisfy if He fed them filet mignon and shrimp scampi! He sent fire on the outside edge of the camp—destroying some of the complainers and hoping it would tame the tongues of the others. The people continued to remind Moses of all the wonderful foods they ate while in Egyptian slavery. If it was so wonderful, why did they cry out for four hundred years to be rescued? Moses had finally had enough... *"LORD, Why have You been so hard on Your servant? And why have I not found favor in Your sight, that You have laid the burden of all this people on me?"* Can you blame Moses for being frustrated? He didn't choose this job; he surely didn't choose these people; and he didn't choose to be their whipping boy for the rest of his earthly days. Finally, he tells God, "Just kill me today if you aren't going to relieve me of their burden."

COMMON GROUND: Moses is like every other leader, who after being put into a position of authority finds out how unappreciative the puppies are of the top dog! How do you treat those who are in authority over you in your home, in your church, in government and in the workplace? **HOLY GROUND:** I know a lot of people who live to gripe and who are never happy with anything those in leadership do. Holy people really need to strive to not complain and cause division or dissatisfaction... for those things spread like a plague.

My Jesus, Silence my tongue, still my whining, and give me gratitude instead of attitude. Help me to be kinder, gentler, and more supportive of those You place in authority over me. Amen.

➤ Day 174: SHARING THE BURDENS
PASSAGE: **Numbers 11:16-17, 24**
VERSE: **Numbers 11:17**

Then I will come down and speak with you there, and I will take of the Spirit who is upon you, and will put Him upon them; and they shall bear the burden of the people with you, so that you will not bear it all alone.

Imagine yourself walking down the side of a busy road carrying the groceries for your family of eight as cars speed by with drivers too consumed with their own distractions to even notice your burden. Would you feel alone, ignored, unimportant and invisible? Imagine then your gratitude if one driver pulled off the road, turned around and came back to offer to load your groceries into his car and drive you home. Now you know how Moses felt as he shouldered the burden of the entire nation of Israel on one pair of bent and tired shoulders. God heard his cries and implemented a relief plan for him. Moses was to gather seventy dedicated men of God who would receive a share of his Spirit and who could share the burden and responsibility for their nation. Moses was seeing the proverbial 'light at the end of his dark tunnel,' but first he had to use wise discernment and judgment to select the right seventy elders and leaders... ones to whom he could entrust his mission.

COMMON GROUND: I have a hard time delegating duties to others... and of course, I think no one can do things as good as I can! Moses had to make a choice of whether to shoulder the burden of the people by himself, or to share the burden. Once he decided to share, then he needed to find responsible, trustworthy and dedicated men for the job. **HOLY GROUND:** Question for the day: Can you offer yourself up to help lighten the load for another person today? Are you willing to help another carry his cross—out of love and not for any kind of glory? Holy people are burden-sharers and burden-bearers.

Jesus, I tend to ignore the needs of others as I worry about my needs and hoard my minutes all for myself. Open my heart to be a sharer and a bearer... and may I do it all for Your glory. Amen.

➤ Day 175: NEEDY AND GREEDY
PASSAGE: **Numbers 11:18-23, 31-33**
VERSE: **Numbers 11:33**

While the meat was still between their teeth, before it was chewed, the anger of the LORD was kindled against the people, and the LORD struck the people with a very severe plague.

I love this passage! You think God didn't hear the whines and complaints? You think He didn't get fed up? Let's revisit an event we discussed in a former entry. In these verses God said to the people, *"The LORD will give you meat and you shall eat. You shall eat, not one day, nor two days, nor five days, nor ten days, nor twenty days, but a whole month, until it comes out of your nostrils and becomes loathsome to you..."* Let me paraphrase this... "You want pizza? I will give you pizza morning, noon and night for the next thirty days. You will gorge yourselves on pizza until it comes out your nose and you cannot stand the thought of another bite of pepperoni. You ungrateful, spoiled, whining child! Pizza you want, pizza you get. Choke on it!" (Now you know why He is God and I am not!) The meat God sent was quail—quail that blew in, landed on the ground and piled up until it was three feet deep. Hmmm... how happy were the gluttonous people who began to stuff their faces—without thanking God for the provision.

COMMON GROUND: Make sure you read all of the verses today. I wouldn't want you to finish this lesson without knowing the ingratitude of the people which led God to send a plague upon the camp. Will Israel ever learn where their provision comes from? Will we? **HOLY GROUND:** Are you always longing for more than you have? Are you satisfied with what God has provided, or do you obsess about what you want? If God were to give you the desire of your heart right now, would that desire lead you away from Him? His policy is to never give us what would become greater in our lives than He is.

Spirit of God, This helps me to understand why some of my prayers seem to fall on deaf ears. You, in Your infinite wisdom, know the things I desire would become the gods of my life. You are keeping me from my own destruction. Thank You, Holy Spirit of God. Amen.

➤ ## Day 176: ALL SHOULD BE MY PROPHETS
PASSAGE: Numbers 11:25-29
VERSE: Numbers 11:29

But Moses said to him, "Are you jealous for my sake? Would that all the LORD'S people were prophets, that the LORD would put His Spirit upon them!"

When the seventy elders were gathered together in order for God to disperse Moses' Spirit upon them, two men decided they didn't have to gather with the rest. The Holy Spirit came upon the sixty-eight and they began to prophesy. The two who didn't attend the gathering also began to prophesy within the camp, speaking the word of God to the people. A young man came and told Moses of the 'evil' these men were doing. Joshua, Moses' right-hand man, wanted him to restrain them. What do you think his response was (caught you if you didn't read the passage)? Moses asked Joshua if he was jealous for his master's sake. Instead of being angry, jealous or restraining... Moses complimented their work and said he wished God would make prophets of all His people. Moses reminds me of John the Baptist—who was willing to give all the glory to Jesus.

COMMON GROUND: Are you a musician, worship leader, Sunday school teacher, usher, librarian, or any other kind of servant in your home church? Have you ever been jealous of someone else who came along and began to do the same job? Did you fight for the position or graciously bless the one who stepped into your shoes? **HOLY GROUND:** If we are the body of Christ all of us have a purpose and use within that body. Moses realized he needed help because he couldn't do it all alone. We must be willing to share the work and share the glory if necessary. How are you measuring up in this area?

Father God, I have been proud and unwilling to share in the duties or service You have called me to. May I realize that others need the same sense of purpose I feel and need to find the same joy in service that I feel. Amen.

➤ Day 177: SIBLING RIVALRY
PASSAGE: **Numbers 12:1-9**
VERSE: **Numbers 12:2**

They said, "Has the LORD indeed spoken only through Moses? Has He not spoken through us as well?" And the LORD heard it.

Moses was willing to delegate authority, but his siblings were jealous of the authority God gave him. One comment led to the next until a full-blown jealous tantrum erupted. I can hear it now... "Who does Moses think he is anyway? Does he think he's the only one God can use? Does he think he is the only one who can climb the mountain and talk to God? It all stems back to him leaving us and living in Midian all those years. That's when he got so full of himself and started talking about a burning bush and a commission from God to rescue our people from Pharaoh's bondage. He is stubborn and proud and has forgotten that we are his sister and brother. Let's confront him." Yes, that is how it began; but here is how it ended. God overheard the conversation and called the three family members to come together before Him. *"My servant Moses, he is faithful in all My household; with him I speak mouth to mouth... openly, and he beholds the form of the LORD. Why then were you not afraid to speak against My servant, against Moses?"*

COMMON GROUND: Ouch! Are your toes being stepped on here? What words have dominated your speech this week? Did your words edify and build up, or destroy and cut down? It is common for us to be drawn into—or even begin—these kinds of conversations. It is rare for us to bring water to douse the gossip fires. **HOLY GROUND:** Jealousy, envy and coveting are sins and usually manifest themselves through the venom which spills forth from our lips. Holy people cannot spew venom and praises from the same lips. One of the two reveals the true condition of the heart. I wonder which one it is...

LORD, May the words of my mouth and the meditations of my heart be wholly acceptable to You, O LORD, my Rock and my Redeemer. Amen.

➤ Day 178: SIBLING MERCY
PASSAGE: Numbers 12:10-16
VERSE: Numbers 12:12-13

"Oh, do not let her be like one dead, whose flesh is half eaten away when he comes from his mother's womb!" Moses cried out to the LORD, saying, "O God, heal her, I pray!"

After God spoke and the cloud of His presence was lifted, Moses and Aaron were stunned to see Miriam's exposed flesh covered with leprosy—a dreaded and highly contagious skin disease. Aaron's first instinct was to apologize for his and Miriam's words to Moses, the target of their venom. *"I beg you, do not account this sin to us, in which we have acted foolishly and in which we have sinned."* Moses, without thought to what his siblings had done, began to plead with God for Miriam's restoration. *"O God, heal her, I pray!"* I can imagine God nodding His head in approval as Moses immediately forgives those who hurt him, who falsely accused him, and who profaned his good name. How could Moses be so.... so... so... merciful, forgiving, selfless, kind... Christlike! What we see in this story is Moses painting an Old Testament picture of what Jesus our Messiah would one day look like when He walked among His own siblings.

COMMON GROUND: Remember a few days ago when I talked about nasty words dividing churches and families? Are you working on improving your words? We see this event and, according to what is socially acceptable behavior, we call him a wimp! We think Miriam and Aaron deserved their suffering for the hurt they inflicted on Moses; but what does Jesus say? **HOLY GROUND:** Matthew 5:39 tells us, *"But I say to you, do not resist an evil person; but whoever slaps you on your right cheek, turn the other to him also."* Moses was walking in Christ-likeness before Christ even appeared.

My Jesus, No wonder Moses was chosen as the redeemer and deliverer of the Hebrew people... he is a perfect Old Testament picture of You—the Redeemer and Deliverer of all men. Amen.

➤ Day 179: MISSION DEFINED!
PASSAGE: Numbers 13:1-24
VERSE: Numbers 13:2

*Send out for yourself men so that they may spy out the
land of Canaan, which I am going to give to the sons of Israel;
you shall send a man from each of their fathers' tribes,
every one a leader among them.*

You thought spying and undercover surveillance began with the thriller novels and movies of the late 20th century... think again. God designed those means of information-gathering way back thousands of years ago when He commanded Moses to choose representatives from each of the twelve tribes to go in and spy out the Promised Land. Well, of course that is what He would command; how else would they know what kind of enemy they would have to overcome or what kind of hard terrain they would have to deal with once they did take possession of that land? The spies went in as commanded and studied the topography of the land and the workings of the nations who lived there. When they returned to those who anxiously and excitedly waited to find out what they had found... *they came to the valley of Eshcol and from there cut down a branch with a single cluster of grapes... they carried it on a pole between two men, with some of the pomegranates and the figs.* How could the news be bad if a single cluster of grapes had to be carried between two grown men? Must be the news would be great and the march toward home could finally begin.

COMMON GROUND: Wouldn't you love to know in advance of every battle just what you were going to come face to face with? Wouldn't it be awesome to see the victory before you fought the battle? It is common to want that kind of assurance. God knew the people would be apprehensive, so He gave them a spectacular preview of the Promised Land. **HOLY GROUND:** God was giving Israel a glimpse of the goodness He was providing for them. I understand those 'previews' because He has given me specific visions several times of things He later brought forth. I am grateful for the glimpses, but I need to step out in pure faith sometimes... trusting Him to lead and guide me. Are you learning to step out in faith? It is time.

Jesus, This preview of the future land of Israel was a kind and generous gift by God to show His children that He had their best interest at heart. That teaches me another facet of His character... compassion. Amen.

➤ Day **180**: MISSION IMPOSSIBLE!
PASSAGE: **Numbers 13:25-33**
VERSE: **Numbers 13:33**

"There also we saw the Nephilim... and we became like grasshoppers in our own sight, and so we were in their sight."

Today is another of those good news/bad news scenarios. The spies came back and told their captive audience, *"We went in to the land where you sent us; and it certainly does flow with milk and honey, and this is its fruit."* The excitement level must have exploded as the members of the wandering camp looked at the huge fruit and heard that the land was everything God had promised... and was everything they had dreamed of during their long journey to Canaan. As visions of flowing rivers, abundant food and sweet honey played across their minds, the spies continued, *"We are not able to go up against the people, for they are too strong for us."* What? Mighty enemies—too strong to fight—Nephilim (giants) so big they made the spies feel like grasshoppers! What kind of joke was God playing on His children? The sense of victory turned into a sense of defeat almost instantly.

COMMON GROUND: Are you a glass-half-full or a glass-half-empty kind of person? Would you have looked at the fruit and found it worth fighting for, or allowed the defeatist words of the spies to wash you in hopelessness? **HOLY GROUND:** Here are a couple of victory verses. *The horse is prepared for the day of battle, but victory belongs to the LORD* (Proverbs 21:31). *One of your men puts to flight a thousand, for the LORD your God is He who fights for you, just as He promised you* (Joshua 23:10). Holy men will learn to stand on the words of God... not on the fears of man.

*Spirit of God, I confess that I am very prone to the latter...
any negativity and I am looking for a means of escape. Yes, I can
relate to the reaction of the people—frustration, doubt, anger
and defeat. Change that about me, Holy Spirit. Amen.*

➤ Day 181: PARALYZING FEAR
PASSAGE: Numbers 13:30-14:6-9
VERSE: Numbers 14:8

*If the LORD is pleased with us, then He will bring us into this
land and give it to us—a land which flows with milk and honey.*

Are you comfortable being in the minority? Is it okay with you to not go with the flow of the masses and to stand out in a crowd? Many people will silence that which makes them peculiar, in order to fit in or be politically correct. Thank God there are some who will simply stand up for what is right. Thank God for Joshua and Caleb. Of the twelve spies who went into Canaan to spy out the land, only these two saw the half-full cup. Only they urged their brethren to fight for that which God had promised them. *Then Caleb quieted the people before Moses and said, "We should by all means go up and take possession of it, for we will surely overcome it."* To whom do you think the people listened? Fear immobilizes the masses. Look at the hateful dictators of the past: Hitler, Stalin, and Lenin—with fear they paralyzed their nations and took mind control of the people. Some things never change. Fear of enemies trumped the fear of disobeying God's direct command. *But the men who had gone up with him said, 'We are not able to go up against the people, for they are too strong for us.'*

COMMON GROUND: Have you ever looked at a seemingly insurmountable mountain? An enemy you couldn't possibly defeat? An addiction you couldn't overcome? A past that held you paralyzed? Our God is a mountain climber, an enemy defeater, an addiction breaker and a past forgiver. **HOLY GROUND:** As you grow, you must begin to look at the mountain as a challenge, not a promise breaker. Find past faithfulness and provisions by the hand of God—lean on them, look at them and remember that He is the same yesterday, today and forever.

Father God, How grateful I am to serve a mountain climbing, enemy defeating, past forgiving God. I need to trust my tomorrows into your hands—because You have been faithful in my yesterdays. Amen.

➤ Day 182: WE WANT NEW LEADERS!
PASSAGE: **Numbers 14:1-5**
VERSE: **Numbers 14:4-5**

So they said to one another, "Let us appoint a leader and return to Egypt." Then Moses and Aaron fell on their faces in the presence of all the assembly of the congregation of the sons of Israel.

Once the hearts were controlled by fear, the people looked for someone to blame for their dashed hopes. Once again—or should I say, as usual—Moses and Aaron were the targets of their anger. *All the sons of Israel grumbled against Moses and Aaron; and the whole congregation said to them, "Would that we had died in the land of Egypt! Or would that we had died in this wilderness! Why is the LORD bringing us into this land, to fall by the sword? Our wives and our little ones will become plunder; would it not be better for us to return to Egypt?"* Yes, here they go again saying they were better off in their bondage—better off being slaves. The next turn is the obvious turn, "We want a new leader. Let's find someone to lead us back into our bondage. Moses and Aaron will lead us to death in this wilderness." In total devastation—and probably total fear of the actions of irrational people—Moses and Aaron fell on their faces before God. And just maybe, that is the only place they felt safe!

COMMON GROUND: Do you remember what your life was like before Christ brought change and liberty? Were you in bondage in any form—alcoholism, drug addiction, gluttony, pornography, sexual sins, pride, self-absorption? Do you ever look back and long for some of those days, forgetting how devastating they really were? God delivered you and you must choose between that life and the one you have today. **HOLY GROUND:** Holy people remember who they are, where they have been, what shame their past brought upon their hearts, and would never, ever, ever want to return to that past. Holy people press on toward the goal of wholeness and holiness.

LORD, I have looked back in remembrance and foolishly thought I would be happy back in my will, as opposed to here in Yours. LORD, cause my spirit to be reminded of the emptiness my former life brought—and the fullness of Your love now. Amen.

➤ Day **183**: TEMPTATION OF MOSES
PASSAGE: **Numbers 14:10-17**
VERSE: **Numbers 14:12**

"I will smite them with pestilence and dispossess them, and I will make you into a nation greater and mightier than they."

As Moses and Aaron lay at God's feet, the wrath of God burned against the weakness of the nation He chose as His own. How could they not trust Him? How could they not trust His provision? How could they doubt His promises... when He had never gone back on a single word He had given them? Moses lay there waiting for the stones to begin to pound his flesh... when he heard God say, *"How long will this people spurn Me? And how long will they not believe in Me, despite all the signs which I have performed in their* midst? *I will smite them with pestilence and dispossess them, and I will make you into a nation greater and mightier than they.*" Those words should have been music to Moses' ears. God knew how hard he had worked, the abuse he had taken, and that he never wavered in his commitment to his LORD'S service. Instead of agreeing and taking his rightful reward, Moses began to tell God why he couldn't do what He said. He stood to his feet, picked up his staff, dusted off the insults and rejection of his fellow Hebrews, and took the burden of Israel back on his bent shoulders.

COMMON GROUND: Today we are at the halfway point in our twelve-month journey from Common Ground to Holy Ground. Are these entries and a renewed commitment to God bringing necessary change in your spiritual life? Are you stronger? Are you willing to do as Moses did and stand up and continue on this journey? Common folk would have closed this book long ago, believing the struggle too long and the requirements too difficult. **HOLY GROUND:** My prayer is that the Potter is molding and shaping you into His clay masterpiece and that you are receiving the rework in a spirit of obedience. Yes, common folk would give up... but then you are not common, are you? You are being molded into holy vessels of great value.

My Jesus, Moses didn't give up... and I won't either. Continue Your work in me for the second half of this transformational year. Honestly, any pain I have suffered has been worth it. Amen.

➤ Day 184: OUR LONGSUFFERING GOD
PASSAGE: **Numbers 14:18-24**
VERSE: **Numbers 14:20-21**

So the LORD said, "I have pardoned them according to your word; but indeed, as I live, all the earth will be filled with the glory of the LORD."

Before Moses could take another step toward the Promised Land, he needed to convince God that the journey would continue. *"Pardon, I pray, the iniquity of this people according to the greatness of Your lovingkindness, just as You also have forgiven this people, from Egypt even until now."* Being fully aware of the failings of his people, Moses doesn't try to sweep their sin under the rug. He addressed it head on and reminded God of His gracious provision and mercy in between the Egyptian bondage and wilderness wanderings. His past history of faithfulness and love would need to be continued in the tomorrows to come. God's response to Moses was, *"I have pardoned them according to your word... but... as I live... **all the men who** have seen My glory and My signs which I performed in Egypt and in the wilderness, yet **have put Me to the test...** and have not listened to My voice, **shall by no means see the land** which I swore to their fathers, nor shall any of those who spurned Me see it. But My servant Caleb, because he has had a different spirit and has followed Me fully, I will bring into the land which he entered, and his descendants shall take possession of it."* What a horrible, horrible price to pay—for the anger provokers would never see the fulfilled promise.

COMMON GROUND: The people who have spit in God's face, doubted His promises and despised His leader would never see the Promised Land. They would begin a forty-year death march... knowing every minute of every day that their rejection of God would keep them from the greatest desire of their heart... a permanent home. **HOLY GROUND:** Stop now and think about your attitudes toward God and His promises. Do you walk in doubt and fear? Are you a grumbler and a whiner? Do you believe the promises of Scripture? Our Promised Land is an eternal home... a place of abundance, love, and the glory of our Jesus. Is any doubt worth losing that promise? Get yourself holy before God.

Jesus, I cannot imagine risking all You have promised by doubting and allowing the fears of this world to paralyze me. This story has opened my eyes to the consequence of 'little faith' and ingratitude for all You have done and all You promise to do in the future. Amen.

➤ Day 185: FORTY YEAR SENTENCE
PASSAGE: Numbers 14:25-38
VERSE: Numbers 14:33

*Your sons shall be shepherds for forty years in the wilderness,
and they will suffer for your unfaithfulness,
until your corpses lie in the wilderness.*

What did God mean in yesterday's devotion when He said those who grumbled against Him and Moses would never step foot into the Promised Land? Today we are given a clearer picture of what the implications of those words would mean. *"...your corpses will fall in this wilderness...all your numbered men, according to your complete number from twenty years old and upward, who have grumbled against Me. Surely you shall not come into the land in which I swore to settle you... your children, however, whom you said would become a prey—I will bring them in, and they will know the land which you have rejected."* Until the last man over twenty was dead, no one would step foot into the land of God's promise to Abraham, Isaac and Jacob. Forty years of wandering aimlessly was God's punishment for the sins of a doubting generation. Caleb and Joshua would be the only exceptions. Notice the last sentence in the verses above... *they will know the land which you have rejected.* God saw the rejection of Him as a rejection of all He stood for—power, glory, honor, promises, safety and life. That condition still holds true today. We cannot have God's benefits without His requirements.

COMMON GROUND: The common ground Israel would walk on for the next forty years was just that... common, dusty, dirty, rough ground. Who would want to walk there instead of in the Promised Land of holy ground? It's really quite simple; those who reject God and choose to walk the ground of this world. **HOLY GROUND:** Most of the world is eager to receive the blessings and protection of God, as long as He doesn't require change, holiness and fruit production. Holy people don't separate the benefits from the requirements. They submit to His pruning to avoid the years in the wilderness apart from Him.

Spirit of God, The thought of forty years outside Your will and provision terrifies me. Create in me a pure heart, change me from the inside out, and walk me gently into the forever land of Your promise. Amen.

➤ Day 186: WE WILL DO IT OUR WAY
PASSAGE: **Numbers 14:39-45**
VERSE: **Numbers 14:40-41**

In the morning, however, they rose up early and went up to the ridge of the hill country, saying, "Here we are; we have indeed sinned, but we will go up to the place which the LORD has promised." But Moses said, "Why then are you transgressing the commandment of the LORD, when it will not succeed?"

Obviously, people thinking they are smarter than God is nothing new. Following God's pronouncement that no one over twenty would live to step one foot into Canaan, the people decided they were sorry for their sin and would repent and go into the land as they had been promised. Moses warned them that going against the word and judgment of God would not work. *"Do not go up, or you will be struck down before your enemies, for the LORD is not among you. For the Amalekites and the Canaanites will be there in front of you, and you will fall by the sword, inasmuch as you have turned back from following the LORD. And the LORD will not be with you."* In other lessons we have talked about being forewarned making people forearmed, but in this case being forewarned made no difference to the stubborn Hebrews. They refused to heed Moses' warning as they started off for the ridge surrounding the plain—without Moses, without the Ark of the Covenant, and without God walking beside them. They made themselves an easy target for the Amalekites and the Canaanites who struck them with great force.

COMMON GROUND: This story is being played out in our nation today. We think we can survive as a nation without God in our homes, our schools, our public forum and our government. My belief is, being the Gentleman He is, our God will not force Himself on us. God has removed His hands, thus removing the hedge of protection America has been blessed with. When we walk out of His will we will naturally reap what we sow. **HOLY GROUND:** In the Sermon on the Mount Jesus says, *"Blessed are the poor in spirit, for theirs is the kingdom of heaven."* The poor in spirit are those who know beyond a shadow of a doubt that they cannot fight battles alone and need Him. Holy people will stop trying to orchestrate their own destiny and will rely on the LORD to write the chapters of the book of their lives.

Father God, I never want to go it alone. I am realizing more every day that in my own flesh I am nothing. Please walk with me into battles and blessings, guiding me and directing my paths. Amen.

➤ Day 187: PRAYER SHAWLS
PASSAGE: **Numbers 15:37-41**
VERSE: **Numbers 15:39**

It shall be a tassel for you to look at and remember all the commandments of the LORD, so as to do them and not follow after your own heart and your own eyes, after which you played the harlot...

Following their defeat at the hands of their enemies Israel decided it was better to walk into the battle with God than without His hedge of protection. He laid down specific laws... and some of the details He reinforced were the laws for honoring the Sabbath. One of the garments a Jewish believer wore was a shawl—a prayer shawl—which when pulled up over the head created a private sanctuary for prayer and worship. The Hebrew name for the garment is *talith* or *tallit* (pronounced tal-eet) and is made up of two Hebrew words of 'tal,' meaning *tent,* and 'ith,' meaning *little.* Thus each man had his own *'little tent'*. In Scripture the prayer shawl is also referred to as a cloak, a skirt or a closet. The shawl blocked the peripheral vision of its wearer, thus helping him to focus more intently on *Adonai* (God). On the corners of the shawl were tassels representing specific truths the wearer was to remember about the character and faithfulness of God. In the passage for today's entry the blue tassel served as a reminder to remember and obey the commandments of the LORD. Jewish and Christian worshippers today often still use these shawls as a means of enhancing their focus during prayer.

COMMON GROUND: How focused is your prayer life? If you are anything like me you are easily distracted by other things in the room you are praying in—dust, cobwebs, mice... just kidding! This distraction is a common tool of the enemy who does not want us to focus on God in prayer and sincere worship. God knew that would be a problem and initiated the prayer shawl as a tool to help us in this vital discipline of our faith. **HOLY GROUND:** If you long for a deeper prayer life, maybe a *tallit* is the answer for you. I also turn off lights, light a candle, play soft background music, or pray before my fireplace to help me better focus. God longs for our focused and intense fellowship and, as His child, we should long for the same.

LORD, As of today I will seek deeper and more intense prayer times. Yes, distractions have kept me from being as focused as I need to be. I want all You have to offer... and likewise to offer all I have to You. Amen.

➤ Day 188: KORAH'S INSURRECTION
PASSAGE: Numbers 16:1-3
VERSE: Numbers 16:3

They assembled together against Moses and Aaron, and said to them, "You have gone far enough, for all the congregation are holy, every one of them, and the LORD is in their midst; so why do you exalt yourselves above the assembly of the LORD?"

If you thought Moses and Aaron were back to being revered and respected by the congregation of Israel, think again! Korah, Dathan and Abiram formed an alliance to overthrow their leaders. Insurrection always starts when one or more people believe those who lead them are inept—or in this case, prideful of their position. Notice their words in the verse above: *"...for all the congregation are holy... every one of them... the LORD is in their midst; so why do you exalt yourselves above the assembly of the LORD?"* The people are holy? I don't think so! Korah played the two hundred and fifty people he could convince like fine fiddles. I can just hear him now: "You are a holy person. God surely approves of how you live your life. Moses and Aaron think they are better than everyone else and constantly LORD their authority over us. Let's overthrow them and take our rightful places as leaders of our people." Jealousy is a bitter and divisive emotion, and Korah was able to find others to join him in his 'bitter pity party.'

COMMON GROUND: Korah's bitterness blinded him to one very real truth... God put Moses and Aaron into their positions; they didn't put themselves there. Who with any sense would choose to be the whipping boys for the ungrateful Hebrew population? Jealousy was the cause of his bitterness. Korah thirsted for power—lots of us deal with the same thirst today. **HOLY GROUND:** How good are you at rejoicing with someone else when they have successes in their lives? *Love is patient, love is kind and is not jealous; love does not brag and is not arrogant, does not act unbecomingly; it does not seek its own, is not provoked...*Honestly, do you walk more like Korah... or more like someone with the characteristics listed in this excerpt from First Corinthians chapter thirteen?

My Jesus, Ouch! Toe stepping time—and mine already hurt so much. Jesus, I have been jealous, proud, arrogant, self-promoting and provoked to anger. I see that holy ground walking will require constant effort and discipline. Bend me, break me. Amen.

➤ Day 189: CHOSEN YET JEALOUS
PASSAGE: Numbers 16:4-18
VERSE: Numbers 16:9

Is it not enough for you that the God of Israel has separated you from the rest of the congregation of Israel, to bring you near to Himself, to do the service of the tabernacle of the LORD, and to stand before the congregation to minister to them...

Korah's insurrection and power play is actually a little hard to understand in the light of the fact that he was from the tribe of Levi and was therefore already chosen by God to serve Him in the tabernacle—and that service was held in high regard within the Jewish nation. Korah's service entitled him to provision for his family from the tithes and offerings of the people, land he didn't have to farm, and a job caring for the holiest place in the Hebrew camp. Korah wasn't satisfied with his lot in life—he wanted the priesthood too. Moses tells Korah, *"Tomorrow morning the LORD will show who is His, and who is holy, and will bring him near to Himself; even the one whom He will choose, He will bring near to Himself."* Wonder how holy and close to God Korah is feeling as he hears those words? Censers, little firepans for offering incense, were to burn in the hands of Moses, Aaron, Korah and all the other men who stood with him. God would reveal His choice as leader of the nation as the censers burned before Him. Korah wants a sign from God... unfortunately for him, he is about to get one!

COMMON GROUND: Some people would complain if you hanged them with a brand new rope... and I think Korah is one of those people. What God gave him was not enough. He had honor and prestige—he wanted the priesthood. He had service in the house of God—he wanted leadership. He wanted to put himself into a new ministry. God will not support ministries we put ourselves into which are contrary to His will. **HOLY GROUND:** When God puts any of us into the ministry of His choosing He will provide for our needs and will open doors before us. When we try to decide how to 'bless God with our amazing talents' He is in no way obligated to come along side us. Let Him place you where He ordains... that is holiness.

Jesus, I have watched man-ordained ministries fail and fall.
I have watched You provide for ministries out of the goodness
of Your heart. I long for Your direction in the ministries of my
hands and the intentions of my heart. Amen.

➤ Day 190: GOD IS STILL IN CONTROL
PASSAGE: Numbers 16:28-35
VERSE: Numbers 16:30

"But if the LORD brings about an entirely new thing and the
ground opens its mouth and swallows them up with all that is
theirs, and they descend alive into Sheol, then you will understand
that these men have spurned the LORD."

Moses made certain he had the attention of the gathered congregation and said, *"If these men die the death of all men or if they suffer the fate of all men, then the LORD has not sent me. But if the LORD brings about an entirely new thing and the ground opens its mouth and swallows them up with all that is theirs, and they descend alive into Sheol, then you will understand that these men have spurned the LORD."* In order for Moses and Aaron to ever truly be the leaders of the Hebrew nation, God needed to once and for all show the people they were His chosen leaders who were put into their positions *for such a time as this.* The ball was in God's court... *As he finished speaking... the ground that was under them split open...the earth opened its mouth and swallowed them up, and their households, and all the men who belonged to Korah with their possessions... they and all that belonged to them went down alive to Sheol...the earth closed over them, and they perished from the midst of the assembly. Fire also came forth from the LORD and consumed the two hundred and fifty men who were offering the incense. The* sign Korah was looking for and the promotion he sought burned up along with him in this judgment of fire by God. Scary, isn't it?

COMMON GROUND: Whenever I teach lessons like this I have people who hate how the stories end. They question why God had to be so decisive and final in His judgment, and why He couldn't have been more patient with Korah or Achan (in a future lesson). God cannot tolerate sin in the camp—it spreads like wildfire. Basing our beliefs on emotions, rather than on a call to holiness, can put us outside the will of God. **HOLY GROUND:** If God had looked past Korah's sin, He would have to look past mine. If He looked past mine, He would have to look past yours. If He looked past yours, He would then be forced to look past everyone's… and chaos would reign. The command to *be holy as He is holy* means we cannot tolerate or sanction sin.

Spirit of God, I must learn to put my emotions aside and base my judgments and beliefs on Scriptural truths. A society operating only on emotion looks a lot like the horrible world we live in today. Call us back to holiness. Amen.

➤ ## Day 191: GOD'S CHOSEN LEADERS
PASSAGE: **Numbers 17:1-13**
VERSE: **Numbers 17:5**

"It will come about that the rod of the man whom I choose will sprout. Thus I will lessen from upon Myself the grumblings of the sons of Israel, who are grumbling against you."

Just in case there is any doubt remaining as to whom God has chosen as His first high priest, He initiates one more test for proving His ultimate decision. One representative for each of the twelve tribes—including Aaron representing the tribe of Levi—is to take a rod or stick and write his name on it. The rods are to be brought into the tabernacle and placed before the Holy of Holies. There God will reveal His will by causing the rod of the man He ordains as high priest to sprout. The next morning Moses entered the house of God and... *the rod of Aaron for the house of Levi had sprouted and put forth buds and produced blossoms, and it bore ripe almonds.* Moses carried the rods outside, proving to the congregation that God indeed chose Aaron's rod over the others. Moses was then instructed to keep Aaron's budded staff as proof in the days to come of what God had ordained. That same staff, along with a jar of manna and the tablets of the Ten Commandments, were the items placed within the Ark of the Covenant for an eternal sign of God's faithfulness.

COMMON GROUND: Why did the nation of Israel continue to challenge Moses' authority and doubt God's promises? Why was God so patient with them? The title of a recent entry was Our Longsuffering God... and He is patient, longsuffering and merciful. We should be grateful for that, for we are a people who surely require His patience, His love and His mercy. **HOLY GROUND:** We can judge Israel or we can look in the mirror and begin to realize how patient He has been with us. Did you come to Christ recently or within the last ten years? Aren't you glad His patience didn't end eleven years ago? Think about it...

Father God, I am beginning to understand that Your patience is allowing others to come into a saving relationship with Jesus Christ. Thank You for each day You linger... that more may live forever in Your presence. Amen.

➤ Day 192: PROVISION FOR LEVITES
PASSAGE: **Numbers 18:21-24**
VERSE: **Numbers 18:24**

For the tithe of the sons of Israel, which they offer as an offering to the LORD, I have given to the Levites for an inheritance; therefore I have said concerning them,
"They shall have no inheritance among the sons of Israel."

During the reiteration of tabernacle duties with Aaron and his sons, God told Aaron, *"Behold, I Myself have taken your fellow Levites from among the sons of Israel; they are a gift to you, dedicated to the LORD, to perform the service for the tent of meeting."* The Levites were to serve as priests, perform the duties of the tabernacle (and later the temple in Jerusalem) and dedicate their lives to God's service. Notice in the verse above that they were not to receive a land inheritance like the other tribes. God was ordaining the Levite tribe as His own, making them His priests, and was making the promise to always provide for their needs. A portion of the tithe of the sons of Israel, which they offered as an offering to the LORD, was given to the Levites for an inheritance. As long as the Levites and priests served, they would receive of the offerings of the other eleven tribes for their wages. Some might think it unfair that God removed the free will of the Levite tribe by forcing them into service. There is always a trade off—free will or endless provision? Which would you prefer?

COMMON GROUND: How do you think you would react if you were a Levite? Would you be grateful that you knew your purpose and that God sanctioned the work before you? Would you be content to do what He ordained for you, or would you feel that somehow you were short-changed? **HOLY GROUND:** I would personally be grateful to know exactly what my ministry was and that God would provide all I needed while I fulfilled His purpose. I also believe He has gifted each one of us for a specific area of ministry. Is that so different from the Levites ordination of tabernacle service?

LORD, Show me the gifts You have given me, the ministry You have ordained for me, and the ultimate will You have for my life. I walk into Your plans willingly and obediently... in pure faith. Amen.

➤ Day **193**: HIGH PRIEST'S PORTION
PASSAGE: **Numbers 18:25-32**
VERSE: **Numbers 18:28**

So you shall also present an offering to the LORD from your tithes,
which you receive from the sons of Israel; and from it you shall
give the LORD'S offering to Aaron the priest.

The Levites were to be provided for by the offerings of the nation—wheat from wheat, meat from animal sacrifices, and wine from the first-fruits of the vineyards. Before the Levites enjoyed their portion, they were to tithe of their 'income' to the High Priest in order to provide for all of his needs. For instance, if a man of Zebulun brought a measure of wheat for a grain offering, the necessary portion was burned with the burnt offering. The remainder was for the Levite worker (priest or worker) who enacted the actual sacrifice. Of that portion, the Levite was to give one tenth to the High Priest. Imagine how much the High Priest would receive. If hundreds of citizens came to the tabernacle each day, the workers inside would receive huge portions and Aaron would receive the tithe of all that. God was simply providing for the workers and their families at the hands of those who were faithful in their sacrifices.

COMMON GROUND: Does the tithe seem like too much for the Levites and high priest? Our modern pastors and church workers are paid in much the same way. Members of a congregation bring their tithes into the church. The funds are divided between salaries, building maintenance, education, missions, outreach, etc. How else would God's workers be provided for? **HOLY GROUND:** Maybe realizing how very important tithes and offerings are is becoming clearer to you as you read these entries. If your pastoral staff wasn't cared for in this way, their focus and work would need to be divided in order to provide for their personal needs, as well as for those of their family. God's system of provision is amazing.

My Jesus, My tithe really is important in the system of the Shepherd, the Kingdom, and the Flock being cared for. I am grateful to be able to be a part of Your implemented plan. Amen.

➤ Day 194: SPEAK TO THE ROCK
PASSAGE: **Numbers 20:1-11**
VERSE: **Numbers 20:8**

Take the rod; and you and your brother Aaron assemble the congregation and speak to the rock before their eyes, that it may yield its water. You shall thus bring forth water for them out of the rock and let the congregation and their beasts drink.

In the wilderness of Zin, Miriam—the sister of Moses and Aaron—died and was buried. The thirsty nation began to accuse Moses of bringing them there to kill them. *"Why then have you brought the LORD'S assembly into this wilderness, for us and our beasts to die here? Why have you made us come up from Egypt, to bring us in to this wretched place?"* Sound familiar? Imagine how familiar it was to Moses' ears. God heard the cries and commanded Moses to *take the rod; and you and your brother Aaron assemble the congregation and speak to the rock before their eyes, that it may yield its water... bring forth water for them out of the rock and let the congregation and their beasts drink.* Moses would likely prefer to strike the people, but instead picks up the staff and strikes the rock twice shouting, *"Listen now, you rebels; shall we bring forth water for you out of this rock?"* Water poured forth and the people drank deeply from the flow and then watered their parched animals. How satisfying that fresh, cool water must have been.

COMMON GROUND: If God punished us for our whining, most of us—me included—would stand in fear before Him. As I wrote this entry Dan and I were facing making important decisions as to our future. Whining is my first instinct. Prayer and seeking His guidance is the correct choice for a believer. It is difficult to look at the current situation, the immediate need, the thirst... and not ask God why He is not providing for that need. **HOLY GROUND:** God will direct our paths—and your paths—but He will do it in His perfect timing and not necessarily on our desired schedule. Holy people must, must, must be trusting, obedient and patient people... well?

Jesus, In God's perfect timing You were born, You came into ministry and You sacrificed Your life for me. How humbling those truths are in the light of my whining about my current needs. Amen.

➤ Day **195**: LEADERSHIP FAILURES
PASSAGE: **Numbers 20:12-29**
VERSE: **Numbers 20:12**

But the LORD said to Moses and Aaron, "Because you have not believed Me, to treat Me as holy in the sight of the sons of Israel, therefore you shall not bring this assembly into the land which I have given them."

Yesterday's story seemed to have a happy ending. The water poured forth, the people's thirst was satisfied and the animals would survive in the wilderness. Those things were all true, but God was not happy. Moses had been directly disobedient and had allowed his anger at the people cause him to react impulsively. Moses spoke to the rock, *"Listen now, you rebels; shall we bring forth water for you out of this rock?"* He also struck the rock... twice. Neither one of these things seems overtly wrong in and of itself. Why then would God say that Moses and Aaron would never lead the people into the Promised Land? What we see as a minor indiscretion, God sees as blatant disregard for His commands and words. What we see as a harmless temper tantrum, God sees as a character flaw. What we see as Moses reacting as he had earned the right to act, God sees as a potential problem with his leadership style. Look honestly at your reaction to Moses' words and the striking of the rock... and you will see how a holy God commands His children to be.

COMMON GROUND: When I teach on God's command for holiness in His disciples, people often feel that I am too absolute, too cut and dried. They usually think God needs to lighten up a little and cut people a little slack. God couldn't allow Moses to lead the people—because they would begin to emulate his blatant disregard for God's basic principles and commands. **HOLY GROUND:** I cannot state too often that God will not accept compromise—in any part of the life of His children. As a holy people we should appreciate His constant reminder of what He requires of us. We should also be grateful that He doesn't allow His leaders to compromise either.

Spirit of God, Your constant reminder is a comfort to me as I strive to walk each day in Your will. I know that the sacrifices I make for obedience will make me righteous in Your eyes. Amen.

➤ Day 196: BALAAM, COME CURSE THEM!
PASSAGE: **Numbers 22:1-14**
VERSE: **Numbers 22:6**

"Now, therefore, please come, curse this people for me since they are too mighty for me; perhaps I may be able to defeat them and drive them out of the land. For I know that he whom you bless is blessed, and he whom you curse is cursed."

Balak, King of Moab, watched the hordes of people who made up the nation of Israel as they camped opposite Jericho. He had heard of their defeat of the Amorites and was afraid of that same defeat in his homeland. Balak sent for Balaam—who was known to pronounce blessings and curses upon people—and Balak wanted the Hebrew nation cursed before they took more land in their journey toward Canaan. *"Behold, a people came out of Egypt; behold, they cover the surface of the land, and they are living opposite me... Please come, curse this people for me since they are too mighty for me."* The messengers of the king told Balaam of Balak's request. The potential curser said he needed the night to seek God's direction and would reveal his plan to them the next morning. God told Balaam, *"Do not go with them; you shall not curse the people, for they are blessed."* The next morning the messengers reluctantly returned to Moab to tell the king he will have to settle for Plan B... if he had one... because Balaam wouldn't go against God's words.

COMMON GROUND: Would you use the same word God did and call the Hebrew people 'blessed'? If we vote with our emotions, we would say that wandering forty years in the wilderness is anything but blessed. We must remember though that the people had a choice every day to walk in God's pathways, be obedient to His commands and be the beneficiaries of His blessing and provision. **HOLY GROUND:** Our being blessed depends entirely on how we respond in obedience to the commands written within the Word of God. How He chooses to bless us is His prerogative; gratefully receiving all He sends is ours.

Father God, I do feel blessed. I am blessed coming in and going out. I am blessed early in the morning and late in the evening. I am blessed with Your unconditional love, as evidenced in the offering of Your Son Jesus for my redemption. Amen.

➤ Day 197: HEY, I CAN'T BE BOUGHT!
PASSAGE: **Numbers 22:15-21**
VERSE: **Numbers 22:18**

Balaam replied to the servants of Balak, "Though Balak were to give me his house full of silver and gold, I could not do anything, either small or great, contrary to the command of the LORD my God."

Balak was not about to give up. His nation's safety and future was at stake and he needed Balaam's curse upon Israel to ensure Moab's victory. Balak sent more influential messengers the second time. *"Thus says Balak the son of Zippor, 'Let nothing, I beg you, hinder you from coming to me; for I will indeed honor you richly, and I will do whatever you say to me. Please come then, curse this people for me.'"* Balaam could name his price because Balak was desperate. Balaam also feared God and stuck to his first answer. *"Though Balak were to give me his house full of silver and gold, I could not do anything, either small or great, contrary to the command of the LORD my God."* He did agree to seek God's will—just in case He had changed His mind. The answer was a little different. God told Balaam to go with the Moabite leaders, but to only speak the words God gave to him. Somehow, I think this will not be easy for Balaam.

COMMON GROUND: What is your compromise price? What would someone have to offer you to get you to disobey God's commands? Don't rush into your answer. All of us would like to think we couldn't fall away from our faith commitment; this is pride and it causes Satan to look at us as a challenge. **HOLY GROUND:** We should never be foolish enough to think we are invincible in our own flesh. God walks with His children, but many times they run ahead of Him, or they walk in ways contrary to His perfect will. Holy people realize that *the spirit is willing, but the flesh is weak.*

> *LORD, I am lost without You. Nothing is worth losing*
> *my place in Your heart... and one day my seat at*
> *Your table in my heavenly home. Amen.*

➤ Day **198**: THIS DONKEY IS NO FOOL!
PASSAGE: **Numbers 22:22-30**
VERSE: **Numbers 22:28**

> *And the LORD opened the mouth of the donkey,*
> *and she said to Balaam, "What have I done to you,*
> *that you have struck me these three times?"*

God must have sensed a change of heart in Balaam because we find in today's passage that God was angry with him. He positioned an angel in his path—an angel Balaam's donkey could see, but Balaam couldn't. When the donkey saw the angel with a drawn sword he veered off the road and went into a field. Balaam struck the donkey and got her back on the road. Next the angel stood in the vineyard path, which caused the donkey to veer off the path and crunch Balaam's foot between her side and the wall. Balaam beat the donkey in anger. Suddenly, *the LORD opened the mouth of the donkey, and she said to Balaam, "What have I done to you, that you have struck me these three times?"* Good question! *Balaam said to the donkey, "Because you have made a mockery of me! If there had been a sword in my hand, I would have killed you by now."* This conversation was going nowhere fast and I have to wonder if Balaam felt like an idiot... talking to a talking donkey. *The donkey said to Balaam, "Am I not your donkey on which you have ridden all your life to this day? Have I ever been accustomed to do so to you?"* (Hey Balaam! Don't you think there must be something different going on here to make your lifelong companion act up?)

COMMON GROUND: No, I am not going to ask you if you ever had a donkey talk to you; that would be way too obvious. Here goes: Have you ever heard God speak through an unlikely source? Did a child speak a truth—did a chance encounter with an old friend reveal God's will to you—or, did you receive guidance through a book, a movie or a song? **HOLY GROUND:** God speaks in many different ways. I haven't heard a talking donkey, but I have heard hard truths spoken in song lyrics. Mostly He speaks to me in the verses of Scripture I study each day. However He speaks, we need to have open ears to hear and open hearts to receive.

*My Jesus, Speak, for Your servant is listening... and
I want to hear whatever You have to say to me. Amen.*

➤ Day 199: BALAAM, GO SPEAK MY WORDS!
PASSAGE: Numbers 22:31-41
VERSE: Numbers 22:35

But the angel of the LORD said to Balaam, "Go with the men,
but you shall speak only the word which I tell you."
So Balaam went along with the leaders of Balak.

Suddenly Balaam's eyes were opened and he could see the angel of the LORD standing with his drawn sword. Balaam recoiled in fear when the angel asked why he had whipped the donkey three times. *"I have come out as an adversary, because your way was contrary to me. But the donkey saw me and turned aside from me these three times. If she had not turned aside from me, I would surely have killed you just now, and let her live."* Can you imagine Balaam's anger toward the animal melting away as gratitude began to fill his heart? He excused his actions by saying he truly didn't know the angel was there because he couldn't see him standing in the pathway. The angel advised him to go on with the Moabites, but reminded him to speak only the words God would give him. Balak came out to greet Balaam, asking why he took so long to come because the problem needed to be addressed quickly. Balaam said, *"Behold, I have come now to you... the word that God puts in my mouth that I shall speak."* The next morning the two men mounted a hill and Balaam had his first glimpse of the Moabite enemy—the nation of Israel scattered before them—a huge enemy indeed.

COMMON GROUND: Once Balaam's eyes were opened to see into the spiritual world, everything that had happened became absolutely clear to him. He could understand the donkey's terror leading him to balk. He could see the weapon in the angel's hand... and he could hear how his life had been in danger. Seeing through spiritual eyes instead of worldly eyes makes all the difference in the world.
HOLY GROUND: Do you see through spiritual eyes? When you are in the midst of battles do you realize the battles are actually spiritual warfare? Our enemy isn't flesh and blood, but demonic forces

sent to stop you from growing in Christ. In the light of Scripture, the holy man can realize who his enemies are and how to fight in a whole new way.

Jesus, So many times You have protected me from falling into sin, falling out of Your grace, and falling right back into the arms of darkness where I once lived. Spiritual warfare scares me—thank you that I do not face these enemies in my own flesh. Amen.

➤ Day 200: CURSING GOD'S ANOINTED!
PASSAGE: **Numbers 23:1-12**
VERSE: **Numbers 23:8**

"How shall I curse whom God has not cursed?
And how can I denounce whom the LORD has not denounced?"

Here is where Balaam's story gets interesting! He told Balak to build seven altars and offer a bull and a ram on each of the altars. Balak was told to stand next to the offerings while Balaam sought the words of God against Israel. Once Balaam had been instructed by God, he returned to Balak and the leaders of Moab and began to speak God's words for Israel. *"From Aram Balak has brought me... 'Come curse Jacob for me, and come, denounce Israel!' How shall I curse whom God has not cursed... how can I denounce whom the LORD has not denounced? As I see him from the top of the rocks, and I look at him from the hills; behold, a people who dwells apart, and will not be reckoned among the nations. Who can count the dust of Jacob, or number the fourth part of Israel? Let me die the death of the upright, and let my end be like his!"* Something had gone terribly wrong... at least in Balak's eyes! Balaam was blessing Israel, talking about how she was different—more blessed—than the other nations, saying how great the number of her people was, and saying he himself would want to die in uprightness like her. Yes, something had surely gone wrong!

COMMON GROUND: Have you ever been so angry at someone that you enlisted another to join in the 'personal crucifixion' of that person—only to have them let the wind out of your sails by saying how kind or good the victim of your attack is? Now you know how Balak felt! **HOLY GROUND:** Before a holy man jumps into the character assassination fray, he needs to stop and think if he has the right to *cast the first stone!* Speaking godly words is like speaking a whole new language. Instead of just Eng-lish, are you ready to learn to speak 'God-lish'?

> *Spirit of God, Balak wanted the curse spoken. You wanted the blessing spoken. Balaam wanted to please both, but chose to please You over man. Help me to always choose to be pleasing to You. Amen.*

➤ Day **201**: GOD CANNOT TELL A LIE
PASSAGE: **Numbers 23:13-26**
VERSE: **Numbers 23:19**

God is not a man, that He should lie, nor a son of man, that He should repent; has He said, and will He not do it? Or has He spoken, and will He not make it good?

Balak was having a very bad day! Nothing was going as he had planned, so he devised a new plan. He would take Balaam to a different mountain, give him a different view of Israel, and get a different response out of his mouth. At the second sight seven altars were built, seven rams and bulls were offered, and Balak stood near the sacrifices as Balaam sought God. Balak was anxious to hear Balaam let the curse fly over the powerful Israelite nation; instead, he heard these words. *"God is not a man, that He should lie, nor a son of man, that He should repent; has He said, and will He not do it? Or has He spoken, and will He not make it good? ...I have received a command to bless... I cannot revoke it... The LORD his God is with him... He is for them like the horns of the wild ox. There is no omen against Jacob, nor is there any divination against Israel... Behold, a people rises like a lioness... and as a lion it lifts itself; it will not lie down until it devours the prey, and drinks the blood of the slain."* Balak's bad day had gone from bad to worse. God was going to fight for His chosen people and no curse against them would stop Him.

COMMON GROUND: Most of us want to fight our own battles in our own time and according to our own strategies. Balak was trying to fight the coming Hebrew battle with spiritual warfare, but was finding out God is also a physical warfare fighter. **HOLY GROUND:** The God of Israel is truthful, dependable, committed, battle-ready and immune to divination's power. He is also a roaring lion ready to fight for His people. That should encourage every holy heart... He will lead us to victory.

Father God, I love the picture in my mind of You prowling around like a lion seeking to protect and defend me from all who would try to harm me. I confess my need for Your intercession against those who wish to stop my service to You. Amen.

➤ Day 202: ISRAEL'S ENEMIES ARE CURSED
PASSAGE: **Numbers 24:1-14**
VERSE: **Numbers 24:9**

He crouches; he lies down as a lion, and as a lion, who dares rouse him? Blessed is everyone who blesses you, and cursed is everyone who curses you.

Balaam was doing exactly as he warned Balak he would do. He was only speaking the prophetic words God gave him to speak over His people. Balak was furious. After a third session of supposed cursing—which actually ended up to be another session of blessing—Balak told Balaam he had planned to give him great honors, but that his God had kept him from receiving those honors.

Balaam seemed somewhat indifferent to those words and reminded Balak that he never promised to say what Balak wanted to hear. *"Did I not tell your messengers whom you had sent to me, saying, 'Though Balak were to give me his house full of silver and gold, I could not do anything contrary to the command of the LORD, either good or bad, of my own accord; what the LORD speaks, that I will speak.'"* Balak's frustration slowly began to turn to fear when Balaam said, *"And now, behold, I am going to my people; come, and I will advise you what this people will do to your people in the days to come."* Could things get any worse for Balak and his nation?

COMMON GROUND: Did Balak really want to know what the future held in store for the Moabite nation? He wanted the problem taken care of—not a warning of how God would use His wandering nation to judge Moab. Why do we so often ask God to take care of a situation without wishing to see the long-range implications of that challenge? **HOLY GROUND:** God's way of resolving troubles in our lives isn't always to remove the thorn. Often He requires us to walk through the thorny places in order for us to come out more in tune with Him in the end. Are you willing to say, "Yes LORD, yes. I will walk where You provide a path."

LORD, Balak was willing for Balaam to consult 'his God' as long as 'his God' said the words that suited Balak's desires. How often have I sought Your answers... really wanting 'my' answers, not Yours? Amen.

➤ Day 203: KEEP BLOODLINES PURE
PASSAGE: **Numbers 25:1-18**
VERSE: **Numbers 25:1-2**

While Israel remained at Shittim, the people began to play the harlot with the daughters of Moab. For they invited the people to the sacrifices of their gods, and the people ate and bowed down to their gods.

Throughout Scripture God cautioned Israel to keep the bloodlines of that nation pure—to not intermarry with the nations around them. Why was that so important that it warranted being repeated so often? God chose Israel to preserve the Holy Scriptures and, more importantly, to be the people who would bring forth the long anticipated Messiah—the Redeemer of all mankind. If God chose Israel as His vessel to deliver the Messiah, He would surely want Him delivered through a pure bloodline. Jesus was to be conceived of the Holy Spirit and born of a virgin; and He was to be born of the Jewish race. While Israel camped in the plains across from Jericho, the men of the nation began to intermingle with the daughters of the Moabites. Once they began forsaking the command to not intermarry, the next command became easier to break... they began to worship Baal, the Moabite god, in order to please their foreign wives. God will not be mocked—and it doesn't matter how you try to justify your sin. He commanded Moses to have those leaders who were dividing their loyalties to Him killed in broad daylight. That may sound drastic, but God knew what unchecked disloyalty would cost in the long run.

COMMON GROUND: *Thou shall not*—have other gods before Me. *Thou shall not*—intermarry with the nations around you. *Thou shall not*—worship idols. Why is *"Thou shall not..."* such a hard command for us to understand? Why do we so commonly think we are smarter than the Author of the *"Thou Shall Not's?"* **HOLY GROUND:** Holy people need to remove 'BUT' from their vocabulary... "I do believe in what the Bible says... BUT... I want to look at dirty books. I do think adultery is sin... BUT... he is so handsome. I know stealing is wrong... BUT... they have lots of money and will never miss a few dollars." If the Author of the *"Thou Shall Not's"* said it... then you *SHALL NOT* do it!

My Jesus, Guilty as charged! I am convicted for the times I have made excuses or rationalized my sins to suit my own liking and completely betrayed Your commands for holiness. Oh LORD, in my flesh I am weak... so weak. Help me to be strong today. Amen.

➤ Day 204: LAND INHERITANCE
PASSAGE: **Numbers 27:1-11**
VERSE: **Numbers 27:4**

Why should the name of our father be withdrawn from among his family because he had no son? Give us a possession among our father's brothers.

In the instruction of how the land of Canaan was to be divided among the Israelite tribes a problem arose. One man, Zelophehad of the sons of Joseph, had five daughters and no surviving sons... and he was dead. Without a son to inherit their family portion and provide for his sisters they would have no place to live once Israel moved in and took up residence. It is important to understand how land inheritance worked. A father left equal portions of his property to his sons, with the oldest son inheriting a double portion—along with the duties of overseeing the family and caring for the elderly. If Zelophehad's daughters couldn't rightly inherit land, their future sons would have no part in the promise God made to Abraham generations before. After they voiced their concerns to Moses, he sought God's guidance and was told, *"The daughters of Zelophehad are right in their statements. You shall surely give them a hereditary possession among their father's brothers, and you shall transfer the inheritance of their father to them. Further, you shall speak to the sons of Israel... if a man dies and has no son, then you shall transfer his inheritance to his daughter."*

COMMON GROUND: Women weren't allowed to be land owners according to Jewish law of the day, but God saw the legitimacy of their request and granted the land. The women were polite and direct in their complaint and didn't resort to badgering or threats. Their dignified manner is rather uncommon in our world today. **HOLY GROUND:** Holy people will seek to approach God or those in authority in a respectful and reverent manner. Our God doesn't react positively to negativity... just a bit of food for thought.

Jesus, Scripture tells me You are just and fair, not a respecter of status or wealth, and that You will judge based on those character- istics. I gladly stand before Your throne of grace. Amen.

➤ Day 205: THEY NEED A SHEPHERD
PASSAGE: **Numbers 27:12-17**
VERSE: **Numbers 27:16-17**

May the LORD, the God of the spirits of all flesh, appoint a man over the congregation, who will go out and come in before them, and who will lead them out and bring them in, so that the congre- gation of the LORD will not be like sheep which have no shepherd.

M oses was nearing the end of his life… and the grief at never being able to walk on the Holy Ground of the Promised Land had to be overwhelming. God told him to go up a nearby mountain, take a long look at the land, and prepare to be gathered to his fathers as his brother Aaron was. God gently reminded His friend Moses of the sin he committed in the wilderness of Zin. Moses turned to God for one of their last earthly conversations and, as always, he put the nation of Israel before his own desires. *"May the LORD… appoint a man over the congregation, who will go out and come in before them, and who will lead them out and bring them in, so that the congregation of the LORD will not be like sheep which have no shepherd?"* God, who was perhaps expecting Moses to try to influ- ence Him to reverse His decision, looked at the heart of a real shep- herd. In every sense of the word Moses was a shepherd leading an unruly flock. God reassured Moses, *"Take Joshua the son of Nun, a man in whom is the Spirit, and lay your hand on him; and have him stand before Eleazar the priest and before all the congregation, and commission him in their sight. You shall put some of your authority on him, in order that all the congregation of the sons of Israel may obey him."*

COMMON GROUND: Moses had every right to be hosting the world's biggest pity party in this passage. Instead, he selflessly lays down his disappointment and sadness to ensure that Israel—ungrateful, unholy and undisciplined Israel—would have a leader to watch over them and protect them from themselves. **HOLY GROUND:** A man seeking to be holy is not perfect and needs to realize that truth. He is striving... seeking... working... being pruned every day toward that goal. He is like Moses who didn't take the pruning as a lack of love, but as proof of God's love.

Spirit of God, Moses is a wonderful picture of the selfless shepherd—a precursor to our glorious Shepherd, Jesus Christ. LORD, may I be willing to suffer disappointment in my own life for the sake of another member of Your flock. Amen.

➤ Day 206: JOSHUA IS COMMISSIONED
PASSAGE: **Numbers 27:18-23**
VERSE: **Numbers 27:18-19**

So the LORD said to Moses, "Take Joshua the son of Nun, a man in whom is the Spirit, and lay your hand on him; and have him stand before Eleazar the priest and before all the congregation, and commission him in their sight."

Today we will overlap with yesterday's entry and use the above verse again. Instead of looking at this verse from Moses' perspective, let's look at what it says about Joshua, the son of Nun. God has a long memory and He had not forgotten Joshua and Caleb and the stand they took for going into Canaan when the other ten spies decried all the reasons for staying out. Joshua is *a man in whom is the Spirit*. He is a man ruled by the Spirit of God, not by the emotions of his heart. Joshua is a man with leadership skills... *At his command they shall go out and at his command they shall come in, both he and the sons of Israel with him, even all the congregation.* God was looking for a rock solid leader to fill the huge sandals of

Moses. He was looking for someone strong and determined. He was looking for someone who would not bow to the weaknesses of his people. He was looking for a man of character and unrelenting faith. He was looking for Joshua, the son of Nun. Fortunately for Israel, Joshua was willing to take the commission from his God.

COMMON GROUND: If you could look at your character and see it the way God sees it, would you like what you see? Do you see the same characteristics that set Joshua apart from the rest of the common people of Israel? Do you see faith, determination and a willingness to serve? Be honest; we are supposed to be growing through these lessons. **HOLY GROUND:** God is looking for a few good Christians to stand up, be brave, remain true to His commands and lead His church into the perilous days ahead. Is He looking at you as someone with those characteristics—or does He have to look beyond you? Isn't it time for you to let Him begin His good work in you.

Father God, I admire Moses and Joshua. I respect David and Abraham. I applaud Ruth and Esther. But, I revere You and Your holy Son. I long to be a hero of the faith… an instrument of Your peace and a tool in the hands of the Master Craftsman. Amen.

➤ Day 207: YOUR WORD IS YOUR BOND
PASSAGE: **Numbers 30:1-2**
VERSE: **Numbers 30:2**

If a man makes a vow to the LORD, or takes an oath to bind himself with a binding obligation, he shall not violate his word; he shall do according to all that proceeds out of his mouth.

Let's look today at how committed you are to keeping your word. As a child I can remember saying, "I swear to God" when I wanted someone to know I was serious about a promise I was making. Other times I would say "I swear on the Bible," not even knowing the significance of the book, but I'd heard someone else say it and it sounded good! My promise meant so much to me that I made half-hearted promises and kept them in an equally half-hearted way. When I began to study that same Bible, I found out we are not to make rash promises... because our word is to bind us like super-glue to the one we make a covenant with. The sheer number of marriages ending in divorce shows us how little weight our word holds. Where is the bond, the covenant, the super-glue, the commitment to marriage vows? The passage for today says an oath or bond is a binding obligation, cannot be violated, and all that was promised must be kept. This is especially true in the promises we make to our Heavenly Father, to His Son and to the Holy Spirit.

COMMON GROUND: Are you keeping the promises you made to honor God, obey His commands and serve Him all your days? Is the passion for Christ the same as it was in your day of conversion, or has it burned hotter or turned cold? Who moved? How are you in your relational commitments? It is common to get lazy in this area... and our society reflects that truth. **HOLY GROUND:** When you make a promise, consider it set in stone—something that cannot be revoked. That should keep us from making rash promises, whether your word is to God or man.

LORD, Curb my tongue from speaking rash promises
and uncommitted commitments. I have failed in the past. Amen.

➤ Day 208: ABRAHAM'S PROMISE FULFILLED
PASSAGE: **Deuteronomy 1:8-15**
VERSE: **Deuteronomy 1:8**

See, I have placed the land before you; go in and possess the
land which the LORD swore to give to your fathers, to Abraham, to
Isaac, and to Jacob, to them and their descendants after them.

Deuteronomy is a book of reminders. At the time of its writing (approx. 1450 BC) only three of the original members of the Exodus were still alive. Moses, Caleb and Joshua alone had survived the forty year wilderness exile. They were standing on the precipice of time and on the edge of Israel's journey into the Promised Land. Most of those alive had never heard the full account of God's provision for His children. They had not seen His amazing miracles or heard bits and pieces from their fathers. Before Moses died he took them on a journey from bondage to freedom. They must never forget the importance of God's faithfulness. They must realize they were about to walk into the covenant God made to Abraham hundreds of years before. Now the nation had grown truly as numerous as the stars in the sky... faithful God. They had wise and discerning leaders... faithful God. They had a code of ethics to live by... faithful God. Let's look at snippets from Deuteronomy and see where the teachings of thousands of years ago still apply today.

COMMON GROUND: God is faithful; we are forgetful. God is gracious; we are unforgiving. God is generous; we are selfish. God is love; we are hard-hearted. God is forever; we are for a breath only. God is constant; we are ever-changing. **HOLY GROUND:** Just as Deuteronomy served as a valuable reminder for the Hebrew people, we need to be reminded of the common truths above. One more—God is holy; we are called to be the same... without excuse or exception.

My Jesus, I need to reread Matthew 5-7 and glean
Your teachings from the Sermon on the Mount, maybe the
greatest single teaching in all of Scripture.
There I will find Your character—and mine. Amen.

➤ Day 209: JUDGES MUST BE JUST
PASSAGE: **Deuteronomy 1:16-17**
VERSE: **Deuteronomy 1:17**

You shall not show partiality in judgment; you shall hear
the small and the great alike. You shall not fear man,
for the judgment is God's. The case that is too hard for you,
you shall bring to me, and I will hear it.

'Judges must be just' sounds like one of those 'Duh' titles, doesn't it? You are likely thinking I have run out of things to talk about and am really stretching today. (Personally, I myself am amazed that I haven't run out of things to say yet—though people who know me are not surprised at all!) In God's command for this holy nation the caliber of its leaders had to surpass all expectation. Recently I have watched as liberal judges have handed down ridiculously small sentences for serious crimes. Why? The judges are activists who are more concerned with making a point than they are with sentencing guidelines. Once the judges begin to compromise the laws, the disregard trickles down to the people. America's system of justice—and the legal system in Israel—are both based on fairness, equality and impartiality under the law. In the book of Exodus we found Moses trying to be the judge over the 600,000 adults who escaped Egyptian bondage. From morning to night he tried to iron out the differences between his people. Finally, God told him to share the responsibility and appoint Godly men to judge under his authority. This lesson is a reminder of the kind of leaders we need in the judgeship.

COMMON GROUND: Wouldn't it be nice to know that the judge and jury you were to stand before in judgment would have the qualities we see in the above passage? Those characteristics aren't very common in our society, but the Supreme Court Justice in Heaven will be fair, kind, impartial, loving, self sacrificing... **HOLY GROUND:** As we strive onward from being common to being holy we must realize that those in positions of authority will not always be perfect... neither are we. Moses could only choose those who exhibited good character—we must do the same as we choose those in leadership.

Jesus, In Heaven You will be my Attorney (defending me before my accuser), my Judge (sentencing me to eternity with You) and my Court Reporter (showing me every thing I have done with my life). What better hands could I be in than Yours? Amen.

➤ Day 210: FEAR NOTHING BUT FEAR
PASSAGE: **Deuteronomy 1:20-21**
VERSE: **Deuteronomy 1:21**

See, the LORD your God has placed the land before you; go up, take possession, as the LORD, the God of your fathers, has spoken to you. Do not fear or be dismayed.

Have you ever stood on the precipice between where you are coming from and where you are going—that uncertain place where the unknown lies before you and safety seems to be behind? Were you afraid? As I write this entry Dan and I are at that place. His health is failing; we are fighting the unknown in a bad Michigan economy; and we are feeling drawn by God to a new ministry—but we don't know where. Been there? Moses was trying to convince the people that the land before them was theirs for the taking. This was the land of the Amorites—not the Promised Land… and the enemies looked big! (Remember, the book of Deuteronomy is a review.) He tried to reassure them… *"You have come to the hill country of the Amorites which the LORD our God is about to give us."* Sounded great… but was the LORD absolutely, positively, without a doubt, assuredly, with no chance of failure, going to give the land to Israel? And what did 'give' mean? Would there be a fight? How big were their weapons? Were their warriors well trained? Are our troops ready to fight? I'm sure you are seeing the picture here. Fear opens the floodgates of doubt and dismay.

COMMON GROUND: Does fear keep you from stepping from the safety of yesterday into the unknown of tomorrow? Can you see lots of reasons to stay put and never venture out of the status quo? God is ready to open new doors... are we willing to step over the threshold? **HOLY GROUND:** I don't know all the answers for Dan and me and our tomorrows, but I do know Who holds them. I didn't know the answers for my yesterdays either, but He has not failed me yet. I walk into the unknown—simply trusting Him.

Spirit of God, In the past, fear has kept me from great blessings and awesome opportunities. No more! I walk forward in faith... in holy boldness into whatever You have planned for me. Amen.

➤ Day 211: GOD'S COVENANTS STAND
PASSAGE: **Deuteronomy 2:1-9**
VERSE: **Deuteronomy 2:5**

Do not provoke them, for I will not give you any of their land, even as little as a footstep because I have given Mount Seir to Esau as a possession.

We talked in an earlier entry about the vital importance of keeping our promises. In order for us to serve a Holy God, God must also be a keeper of His promises. In this entry I must take you back to the book of Genesis where we find the story of twin brothers—Esau and Jacob. You may know the story of the sibling rivalry between these brothers which was fueled by their parents who chose favorites and played one brother against the other. Jacob, the second born twin, received his brother's blessing and went on to father the twelve tribes of Israel. Esau, who was betrayed by his mother and Jacob, was left without his rightful double-portion and was told he would live by the sword and serve his brother all his days. As you can imagine, that went over like a lead balloon! Jacob was secreted away to protect him from Esau's rage. Esau was given the land of Seir and became the father of the Edomite nation.

Here, hundreds of years later, we see God telling Jacob's descendants (Israel) that they are not to take any part of the land of Seir. Why? Because God made a promise to Esau and, as we learned in an earlier lesson, *God is not a man, that He should lie.*

COMMON GROUND: Do you believe the promise Scriptures of the Bible? Do you believe God fights for you, prepares a way for you, defends you, strengthens you, and is your refuge? Commonly, we look at what our eyes see and base our judgments on that— forgetting that God's promises are as sure as the sunrise. **HOLY GROUND:** Until you completely believe that God will do all He has promised for you, you cannot walk in holiness. Yes, my friend, that requires faith… and *without faith it is impossible to please* Him.

Father God, I know that I cannot trust man to have my best interest at heart. I know man will always let me down. I also know that You are the same yesterday, today and forever—thank You! Amen.

➤ Day **212**: A NEW GENERATION IS HERE
PASSAGE: **Deuteronomy 2:14-16**
VERSE: **Deuteronomy 2:14**

Now the time that it took for us to come from Kadesh-barnea until we crossed over the brook Zered was thirty-eight years, until all the generation of the men of war perished from within the camp, as the LORD had sworn to them.

Yesterday we talked about God keeping the promise He gave to Esau, and today we see Him keep a promise He made to the Hebrew people. In this case He was keeping a promise they wished He would break. Remember God telling His doubting people that all of their generation would die and never see the Promised Land? Now we see the fulfillment of that promise. Thirty-eight years have passed… and so have all members of the generation who believed their fears and emotions instead of God's commitment to their nation.

Imagine this: Everyone knew that no one over twenty during those days would survive… thus they began to watch the 'old folks' die. A day came when there were twelve left, eleven, ten, nine, eight… The new generation knew the Promised Land was theirs, once the other seven were gone. They watch… seven, six, five, four, three, two… Imagine being the last one living from that generation with everyone looking at you and waiting for you to die!

COMMON GROUND: For the new generation, the death of the last member of the old one ushered in a whole new paradigm. The comfort of wandering in the wilderness with every need provided for was about to end. God was keeping His promise, but moving forward would require an even greater degree of faith. **HOLY GROUND:** As God closes a door, He usually opens a window of opportunity. Are you so busy staring at the closed door that you fail to see the wide-open window next to it? Do you trust the Door Closer?

LORD, There is a certain degree of comfort in sameness
and ritual. I confess that I am reluctant for change;
but if You want to close that door and open a new window for me—
I will climb through it. Amen.

➤ Day 213: NATIONS WILL FEAR YOU
PASSAGE: **Deuteronomy 2:25**
VERSE: **Deuteronomy 2:25**

"This day I will begin to put the dread and fear of you upon the peoples everywhere under the heavens, who, when they hear the report of you, will tremble and be in anguish because of you."

If you talk to the World War II generation in America, most of them will speak glowingly about their homeland and the service they gave to preserve her independence. They will also tell you that all nations around the world once stood in awe of the United States because surely she was blessed by God—in every way. The reputation of a nation means everything when it comes to military negotiations, business dealings and international trade. In this session we see God assuring Israel that he would put dread and fear of her in the hearts of every nation under the heavens. Why did God want other nations to dread and fear Israel? This sort of dread and fear isn't terror; it is respect and reverence. God's hand was firmly holding onto His chosen nation—and He wanted everyone to look at her, see her strength, admire her fortitude, observe her miraculous story... and receive her Son Jesus for their salvation. Israel had to be different from the pagan nations around her. She had to be peculiar, unique, set apart... uncommon.

COMMON GROUND: My friend, we are called to be like Israel. People should look at us and see God's hand holding us, His provision for us, His character on us... and they should hear His Word flowing from our lips. How else will others know they need what we have? How will they ever learn to revere our God? **HOLY GROUND:** When Israel walked with God they were blessed. When they walked away from God they were cursed. There were no gray areas or compromises. We cannot serve Him and the world. Look at Israel's history to find support for this truth.

My Jesus, I choose to be blessed, thus I walk with You, talk with You, glorify Your Name and praise You with all I have in me. Amen.

➤ Day 214: GOD FIGHTS FOR HIS OWN
PASSAGE: **Deuteronomy 3:21-22**
VERSE: **Deuteronomy 3:22**

*Do not fear them, for the LORD your God
is the one fighting for you.*

Let's take a slight detour today and look at why we need to know the Old Testament foundational stories, promise Scriptures and prophetic words. If I wanted to sell you my used car today, you (if you were a wise buyer) would ask me to tell you how the car runs. You might check to see if it had been in any accidents, and you might even take it to a mechanic for a check-up. Why? You want to make sure you are buying a good car. Right? How can a fledgling believer being drawn by the power of the Holy Spirit find out if God is faithful and if His promises are true before they 'buy' the gospel message? Simple. They look at the stories of His provision for Noah and Moses, His mercy toward David and Samson, His blessings upon Ruth and Esther... and see a proven history of faithfulness. They see how God fought along side Gideon, Joshua and Daniel. Without those Biblical foundations, the seeker has only your word to go on when you tell him God is real and wants to save him from eternal destruction. There is a greater purpose for those Bibles in most homes than merely collecting dust on a shelf. They give us a rock solid foundation for our faith... and assure us that God has not changed in His commitment to His own.

COMMON GROUND: Checkpoint Question: Have you been using your Bible in conjunction with this devotional? Let me encourage you to start today if you haven't in the past. My goal isn't to get rich or get famous. It is to get you right with God... and the very real truth is that you need what His Word has to offer. **HOLY GROUND:** Holy people who are hungry for a deeper, more intimate relationship with Jesus Christ will do everything in their power to learn more about Him, His teachings and His life... thus we read the Bible.

Jesus, Open my heart to hunger for Your Word, my eyes to look eagerly to see more of You and my ears to hear what You have to say to me. I am hungry for our intimacy, Jesus. Amen.

➤ Day 215: MY WORD IS PERFECT
PASSAGE: **Deuteronomy 4:1-2**
VERSE: **Deuteronomy 4:2**

*You shall not add to the word which I am commanding you,
nor take away from it, that you may keep the commandments
of the LORD your God which I command you.*

Oh Goody! Today I get to rant and rave about lack of sound Bible teaching! See what it says in the verse... *You shall not add to the word which I am commanding you, nor take away from it.* In other words... teach it, teach it as written, and don't pick and choose what you teach!!! Get the point? (Boy, I feel better already!) God's Word is perfect. It is complete; it is holy; it is truth; it is preserved for you; and it is a perfect picture of our LORD Jesus Christ! Which part of Him don't you want to know about? If you want to know the real Jesus, you need to know the Old Testament prophesies of His life, as well as the New Testament details of His teaching and ministry. You need to know He is Love—but that righteous anger led Him to turn over the tables of the temple's moneychangers. You need to know that He didn't come to abolish the commandments of God, but to be the perfect fulfillment of them. You need to know that He spoke out against hypocrites, religiosity and false prophets. If you need to know all those things—why aren't they being talked about in today's houses of worship? Remember—add to or take away from it at your own peril!

COMMON GROUND: Those who hunger after ear-tickling drivel will love what they hear in our 'Seeker-friendly' churches today. They will love hearing that they are okay just as they are and no change is required for them to be a Christian. But wait! That isn't the whole truth. Someone is leading people to believe they can create their own 'more palatable' God. **HOLY GROUND:** Are you mad yet? Is your anger at me, or at those who teach drivel? If you don't like my words, take it up with the One who wrote them. I am just teaching as they are written... no adding, no subtracting.

Spirit of God, I want more... more of You and Your Word.
I don't want a dumbed-down message or ear-tickling drivel.
Teach me all You want me to know. Amen.

➤ Day 216: HOW GREAT IS 'THEIR' GOD
PASSAGE: **Deuteronomy 4:6-8**
VERSE: **Deuteronomy 4:7**

For what great nation is there that has a god so near
to it as is the LORD our God whenever we call on Him?

God Calling... *"Hello, My child. Just wanted to get in touch with you—haven't heard from you in a while. Are you missing our conversations—our quiet times together? I am. Oh, I know you are busy—money to make, friends to entertain, careers to work, houses to clean—but I have never been too busy for you. Remember when you cried out to Me the night your heart was breaking and I stilled your sobs and brought you much needed rest? Or, do you remember when the doctors said your cancer was terminal and I said 'terminal-sherminal—I made that body and I will heal it.' I did—and I held your hand through those brutal treatments. It is so good that every hair I numbered has been replaced on your head. Have you told others about how I never leave you... never forsake you... never turn My back on you? They won't know if you don't tell them. They will never hunger for Me if they don't see My blessings showering upon you. What? You don't feel the blessing shower? Feeling a little dry? I didn't move; I'm still here. I love you. Let's get together soon, very soon."*

COMMON GROUND: Today's verse tells us God is so near He hears our call—whether it is a shout or a whisper. Do you believe that? Do you live like that? Do you call His Name in worship, or only to give Him your prayer requests? He is waiting. **HOLY GROUND:** Prayer is interaction, conversation between God and His children. You get out of any relationship exactly what you invest into it. How much time have you invested in your relationship with Christ lately?

Father God, Holy, Holy, Holy, LORD God Almighty! Early in the morning our song shall rise to Thee; Holy, Holy, Holy, merciful and mighty! God in three persons blessed Trinity. Amen.

➤ Day 217: BE DILIGENT, BE ALERT!
PASSAGE: **Deuteronomy 4:9-10**
VERSE: **Deuteronomy 4:9**

Only give heed to yourself and keep your soul diligently, so that you do not forget the things which your eyes have seen and they do not depart from your heart all the days of your life; but make them known to your sons and your grandsons.

A re you diligent? Do you know what I mean by that in regard to your relationship with the LORD? Someone who is diligent is constant in their effort to achieve a goal. Hmmm... are you diligently striving to work out your salvation and to attain a higher level of intimacy with God? Are you on the alert for anything that would lessen your diligence or hinder your progress? These are all good questions to ponder. They were good words when Moses spoke them thousands of years ago as a warning before the people ventured into the Promised Land. God was taking them from common to holy ground and—knowing the heart of those He created—He felt it was necessary to repeat these oft-spoken words of caution. *Keep your soul diligently... do not forget the things which your eyes have seen... make them known to your sons and your grandsons...let them hear My words so they may learn to fear Me all the days they live on the earth, and that they may teach their children.*

COMMON GROUND: The opposite of diligence is apathy. Apathy is the absence or suppression of passion, emotion or excitement. Which better describes your current spiritual level? I will say that apathy in any relationship leads to indifference, drift and compromise. **HOLY GROUND:** God wants His children to have a burning passion for Him. Do you want an apathetic response toward you from your spouse, your family or your friends? Of course you don't. The road to holiness also requires diligence and dedication.

LORD, Diligence will keep me focused and growing in my faith. Show me any apathetic areas, perform spiritual surgery on them, and create in me a passionate heart. Amen.

➤ Day 218: WHEN (NOT IF) YOU SIN AGAINST ME
PASSAGE: Deuteronomy 4:25-26
VERSE: Deuteronomy 4:25

When you become the father of children and children's children and have remained long in the land, and act corruptly, and make an idol in the form of anything, and do that which is evil in the sight of the LORD your God so as to provoke Him to anger...

Notice that the word used in the above Scripture is 'when'—not 'if.' This is important because the rest of the verse says the nation of Israel *will* act corruptly, make idols and do that which is evil in the sight of the LORD... and provoke Him to anger. What difficult words these must have been for God to have to speak to a people He delivered from bondage, performed miracles for, provided manna and water for in the desert, and promised a whole new land flowing with milk and honey. Look at verse 26. *"I call heaven and earth to witness against you today, that you will surely perish quickly from the land where you are going over the Jordan to possess it. You shall not live long on it, but will be utterly destroyed."* Can you believe this? God was predicting the destruction of Israel before they ever set foot in the land. Why? It all comes back to a little thing called 'free will.' God created man with a spirit to bind him to His Creator. He also gave him free will to accept that binding or reject it. Since the beginning of time—in a lovely Garden called Eden—man has chosen to reject God, worship other gods, do evil and follow the lust of the flesh. Some things never change.

COMMON GROUND: Maybe I am different from other people, but if God told me I *would* sin... I'd do everything in my power to prove Him wrong! What is it that causes forewarned people to fall into the very traps they were warned about? **HOLY GROUND:** The answer to those questions goes back to yesterday's lesson... we are not diligent. We are not prepared to withstand temptation. We are convinced in our little human brains that we are smarter than God. Only when we admit that we are helpless without Him will we ever become strong enough to resist sin.

My Jesus, The Father knew Israel would sin... and knew I would sin, and knew every man except You would sin. He still sent You— to cover our sin, to assume our sin and to wash our sins away. All my gratitude goes to You. Keep me strong in Your power. Amen.

➤ Day 219: I WILL SCATTER YOU
PASSAGE: **Deuteronomy 4:27-28**
VERSE: **Deuteronomy 4:27**

The LORD will scatter you among the peoples, and you will be left few in number among the nations where the LORD drives you.

God not only told Israel they *would* sin, but that the consequence of their sin would be a scattering—a disbursement of them throughout pagan nations. Remember, these words are spoken before the battle for the land of Canaan even began. As of that moment, the sons of Jacob—the twelve tribes of Israel—had always been together. They were raised together, moved together, had worshipped together, and probably foolishly believed nothing would ever change that. Being scattered is not something to be taken lightly. Families would be shattered; the people of the nations where they were to reside would worship other gods and idols; and they would be persecuted for their faith in the God of Abraham. Worse yet, they would reject that faith and serve other gods. Observe these crushing words: *There you will serve gods, the work of man's hands, wood and stone, which neither see nor hear nor eat nor smell.* Not only *will* they sin, but they *will* be scattered, and they *will* serve dead idols that were built from the materials their Creator's hands had made—and they *will* lose the abundant life they had while serving the living God.

COMMON GROUND: Because of the prophetic words of Moses, Israel knew the pitfalls before them and the dire consequences of falling into them… yet they still fell. Here is a hard truth to ponder. The same prophetic words are sent to warn the Christian church today of the pitfalls—lukewarm commitments, creating self-pleasing gods and teachings contrary to Scripture—and just like Israel before us; we are falling right into those pitfalls. **HOLY GROUND:** Holy people who seek to please God must heed His warnings, commands and teachings. If that doesn't happen, we too will be scattered among the evil of this world. Dear God, it is already happening… we are following wolves… not Your Word.

Jesus, I cannot imagine anything emptier than the life I would live serving other gods after having served the living God all these years. Keep me ever mindful of Your truths. Amen.

➤ Day 220: REPENT, AND I WILL HEAR
PASSAGE: **Deuteronomy 4:29-31**
VERSE: **Deuteronomy 4:30-31**

When you are in distress and all these things have come upon you, in the latter days you will return to the LORD your God and listen to His voice. For the LORD your God is a compassionate God; He will not fail you nor destroy you nor forget the covenant with your fathers which He swore to them.

In Moses' prophetic word Israel may be scattered and under the authority of enemy nations, but they will not be destroyed. God still had a plan—a plan to bless them after years of lessons learned the hard way. *For the LORD your God is a compassionate God; He will not fail you nor destroy you nor forget the covenant with your fathers which He swore to them.* God's promises stand strong even when His children's commitment is weak. The words He spoke to Abraham hundreds and hundreds of years before are the words He would keep in the days ahead. God buried a faith seed deep in the hearts of His children. They could ignore or reject the seed for a season, but one day the seed would begin to sprout and the people would begin to hunger for something more. Moses told his flock that in that seed sprouting day ...*you will seek the LORD your God, and you will find Him if you search for Him with all your heart and all your soul.* From that foreign land, in spite of all their shortcomings and through all of the hardships their choices have created, the faith seed will grow, they will remember His past faithfulness and they will call once again upon their God. They *will* call... and He *will* hear.

COMMON GROUND: It is common for us to look at others and believe they are beyond hope. God planted the faith seeds—who are we to judge where the seeds are buried? **HOLY GROUND:** For those who believe God to be harsh and unloving, they need to study this portion of Scripture. God is not harsh; He is love. He is also *El Qanna*, our Jealous God, and has every right in the world to fight for the perfection and the protection of His children.

Spirit of God, Knowing that God will hear the sincere cries of the repentant heart is a reassurance to me. I have loved ones who are lost. May You stir their hearts, bring that seed to life, and bring them into right standing with the Father. Amen.

➤ Day 221: HE ALONE IS YOUR GOD
PASSAGE: **Deuteronomy 4:35-39**
VERSE: **Deuteronomy 4:39**

Know therefore today, and take it to your heart, that the LORD, He is God in heaven above and on the earth below; there is no other.

Did God truly choose Israel and set her apart from all other nations? Let's look at today's passage for answers to that question. *To you it was shown that you might know the LORD.* Look closely. The miracle and plan of God was shown to Israel (and Israel alone at the time) so they would know who God was. *Out of the heavens He let you hear His voice.* God let Israel alone hear His voice. *On earth He let you see His great fire, and you heard His words from the midst of the fire.* God manifested Himself in the clouds and fire to Israel alone. *He loved your fathers, therefore He chose their descendants after them.* God's promises were to Abraham and his descendants—the sons of Jacob (whose name later became Israel). *He personally brought you from Egypt by His great power. Driving out from before you nations greater and mightier than you, to bring you in and to give you their land for an inheritance...* Israel stood on the edge of seeing the land of promise—a land given to them and no other nation by their God. I would say God surely chose Israel from among all other nations, and if anyone should fully understand the love of God... it should have been Israel.

COMMON GROUND: You might not be a student of Israel's history and the proven legacy of God's provision for this tiny nation. You might think what happens in the Middle East has nothing to do with you. Nothing could be further from the truth! As Gentile (non-Jew) believers, we are grafted into the tree of Israel. What affects her affects us. What God promised her He also promises us. **HOLY GROUND:** In order to more fully understand prophecy we need to be informed on what is happening regarding our sister Israel. We need to pray for that tiny nation situated among huge enemies; and we need to process the truth that those who live there are indeed our brothers and sisters.

Father God, Help me to understand the implications of what is happening between Israel and her neighbors and how it plays out in prophetic messages in Your Word. Amen.

➤ Day 222: OBEY FOR LONG LIFE
PASSAGE: **Deuteronomy 4:40**
VERSE: **Deuteronomy 4:40**

So you shall keep His statutes and His commandments which I am giving you today, that it may go well with you and with your children after you, and that you may live long on the land which the LORD your God is giving you for all time.

Is 'obedience' a word that sticks in your craw and makes your hackles rise? Does the thought of being held by a bunch of rules feel a little like living in a straight-jacket? I have talked before about us thinking we are free to make our own decisions, yet being held in sin's bondage and continually returning to the same ones over and over. Is that freedom? Are you free when alcohol, drugs, food or pornography become an obsession and take control of your life? Freedom from sin comes from obedience to holiness. Holiness comes from knowing God's commands and obeying them. Obedience is a choice—freedom is a blessing—holiness is a goal. The man who learns to walk each day in the footsteps of Jesus will understand that true freedom comes from the realization that you don't have to do the things which used to hold you in bondage. Less stress, fewer struggles and greater freedom will lead to life—real life. God was trying to explain that truth to Israel... before they took their first step into the freedom of the Promised Land.

COMMON GROUND: The desire of Israel's heart was to enter into and live in the land of God's promise to Abraham. God was about to give them the desire of their heart. The truth God faced was that giving them the desire of their heart could tear them away from Him. **HOLY GROUND:** God shouldn't have to wonder if His blessings will tear us from His hands. Holy people should be able to receive blessings and remain firmly grounded in obedience to the One who sends the blessings.

LORD, I fully understand that obedience requires effort and a different degree of faith than in other areas in my Christian walk. May I never receive from Your hands anything that would remove me from the shelter of those same hands. Amen.

➤ Day 223: MOSES, YOU PLAY MIDDLE-MAN
PASSAGE: Deuteronomy 5:24-28
VERSE: Deuteronomy 5:27

Go near and hear all that the LORD our God says; then speak to us all that the LORD our God speaks to you, and we will hear and do it.

"Here we are; send Moses!" That is the cry of the nation of Israel as they stood before *El Elyon* (the Most High God). They wanted His words—or did they? They wanted the guidance of *Jehovah-Raah* (the Shepherd)—or did they? They wanted His hedge of protection—well, of course they wanted that! The people were afraid of real contact with *Elohim* (God the Judge)... thus they wanted a "Middle-Man" to stand in the gap. Let Moses get zapped with a lightning bolt if *Adonai* (the LORD) gets angry. Let Moses stand in the presence of *Jehovah Tsidkenu* (the Righteous God). Moses is a good choice to encounter *Jehovah-Shalom* (the God of Peace) or *El Shaddai* (Almighty, all-Sufficient God). Yes, Moses was the one to send, but imagine what the rest of the congregation missed out on when they didn't have a personal encounter with *Jehovah Shammah* (the God who is always there) or *Jehovah Jireh* (their Provider God).

COMMON GROUND: Don't get hung up on the difficult to pronounce names of God. Just look at how He defines Himself—always there, Provider, Source of Peace, Shepherd, Master, Healer and Righteousness. If you want to get off common ground, learn who God really is. He is not a benevolent white-haired grandfather. He is power and majesty. **HOLY GROUND:** Study these names and begin to pray them back to the Father. Prepare your hearts for a genuine encounter with *Jehovah Sabaoth* (the LORD of Powers) and *Jehovah Nissi* (the God of Miracles). Rest in the arms of *Jehovah Rapha* (the God who Heals)… are you seeing what you have missed? We will study each Name of God in greater detail in later entries.

My Jesus, How can I forget Your Name? Yeshua! Jesus,
oh my Yeshua. You are the fullness of the prophets,
the Law and the love of Adonai. Amen.

➤ Day 224: IF ONLY THEY HAD MY HEART
PASSAGE: **Deuteronomy 5:29-33**
VERSE: **Deuteronomy 5:29**

"Oh that they had such a heart in them, that they would fear
Me and keep all My commandments always, that it may
be well with them and with their sons forever!"

Now that you know more about the character and names of God, we come to a place where you really encounter His heart. When Adam was created at the hands of his Creator, he was God's highest form of creation. Unlike everything else created, Adam had the image (or soul) of God within him. He could feel emotions, seek relationships, hunger for a deeper spiritual meaning, and not follow his flesh desires like the animals… because he had a sense of conviction, an inherent sense of right and wrong. God created man to fellowship with Him, to walk in obedience to Him, and to honor and revere Him as they walked forever together. Then sin entered the garden and man was separated from God. In today's passage we see God's heart breaking as He speaks the truth of how man would always be pulled away from holy fellowship with God by his flesh. *"Oh that they had such a heart in them, that they would fear Me and keep all My commandments always, that it may be well with them and with their sons forever!"*

COMMON GROUND: Can you hear the cry of God's heart? Do you realize how much He wants to have an intimate relationship with you? He is asking you to give your heart to Him, to share cherished fellowship and to walk in obedience. Don't give the common response and ignore the cry. **HOLY GROUND:** Our God is *El Qanna* (the Jealous God) who will fight for the hearts of His people. He will fight for your heart as surely as He will fight your battles beside you. Think about this—something not loved will not be fought for. We are so blessed to have a living God to serve.

Father, You longed so much for the hearts of man that You became flesh, dwelt among us and died to remove our sins. You were jealous for us. I am beginning to understand this in a new 'eyes-wide-open-to-see' light. Amen.

➤ Day 225: HOW TO LOVE GOD
PASSAGE: **Deuteronomy 6:3-5**
VERSE: **Deuteronomy 6:5**

You shall love the LORD your God with all your heart and with all your soul and with all your might.

As I wrote this entry and the two previous ones, I was humbled and filled with the overwhelming urge to tell you not to take one word too lightly. Do not read these devotionals without really absorbing them and asking God why you are reading them... *for such a time as this.* Going into a deeper walk with *Adonai* will require effort and a willingness to change your walking habits. Change is required because God will not settle for less than your all.

You shall love the LORD your God with all your heart and with all your soul and with all your might. What does that mean? He must become *El Shaddai* — all sufficient — in your life. He must be your first and last thought. He must be the single most important focus of your life. He must be the 'audience of One' you seek to please. He must be enough. Is He that important to you? If not, this is the day for change. Notice the requirements... *all your heart and with all your soul and with all your might*. Why love Him that way? Look at the promise of Matthew 6:33 "*...seek first His kingdom and His righteousness, and all these things will be added to you.*"

COMMON GROUND: Bend, stretch, breathe in, breathe out... are you exercising new faith muscles? Don't stop... feel the burn. That is your old half-hearted commitment — your lukewarm faith — being stretched and tested. Give Him your anemic past and walk into fullness and richness. I am your trainer... He is your source of strength. **HOLY GROUND:** We needed a little humor there... briefly... but the message is **dead serious**. Lukewarm, uncommitted, unchanged people will not be strong enough to walk into battles and fight mighty enemies. Just like in Moses' day, this is what we are called to do.

Spirit of God, You are Ruach HaKodesh (Spirit of God) and I will need all of Your teaching and insight as I step out in faith onto Holy Ground. Guide me, direct me, protect me, keep me... Amen.

➤ Day 226: HIDE MY WORD-USE IT!
PASSAGE: **Deuteronomy 6:6-9**
VERSE: **Deuteronomy 6:6-7**

These words, which I am commanding you today, shall be on your heart. You shall teach them diligently to your sons and shall talk of them when you sit in your house and when you walk by the way and when you lie down and when you rise up.

In the days of Jesus, the Jewish leaders seemed to have been keeping the words of the commands given in today's passage. They looked like they had God's word on their hearts. They were teaching them to Jewish youth in the synagogues. They talked about the laws of God endlessly... debating and debating... adding to it as suited their needs. They made sure to *bind them as a sign... as frontals on (their) foreheads*. The Pharisees and Sadducees wore small black boxes (phylacteries) strapped to their foreheads with portions of Scripture copied and placed inside. They wrote the Mosaic Law on their doorposts. Why then did Jesus challenge them and call them *whitewashed tombs which on the outside appeared beautiful, but inside were full of dead men's bones and all uncleanness?* (Matthew 23:27) Jesus challenged because He knew their hearts. He knew they were practicing religiosity, not faith. They had head knowledge but not heart knowledge.

COMMON GROUND: I believe that knowledge of the Word of God is absolutely vital to the effective Christian walk, but it has to go deeper than knowing some Scripture verses to recite. Memorized verses are no more life-changing than the Pledge of Allegiance—unless they enter into your heart and change your life. **HOLY GROUND:** The Bible is the life-transforming, truth-revealing, firm foundation-building, heart-strengthening, God-inspiring and spirit-building Word of God. Only a wholly dedicated, holy focused man will allow it to become his identity. Don't try to read it fast; it is not fast-food. It is sweet like honey to the tongue and is meant to be savored.

Father God, Make Your Word alive in my heart. Transform me from common to holy, from smoldering embers to a bright burning flame. Sanctify me in truth; and Your Word alone is truth. Amen.

➤ Day 227: BEWARE, LEST YOU FORGET
PASSAGE: **Deuteronomy 6:10-12**
VERSE: **Deuteronomy 6:12**

Then watch yourself, that you do not forget the LORD who brought you from the land of Egypt, out of the house of slavery.

It is time for a review of the past faithfulness of God in your life. Why do we need the review? Could it be because we are so quick to forget? Did you have breakfast this morning, dinner last night and food on the table last week? Do you have a roof over your head and a place to lay your head down at night? Do you have at least one person who loves you and cares about what happens to you? Can you see, hear, taste, touch, smell, walk, talk, laugh and cry? Is your heart beating? Are your lungs breathing? Is your blood circulating? How long has it been since you thanked Your Creator for those things—things we often take for granted? You forgot where those blessings came from, didn't you? *Then it shall come about when the LORD your God brings you into the land which He swore to your fathers... to give you, great and splendid cities which you did not build, and houses full of all good things which you did not fill, and hewn cisterns which you did not dig, vineyards and olive trees which you did not plant, and you eat and are satisfied, then watch yourself, that you do not forget the LORD.*

COMMON GROUND: This is sad but true, God knows each and every weakness in our lives. He knew before you were created that you would forget His myriad blessings. He knew you would take all He has provided for granted. He knew you would be like an ungrateful child asking, "Is that all the presents?" instead of someone who would be satisfied with what he has been given. **HOLY GROUND:** If you are reading this book you are richer than ninety-percent of all the people on the face of the earth! Do you feel rich? Do you feel blessed? Have you thanked Him today for all you have so graciously been given?

LORD, As I said in a former lesson... Thank You. Amen.

➤ Day 228: SIMPLE—DO WHAT'S RIGHT!
PASSAGE: **Deuteronomy 6:16-19**
VERSE: **Deuteronomy 6:18**

You shall do what is right and good in the sight of the LORD, that it may be well with you and that you may go in and possess the good land which the LORD swore to give your fathers.

What a revolutionary thought today's verse conjures up in our minds. Do it right; do it that way the first time and enjoy the fruits of your obedience. This reminds me of the words from Exodus chapter twenty in regards to the Fifth Commandment: *Honor your father and your mother, that your days may be prolonged in the land which the LORD your God gives you.* A common thread is woven through these calls for respect and compliance... they bring blessings! Long life, victories, possession of new lands, and enemies driven out from before the child of God are just a few of the generous gifts of God. Before you think obedience is all about getting blessings from *Jehovah Jireh* (God the Provider), remember this very real truth... we obey out of love and respect. Even if there were no blessing for obedience, we would still be called to observe and comply with His words.

COMMON GROUND: Do you understand better today than you did seven months ago when we started this journey together about how vitally important an obedient heart is in the hands of a loving God? Dig deeper; ask the Holy Spirit for wisdom; seek His face. **HOLY GROUND:** Here is a verse to get you started in seeking Biblical wisdom. *But if any of you lacks wisdom, let him ask of God, who gives to all generously and without reproach, and it will be given to him* (James 1:5). Let's go way back to the basics... ask—seek—knock—receive.

My Jesus, I desire a new wisdom, a spirit altering wisdom that comes only from You and Your awesome holy Word. Teach me until I am full and overflowing... You are my Instructor. Amen.

➤ Day 229: NO UNHOLY ALLIANCES!
PASSAGE: **Deuteronomy 7:2-4**
VERSE: **Deuteronomy 7:4**

For they will turn your sons away from following Me to serve other gods; then the anger of the LORD will be kindled against you and He will quickly destroy you.

Are you tired of sessions on obedience? Okay, I will talk about disobedience instead! God is abundantly fair. He gives the command; He tells why He is giving it; and He forewarns of the consequences of disobedience. Divided loyalties never work. God forbids intermarriage between believers and non-believers (unequal yoking), and throughout Scripture He cautions what happens when that command is disobeyed. In the days of Moses the command to not intermarry was to preserve the bloodline for the coming Messiah and to keep Israel single-minded and fully devoted to God. *You shall not intermarry with them; you shall not give your daughters to their sons, nor shall you take their daughters for your sons. For they will turn your sons away from following Me to serve other gods; then the anger of the LORD will be kindled against you and He will quickly destroy you.* Notice that God was very emphatic about how foreign wives would lead their husbands astray—thereby incurring His wrath and causing Him to destroy them.

COMMON GROUND: Why, when God explains the very real consequences of sin, do we still walk into right into it and then act surprised when the outcome is as promised? Why do people think they can get away with unequal yoking in marriage, friendships and business partnerships… when God has told them ahead of time that these alliances will bring destruction? **HOLY GROUND:** It is time in your journey of transformation for you to realize God loves you, wants the best for you, and warns you in advance about the high price of sin. Just like your earthly father may have said, "I am the father; do it because I love you—that's why. No negotiation required."

Father, Sin hurts me as much as it hurts our relationship.
Help me to make holy decisions at the start and avoid
paying for wrong ones later. Amen.

➤ ## Day 230: ABOVE ALL NATIONS
PASSAGE: **Deuteronomy 7:5-8**
VERSE: **Deuteronomy 7:6**

For you are a holy people to the LORD your God; the LORD your
God has chosen you to be a people for His own possession out of
all the peoples who are on the face of the earth.

Earlier we discussed whether or not Israel was truly special, chosen of God, set apart, and a blessed nation. Let's look at what God Himself said about choosing them. *For you are a holy people to the LORD your God; the LORD your God has chosen you to be a people for His own possession out of all the peoples who are on the face of the earth.* I would say that this verse in itself removes any doubt as to Israel being God's chosen possession. *The LORD did not set His love on you nor choose you because you were more in number than any of the peoples, for you were the fewest of all peoples...* Moses was making it clear that Israel wasn't the biggest, or the strongest, or the most prominent of all nations. He stated they were the smallest of all people groups when He selected them. *...because the LORD loved you and kept the oath which He swore to your forefathers, the LORD brought you out by a mighty hand and redeemed you from the house of slavery, from the hand of Pharaoh king of Egypt.* God had the nation of Israel standing at the entrance to the Promised Land for one reason and one reason only... He gave His promise to Abraham and, in spite of the shortcomings of his heirs, He would keep it. Plus, we already know that *God is not a man that He should lie.*

COMMON GROUND: Are you struggling with believing that out of all the people on the earth, all who ever lived or ever will live, that

God chose you? Do you sometimes doubt your salvation? (Salvation: see special section near back of this book.) In addition to just being foolish, I think Israel had a real issue with self-doubt. You know... a feeling of inadequacy before a holy, holy God. **HOLY GROUND:** *You formed my inward parts; You wove me in my mother's womb. I will give thanks to You, for I am fearfully and wonderfully made... my frame was not hidden from You, when I was made in secret... Your eyes have seen my unformed substance; and in Your book were all written the days that were ordained for me, when as yet there was not one of them.* (Psalms 139)

Father God, You did choose me! You did choose me! Amen.

➤ Day 231: CHOOSE HEAVEN OR HELL
PASSAGE: **Deuteronomy 7:9-11**
VERSE: **Deuteronomy 7:10**

...but repays those who hate Him to their faces, to destroy them;
He will not delay with him who hates Him,
He will repay him to his face.

God's abundant faithfulness is a recurring thread throughout these entries. He showed mercy—the people rebelled. He showed kindness—the people rejected Him. He showed love—they turned their backs to Him. He showed anger—and they didn't understand. For thousands and thousands of years, God has patiently dealt with the dismissal and rebuff of His people. In today's entry He reminds them of that past faithfulness. *He is God, the faithful God, who keeps His covenant and His loving-kindness to a thousandth generation with those who love Him and keep His commandments.* The covenant Adonai made with Abraham was renewed with Isaac, Jacob, Joseph, and all subsequent generations until Jesus came to completely fulfill the promise. During those years many rejected His commands and refused to honor Him... and the verse for today reveals to us that disobedience for His commands is hatred or irreverence for Him and will surely be punished.

COMMON GROUND: Do you have loved ones who reject God's command for holiness and choose not to serve Him? They may take that lightly, but after reading the verse of the day you shouldn't. **HOLY GROUND:** On their behalf you need to pray and intercede for them, seeking for the Holy Spirit to open their eyes to the truth before it is too late. They are one breath away from realizing their greatest nightmare.

Father God, I have loved ones who have chosen the purpose for their lives from the things of this world. LORD, they need You... not money, alcohol, sexual impurity or drugs. I lift up before Your throne. Father, call them to You, please. Amen.

➤ Day 232: BE BLESSED, BE LOVED
PASSAGE: **Deuteronomy 7:12-16**
VERSE: **Deuteronomy 7:13**

He will love you and bless you and multiply you; He will also bless the fruit of your womb and the fruit of your ground, your grain and your new wine and your oil, the increase of your herd and the young of your flock...

In a series of entries quite some time ago, we learned of the blessings and curses of God in great detail. Time for one of my not-so-gentle reminders. Actually, you will like being reminded of the blessings! *He will love you and bless you and multiply you; He will also bless the fruit of your womb...* That sounds great— lots of kids! *...and the fruit of your ground, your grain and your new wine and your oil...* Who wouldn't want plenteous gardens, rich grain harvests, lush vineyards and healthy fresh olive oil? *...the increase of your herd and the young of your flock...* Lots of cattle, plenty of milk to drink and beef to eat, lambs for warm wool for clothing—who would complain about that? *You shall be blessed above all peoples...* More blessed than any other people. This alone is worth the price of serving God. *The LORD will remove from you all sickness; and He will not put on you any of the harmful diseases of Egypt which you have known, but He will lay them on all who hate you.* No pestilence, plagues, disease or famine for those who are His, but all would come upon their enemies. *You shall consume all the peoples whom the LORD your God will deliver to you...* Victory in all the battles we face! The blessings of God are amazing and abundant. Who wouldn't want to be on the receiving end?

COMMON GROUND: Here is the rub. The blessings come when you <u>listen</u> to these judgments and <u>keep</u> and <u>do</u> them... *that the LORD your God will keep with you His covenant and His loving-kindness which He swore to your forefathers.* **HOLY GROUND:** No free lunch offered here either. Effort is mandated, obedience demanded, and change required. How else would our Lord know we are sincere?

LORD, Looking at what I can <u>get</u> from You instead of what I can <u>do</u> for You has been my past motivation. As of today, I will seek to hear, keep and carry out the charges You give to me. Amen.

➤ ## Day **233**: NO PLACE WITH OTHER GODS
PASSAGE: **Deuteronomy 7:25-26**
VERSE: **Deuteronomy 7:25**

The graven images of their gods you are to burn with fire; you shall not covet the silver or the gold that is on them, nor take it for yourselves, or you will be snared by it, for it is an abomination to the LORD your God.

As Israel prepared to move into the land of God's covenant, God knew they would be tempted by the things they would see in these pagan nations. Natural curiosity would have to be curbed or they would be inclined to pick up idols of gold and silver and keep them as souvenirs from the journey. Israel had already proven their lack of self-discipline—remember the golden calf incident while Moses was on Mount Sinai receiving the Ten Commandments from God? These idols would be an abomination amidst the Israelite nation which was committing to be holy before their God. The command was given for them to crush and burn every idol, image, altar, pole and high place they encountered. *You shall not bring an abomination into your house, and like it come under the ban; you shall utterly detest it and you shall utterly abhor it, for it is something banned.* Knowing the history of the Hebrew people, do you think the command kept them from this sin?

COMMON GROUND: Dabbling with any religion or spiritual belief other than those of the Christian faith is the same as picking up the abominations mentioned above. Wicca, sorcery, tarot cards, psychic practices, palm readings and astrology are all abominations before our LORD. **HOLY GROUND:** No more dabbling. You can't serve two gods... and the One I serve is not willing to share you with anyone or anything else—especially another god!

My Jesus, Show me what needs crushed or removed. Show me anything I have made an idol in my heart. No divided loyalties... and no abhorrent practices... I am all Yours. Amen.

➤ Day 234: NOT BY BREAD ALONE
PASSAGE: **Deuteronomy 8:1-3**
VERSE: **Deuteronomy 8:3**

He humbled you and let you be hungry, and fed you with manna which you did not know, nor did your fathers know, that He might make you understand that man does not live by bread alone, but man lives by everything that proceeds out of the mouth of the LORD.

W hy the wilderness? Why would God put someone in the wilderness for forty years... away from comfort, home, abundant provision and every desire of the heart? Maybe—just maybe—that is the only way to get their attention. Maybe all the comforts have to be removed in order for us to recognize our utter dependence on Him. Why do we have to come to the end of our own abilities and strength before we call upon *Jehovah Jireh*, our Provider God? The simple truth is that we forget where our next bite of bread, our next breath, our next drink of water, and the next beat of our heart comes from. He is our Source... yet we, like Israel, forget this deep and abiding truth. Hindsight will be a powerful reminder of God's provision for the Hebrew nation. *He **humbled you** and **let you be hungry**, and **fed you with manna** which you did not know, nor did your fathers know, **that He might make you understand** that man does not live by bread alone, but **man lives by everything that proceeds out of the mouth of the LORD**.*

COMMON GROUND: *You shall remember all the way which the LORD your God has **led you in the wilderness** these forty years, that He might **humble you, testing you, to know what was in your heart**, whether you would keep His commandments or not.* **HOLY GROUND:** Wilderness journeys are difficult, unpleasant, dry, and often heartbreaking. But then, isn't that the whole purpose of the journey—to break hard hearts and cause man to realize his need for his God?

Father, Humble me. Let me be hungry; feed me with Your
provision; and make me understand that I live by Your Word.
The wilderness is where You lead me to test my commitment and
my obedience. Just please don't leave me there, Jehovah Shammah.
Amen.

➤ Day 235: INDESTRUCTIBLE GARMENTS
PASSAGE: **Deuteronomy 8:4-5**
VERSE: **Deuteronomy 8:4**

Your clothing did not wear out on you,
nor did your foot swell these forty years.

J.C. Penney would hate this entry! Imagine forty years without new clothes! People in Moses' day didn't have walk-in closets full of clothes for different seasons. Most had one change of clothing and, because the weather didn't vary much in the Middle East, they had no need for anything other than an additional cloak during cooler times. Even if they weren't clothes hounds, their garments had to wear out from every day use. The amazing verse above tells us: *Your clothing did not wear out on you... these forty years.* Remember, these were not forty years in bed. Rather, they were forty years of days with repeated packing, moving and resetting camp. This was a nomadic nation on the move (and really going nowhere). How was this possible? They served a big God who re-knit frayed fabrics, strengthened weak seams, grew the clothes as the children grew, and kept His people clothed for forty years... without a Wal-Mart in the middle of the wilderness! As a woman with persistent foot problems, the non-swelling feet sound wonderful to me; but I don't want to go into the wilderness to have Him prove He cares about my feet.

COMMON GROUND: Do you believe in God's complete provision for your every need? I didn't say your every *desire*, but your every *need*. As common people do, the Hebrews probably gave no thought whatsoever to their clothes not wearing out; they were too focused on their lack of food and water to see God's provision for their protection from the scorching sun. **HOLY GROUND:** Look backward over your lifetime at things God has supplied and you have failed to acknowledge or thank Him for. Holy people are grateful for everything. They are always looking for things to praise Him for... breath, vision, food, shelter, family, sunshine, puppies, children's laughter, rainbows, gentle breezes...

Spirit of God, If gratitude is a requirement for holy living… please open my eyes to any ingratitude within my distracted heart. Amen.

➤ Day 236: ADULTEROUS HEARTS
PASSAGE: **Deuteronomy 8:6-14**
VERSE: **Deuteronomy 8:14**

Then your heart will become proud and you will forget the LORD your God who brought you out from the land of Egypt, out of the house of slavery.

If I were to ask you to define adultery, how would you define it? If you are like most other people you would say it is sharing intimacy with someone you aren't married to, while still married to another. Marital adultery can be both physical and emotional. You can love and lust over someone and be guilty of adultery just as if you acted physically to consummate the relationship. Emotional adultery is just as damaging as is physical adultery. Christians are referred to in Scripture as the Bride of Christ. He is our Bridegroom and expects fidelity from us to maintain our covenant relationship. Spiritual adultery—having a relationship with other gods, other forms of religion, or someone who takes us away from Him—destroys our covenant union. Today's passage states …*your heart will become proud and you will forget the LORD your God.* He was cautioning Israel—not that they *might* forget His faithfulness after He sent them water, rich harvests, precious metals, shelter and the like, but that they *would* do that. I am certain God is issuing that same warning to us today. "You may live in a land of great abundance and freedom, but you are not free to worship other gods, serve money or obsess with self. I alone am your God, your Provider."

COMMON GROUND: If you have watched someone deal with an adulterous spouse you know how devastating it is for the one who has been betrayed. Imagine then how Jesus (the perfect picture of marital covenant relationships) feels when He is cast off for the latest religious craze or self-absorption in your life. **HOLY GROUND:** *El Qanna*—our Jealous LORD—requires fidelity, devotion, dedication and commitment from us. After all, we required the same of Him when we called upon His precious blood to redeem us from our sins.

Father God, Remind me constantly of who You are... lest I forget and commit spiritual adultery. My heart breaks at the thought. Amen.

➤ Day 237: PRIDE WILL DIVIDE US
PASSAGE: **Deuteronomy 8:15-20**
VERSE: **Deuteronomy 8:17**

Otherwise, you may say in your heart,
"My power and the strength of my hand made me this wealth."

How does the spiritual adultery we talked about in entry 236 manifest itself in our relationship with Christ? When does total dependence on Him turn to no need for Him? The verse above gives us a great glimpse of that transition. When we forget that He is our supplier and provider and begin to take credit for all that happens in our lives, we become self-sufficient—and self-sufficient people don't need anyone else. God knew that Israel would forget He gave them wells they didn't dig, houses they didn't build and vineyards they didn't plant. He knew and still gave them those things. He also knows we will forget that He gives us miraculous bodies with muscles to work, brains to calculate, gifts and abilities to perform as we need to, and that He opens doors of opportunity before us. Instead of giving Him all glory, we suffer with 'I Disease.' I did it—I am so good—I am successful—I built this business—I led my son to Christ. And we find fault with Israel, how hypocritical?

COMMON GROUND: Today I want you to look in the spiritual mirror. Weigh yourself against this entry and the passage of Scripture it is lifted from. What do you see in the mirror? Are you suffering with 'I Disease' and self-glorification? Is it time for a spiritual heart surgery? **HOLY GROUND:** Until we realize that without Him we can do nothing, and that apart from Him we have nothing but a temporary identity here on this earth, we will never measure up. Jesus, the perfect Son of God, said in John 15, *"I am the vine, you are the branches; he who abides in Me and I in him, he bears much fruit, for **apart from Me you can do nothing."***

Yes, LORD, that disease plagues me. So does my reluctance to give You credit for my successes. Instead I take credit for my own glory. You have begun the good work—please continue until it is completed. Amen.

➤ Day 238: GOD GOES BEFORE YOU
PASSAGE: **Deuteronomy 9:3-6**
VERSE: **Deuteronomy 9:3**

Know therefore today that it is the LORD your God who is crossing over before you as a consuming fire. He will destroy them and He will subdue them before you, so that you may drive them out and destroy them quickly, just as the LORD has spoken to you.

*I*t is not for your righteousness or for the uprightness of your heart *that you are going to possess their land, but it is because of the wickedness of these nations that the LORD your God is driving them out before you, in order to confirm the oath which the LORD swore to your fathers, to Abraham, Isaac and Jacob.* Maybe the reminder God was giving to Israel in this passage is one we need to hear today. God was making certain His people realized that the nations they were to dispossess were evil—and that alone was the reason they would defeat them. Israel had no room to feel smug, because they had proven their own unrighteousness many times over. God was keeping His promise to Abraham—the covenant from hundreds of years before—for his heirs to have the Promised Land. He would keep His promise, but would never excuse the failures of the

Hebrews. The people also needed to remember that any victories were because God went before them and subdued those nations.

COMMON GROUND: Have you faced mighty enemies since you began your walk with Christ? Have you had victories? Look closely; can you see where He opened doors, prepared pathways and fought for you? If you don't see that, then perhaps you are looking through 'self-tinted' eyeglasses. **HOLY GROUND:** God will fight for you and will open doors before you, but only for so long. Holy people are aware that He goes before them... blazing new pathways.

My Jesus, I love the thought of You charging in front of me into foreign territories, blazing before me clear paths and guarding over me like a protective mother hen. Amen.

➤ ## Day 239: FORTY DAY INTERCESSION
PASSAGE: **Deuteronomy 9:9-18**
VERSE: **Deuteronomy 9:18**

I fell down before the LORD, as at the first, forty days and nights; I neither ate bread nor drank water, because of all your sin which you had committed in doing what was evil in the sight of the LORD to provoke Him to anger.

Intercessory prayer, coupled with fasting, is a powerful tool in the hand of the believer. Praying for spiritual breakthroughs, deliverance from addictions, relationship problems and restored health are examples of when deep intercessory prayer is needed. In this entry we hear Moses tell how he spent forty days on Mt. Sinai interceding for the people God gave him charge over. *When I went up to the mountain to receive the tablets of stone, the tablets of the covenant which the LORD had made with you, then I remained on the mountain **forty days and nights; I neither ate bread nor drank water**.* Moses then descended the face of the mountain, only to find the people cavorting shamelessly in their sin and worshipping a golden idol they had formed and ordained their new god. In anger he threw the stone tablets of the Commandments to the ground—smashing them and shattering any dreams he had that Israel would ever change. We talked about this earlier in this book, but look at today's key verse. *I fell down before the LORD, **as at the first**, forty days and nights; I neither ate bread nor drank water, because of all your sin which you had committed in doing what was evil in the sight of the LORD to provoke Him to anger.* Sounds to me like Moses was one of the most committed intercessors of all time... and for people who did not care!

COMMON GROUND: Are there people you have prayed for over the years without seeing visible breakthrough? Can you imagine forty days of fasting and praying, having your hopes dashed, and then forty more days of intercession? Does this make you realize how much prayer is sometimes required? Does it step up your previous commitment to *pray without ceasing*? **HOLY GROUND:** If all prayers were answered immediately, we would treat God like a jolly Santa Claus—you know how it goes, write it on a list and get it under the tree. Intercessory prayer is selfless and thankless work. Couple that with self-denying fasting for genuine spiritual breakthrough.

Father, I have given up far too easily in my intercessions. I have a whole new dimension of respect for Moses, who loved Israel in spite of Israel. Make me an intercessor for the salvation of my friends and loved ones, for healing and for liberty. Amen.

➤ Day 240: CIRCUMCISE YOUR HEART
PASSAGE: **Deuteronomy 10:12-19**
VERSE: **Deuteronomy 10:16-17**

So circumcise your heart, and stiffen your neck no longer. For the LORD your God is the God of gods and the LORD of LORDS the great, the mighty, and the awesome God who does not show partiality nor take a bribe.

What a strange command *circumcise your heart* is! The Hebrew circumcision ritual was performed on all males on the eighth day of life, placing a sign upon their flesh to signify that they belonged to *Jehovah* God. We understand that, but what does circumcision have to do with the heart? *Dictionary.com* gives a secondary definition for circumcision as *a process to purify spiritually*. That makes much more sense. God repeatedly told people they had hardened hearts which kept them from obedience to His commands. If circumcise literally means to cut around (circum) and cut away (cise), then we see how that process could be used to remove the hardened exterior of a stubborn heart. A proud stiffened neck would also need spiritual surgery… the kind God alone can do.

COMMON GROUND: Is there any part of your life needing circumcision? Do you have hidden sin? You know, it really isn't hidden from your Creator. Are you dealing with a poisonous tongue, a critical spirit, a judgmental attitude, or an abundance of pride? That tongue needs to be tamed; that criticism needs be tempered; your judging others needs to stop; and your pride—if not broken—will keep you from full fellowship with God. **HOLY GROUND:** I have stated before that the journey I have made while writing has not always been an easy one. I have been made fully aware of my tongue and the fires it starts, of how I judge and criticize others, and how my pride and self-sufficiency keep me from being fully subservient to the LORD. The journey is quite treacherous, but the destination is perfect.

Spirit of God, I have mistakenly thought I could keep some of my sins hidden. Unfortunately—or should I say fortunately—these entries have made that sin blaringly obvious. Circumcise my heart. Amen.

> # Day 241: HE IS YOUR PRAISE!
PASSAGE: **Deuteronomy 10:20-22**
VERSE: **Deuteronomy 10:21**

He is your praise and He is your God, who has done these great
and awesome things for you which your eyes have seen.

Let's take today's lesson and simply praise God our Father, Jesus His Son, and the Holy Spirit, for they are worthy of all our praise. Father God of all creation, indeed the universe does declare Your majesty. From the smallest creature to the greatest mountain, Your glory is there. From the depths of the oceans to the tops of the highest clouds, Your wonder is revealed. When I look upon the first flowers of spring, the colored patchwork You paint in the Fall, and the first tiny perfect snowflake of winter—Your imagination is unveiled. When I think You created man in Your image and gave him free will instead of forcing him to love You—I am bowled over by Your love. And my sweet Savior Jesus, I thank You for Your obedience and Your willingness to leave the splendor of Heaven, to come here under humble and difficult circumstances and to suffer rejection by those You came to save. I praise that You are the perfect fulfillment of the Old Testament prophetic Word. No... that You are the perfect fulfillment of all of God's Holy Word! How can a heart saved by grace ever forget what that first moment of freedom from sin felt like? I praise You, Lamb of God, Prince of Peace, LORD of LORDS, Bright Morning Star, Redeemer, Suffering Servant... *Yeshua*—my Jesus. Lastly, to You, sweet Holy Spirit, my Teacher, my Conviction, my Guide, my Wisdom... I praise You. How could I ever wish to walk through this dark world without the presence of the *Ruach HaKodesh*... the Holy Spirit of God, living within my heart? *Jehovah* God, *Yeshua* my Messiah and *Ruach HaKodesh*... my heart bursts with praises for You!

COMMON GROUND: Did that feel uncomfortable for you? The goal of this passage is to bring you to a place where praise and worship naturally flow from your lips to the throne room of God. Work on this aspect of your faith walk. **HOLY GROUND:** Praise and worship flow from grateful hearts... praise, praise, praise His Name! You may need to reread this entry several days in a row to become familiar with this kind of worship and prayer, yes, it is a form of prayer.

Father God, You are worthy of all my praise. Amen.

➤ Day 242: YOUR EYES HAVE SEEN
PASSAGE: **Deuteronomy 11:1-7**
VERSE: **Deuteronomy 11:2 & 7**

Know this day that I am not speaking with your sons
who have not known and who have not seen the discipline of
the LORD your God—His greatness, His mighty hand and His
outstretched arm; but your own eyes have seen all the
great work of the LORD which He did.

As Moses reminded the Hebrew nation of all they had to be grateful for and for all the reasons they should obey God's commands, he reminded them that they weren't basing their faith upon past stories handed down through the generations. Some of them were children who actually watched their deliverance from Pharaoh's bondage. They watched the Red Sea part, the Egyptian army drowned, the manna fall from heaven, and the water flow from the rock. They watched Moses come down the mountain after an amazing encounter with God, heard the Law defined, listened to the negative spy report, and heard God pronounce forty years of wandering in the wilderness for the generations over age twenty. They had wandered those forty years, had their clothes remain sturdy, and had watched as Moses interceded time and time again for Israel. They had watched the miracles and the work of God on their behalf... yet they had rejected Him time and time again. Somehow it makes no sense at all.

COMMON GROUND: It is easy to understand uncertainty and doubt by people who have never seen the hand of God or felt the presence of God in their lives. I find it harder to comprehend of someone walking for a while with Him and then turning their back or being led astray. Maybe 'drift' is the cause. We slowly drift away from our early passion and don't even realize we have lost our anchoring. **HOLY GROUND:** A recounting of God's past blessings can be the prescription for avoiding that drift. When we are faithful to remember His amazing works He is faithful to prepare new ones for us. Look back—as a reminder; live in the present; and press on toward the goal.

*LORD, I remember the time when You _____,
and the times when You_____ , and I haven't
thanked You recently for_____. Amen.*

➤ Day 243: A LAND GOD CARES FOR
PASSAGE: Deuteronomy 11:8-12
VERSE: Deuteronomy 11:12

*...a land for which the LORD your God cares; the
eyes of the LORD your God are always on it,
from the beginning even to the end of the year.*

When God promised Israel a land of milk and honey, what was He actually promising? *The land into which you are about to cross to possess it... drinks water from the rain of heaven, a land for which the LORD your God cares; the eyes of the LORD your God are always on it.* Israel, though in a region of the world known for being arid is promised to be a land where rain would fall from God's heaven. A well-watered land affords bountiful crops, healthy livestock and satisfied thirsts. Most of the people preparing to enter into the land of Canaan have never seen abundant rain. God reminds them how difficult the work is in arid lands... *not like the land of Egypt from which you came, where you used to sow your seed and water it with your foot like a vegetable garden.* In Egypt, 97% of the population lived within three miles of the Nile River—the sole source of water in a land which saw little or no rainfall each year. Water had to be hauled from the Nile to cook, clean, water animals and water gardens. The land was abundantly fertile, but people in Moses' day had not devised modern irrigation systems to store water from spring floods to last in times of draught. The Hebrew slaves likely carried the water for those they served, as well as for their own needs. A land flowing with milk and honey—and falling rain—had to sound wonderful to them.

COMMON GROUND: Do you believe God only wants the best for His children? Notice that He delivered them from the draughts of Egypt in order to deliver them to the watered land of Israel. He only wanted the best for them... yet they fought Him every step of the way. **HOLY GROUND:** Are you missing out on the best God wants for you—by settling for less than His perfect will? Talk to Him today about any stubborn streaks left in your spirit. Like an earthly father, He wants to care for your every need, but will not force you to accept His grace, mercy and blessings.

My Jesus, I confess that I still settle for less than Your best and Your perfect will for me. I run ahead of You, think I know better than You, and take matters into my own hands. Then... I fail. Amen.

➤ Day 244: LATTER RAIN
PASSAGE: **Deuteronomy 11:13-15**
VERSE: **Deuteronomy 11:14**

*That He will give the rain for your land in its season,
the early and late rain that you may gather in your grain
and your new wine and your oil.*

As you read the passages of Scripture for each entry, I pray that you are seeing the *ifs* and *thens* within the verses. God was calling the people to obedience and *if* they followed His commands and did things the way He ordained, *then* they received His bounty. In today's verse we see His promise to send the early and latter rains upon the land. As we learned yesterday, rain is vital for the land to flourish. The early rain falls in October or November and brings with it the celebration of *Rosh Hoshanah* (the beginning of the year in the Hebrew calendar). During that time the people would harvest grapes, olives, and other fruits. It was also when the barley was sown. The late (latter) rain was the spring rain which fell in March and April when Passover and the Feast of Unleavened Bread were celebrated. The barley was harvested then, and seven weeks later the wheat was harvested. These crops would only thrive if the rains came in their respective seasons. God would be faithful *if* the people remained faithful to Him. He would send drought and famine *if* they didn't. Unfortunately, they would see many periods of drought and famine.

COMMON GROUND: We want God's blessing and provision without His requirements, and Israel was no different. If you knew your food six months from now depended on obedience today... would you obey? Or, would you compromise and worry about the consequences later? Israel gave little thought to long-term consequences of sin. **HOLY GROUND:** Every sin has a subsequent consequence. Some are short-term, immediate and quickly rectified. Others seem to impact our lives forever, bringing unimaginable hardship. If you could look ahead and see your consequences before you sin, would it keep you from sinning? We need to walk as if we can see them—and choose obedience.

Father, There are things I have done which still cause me pain and shame. Father, from this day on help me to be forward-thinking. I want Your rains in their season. Amen.

➤ Day 245: BE NOT DECEIVED
PASSAGE: **Deuteronomy 11:16-17**
VERSE: **Deuteronomy 11:16**

*Beware that your hearts are not deceived, and that you
do not turn away and serve other gods and worship them.*

Let me start this entry with a serious question... don't be too quick to respond... think before you answer. Do you think your heart could be deceived into serving other gods? You probably think other gods would be from other religions—Wicca, Hindu, Islam or Buddhism, but other gods don't always manifest themselves in the form of religion. Let me rephrase the question. Do you think money, fame, material possessions, beauty, flesh lusts, drugs, alcohol or pornography could draw you away from your worship of God? Notice the first word of the verse above: Beware! That word is an explicit warning that reveals a sad truth—we can be deceived! Even the most dedicated Christian can be drawn into Satan's web of deceit—and make no mistake about it... that is his ultimate goal. John 10:10 tells us, *The thief comes only to steal and kill and destroy; I came that they may have life, and have it abundantly.* Jesus is warning you. Jesus Christ is telling you to be aware that the enemy is plotting to *kill* your commitment to Him, *steal* your peace and *destroy* your eternal reward. No wonder God so often warned the nation of Israel to beware, guard their hearts, remain alert, be vigilant, and watch that they not be deceived.

COMMON GROUND: Let me ask the question again. Do you think your heart could be deceived into serving other gods? When any man says he cannot be deceived, he is putting a target on his back and inviting the arrows of the Devil. **HOLY GROUND:** We must remain poor in spirit—realizing that only through the strength of God can we survive the battle with the Enemy's unseen forces. Without the shield of faith, the breastplate of righteousness, the helmet of salvation and the sword of the spirit (the Holy Bible)—we are powerless.

Spirit of God, Arm and equip me to be strong in the fiercest tempta-
tion, the greatest testing, and in the deceitfully calm and safe days
when I let my guard down. I can be led astray—that is why I need
You, Holy Spirit, to walk with me into each battle. Amen.

➤ Day 246: MY WORD—YOUR HEART
PASSAGE: **Deuteronomy 11:18-20**
VERSE: **Deuteronomy 11:18**

You shall therefore impress these words of mine on your
heart and on your soul; and you shall bind them as a sign on your
hand, and they shall be as frontals on your forehead.

George, a customer at our bookstore, came in and asked for a poster or large plaque with the Ten Commandments on it to hang near the door of his house. He had been studying Deuteronomy and wanted God's moral law written on the doorpost of his house as God commanded. George wanted to be reminded every time he came in or went out the door that he was to *love the LORD His God with all his heart and soul* (the first four Commandments) and *to love his neighbor as himself* (the last six). This dedicated Christian man wanted this not only for himself but for his sons and anyone else who stepped through his door. Folks, there is only one way to *impress these words of mine* (God's) *on your heart and on your soul*, and that is through committed study of the Bible. Scripture doesn't enter your spirit through osmosis. It doesn't change your life by hearing it for an hour on Sunday morning. It doesn't transform you into God's image because your grandmother was a believer. Scripture must be pored over, studied, meditated upon, digested and loved in order for it to change your life and reveal truth to you.

COMMON GROUND: Do you dedicate time every day to reading the Bible... other than what you are getting in these devotionals? Have you convinced yourself you cannot understand it, or that history is boring? Have you learned anything here that shows you that Bible history is applicable in your life today? Are you ready to commit to growing through study of the Word? **HOLY GROUND:** You will get out of your relationship with the LORD a measure equal to that which your pour into it. Pour in half-hearted effort—get out a half-hearted commitment. Holy people have an eager desire (hunger) for Him. Do you hunger?

Father God, I am ready to go to a higher level in my relationship with You. I will need the Spirit to reveal all truth to me on this journey. Give me sound judgment, deep discernment, godly wisdom and eye-opening instruction. I am hungry! Amen.

➤ # Day 247: CHECKPOINT #2
PASSAGE: **Philippians 3:7-14**
VERSE: **Philippians 3:14**

I press on toward the goal for the prize of the upward call of God in Christ Jesus.

Unless you are sleeping, you see that I have taken you into a New Testament passage and verse. Now that you are two-thirds of the way finished with this book, let's evaluate how you are growing through this *Transforming Journey.* Are you better able to understand how to study and apply Scriptural applications to your personal faith walk than you were on Day One? Can you see the personal involvement God longs to have with His children—and can you see where He has proven Himself to be involved in your life? The letter to the church at Philippi was written by the Apostle Paul who had a life-changing encounter with Jesus Christ which left him broken, blinded, humbled, convicted and forever ruined for the ordinary. In this Bible passage we see that all the things he once counted as gain he was willing to lose in order to become a servant of Christ. He admitted that his righteousness didn't come from Mosaic Law, which he had fought hard to protect, but instead from his encounter with Jesus and his commitment to follow Him. Lastly, Paul says, *"I*

314

press on so that I may lay hold of that for which also I was laid hold of by Christ Jesus."

COMMON GROUND: Paul was never satisfied with the medi-ocre or lukewarm. He burned hot for Christ. That burning passion led him to be beaten, shipwrecked, despised and imprisoned—and to count those things blessings—for he was worthy to suffer for the cause of Christ and the spread of the Gospel message. **HOLY GROUND:** My prayer is that you are more willing to *press on toward the goal* so you too may *lay hold of that for which Christ laid hold on you.* Holy people don't give up... they fight to the finish... to get their reward!

LORD, I press on toward perfection in You. Amen.

➤ Day 248: GOD'S CHILDREN FEARED
PASSAGE: **Deuteronomy 11:24-25**
VERSE: **Deuteronomy 11:25**

No man will be able to stand before you; the LORD your God will lay the dread of you and the fear of you on all the land on which you set foot, as He has spoken to you.

After our brief detour for a Checkpoint, let's turn our focus back to the Hebrew people who were being reminded of God's past faithfulness, being encouraged about His future provision and being strengthened in the knowledge that *El Shaddai* (God Almighty) was going to walk with them in the journey ahead. What an amazing promise this is... *Every place on which the sole of your foot treads shall be yours.* The land before them likely seemed formidable and vast, but in reality all of Israel's land holdings equal 10,762 square miles—as compared to 96,810 square miles in the state of Michigan alone. Land size didn't seem so overwhelming—but the people living on the land did not want to give it up. Israel was walking into a battle for the land of God's covenant with Abraham, but they were assured by Moses that no man would be able to stand up to them and that God would put a fear (dread) of them in the hearts of their enemies. Imagine God dropping you in the middle of Lower Michigan and saying, "Take off walking. Every place you lay your foot will belong to you. Don't worry about those who own the land and don't wish to give it up... because I have given it to you... and I am God!"

COMMON GROUND: If you were given the mission to stake out the land, how far and how fast would you walk? The question may seem foolish, but the reality is that some of us are so firmly situated in our comfort zones that we would say, "No thanks, God. Send someone else to take the land." Is that you, or would you take off on a dead run to claim all the ground you could cover? **HOLY GROUND:** God has given you a testimony of His faithfulness so you can share it, causing the people around you to be amazed at His provision. If you use your witness you will take ground for Christ... and then others will learn to fear, revere and serve Him as you do.

My Jesus, The fertile land is before me; now the seed needs to be sown. I claim for You all the land I seed... and all the hearts I seed it in. LORD, harvest hearts, take Satan's ground, and show your face. Amen.

➤ Day 249: BLESSINGS & CURSES
PASSAGE: **Deuteronomy 11:26-32**
VERSE: **Deuteronomy 11:26**

See, I am setting before you today a blessing and a curse.

We have discussed in previous entries about blessings for obedience and curses for disobedience. Today we see God telling the people very emphatically that the choice is theirs. *"I am setting before you today a blessing and a curse: the blessing, if you listen to the commandments of the LORD your God... and the curse, if you do not listen to the commandments of the LORD your God, but turn aside from the way which I am commanding you today."* God was putting the proverbial ball in Israel's court. They could dribble it, handle it well, guard it and ultimately score the goal of all the blessings God had in store for their obedience. Or... they could fumble it, trip over their own shoelaces, and ultimately pass the ball off to the enemy. If you know anything about Israel's history, you already know they will drop and dribble and score victory after victory for the enemy. Why, when God is so generous as to give His children free will, do we so rarely choose the blessings through obedience? The answer is we allow our flesh to control our lives. What power the flesh has!

COMMON GROUND: We can judge the Hebrew people, but then we had better not look in our own spiritual mirror. God says to honor marriage vows and He will bless the family unit... and we commit adultery. He promises to provide all we need if we trust Him... and we seek instead after what we want and reject Him. **HOLY GROUND:** The obedience ball is in your court. It will not always be easy to dribble—and the enemy players will try to snatch it from you—but press on down the court within the boundaries and S-C-O-R-E the goal! Eternal victory is waiting at the final buzzer.

Father, I need to develop my handling skills if I want to win this game. I cannot afford for anyone to steal my relationship with You from me through my disobedience, or from my being caught off guard. Amen.

➤ Day 250: MAN-MADE RELIGIONS
PASSAGE: **Deuteronomy 12:1-14**
VERSE: **Deuteronomy 12:8**

You shall not do at all what we are doing here today, every man doing whatever is right in his own eyes...

Today I want to tackle the difficult topic of politically correct Christian practices. Since coming to know Christ in 1996, I have heard hundreds of believers talk about not wanting to force their beliefs on others, not wanting to be 'intolerant' to others' beliefs, and being afraid of retribution if they do share faith 'with the wrong person.' To start off, is there a wrong person to witness to? Who are we to judge whether they are wrong or right for God's kingdom? If we look at today's passage we see what God thinks about political correctness when it comes to being tolerant to other practices... like sorcery, witchcraft, psychic practices, tarot card readings and such. In Moses' day God was telling the Hebrews to not allow any of the evil practices and idols of the nations to survive when they went in to take the land. *You shall tear down their altars and smash their sacred pillars and burn their Asherim with fire, and you shall cut down the engraved images of their gods and obliterate their name from that place.* Hmmm... that doesn't sound very 'tolerant' to me! It actually sounds like a command to speak out, get rid of, and fight against the promotion of evil in our land—and to remove the temptation of compromise.

COMMON GROUND: When we allow the political correctness doctrines so prevalent in society today to dictate with whom and when we can share Christ, we are bowing to the gods of nationalism and disobeying the God of the Christian church. You don't have to be obnoxious... but you are called to Go and Tell! **HOLY GROUND:** Being discreet is not the same as being silenced. I didn't hear God telling the nation of Israel to ask permission to tear down those altars... they already had permission. If we know people caught up in occult practices, we are obligated to speak truth into their lives and hopefully move them from dangerous altars at which they worship.

Spirit of God, Give me open doors, opportunities, and Your wisdom as I expand my boundaries and share Jesus with those who are seeking after other gods and religious practices. Make me bold yet kind, strong yet gentle, and straightforward yet loving. Amen.

➤ Day **251**: BEWARE! FALSE PROPHETS
PASSAGE: **Deuteronomy 13:1-5**
VERSE: **Deuteronomy 13:3**

You shall not listen to the words of that prophet or that dreamer of dreams; for the LORD your God is testing you to find out if you love the LORD your God with all your heart and with all your soul.

As you grow in your personal faith walk, and you diligently apply yourself to learning the Scriptures, you will develop a new level of discernment which will help you to readily recognize false prophets and false doctrines when they present themselves before you. I dedicated a whole chapter to this topic in *About Face!* but will touch on it here. Warnings about false prophets and false teachers are ubiquitous throughout the Bible, but I like the dire warnings of Jesus in Matthew 7:15: *Beware of the false prophets, who come to you in sheep's clothing, but inwardly are ravenous wolves.* As long as there are people on the earth there will be false teachings and new religions—a virtual smorgasbord where man can pick and choose their *Religion D'Jour.* These false teachers' messages speak to who we want God to be, as opposed to whom He truly is. They are soft-selling a manufactured god because they think the God who requires holiness is too hard to please. Some things never change. This was happening thousands of years ago in Moses' day... and is happening across the world (and in the Christian church) today.

COMMON GROUND: The Matthew verse above is followed by *You will know them by their fruits.* To be able to identify good fruit and differentiate between it and bad fruit, you need to grow and learn. If you want to be in God's will you must be equipped to not fall for false doctrines. **HOLY GROUND:** Growth always presents a challenge. Those who are challenged and wish to grow will stay and keep feeding at the growth trough. Those who don't want to step up to the challenge will find a less challenging place to feed.

Father God, Give me the knowledge and instincts to discern between false prophets and Your prophets, false teachers and Biblical teachers, false doctrines and Your doctrines. I want to feed at the growth trough. Amen.

➤ Day 252: STILL PECULIAR!
PASSAGE: **Deuteronomy 14:1-2**
VERSE: **Deuteronomy 14:2**

For you are a holy people to the LORD your God, and the LORD has chosen you to be a people for His own possession out of all the peoples who are on the face of the earth.

While the NASB version above says Israel is to be a *holy* people, I prefer the King James Version which reads... *and the LORD hath chosen thee to be a **peculiar** people unto himself.* We talked before about being *peculiar* for the LORD, but you should be in a different place in your faith walk after eight months of Bible reading and studying these devotional entries. Are you feeling more *peculiar* and different about the things of this world than you were when this journey began? Being *peculiar* doesn't mean you stand on the street corner dressed in mourning clothes and hit total strangers over the head with your Bible. It does mean that you stand out in the crowd—not because of flash and panache—but because you speak, act and interact with people differently than worldly people do. When Jesus moves into your heart every single thing about your life should change. Think about that statement. When the Holy Spirit placed Jesus within Mary's womb... every single thing in her life changed. She was *peculiar* because the Son of God was firmly ensconced within her. That same Spirit placed Jesus within your heart... how *peculiar* are you?

COMMON GROUND: Hard truth: If the presence of Jesus in your heart has not manifested itself in outward change, you need to talk to Him about what is missing. Where you walk, how you talk, how you love, the light in your eyes, and the bounce in your step should let others know the Spirit of Jesus dwells in you. **HOLY GROUND:** Holy people seed, salt, speak and shine.

LORD, May You fill me and change every single aspect of my life.
I am amazed to be carrying You within me just as
Mary of Nazareth did. Amen.

➤ ## Day 253: A LENDER, NOT A BORROWER
PASSAGE: **Deuteronomy 15:1-6**
VERSE: **Deuteronomy 15:6**

For the LORD your God will bless you as He has promised you, and you will lend to many nations, but you will not borrow; and you will rule over many nations, but they will not rule over you.

Among all the wonderful promises God made with Israel was that they would be an immensely wealthy nation. Loans made among their own people were to be forgiven every seven years in the year of release. The lender could not pursue collection of a fellow Jew's debt after that time. A loan made to a non-Hebrew was still due and could be collected. Look at what God is telling the people in the verse above... *you will lend to many nations, but you will not borrow.* Not only is that a wonderful promise—it just makes sense. Owing others is an uncomfortable feeling; and if Israel was obedient to that command they would not be overwhelmed with debt. Notice also that God promised Israel they would *rule over many nations.* Because of their sin history, that promise hasn't yet been fulfilled... but Jesus is still on the throne.

COMMON GROUND: Are you a borrower or a lender? For the first twenty years of our marriage Dan and I were always in debt and worrying about how to get out from under that burden. Add to that debt the additional financial burden when we opened His House and there were many days we felt like we were drowning in the debt-sea.

In 2007 we worked hard and eliminated our credit card debt. No longer being suffocated with credit card debt is one of the greatest freedoms in the world. That was God's plan. **HOLY GROUND:** Debt is bondage. Bondage is never God's choice for His children. Seek His will to find freedom through being debt free. Learn delayed gratification practices of saving for that which you want or need.

My Jesus, Only with Your provision can I eliminate my debt and be free. LORD, You came to deliver us from every form of bondage... and whom the Son sets free is free indeed. I choose freedom. Amen.

➤ Day 254: REMEMBER YOUR BONDAGE
PASSAGE: **Deuteronomy 15:11-15**
VERSE: **Deuteronomy 15:15**

You shall remember that you were a slave in the land of Egypt, and the LORD your God redeemed you; therefore I command you this today.

Most of you have never been a slave—though if you are a mother you sometimes feel like one! God was reminding Israel to never **ever** forget where they came from and what they had been delivered from. He wanted them to remember what hunger felt like, what serving difficult taskmasters did to their morale, and how powerless they were in their bondage. He wanted them to never take freedom for granted, and in that gratitude to extend mercy to others. If only they'd had memories as strong as their desire to rebel. *For the poor will never cease to be in the land; therefore I command you, saying, 'You shall freely open your hand to your brother, to your needy and poor in your land.'* Gratitude should naturally create a compassionate attitude.

COMMON GROUND: Somehow, many of us—even those of us who came from humble circumstances—turn a blind eye to the needs of the poor in our country and in the world. God's heart must break when He sees how much we have received—forgiveness of sins leading to eternal life—and how little we give. **HOLY GROUND:** I confess that I need to work on this area of my faith walk. If you do too, let's come into agreement to step up our compassion levels and be more generous with our money, time and service.

Father, I have looked away from the hardship of others and remained self-focused. Break my heart with compassion. Amen.

➤ Day 255: GIVE AS YOU ARE ABLE
PASSAGE: **Deuteronomy 16:15-17**
VERSE: **Deuteronomy 16:17**

Every man shall give as he is able, according to the blessing of the LORD your God which He has given you.

In this entry we will look at how much believers are required to offer to God. Most of you probably come from tithing churches where members of the congregation give one-tenth of their income. That offering is used for administration fees, pastoral salaries, missions programs, education and community outreach. That same required offering was commanded in the law of Israel where the people were to offer the first-fruits of all things...the first animal from its mother's womb, the first of the grain harvest, the first of the vineyard, etc. What we are looking at today is a different offering altogether. Three times each year the adult males of the Hebrew nation were to go to Jerusalem to worship at the temple there. Remember, the twelve tribes of Israel were dispersed from one end of the land to the other and couldn't come on each Sabbath to Jerusalem. During these three annual visits each man was to give an additional offering as *he was able*. How did he know how much to give? It depended on how much he felt God had blessed him and how much he wanted to give back to God.

COMMON GROUND: Do you think tithing is about monetary income only? Think about this concept: If tithing is to be on the first-fruits of everything, then we should tithe of our time too. Imagine the impact in the world if believers gave one-tenth of each 24-hour day in service to God! What could you accomplish if you offered even two hours per day? **HOLY GROUND:** God wants you to give the best of your service, time, money and talents. Holy people give because they have received.

*Spirit of God, I am not as generous with my money as I should be,
and I am even less generous with my time and service.
I know where changes need to be made and I will need You
to guide me in making those changes. Amen.*

➤ Day 256: NO PERVERTED JUSTICE
PASSAGE: **Deuteronomy 16:18-20**
VERSE: **Deuteronomy 16:19**

*You shall not distort justice; you shall not be partial,
and you shall not take a bribe, for a bribe blinds the eyes of the
wise and perverts the words of the righteous.*

You would think keeping the justice system honest would be easy; after all, it's the *justice* system! Before Israel moved in and took Canaan God wanted to remind them that honest business practices and an honest judicial system would be the key to growing an honest nation of believers. Look at the following quotes: *"It is impossible to rightly govern a nation without God and the Bible. Observe good faith and justice toward all nations. Cultivate peace and harmony with all. Let us raise a standard to which the wise and honest can repair; the rest is in the hands of God."* These words are all taken from speeches by America's first president, George Washington. A careful study of Mr. Washington's words reveals how seriously our founders took the Bible as a rulebook and guidepost and how they recognized that obedience to a code of laws would result in a moral nation. Our entire legal system is founded upon Mosaic Law. Bribes and compromises in business and the justice system have ruined the perfect construction of our Constitutional Republic.

COMMON GROUND: Any detours from that code of laws would lead to chaos and anarchy. Lack of regard for laws and believing they apply to others and not to us has cheapened the moral fiber or out nation... as it did Israel. If there are any moral, ethical and/or spiritual laws you are breaking, today is the day for reformation. **HOLY GROUND:** As holy people, we must keep ourselves immovable and steadfast in our morality, or we will compromise our identity in Christ and contribute to the immoral sewage our brothers and sisters are drowning in.

Father God, The immorality of our world is a horrible plague upon us... and I want no part of it. Give me a steel-girded heart of hunger for You and self-discipline in my members. Amen.

➤ Day 257: CASTING FIRST STONES
PASSAGE: **Deuteronomy 17:2-7**
VERSE: **Deuteronomy 17:7**

The hand of the witnesses shall be first against him to put him to death, and afterward the hand of all the people. So you shall purge the evil from your midst.

In order to prevent the sin-sewage and chaos we talked about in yesterday's entry, justice had to be handed out fairly and a punishment system had to be instated. You may be uncomfortable with the words in today's Scripture passage, but you must never forget that unpunished sin spreads like a wildfire in a community, in a group of people and in the church itself. We see that stoning was the punishment for those who *served other gods and worshiped them, or the sun or the moon or any of the heavenly host.* (Ouch! That must mean following astrology and the signs in the sky.) On the testimony of two or more witnesses the one found guilty of these practices was to be stoned to death, but never on the testimony of only one witness. Why was God so specific? He knew that false testimonies of vengeful enemies could lead to the death of innocent people. To further prevent false accusations, God said the witnesses were to cast the first stones. What a sobering thought that is. You accuse—and you are the first to initiate the death penalty.

COMMON GROUND: Our Creator knows us intimately enough to know that jealousy, envy, personal hatred and vengeful hearts could lead us to falsely accuse another person. Would you speak the words you speak against others if Jesus was standing next to you—knowing the motives of your heart? **HOLY GROUND:** The sobering thought of casting that very first stone against another human being should serve to wake all of us up. Our words—gossip and false accusations—are the stones we cast at others... and they can sometimes inflict more pain than stones against the flesh. Holy people think before casting stones.

LORD, What a sobering passage this one is. I confess that I have cast stones, thrown gossip darts, hurled false accusations and heaped coals upon the heads of others... for my own personal agenda. Silence me, hold my arms at my side, and lead me into a holy life. Amen.

➤ Day 258: YOU WILL SEEK A KING
PASSAGE: **Deuteronomy 17:14-17**
VERSE: **Deuteronomy 17:14**

When you enter the land which the LORD your God gives you, and you possess it and live in it, and you say, 'I will set a king over me like all the nations who are around me.'

God's prophetic knowledge and words about what we will do and how we will act is really quite startling. In this passage He says that *when* Israel enters the land *they will **ask for a king*** like the nations around them had. Approximately five hundred years later that specific prophecy was fulfilled in 1 Samuel 8:5 when the people said, *"Behold, you have grown old, and your sons do not walk in your ways. Now **appoint a king** for us to judge us **like all the nations.*** " God was angry at the request and told the people exactly what the downfalls would be of serving an earthly king instead of allowing Him to be their King. They ignored Him—and He gave them Saul who affirmed each downfall He had spoken. Also in this passage we see God talking about a king who would *multiply horses for himself... multiply wives for himself... and greatly increase silver and gold for himself.* These words all came to pass in the lives of the kings who would reign over Israel, and most notably in the actions of King Solomon, the wisest man who ever lived. His foreign wives led him away from service to the Hebrew God and into worship and offering to the gods of their nations.

COMMON GROUND: Watch what you ask for. Sometimes we desire things, even good things, which will take us away from God. Oftentimes those desires of our heart—wealth, fame, power, thriving ministries—take us away from Him. Guard your heart. If wise, wise Solomon could drift away, what makes you think you are immune to drift? **HOLY GROUND:** Some of God's greatest blessings are unanswered prayers. We may question why He withholds what we ask for, but He knows the difference between want and need. Trust Him.

My Jesus, You alone are the King I want to reign over my life and my heart. You alone are upon the throne of Heaven and the throne of my heart. You are my source of blessings and riches. No man, nor money, nor fame, nor ministry can take Your place. Amen.

➤ Day 259: THE LAW BRINGS AWE
PASSAGE: **Deuteronomy 17:18-20**
VERSE: **Deuteronomy 17:19**

*It shall be with him and he shall read it all the days of his life,
that he may learn to fear the LORD his God, by carefully
observing all the words of this law and these statutes.*

Maybe the passage for today's devotional will give us a bit of a glimpse into what went wrong in the lives of the human kings who ruled over the nation of Israel. God spoke that each king was to *write for himself a copy of this law on a scroll in the presence of the Levitical priests. He shall read it all the days of his life, that he may learn to fear the LORD his God, by carefully observing all the words of this law and these statutes.* Scripture tells us in Mark chapter fourteen that *the spirit is willing, but the flesh is weak.* Saul, David and Solomon may have had the best intentions when they assumed the throne. They may have indeed written the law on the scroll and even committed to read it each day, but at some point they skipped a day... and then another... and then another... until they had gone long periods of time without the moral reminders of that law. Their weak flesh succumbed to drift, and that drift took them out of God's will. God's warning signs failed to get their attention and they turned *aside from the commandment, to the right or the left...* bringing the nation along with them into apostasy.

COMMON GROUND: Reverence and awe for the amazing power of the Scriptures will never be developed if you are not digging in and mining the nuggets there each day. Without the constant affirmation of God's presence, His direction, and His wisdom for our lives, we will turn aside to the right and to the left... and eventually turn right out of the will of our LORD. **HOLY GROUND:** Biblical study should never grow old or mundane in the life of believers. The Word of God is alive, sharp, peace-giving and life-changing... and it does no one any good if it is a sheathed sword sitting on a shelf collecting dust!

Father, May awe, reverence, worship, praise and adoration spring forth from my heart as I feast upon the honey-like sweetness of Your Holy Bible. Amen.

➤ Day 260: CHARMER'S CHARM
PASSAGE: **Deuteronomy 18:11-14**
VERSE: **Deuteronomy 18:11**

...or one who casts a spell, or a medium, or a spiritist, or one who calls up the dead...

Let's look one more time at what God says about the occult, about psychic practices, and about necromancy (calling up the dead). These words are not my words—they are from the Word of God—as are the perilous consequences resulting from their practices. *There shall not be found among you anyone who makes his son or his daughter pass through the fire, one who uses divination, one who practices witchcraft, or one who interprets omens, or a sorcerer, or one who casts a spell, or a medium, or a spiritist, or one who calls up the dead. For whoever does these things is detestable to the LORD... You shall be blameless before the LORD your God. For those nations, which you shall dispossess, listen to those who practice witchcraft and to diviners, but as for you, the LORD your God has not allowed you to do so.* (NIV) That is God's final word on the topic... none of it is acceptable!

COMMON GROUND: I am absolutely amazed at the number of professing Christians who sanction these practices and honestly believe God will overlook their tolerance for or practice of sorcery. Hard truth: God is telling you to repent of these sins and run the other way. Do you want to risk His judgment and wrath for a little fun at tarot card readings or psychic encounters? **HOLY GROUND:** How heartbreaking it must be to our Creator when He sees those who profess to believe in Him practicing things totally contrary to

His words and His teachings. People walking in holiness don't spit in God's face.

> *Spirit of God, Make me so aware of what is wrong that*
> *I will instantly be on alert. Keep my feet from falling on these*
> *pathways. Keep my mind aware and alert. Keep my spirit from*
> *seeking anything displeasing to You. Amen*

➤ Day 261: JOSHUA TO YESHUA!
PASSAGE: **Deuteronomy 18:15-19**
VERSE: **Deuteronomy 18:15**

The LORD your God will raise up for you a prophet like me from among you, from your countrymen, you shall listen to him.

In the passage of Scripture for this lesson, God refers to a prophet He will raise up from among the Hebrew people, to whom they are to listen because God Himself will speak His words through that prophet's mouth. He also said anyone refusing to listen to the words would die outside God's ultimate will. If we look at that prophetic word on the surface, Joshua (Moses' protégé) fulfilled it. He would take over leadership, speak God's words to the people and, at their own peril, they would disregard his commands. If we look deeper though, we see that God was actually prophesying about an event to take place in the far distant future — approximately 1400 years in the future. The prophet He is speaking of is Jesus Christ! If you know the New Testament accounts of His life, Jesus was a Jew (Hebrew) and was raised up from among His own people to speak the words of God to the people. Not believing in Him or receiving His truths leads to death apart from the Father. *He who does not love Me does not keep My words; and the word which you hear is not Mine, but the Father's who sent Me.* (John 14:24) Hidden here in the Old Testament book of Deuteronomy we are given a glimpse of *Yeshua* (Jesus), not Joshua. Did you know that Joshua is a version of the Hebrew name *Yeshua*?

COMMON GROUND: Are you amazed at how the Bible reveals itself to be the inspired Word of God over and over again? Who would think *Adonai* would use the Old Testament character Joshua (the deliverer of His people to the Promised Land) as a preview of His greater purpose through Jesus to deliver His children to the eternal Promised Land! God is amazing! **HOLY GROUND:** Are you amazed? Tell Him…

Father God, You have woven Jesus into the Old Testament stories.
He is Abraham, the obedient servant; Noah, the refuge
from the judgment flood; Joseph, feeder of His hungry children;
Moses, intercessor for undeserving souls; and Joshua,
deliverer unto the Promised Land. Amazing! Amen.

➤ Day 262: TESTING PROPHETS
PASSAGE: **Deuteronomy 18:20-22**
VERSE: **Deuteronomy 18:22**

When a prophet speaks in the name of the LORD, if the thing does
not come about or come true, that is the thing which the LORD
has not spoken. The prophet has spoken it presumptuously;
you shall not be afraid of him.

How do you know whether a person is a true prophet speaking for God, or a false prophet promoting an artificial agenda? Without spiritual discernment you will never know. Look with me at these excerpts from Proverbs 2. *Make your ear attentive to wisdom, incline your heart to understanding…cry for discernment, lift your voice for understanding…seek her as silver and search for her as for hidden treasures; then you will discern the fear of the LORD and discover the knowledge of God. For the LORD gives wisdom; from His mouth come knowledge and understanding. He stores up sound wisdom for the upright; He is a shield to those who walk in integrity.* Notice how the wisdom and discernment of God come—they are sought after, searched out and cried for. Why would we want them?

Discernment will guard *the paths of justice... preserve the way of His godly ones... guard you... watch over you, to deliver you... from the man who speaks perverse things.* Wow—protection, direction and spiritual detection!

COMMON GROUND: Without godly wisdom and discretion it will be difficult to not fall for false teachings. Remember, false prophets work for the Enemy—and they will tickle your ears and speak all the right words to lead you down wrong paths. **HOLY GROUND:** Read the second Proverb, mark it, study it, feed upon it and equip yourself. You must prepare your spirit with discernment.

LORD, Make me a Seeker, a Searcher, a Miner and a Finder!
I want to understand and be filled to overflowing with godly
wisdom and spiritual discernment. Help me to hit
the target—my aim is high! Amen.

➤ Day 263: BIG ENEMIES
PASSAGE: **Deuteronomy 20:1-4**
VERSE: **Deuteronomy 20:1**

When you go out to battle against your enemies and see horses
and chariots and people more numerous than you, do not be
afraid of them; for the LORD your God, who brought you
up from the land of Egypt, is with you.

Have you ever had a day or a week when the spiritual attacks seemed endless and you felt like you were drowning in them? I had that week while writing this entry. My video camera which is used to tape Bible programming for television messed up. We purchased a new one out of necessity, not financial abundance, and taped two hours of programming. I worked for two weeks trying to get those sessions from the camcorder into my DVD burning program... with no success. I prayed, ate junk food, screamed, cried, prayed some more, ate more junk food and finally told Dan the Enemy had won.

I was not getting writing done because I was determined to write those DVDs. At the end of my thin and very well-worn rope I called tech support for the camera and was told that any DVD program over a year old would never work because of the type of files on the camcorder's hard drive. What? Two Weeks! What? All those empty calories! What? The Enemy was too big... he had won... I returned the camcorder to the company I purchased it from. We purchased a less technically challenging model... you know, a no-brains-necessary one. Go ahead and smile... you know you have been there and done the same thing.

COMMON GROUND: How big are your enemies? Which part of your life are they attacking? Don't be too quick to give in and cede ground. That is what the Enemy of your soul wants... victory over the children of God. **HOLY GROUND:** *"You are approaching the battle against your enemies today. Do not be fainthearted. Do not be afraid, or panic, or tremble before them for the LORD your God... is with you."*

My Jesus, You are bigger than my greatest enemy. You are my strength in testing, my shelter in the storm, and victory over death. Amen.

➤ Day 264: WEED OUT THE WEAK
PASSAGE: Deuteronomy 20:5-7
VERSE: Deuteronomy 20:5

The officers also shall speak to the people, saying, "Who is the man that has built a new house and has not dedicated it? Let him depart and return to his house, otherwise he might die in the battle and another man would dedicate it."

Armies must be trained for battle and equipped to fight the enemy they are preparing to engage... before they get to the sight of the conflict. The battlefield is not the place to weed out weak or non-committed warriors. A distracted soldier is a danger to those he is supposed to fight alongside. Even if you have never served in the military, these truths should be obvious. In the Scripture verses for this entry we see Moses excusing three groups of men from voluntary service in Israel's army. *The man that has built a new house and has not dedicated it... the man that has planted a vineyard and has not begun to use its fruit...and the man that is engaged to a woman and has not married her.* Why excuse them? God and Moses knew the loyalty and focus of the man would be on the house, crops and woman—not on the battle itself.

COMMON GROUND: What does this entry have to do with you? God is looking for focused warriors, intent witnesses and committed servants. Lukewarm commitments will never grow the kingdom and may even serve to hinder its growth. Do you want half-hearted people in this fight with you? No, if you are honest you want people who are fully focused and who will cover your back as the Enemy sends his attack arrows. **HOLY GROUND:** Holy people are battle-ready and have committed hearts. Are you distracted? Ask for concentration and intent on purpose.

Father, Yes, I have been a distracted warrior and have to confess that I have let earthly things hold my attention and take it off heavenly missions. No more. As of today I am intent on the battle. Amen.

➤ Day 265: WEED OUT FEAR
PASSAGE: Deuteronomy 20:8-9
VERSE: Deuteronomy 20:8

Then the officers shall speak further to the people and say, "Who is the man that is afraid and fainthearted? Let him depart and return to his house, so that he might not make his brothers' hearts melt like his heart."

Fear paralyzes the heart. My husband is a Vietnam veteran who was wounded in battle after being drafted into the military just after his high school graduation. He could tell you more about fear than I could, but suffice it to say that someone afraid before they ever get to the battlefield will be afraid when the battle begins. That fear—and who wouldn't be afraid of war—can manifest itself in the flight response, leaving fellow soldiers without the backup they need. Some men can overcome that fear, charge headlong into battle and stun the enemy with their determination. Moses was looking for those kinds of leaders to appoint over the army of Israel. Fear is a normal emotion, yet over and over again God tells His children to *"Fear not and be of good courage."* How can we do that? How can we overcome in the spirit what manifests itself so much in the flesh?

COMMON GROUND: Look at lessons from Psalms 34 for how to overcome your natural fear. *I sought the LORD, and He answered me, and delivered me from all my fears... the LORD heard him and saved him out of all his troubles... the angel of the LORD encamps around those who fear Him, and rescues them.* **HOLY GROUND:** There is only one answer and one way to combat fear—trust in God. He alone can deliver you from your fears, to save you out of your troubles and to rescue you from that which causes you fear.

Spirit of God, I cannot promise to never fear again,
but I can promise to call upon You in those moments when my
natural man falls back into natural habits of life—fear,
discouragement and doubt. Amen.

➤ ## Day 266: HANGED-CURSED
PASSAGE: **Deuteronomy 21:22-23**
VERSE: **Deuteronomy 21:22-23**

If a man has committed a sin worthy of death and he is put to death, and you hang him on a tree, his corpse shall not hang all night on the tree, but you shall surely bury him on the same day (for he who is hanged is accursed of God), so that you do not defile your land which the LORD your God gives you as an inheritance.

During the reiteration of God's laws for the blossoming Jewish nation, the sentence of death by hanging was again addressed. Notice that the body of the hanged man was not to be left on the cross or tree all night, even though it was to be displayed during the daylight hours on the day of hanging in order to serve as a deterrent. Even in punishment, God would leave the criminal some dignity and not allow the animals and birds to eat the flesh. Also, according to Jewish law a dead body defiled the one who touched it and would defile the land it was laid upon, thus the cross where the body was suspended between earth and heaven—seemingly unfit for either place. *He who is hanged is accursed of God...* think about what you just read. Does that mean Jesus was cursed? Absolutely. He hung between heaven and earth—fully God, yet fully man. He carried our sins—not one of His own on those shoulders. We nailed His hands and feet to that cross with our transgressions. We sent Him there... and He willingly went because of His great love for us.

COMMON GROUND: The above teaching wasn't written to upset you, but to remind you. When we get full of ourselves, when we judge others and think we are better than they are, and when we condemn them with our words... we nail Jesus to that cross over and over again. **HOLY GROUND:** His sacrificial death should cause every one of us to fall on our knees before Him in absolute gratitude. In actuality, we all deserve that sinners' cross.

Father God, No dignity, No anger, No hatred, No retribution, No selfishness... No one, but Jesus. Amen.

➤ Day 267: CROSS-DRESSING
PASSAGE: **Deuteronomy 22:5**
VERSE: **Deuteronomy 22:5**

A woman shall not wear man's clothing, nor shall a man
put on a woman's clothing; for whoever does these things is an
abomination to the LORD your God.

Some of you are going to hate—and I do mean hate—this entry. Actually, there are things I don't even like about it! Step back with me into the 1950's when females dressed like females and men dressed like men... and no one thought those things would ever change. You remember... June Cleaver cleaned house in a dress and heels! I love looking at pictures from those days when children were allowed to dress like children (instead of prosti-tots) and teen-agers still dressed like two different sexes. Men looked handsome in their shirts and ties; and ladies looked pretty and feminine in their dresses. Life was easier then, but we progressed into the 20th century where girls dressed like guys, and guys began to wear jeans they bought in the junior girl's department. Go figure! The verse above is not about these changes, but is a reference to sexual tendencies for males to dress like females and vice-versa. In our permissive and ultra tolerant society, everything goes. The problem is that children are being drawn into these sexual changes and are being told that these are normal practices. God help us. He was warning us thousands of years ago to not sanction sexual aberrations.

COMMON GROUND: First things first, as we are always to love the sinner and hate the sin—in any situation. We must not repulse or rebuff people who are being deceived by the Enemy who is telling them to act out their fleshly fantasies. We are also not to tolerate the sin—not to make it acceptable and not to partake in it in any way. **HOLY GROUND:** A friend's grand-daughter told her she was too old fashioned, too set in her ways and she needed to loosen up. She said those things because her grandmother was challenging her life-style choices. That is what the world will always say, but nowhere in Scripture do I find that we are to compromise our moral stands.

*LORD, Teach me to love the sinner as a child You created, but to
never sanction sin in my home, my community and my church.
I may stand alone in this battle, but You are there. Amen.*

➤ Day 268: CROSS-POLLINATION
PASSAGE: **Deuteronomy 22:9-11**
VERSE: **Deuteronomy 22:9**

*You shall not sow your vineyard with two kinds of seed,
or all the produce of the seed which you have sown and the
increase of the vineyard will become defiled.*

Following a lesson on cross-dressing, what could be more appropriate than one on cross-pollination! God elaborates on some
of the rules He had set forth for Israel... *You shall not sow your
vineyard with two kinds of seed, or all the produce of the seed which
you have sown and the increase of the vineyard will become defiled.*
Why would God care about mixing seeds for the vineyard? He
made each thing perfect in its created form. Today's botanists and
horticulturists would hate this law, but think about things in their
purest form—not those maneuvered by human hands. Two different
seeds sown in one field could lead to one choking the other out and
would be a waste of good seed. *You shall not plow with an ox and
a donkey together.* Why would God care about plowing with an ox
and donkey together? They cannot plow equally together; because
they are not the same size and strength. Crooked furrows are hard
to harvest. This is a common sense law. It also brings to mind God's
warning against unequal yoking between believers and unbelievers.
You shall not wear a material mixed of wool and linen together.
Now we have offended the fashion designers! Two different fabrics
wear and are washed differently; they may pull one another apart.
In Moses' day, there weren't dry cleaners to care for mixed fabric
clothing... thus again, the law was practical.

COMMON GROUND: Rules like these may seem foolish to you because of the time period we live in. God was speaking one very simple truth: "Keep things pure, Keep them as I created them and Keep your eyes on Me." **HOLY GROUND:** When you give your own children basic household rules, do you give them to protect them or restrict them? God was trying to protect His children from too much change which would draw them away from Him. He knew what worldly influences would lead to... and He was right.

My Jesus, I understand the rationale for these laws which at first seemed silly. Father God was setting limits for obedience—not restricting fun or freedom. He was doing the same thing I tried to do for my own children. Amen.

➤ Day 269: PURE CAMPS
PASSAGE: Deuteronomy 23:1-11
VERSE: Deuteronomy 23:9

When you go out as an army against your enemies, you shall keep yourself from every evil thing.

Deuteronomy is a reminder, or a rehashing, of past laws that could possibly have been forgotten or not passed down from one generation to another. Remember that the generation who first received the laws at Mount Sinai had died. Any tolerance for sin within the camp would lead to a pollution of the entire camp. It all goes back to the picture of sin being like a leavening agent and Jesus' teaching that a little sin-leaven ruins the whole batch. Some of these laws are common sense. Some are reminders of past promises and covenants God's people made with the nations around them. Some have to do with sexual purity, physical purity and moral purity. We will see in a later entry how seriously God takes sin in the camp. If God's people were to indeed be holy and set apart, they would have to reject the sins of the flesh and the sinful practices of the nations around them. God was preparing them for battles to be followed by times of great blessing and promise. He knew that allowing them to forget basic laws would lead to anarchy—thus the reminders in this chapter.

COMMON GROUND: I am amazed at the conversations I have with believers who are tolerating sin in their families, homes, churches and even their own flesh. Jesus said in 2 Corinthians chapter six ... *for what partnership have righteousness and lawlessness, or what fellowship has light with darkness?* **HOLY GROUND:** Holy people must live **in** this world, however we do not have to be **of** it and allow it to influence our decisions, affect our opinions, and silence us to what is wrong. Are you standing tall in battles where holiness is challenged? We cannot serve both light and darkness... we have to serve one or the other.

Father, I need to stand taller, speak louder and hold tighter to what I know is right according to Scripture. Give me a backbone of steel. Amen.

➤ Day 270: GOD WALKS AMONG YOU
PASSAGE: **Deuteronomy 23:12-14**
VERSE: **Deuteronomy 23:14**

Since the LORD your God walks in the midst of your camp to deliver you and to defeat your enemies before you, therefore your camp must be holy; and He must not see anything indecent among you or He will turn away from you.

If you thought the Bible was a boring old book with lots of hard to pronounce names and stories that have nothing to do with life in America in the 21st Century—you are wrong. Look closely at the passage for today. I laughed myself to tears when I first read this one. God says to have a place outside the city gate—a public outhouse if you will—and the people are to carry a digging instrument to bury their excrement. What? God is talking about personal body functions! Who do you think made the body function in the first place? Why would this be important enough to address in the middle of recitations of Mosaic Law? Look at verse fourteen for a clue: *God walks in the midst of your camp... therefore your camp must be holy... He must not see anything indecent among you.* Before you get too far off track with mental pictures of the community outhouse, I want you to think about this truth in the light of yesterday's lesson on sin in the camp. If God walks in the camp and expects it to be holy, then anything at all which is unholy will cause Him to *turn away from you.*

COMMON GROUND: What is God seeing that is filthy or indecent in your camp? What is it that would cause Him to turn away from being there with you? **HOLY GROUND:** Whatever came to mind when I asked that question is what you need to surgically remove. In my case—the filth is a biting tongue, a judgmental spirit and a boatload of pride. I was honest—will you be too?

Spirit of God, Anesthesia, Scalpel, Suction, Sponge, Sutures, Antiseptic... Spiritual Surgery complete... Amen.

➤ Day 271: SEXUAL SIN REMOVED
PASSAGE: Deuteronomy 23:15-18
VERSE: Deuteronomy 23:17

None of the daughters of Israel shall be a cult prostitute, nor shall any of the sons of Israel be a cult prostitute.

Sexual purity may seem old-fashioned in our liberated and sexually free society, but God still commands obedience in this area of our lives... and that will never change, no matter what society's values are. You may be asking what sexual purity has to do with serving the LORD completely. Glad you asked; I have lots of answers! (Like you had any doubt!) First Corinthians gives us insight into this topic. *Do you not know that **your body is a temple*** *of the Holy Spirit who is in you, whom you have from God, and that you are not your own?* That is a good start! *Food is for the stomach and the stomach is for food, but God will do away with both of them. Yet* **the body is not for immorality, but for the LORD**, *and the LORD is for the body.* Sounds like God made our bodies for a higher purpose. Lastly *...this is the will of God, your sanctification; that is, that you abstain from sexual immorality; that each of you know how to* **possess his own vessel in sanctification and honor**, *not in lustful passion, like the Gentiles who do not know God.* Contrary to the propaganda in our media and in the field of education, we are not animals; we can control our fleshly lusts and we are to treat our bodies as the temple of the Holy Spirit... no exceptions.

COMMON GROUND: Sexual impurity manifests itself in many forms, but is commonly described as any sexual practices outside the bonds of marriage. Homosexuality, pornography, transsexual lifestyles, adultery and fornication (sex outside of marriage) are all included in this impurity which must be addressed. **HOLY GROUND:** Compromise in this area will surely lead to compromise in other areas of our lives. If you take sin and God's definitions of sin seriously, you cannot continue in sexual sin and fully serve Him. You were created in the image of Creator God and do not have to act like an animal which cannot control its flesh.

Father God, This, like other areas of my life, requires self-control and self-discipline. I need both, LORD. Please teach me to control my flesh and my lusts. In my flesh, I am weak... in You I am strong. Amen.

► **Day 272: DON'T CHEAT BROTHERS**
PASSAGE: **Deuteronomy 23:18-20**
VERSE: **Deuteronomy 23:19**

You shall not charge interest to your countrymen: interest on money, food, or anything that may be loaned at interest.

In a day when buying on credit is a way of life, and when current statistics prove that the average American family has approximately $10,000 in credit card debt, we could hardly imagine a law telling lenders they couldn't collect interest on loans. The law for today's entry is that the Hebrew people could lend to foreigners and charge interest, but they couldn't collect a usury fee on money lent within the twelve tribes. Why would God institute such a rigid law? Didn't those who *had* deserve to collect interest from those who *had not*? Was God limiting the 'free enterprise system' of Israel? No. He knew that borrowing money put someone in bondage and subjection to a fellow citizen. He wanted His people to honor, value and respect one another. He wanted them not to grow or gain off the sweat of one another. God was trying to keep *the love of money* from dividing His people. Sin in this one financial area would open the door to other sin.

COMMON GROUND: In the days these laws were being written, most money was lent because someone's crops failed or they fell into poor health. They were already humiliated at having to seek the loan, so adding interest was like rubbing salt into a gaping wound. God's goal of a united brotherhood couldn't afford division like that. **HOLY GROUND:** Pity must be shown to someone who is in deep enough need that they will humble themselves and ask for a loan. I am not talking about the needless spending and borrowing of today, but I am addressing a hurting need. We must not take advantage of a Christian brother who is humbled and broken and asking us for help.

LORD, I have been the borrower and the lender. I far prefer to be the latter. May I never forget what the burden of owing another felt like on my shoulders and in my spirit. Amen.

➤ Day 273: BUILD MARRIAGES
PASSAGE: **Deuteronomy 24:1-5**
VERSE: **Deuteronomy 24:5**

When a man takes a new wife, he shall not go out with the army
nor be charged with any duty; he shall be free at home one year
and shall give happiness to his wife whom he has taken.

Let's start with a question for this devotional. How important is the marriage union of one woman and one man in the strength of a community, nation and church? Do you understand why God designed the union of marriage as the foundational norm for all time? Both parties were required for conception, birth and multiplication to take place. The woman was taken from the side of man—not to be at his head—and not to be at his feet—but to walk beside him. The two would share the charge to raise their offspring and provide for their home. God knew that little boys would need a father to emulate in their adult lives. He knew little girls would need a mother to pass on nurturing skills to them, so that one day they could do the same for their children. He knew little children would need to understand parental love and discipline. Society can define marriage any way it wants, but God ordained the union of marriage in one of His first interactions with His human creation. The law we read today was designed to give the marriage union a strong start and a firm foundation.

COMMON GROUND: God knew marriage would be a union between two very different creatures—each driven by unique instincts and strengths. He knew it would require effort and a strong commitment. Let me ask again, how important is the marriage unit in our homes and churches? In our society marriage is made to look unnecessary and inconvenient... shame on us. **HOLY GROUND:** I am asking you today to help strengthen the marriages of your family and friends, along with your own if you are married. The hardest vows to keep are the marriage vows of fidelity, commitment and support. These marriages need the prayer covering of holy people.

My Adonai, I have failed to pray for marriages and have even been known to encourage others to give up on theirs. Father, You ordained marriage as the perfect union. I give You my promise to help marriages survive through prayer support. Amen.

➤ ## Day 274: COLLECTIONS DEPARTMENT!
PASSAGE: **Deuteronomy 24:10-13**
VERSE: **Deuteronomy 24:10**

When you make your neighbor a loan of any sort, you shall not enter his house to take his pledge.

We talked recently about the bondage of debt. As I wrote this book... America and Michigan especially, was going through a difficult economic downturn leading to increased bankruptcies and foreclosures. From past personal experience I know the dread of answering the phone to potential collection calls. (Personally I cannot imagine a worse job in the world than being in the collection department of a company and having to call for payments from people suffering in hard times.) For most of us, our debt is owed to a faceless entity in a far away city. Imagine living in the days of Moses and owing borrowed money to people you passed on the street, or worked for, or were related to. God set down specific collection and collateral laws. *When you make your neighbor a loan of any sort, you shall not enter his house to take his pledge...the man to whom you make the loan shall bring the pledge out to you. If he is a poor man, you shall not sleep with his pledge. When the sun goes down you shall surely return the pledge to him that he may sleep in his cloak...* The man who gave his cloak as collateral for a loan was to be given the cloak back at the end of the day, as it was likely his sole covering for the night temperatures. Does that seem fair to you?

COMMON GROUND: It may seem unfair that God would require the lender to return the collateral to the borrower. Think about this... the lender obviously had enough to lend in the first place. He wouldn't miss the cloak, but the man who gave it to him would. Even in lending we are to be people of compassion. **HOLY GROUND:** I said before and will say it again that some *loans* are *gifts*—especially to family members—and we need to treat them as such. How tragic it would be for holy people to allow money to separate them from those they love.

Jesus, I am the borrower of Your grace and mercy. How would I feel if it were withheld from me because I couldn't repay the cost of my sins? I owe You everything I have and more. Amen.

➤ Day 275: FAIR COMMERCE
PASSAGE: **Deuteronomy 25:13-16**
VERSE: **Deuteronomy 25:15**

You shall have a full and just weight; you shall have a full and just measure, that your days may be prolonged in the land which the LORD your God gives you.

This will make me sound like your mother but, *"When I was a child* business revolved around customer service, fairness and quality products." I can remember walking into stores where the sales clerk greeted my mother by name and some even knew my name. How far we have fallen! Today we are a nameless consumer with a credit card number who needs to be herded through the check out process because hundreds of other nameless consumers are waiting behind us. Customer service is a foreign concept and low quality imported products have replaced those made, grown and produced by our fellow countrymen... and we think we are better for it! God knew that even a little cheating with weights and scales would lead to corruption in commerce. Throughout the Bible He warns about keeping fair weights and very seriously states *everyone who acts unjustly is an abomination to the LORD your God.* I don't believe we will ever return to the days of my fond childhood memories—the days modern progressives see as backward and passé. Unfortunately, compromise in business has seeped into compromise in all parts of our society. And to think it all started with those fair weights God spoke about!

COMMON GROUND: Compromise most often begins small and grows as we become more comfortable with it. Reread that statement. As we become less convicted by our sins, they are fertilized and begin to grow. Without the check of the Holy Spirit, they will soon take over like weeds in the garden of our heart. **HOLY GROUND:** Ask God to reveal any hidden area of compromise—even the smallest, least significant thing. Bare yourself before Him... and expect to be ashamed. Only then can He remove the sin nature you harbor deep inside.

Spirit of God, In my journey toward holiness I see latent sins, even unintentional sins, in my life. You can reveal and repair these areas. I humbly and fearfully submit to Your microscopic exam, my Ruach HaKodesh! Amen.

➤ Day 276: WE CRIED-HE LISTENED
PASSAGE: **Deuteronomy 26:1-11**
VERSE: **Deuteronomy 26:7**

Then we cried to the LORD, the God of our fathers, and the LORD heard our voice and saw our affliction and our toil and our oppression.

So Israel would not forget the past faithfulness of God, when they arrived in Canaan they were to take the first produce from their new ground to the priest and relate to him the story of their bondage, their redemption, their deliverance and the faithfulness of God. They must never forget that when they cried out He listened... and He responded. In this lesson we begin a more in-depth study of the names of God which will continue for the next few weeks. Today we look at *El Elyon* (el el-yone'), the Most High God. How tragic that our generation has forgotten, and those to come will have forgotten, the glory of *El Elyon. El* is a word translated simply as God. *Elyon* reveals the extreme sovereignty and majesty of the God of creation. It can be translated as 'the Most Exalted God' and is used twenty-eight times in the Old Testament—mostly in the Psalms. In a day when we are seeking a touchy-feely, goose bump creating kind of God, I believe we have lost the awe and reverence for *El Elyon*. That which we make too common tends to lose its awe-inspiring power to move us.

COMMON GROUND: Seeking God for emotional encounters will never bring you the relationship you need. Your soul needs to daily realize that the Most High God of all creation chose you, loves you and died for you. Surely that deserves a degree of reverence and awe that nothing else in your life merits. **HOLY GROUND:** When is the last time you stood before *El Elyon* and praised Him for who He is? If you want a true relationship… reverence is a requirement.

Father God, You are El Elyon, the Most High God, higher
than all other gods, more powerful than any idol man can fashion,
and more committed to me than any man could ever be.
I praise You, El Elyon. Amen.

➤ Day 277: I HAVE OBEYED
PASSAGE: **Deuteronomy 26:12-15**
VERSE: **Deuteronomy 26:14b**

I have listened to the voice of the LORD my God;
I have done according to all that You have commanded me.

There is only one way to shed our sinful flesh and become holy people. This way involves a journey from a spiritual awakening where God's Spirit begins to commune with yours, and concludes when you are glorified before Jesus' throne. *Jehovah Mekoddishkem* (yeh-ho-vaw' M-qadash) is the LORD Who Makes Holy or Who Makes Righteous. Good hearts, generous spirits and busy hands do not make us holy. Sincere obedience and a striving to follow God's direction do. *Jehovah Mekoddishkem* gave Israel commands to tithe of the increase of their flock, herd and crops, and to provide for the Levites who served in the temple. Only when they could stand before Him and say, *"I have listened to the voice of the LORD my God; I have done according to all that You have commanded me,"* would they be considered righteous in the eyes of a holy God. This name of God is used twice in the Scriptures (Exodus 31:13 and Leviticus 20:8) in the original Hebrew. *Jehovah* means LORD or the Existing One. *Mekoddishkem* is the Hebrew word meaning sanctify, make holy or dedicate.

COMMON GROUND: In our own power we cannot make ourselves holy—and that should be reassuring to each of us on this journey. I am no more holy than you because I write books. You are not more holy than your neighbor because you attend church. Romans 3:23 teaches us... *all have sinned and fall short of the glory of God.* **HOLY GROUND:** We are nothing without the God who makes us holy—*Jehovah Mekoddishkem.* Is He working in your heart to make you more holy as we journey through these pages together? God's ideal for you is higher than you could ever imagine!

LORD, You are my Jehovah Mekoddishkem—the Source of my holiness, the Initiator of my righteousness and the Perfecter of my glorified self. Without You, I am so far from holy. Amen.

➤ Day 278: YOU CALLED HIM GOD
PASSAGE: **Deuteronomy 26:16-18**
VERSE: **Deuteronomy 26:17**

You have today declared the LORD to be your God, and that you would walk in His ways and keep His statutes, His commandments and His ordinances, and listen to His voice.

When Jesus described Himself as the Good Shepherd and told how vital the relationship was between a shepherd and his flock, we were given a picture of Him guiding and directing us, His protection over us, and His expectancy that we would follow Him, trusting that He had our best welfare at heart. In today's Bible passage we find these words: *You have today declared the LORD to be your God... that you would walk in His ways... and listen to His voice. The LORD has today declared you to be His people, a treasured possession, as He promised you... Jehovah-Raah* (yeh-ho-vaw' raw-aw') is the name of the LORD My Shepherd. Picturing God shepherding and protecting His flock is a comforting thing to me and doesn't feel even a bit restrictive. *The **LORD is my shepherd**, I shall not want. He makes me lie down in green pastures; He leads me beside quiet waters. He restores my soul; He guides me in the paths of righteousness for His name's sake. Even though I walk through the valley of the shadow of death, I fear no evil, for You are with me; Your rod and Your staff, they comfort me...*

COMMON GROUND: Does the idea of a shepherd directing your paths—rather than allowing you to run headlong into sin, danger and trouble—feel restrictive to you? Are you ready to let *Jehovah-Raah* shepherd your wandering heart today? **HOLY GROUND:** That would mean He leads, feeds, waters, guides, disciplines, shelters, moves and protects. How can that be bad? It is only bad if you want to remain on the common ground He is trying to deliver you from.

My Adonai, I am realizing more every day just how much I need a shepherd. In the past I have walked on rough, rocky crags, drifted into dangerous dry places and wandered from the sheepfold. Today I ask Jehovah-Raah to be my forever Shepherd—why would I not? He was willing to die for me. Amen.

➤ Day 279: YOU WILL BE HIS NATION
PASSAGE: **Deuteronomy 26:19**
VERSE: **Deuteronomy 26:19**

...He will set you high above all nations which He has made, for praise, fame, and honor; and that you shall be a consecrated people to the LORD your God, as He has spoken.

As I have been studying these names of God in my own personal devotion time, I have been praying the meanings back to Him. Here is an example. *"Adonai (LORD) you are the Master of my heart, the LORD of my life and the Name I praise above all other names. I relinquish my plans, thoughts and wishes and willingly submit to Your LORD-ship in my life. I do this in peace, for I know You are Jehovah-Shalom, the LORD of Peace."* I pray you are learning about the very character of *Jehovah* God from these entries. I am thoroughly enjoying writing them for you and believe they can take you to a higher worship level if you will study them and apply them to your own worship and prayer time. Notice in the verse for today that Israel was set aside as a *consecrated* (set apart for righteousness) nation of God. *Jehovah-Tsidkenu* (yeh-ho-vaw' tsid-kay'-noo) is a name I am clinging to as I strive to climb from common to holy ground. The LORD our Righteousness is used twice in the book of Jeremiah and literally means to be *stiff, straight or righteous.* I want to be stiff and straight if that means not yielding to sin or falling into temptation.

COMMON GROUND: Are you consecrated to God? Do you believe you have been set apart for holy service? Are you fighting the idea of being ramrod-straight in your steadfastness and commitment to righteousness? **HOLY GROUND:** Stiff and straight for the sake of holiness sounds better to me than being floppy and lax and being carried every way the wind blows. *Jehovah-Tsidkenu* is calling you to His Righteousness. The good news is that all of us have to make that same journey; remember, none of us are born holy.

Jesus, Righteousness came upon You through Jehovah-Tsidkenu and You wore it well. As I strive to allow this transformation of my life, and as I bend my will to match Your will for me, be my source of strength. This is all new to me... and surprisingly painful. Amen.

➤ Day 280: WRITE DOWN MY LAWS
PASSAGE: **Deuteronomy 27:1-10**
VERSE: **Deuteronomy 27:3a**

...write on them all the words of this law...

In order for the nomadic Hebrew population to take the land promised throughout their history to their forefathers, they would first have to cross the Jordan River. In order to keep them from rushing headlong into battle—and likely defeat, God gave commands for them to stop immediately on the other side, build a memorial altar, write out the Mosaic Law on whitewashed stone tablets, and offer burnt offerings upon that altar. They were to use uncut stones—just as God made them. This altar would serve to remind them of the miracles they had witnessed at the hand of their God. Today's name to study is *Jehovah Nissi* (yeh-ho-vaw' nis-see') and means The LORD my Miracle, or the LORD is my Banner! How awesome to have seen His myriad miracles with their own eyes! Imagine watching the plagues of Egypt, the parting of the Red Sea, the first morning of Manna, and Moses descending from Mount Sinai with his face literally shining from being in the presence of God! This name is used only once in Exodus 17:15 where we read, *Moses built an altar and named it **The LORD is My Banner**.* Moses, the dedicated servant of God, wanted everyone to see as he proudly waved his God before the Egyptians, Pharaoh, foreign kings and pagan nations. Indeed, he served a Miracle-working God!

COMMON GROUND: What has God delivered you from or carried you through? What miracles have your eyes witnessed? Are you waving His banner? Are you telling every one of the miracles

He has wrought in your life? **HOLY GROUND:** Those who have tasted the redemption of Jesus Christ should be the most passionate, most vocal, most unquenchable people in the world. There is nothing quiet about being redeemed! They should be waving *Jehovah Nissi* constantly for a lost world to see.

Spirit of God, No more silence for me. With Your guidance and direction I will proudly wave Jehovah Nissi as my banner, my miracle-worker and my redeeming grace. I must never forget where I was before You wrought miracles in my life. Amen.

➤ Day 281: LEADING THE BLIND ASTRAY
PASSAGE: **Deuteronomy 27:11-19**
VERSE: **Deuteronomy 27:18**

*Cursed is he who misleads a blind person on the road.
And all the people shall say, "Amen."*

As another reminder to the people of God's command for holiness, He commanded them to perform what might seem a bizarre exercise before they took the land. Some tribes—Simeon, Levi, Judah, Issachar, Joseph, and Benjamin—were to stand on Mount Gerizim. The remaining tribes—Reuben, Gad, Asher, Zebulun, Dan, and Naphtali—were to stand on Mount Ebal. They were to shout back and forth warnings and curses for disobedience to God's laws. I used the verse above as an example to show that anyone leading a blind man into danger would be cursed. In order to agree to obey the law, the people's '*Amen*' signified assent. *Elohim* (el-o-heem') is the name of God we will study today. *Elohim* means God, Judge or Creator, and is used over 2,000 times in the Old Testament books. The exercise of stating the sins and warning with the curses was actually very fair on the part of God. If He was calling for holiness, He needed to define it—or define that which defiled it. After all, He was the Judge who would have ultimate authority when days of discipline and punishment would come.

COMMON GROUND: Think about a family writing a list of house rules and each night reciting them—along with the consequences of breaking them—between parent and child. The child would grow up knowing what was expected and the cost of disobeying the rules. It sounds fair to me. Are there too many rules for you? **HOLY GROUND:** Even with the rules read and debated, the Hebrew people would stand before *Elohim* seeking mercy when they blatantly disobeyed His commands. Creator God does everything in His power to equip us to walk in His fullness. Holy people need to accept His Word as truth.

> *Father God, You are Creator, Judge, Elohim and Adonai.*
> *When will we learn to simply do it Your way the first time?*
> *When will I learn that it is harder to pick up broken pieces*
> *than to do it right the first time? I know the way—yet often*
> *choose to not walk in it. Melt me. Amen.*

➤ Day 282: OVERTAKEN BY BLESSINGS
PASSAGE: **Deuteronomy 27:26/28:2**
VERSE: **Deuteronomy 28:2**

All these blessings will come upon you and
overtake you if you obey the LORD your God.

If you diligently obey the LORD your God, being careful to do all His commandments which I command you today, the LORD your God will set you high above all the nations of the earth. What an amazing promise that is. Obey and be set high above all the nations of the earth! Israel had that promise. I believe America once had a similar promise because we stood as an ally with Israel and shared the same faith foundations as her children. How do those blessings come upon a people? They come from the hand of *Jehovah-Jireh* (yeh-ho-vaw' yir-eh') the LORD who Provides. This name of God is used only once in all of Scripture and is the symbolic name Abraham gave to Mount Moriah when God 'provided' a ram for him to offer to

God instead of his son Isaac. Genesis 22:14 reads, *Abraham called the name of that place **The LORD Will Provide**, as it is said to this day, "In the mount of the LORD it will be provided."* I'd bet Abraham never forgot who provided that ram. The story would have passed down through the generations until Moses, the author of the first five books of the Bible, wrote them down by the inspiration of God to preserve the history and affirm His moral and civil laws. *Jehovah-Jireh* provided everything His children needed... yet they would not remain satisfied and their eyes would wander to foreign gods. Why?

COMMON GROUND: How could Israel be so foolish as to forget their Provider? How could they so brazenly and so often spit in His generous face? Before you judge them, you (and I) need to look again at that spiritual mirror to see where we have failed to obey and failed to be grateful for blessings generously bestowed upon us. **HOLY GROUND:** Do you look at yourself or at *Jehovah-Jireh* as your provider? Holy people realize that all they have comes from the hands of Provider God—giftings, abilities, talent, food, shelter, family, wisdom, mercy, sight, vision, health, breath, prayer, forgiveness, redemption...

LORD, You have blessed me beyond my wildest dreams. Jehovah-Jireh, You are my Supplier and You always supply just enough... just enough to keep me hungering for more of You! Amen.

➤ Day 283: BLESSED EVERYWHERE
PASSAGE: **Deuteronomy 28:3-5**
VERSE: **Deuteronomy 28:3**

Blessed shall you be in the city,
and blessed shall you be in the country.

Peace is the greatest blessing a heart can receive. How do you define peace? I don't mean the hip 1960's peace signs. I am talking about real, heart deep, unshakable peace? Absence of conflict can be defined as peace. Living in harmony among your brothers can result in peace. What if I told you the only real peace you will ever know is *Jehovah-Shalom* (yeh-ho-vaw' shaw-lome'), the LORD is Peace. I am going to drop some verses before you defining Biblical peace. *I shall also grant peace in the land, so that you may lie down with no one making you tremble. The LORD lift up His countenance on you, and give you peace. God is not a God of confusion but of peace. Peace I leave with you; My peace I give to you; not as the world gives do I give to you. Do not let your heart be troubled, nor let it be fearful.* Do you see the kind of peace *Jehovah-Shalom* wants for you. Not surface quiet and calm, but soul-deep inner peace. You will never find that peace in the things of this world.

COMMON GROUND: How much peace do you have in your personal life? Is your peace dependent on external factors? More importantly, does peace reign in your heart in spite of circumstances around you? I lost my peace last week when I had camera, email and business concerns. I allowed the Enemy to replace *Jehovah-Shalom* as my source. **HOLY GROUND:** Holy people find peace in a crowd and peace on a seashore. They can find peace in a church pew and peace in the Word of God—the Author and Finisher of our peace.

My Adonai, Come flood my heart with unmistakable and indescribable peace—that peace which surpasses all human understanding. All praise to You, my Prince of Peace. Amen.

► Day 284: BLESSED IN BATTLES
PASSAGE: **Deuteronomy 28:6-7**
VERSE: **Deuteronomy 28:7**

The LORD shall cause your enemies who rise up against you to be defeated before you; they will come out against you one way and will flee before you seven ways.

Wouldn't it be nice to be a military leader and know beyond a shadow of a doubt that you could not be defeated, no matter how mighty the enemy or how steep the ascent to victory? *Jehovah Sabaoth* (yeh-ho-vaw' sa-ba-ot') gives that promise as the LORD of Hosts and the LORD of Powers. It is He who fights for His children and fights beside them. It is *Jehovah Sabaoth* alone who defeats mighty enemies, sows confusion in their camps, makes the sound of thundering chariots in the treetops and directs the battle plans. It is no wonder this name of God is used more than 285 times, mostly in the prophetic books of Jeremiah and Isaiah. *Sabaoth* literally means armies or hosts and signifies God's universal sovereignty over every army. What a promise for us today—because He is sovereign over spiritual as well as earthly enemies. We can be victorious when we have the right General in charge, the right Commander giving the orders, and the right Privates obeying the commands. Here is an example of this name used in Psalm 24:10. *Who is this King of glory?* **The LORD of hosts**, *He is the King of glory.*

COMMON GROUND: It almost makes you feel sorry for Israel's enemies—or even Satan—that we are assured victory in every battle. Do you feel victorious? Or, are you walking in utter defeat instead? That is not from God... and the battle belongs to Him. **HOLY GROUND:** Do you find it comforting that you never need to walk into a battle unprotected? How is your spiritual armor? Does it need some polishing? Got a few dents and bangs? Ask *Jehovah Sabaoth* to train you for any assault that may come.

Jesus, I feel strong. I feel empowered. I feel more prepared to face enemies than I have felt in a long time. How could I not feel this way when I have Jehovah Sabaoth on my side? Amen.

➤ ## Day 285: EVERYONE WILL SEE
PASSAGE: **Deuteronomy 28:8-11**
VERSE: **Deuteronomy 28:10**

So all the peoples of the earth will see that you are called by the name of the LORD, and they will be afraid of you.

Try to picture being so showered with blessings that the other people around you cannot help but be in total awe because of your God and His amazing provision for you. How would you answer their questions as to why you are favored so highly? Here is a hint... tell them *El Shaddai* (el shad-di'), the LORD God Almighty, chose you before time began and set you apart for his service. Top that off by adding that because He is the All Sufficient One and owns everything in the world, He has chosen to pour out His amazing love on you. Think they would be jealous? Maybe they would just be curious—and that would give you opportunity to give Him glory. *El Shaddai* is used seven times in the Old Testament—mostly in Genesis. Look at its first use in that text. *Now when Abram was ninety-nine years old, the LORD appeared to Abram and said to him, "I am God Almighty; Walk before Me, and be blameless. I will establish My covenant between Me and you, and I will multiply you exceedingly."* What an amazing reward for a life of obedience.

COMMON GROUND: When we speak of promise verses in these devotions, do you ever doubt that they are true? Do you think God is real but not involved in your daily activities? Time and time again He promised... and He followed through exactly as He promised. **HOLY GROUND:** If we serve an All-Sufficient God, *El Shaddai*, why are we so quick to doubt His provisions? His Words tells us He is no respecter of persons, so Abram is no more valuable to Him than you are. Humbling, isn't it?

El Shaddai, You truly do own the cattle on a thousand hills. You truly did cast the stars into the sky and the planets into their orbit. Why are you mindful of me? Oh yes, how could I forget?

*I am made in Your image. You breathed the breath of life into me.
Thank You, LORD. Amen.*

➤ Day 286: THE HEAD, NOT THE TAIL
PASSAGE: **Deuteronomy 28:12-14**
VERSE: **Deuteronomy 28:13**

*The LORD will make you the head and not the tail, and you
only will be above, and you will not be underneath, if you listen
to the commandments of the LORD your God, which I
charge you today, to observe them carefully.*

As God bestowed upon Israel the blessing of being the head—the leader in front of others—and not the tail, He honestly told them too about the price of being first. That price is obedience to Him, loyalty to Him, and refusal to serve any other god but Him. *Do not turn aside from any of the words which I command you today, to the right or to the left, **to go after other gods** to serve them.* Why does He command this undivided loyalty and love from His children? He is *Qanna* (kan-naw'), the Jealous and Zealous God. I would think He has every right to be a jealous God because He created us in His image to honor Him, love Him, and fellowship with Him. When we commit our lives to *Qanna* we enter a covenant relationship with Him; we promise to be His people and He promises to be our God. He has every right to demand fidelity. This is no different than a covenant marriage vow between two people. If someone threatens that covenant relationship, the partners in it are bound by their vows to each other to fight for that marriage. The marriage of our hearts to *Qanna* God is no different. He will jealously and zealously defend that which belongs to Him. This name is used six times, mostly in Exodus and Deuteronomy.

COMMON GROUND: Would you rather serve a god who doesn't care enough to fight for your commitment, or the One who demands fidelity? Would you want to be in a marriage relationship with a spouse who doesn't care whether you stay or go? If you would settle for that, I would have to ask how committed you were to the relationship in the first place. **HOLY GROUND:** I am comforted to know that *Qanna* will fight for me. He will require my loyalty and will not tolerate spiritual infidelity. That means our relationship is of value to Him.

Father God, Your commitment to me and to our covenant
is a secure feeling—not a threat to me. I will gladly stand by the
Qanna God who stands by me, seeks after me, and draws
me back when I drift. Amen.

➤ Day 287: YOU SIN—YOU SUFFER
PASSAGE: **Deuteronomy 28:36-37**
VERSE: **Deuteronomy 28:37**

You shall become a horror, a proverb, and a taunt among
all the people where the LORD drives you.

I cannot imagine anything worse than being falsely accused of something and having everyone believe you were guilty, no matter how you tried to defend yourself. I have a friend who went through that very situation and it destroyed five years of her life. When she was exonerated there was no media press to proclaim her innocence. The damage was done. This is a very different situation than that of my friend who was innocent and thought guilty. God warned Israel that they *will* sin and *will* turn against Him to serve other gods. He also said they *will* become a horror to those who look upon them and who were once amazed at the blessings of God on that nation. Israel *will* commit the sins... and *will* pay for their compromises. Part of the cost would be very public national humiliation. They would become a common proverb—a saying like, "Watch what you do to dishonor your gods. Remember what happened to Israel!" How horrible that God's chosen people would bring this shame upon them and upon His name as well.

COMMON GROUND: How hard it is to honestly confess our shortcomings and face the consequences. Israel was no different than you and I. We fail; we pass the buck; we attempt to explain our actions; we seek to condone them; and we still pay the price. **HOLY GROUND:** Confession of sin is a mandatory part of a full walk with God. As long as there is unconfessed sin of any sort, there is a wall of separation between a holy God and His unholy children. It is time for spiritual cleansing on this journey. Wipe the slate clean by confessing those latent sins.

LORD, The sin I am dealing with is_____.
I have tried in my own flesh to overcome it, but it controls me.
LORD, I ask Your strength and Your mercy. Help me to begin anew today. Amen.

➤ Day 288: CHECKPOINT #3
PASSAGE: **Proverbs 2:1-11**
VERSE: **Proverbs 2:3**

For if you cry for discernment, Lift your voice for understanding...

I was preparing to write another entry of warning and caution from the book of Deuteronomy, but decided instead to ask you an important question in this 3rd Checkpoint. Are you hungering for Biblical discernment, Godly wisdom and spiritual knowledge? In this proverb we learn that gaining these things requires effort—sometimes even physical effort—on the part of the Seeker. *My son, if you will **receive** my words and **treasure** my commandments within you, **make your ear attentive** to wisdom, **incline your heart** to understanding... if you **cry** for discernment, **lift your voice** for understanding... **seek** her as silver and **search for** her as for hidden treasures... then this is the reward you will receive... You will **discern** the fear of the LORD and **discover the knowledge of** God. For the LORD... **stores up sound wisdom** for the upright; He **is a shield** to those who walk in integrity, **guarding the paths*** *of justice, and He **preserves the way** of His godly ones. Then **you will discern righteousness and justice and equity** and every good course... **knowledge** will be pleasant to your soul; **discretion will guard you... understanding will watch over you...***

COMMON GROUND: Please don't take this devotion lightly. Most people will never put the effort required into gaining this kind of life-changing and life-protecting wisdom. Are you hungering, thirsting, seeking, craving and mining for God's discernment and knowledge? **HOLY GROUND:** Ordinary book smarts will never save your soul, but The Good Book smarts will guard your heart and keep your feet on right paths. My prayer for you today is that these entries I have agonized over have awakened a new desire for more of *Adonai, Yeshua,* and the *Ruach HaKodesh* in your spirit.

My God—in all Your generosity, may I receive wisdom equal to the effort I am willing to put forth to know You more. This deeper level of commitment is new to me... and I am amazed by Your love. Amen.

➤ Day 289: FEW IN NUMBER
PASSAGE: **Deuteronomy 28:62-66**
VERSE: **Deuteronomy 28:62**

Then you shall be left few in number, whereas you were as numerous as the stars of heaven, because you did not obey the LORD your God.

Let's get back to our lessons as we near the end of Deuteronomy. When God told Israel He would punish them for the sins they would commit against Him, He also said He would scatter them in enemy nations where they would serve the gods of their pagan captors. Their suffering would be great and their loss of life even greater until the once mighty nation would be but a remnant—a shadow of who they once were. Numerous times God made it clear

He wouldn't destroy them completely—though their sins warranted Him doing so. Instead, because of a promise made to Abraham, He would keep the Hebrew line alive and would one day return them to their homeland. Before that day they would face the horrible consequences of their sins. *Among those nations you shall find no rest, and there will be no resting place for the sole of your foot; but there the LORD will give you a trembling heart, failing of eyes, and despair of soul. So your life shall hang in doubt before you; and you will be in dread night and day, and shall have no assurance of your life.* Going from a chosen people as numerous as the stars to a starving remnant... how hard the mighty would fall when they fell away from their God.

COMMON GROUND: Israel knew what was required, chose to compromise and cut corners, found they hated the consequences, thought they didn't deserve the discipline, and probably whined about how unfairly God was treating them. **HOLY GROUND:** Does that sound familiar? None of us likes discipline and correction. None of us willingly tells God to prune us and bring us into right standing with Him. None of us learn without that necessary pruning.

Jesus, Snip, Clip, Lop, Pluck, Pinch and Chop away anything growing contrary to Your will in me. You are the Master Gardener... I am but Your plant waiting to be groomed. Amen.

➤ Day 290: COVENANT WITH GOD
PASSAGE: **Deuteronomy 29:1-13**
VERSE: **Deuteronomy 29:12**

...That you may enter into the covenant with the LORD your God, and into His oath which the LORD your God is making with you today.

It has been a few days since we looked closer at another name of God, but I think you will want to know this one. *Jehovah Shammah* (yeh-ho-vaw' shawm'-maw) is the LORD Who Is There. This name occurs only once in Ezekiel 48:35, but could be used hundreds of times in the story of Moses leading the Hebrew people from Egypt to the Promised Land. God was *there* when the people cried in their bondage. He was *there* when Moses was chosen as their deliverer. He was *there* to send the plagues against Pharaoh. He was *there* in the signs and wonders of Moses and Aaron. He was *there* to protect Goshen during the Passover. He was *there* to spoil the Egyptians of their wealth. He was *there* to part the Red Sea. He was *there* to send the manna; *there* to send water from the rock, *there* to listen to their whining, *there* to see the golden calf they worshipped, *there* to watch their disobedience... Yes, *Jehovah Shammah* was *there*... and He would still be *there* to usher them home into their land. He was *there* ... but will Israel be there for Him?

COMMON GROUND: God was ready to make a once and for all time covenant with His children. He had chosen them long before and loved them in spite of their foolishness. He wanted to be enough for them. He wants the same thing with you. Is His being *there* enough for you? **HOLY GROUND:** Jesus was *there* to take your sin upon His flesh, to die on a sinner's cross, and to be separated from heaven and His Father. He was *there* for you—what can you give Him in return but total dedication.

Jehovah Shammah, In my every need, You are there. I am never alone, never abandoned and never forsaken. Thank You. Amen.

➤ Day 291: GOD'S BOOK OF CURSES
PASSAGE: **Deuteronomy 29:14-21**
VERSE: **Deuteronomy 29:20**

The LORD shall never be willing to forgive him, but rather the anger of the LORD and His jealousy will burn against that man, and every curse which is written in this book will rest on him, and the LORD will blot out his name from under heaven.

Division, dissention and defection begin with a tiny root of dissatisfaction with how things currently stand. *El Shaddai* was warning the people against that bitter root which, if left intact, would grow up, multiply, begin to produce bitter fruit and eventually lead to bitterness and dissention within a nation. Sometimes that bitter root would start in rebellion to a creed or doctrine, a set of laws or a command to holiness. The root was to be removed, dug up and taken from where it was growing. *There will not be among you a man or woman, or family or tribe, whose heart turns away today from the LORD our God, to go and serve the gods of those nations; that there will not be among you a root bearing poisonous fruit...* Why remove it? Because the poisonous fruit is like the leaven Jesus warned of in the New Testament. A little jealousy leavening will compound itself throughout the whole body. An iota of compromising leaven will be slowly accepted by others, and soon the whole body would be compromised. A tiny amount of idol worship leaven would open the door to other forms of worship contrary to God's words. The person feeding and fertilizing the root and helping it to grow will one day face *every curse which is written in this book.*

COMMON GROUND: Picture two gigantic books resting on a table near the throne of Jesus in Heaven. One book is labeled '*God's Blessings for the Righteous*' and the other '*God's Curses for the Rebels.*' Your name can only be written in one of them. Your decision is which will it be—rebel or righteous? **HOLY GROUND:** Look closely for roots of anything contrary to Biblical holiness. Do you see anger, unforgiveness, pride, rebellion or ingratitude? Get out that shovel and begin to dig! Dig deep and leave no feeder roots at all. That poisonous root must be completely removed.

Father God, Pulling weeds in my garden is a whole lot easier than uprooting that which is buried deep within the soil of my heart. I confess I have fertilized and watered the poisonous root for many years and will need Your help to get it all out, for it has grown very deep. Amen.

➤ Day 292: SECRET THINGS OF GOD
PASSAGE: **Deuteronomy 29:29**
VERSE: **Deuteronomy 29:29**

The secret things belong to the LORD our God,
but the things revealed belong to us and to our sons forever,
that we may observe all the words of this law.

What if I were to tell you—nearly three hundred entries into this book—that when you are finished with it, or when you are finished studying your way through the entire Bible, you will not have absorbed even an iota of the wisdom of God? Honestly! Hidden within are things so infinite that our finite minds cannot comprehend them. Isaiah 55:8-9 states that truth quite succinctly. *"For My thoughts are not your thoughts, nor are your ways My ways," declares the LORD. "For as the heavens are higher than the earth, so are My ways higher than your ways and My thoughts than your thoughts."* Some things we couldn't comprehend and others we do not need to know at this time. When you were six years old you didn't know how to balance a checkbook because you didn't need to balance one. Today you don't need to have all the answers because you aren't in need of them. God gives us what we need when we need it. Our job is to trust that He gives what we need in His perfect timing. He has given us enough knowledge, wisdom and discernment for the step we are on, and He will provide more as we ascend higher and higher... until everything will be revealed when we stand before Him.

COMMON GROUND: The promise of God, as in the verse for today, wasn't to tell Israel everything before they crossed into Canaan. If He had been that open, they would never have crossed because He would have told them of mighty enemies, fierce battles and hard work which lay before them. **HOLY GROUND:** Holy people must be content to step in faith without knowing everything lying before them. They must trust that the Tour Guide knows where the deep crevices, the high barriers and the raging torrents are... and trust Him enough to get them safely to their destination.

LORD, The Bible is my source for wisdom, the Holy Spirit my guide for discernment, and Your past provision the manual for my knowledge. I trust you to show me just enough to get me through this day... and safely into my tomorrow. Amen.

➤ ## Day 293: RECIRCUMCISED HEARTS
PASSAGE: **Deuteronomy 30:3-9**
VERSE: **Deuteronomy 30:6**

Moreover the LORD your God will circumcise your heart and the heart of your descendants, to love the LORD your God with all your heart and with all your soul, so that you may live.

Why would a heart once circumcised—one that had the hard outer layer removed in obedience to the commands of God—have to be recircumcised at a later date? The answer is painfully obvious. The hard outer crust was allowed to grow back, placing a shell between God and the heart He longs to reside within. In true prophetic fashion Moses related *Adonai's* words that Israel would accept His covenant, turn and serve other gods, be scattered like sheep without a shepherd in a foreign land, realize the damage their sin had done, cry out to the God of their fathers and be restored to His full grace. The promise was for all the descendants of Abraham—for all of eternity. *If your outcasts are at the ends of the earth, from there the LORD your God will gather you, and from there He will bring you back. The LORD your God will bring you into the land which your fathers possessed, and you shall possess it; and He will prosper you and multiply you more than your fathers.* This prophecy must have been hard to accept, but that did not make it less true or less accurate. God wants circumcised hearts, willing and open hearts, honest and genuine hearts, and He will reject all others.

COMMON GROUND: I believe the crustiness on the outer shell of the human heart creeps on a little at a time. One business failure... a fine layer of crust; one marriage ending in divorce... another layer;

one rebellious child... the crust is getting thicker; one church division... the barrier between you and God is now nearly impenetrable. God hasn't moved. He is still faithful. He still has a promise for you. **HOLY GROUND:** *Then the LORD your God will prosper you abundantly in all the work of your hand, in the offspring of your body and in the offspring of your cattle and in the produce of your ground, for the LORD will again rejoice over you for good, just as He rejoiced over your fathers.* Awesome promise, isn't it?

My Adonai, I can sense those crust layers of anger, disillusionment, suffering, rejection, loss and dashed hopes. But guess what, Adonai? I realize they are there because of man... and never because of You or Your lack of faithfulness. Help me, LORD. Amen.

➤ Day 294: CHOOSE LIFE
PASSAGE: **Deuteronomy 30:10-20**
VERSE: **Deuteronomy 30:19**

I call heaven and earth to witness against you today, that I have set before you life and death, the blessing and the curse. So choose life in order that you may live, you and your descendants...

I love the passage of Scripture for today's message. God is telling His people, "Don't think what I am requiring of you is too far out there or too hard to achieve. Holiness is possible—if you apply My Word to your life." Look at the exact words as to where the answers to all life's situations are. Holiness *is not in heaven, that you should say, "Who will go up to heaven for us to get it for us and make us hear it, that we may observe it?" Nor is it beyond the sea, that you should say, "Who will cross the sea for us to get it for us and make us hear it, that we may observe it?" But* **the word is very near** *you,* **in your mouth** *and* **in your heart**, *that you may observe it.* Israel didn't have to jump through hoops to find holiness; they merely needed to read, study, meditate upon and apply Scriptural truths to their everyday lives. God didn't put it out of our reach either in some mystical, transcendental or psychic experience. He put it right before us. He inspired it into the spirits of those He commanded to write it. He saw to it that it was transcribed and translated so you could hold it in your hand and write it on your heart today. Are you excited about that truth? Their truth is your truth—you are a joint heir to the promises God made to His children, Israel.

COMMON GROUND: Moses went on to conclude this passage with an option—a chance for the people to exercise their free will. *I have set before you* **life** *and* **death***, the* **blessing** *and the* **curse***. So* **choose life** *in order that you may live.* As joint heirs, we must also make that choice between eternal life and eternal separation from our Creator in death. Common people will fail to choose. **HOLY GROUND:** Choose life! Choose life! Choose life! Choose life! Choose life! Choose life! Choose life!

Jesus, Faced with this decision, I will always choose life! Amen.

➤ Day 295: JOSHUA, YOU'RE UP!
PASSAGE: Deuteronomy 31:1-8
VERSE: Deuteronomy 31:8

The LORD is the one who goes ahead of you; He will be with you; He will not fail you or forsake you. Do not fear or be dismayed.

Moses had poured himself out as an offering for the hateful and ungrateful nation of Israel. He had sweat blood for them, cried tears over them and defended them when God had had enough. Moses is old and all he wants is to cross that river, stand on the land of God's promise and breathe the air of freedom. Instead, he was to pass the baton on to Joshua. Moses—in his flesh—had to want to remind the people that he would never receive the desire of his heart because he reacted in anger to their whining. He didn't do that—it would serve no good purpose. For the first time in his adult life Moses must let someone else take charge. He knew that as hard as it was, he must convince the people to honor and obey Joshua, his faithful friend and protégé. *Then Moses called to Joshua and said to him in the sight of all Israel, "Be strong and courageous, for you shall go with this people into the land which the LORD has sworn to their fathers to give them, and you shall give it to them as an inheritance. The LORD is the one who goes ahead of you; He will be with you, He will not fail you or forsake you. Do not fear or be dismayed."*

COMMON GROUND: Moses was the most gracious 'baton-passer' in the Bible. He was passing authority, handing over his flock and entrusting them into the hands of another... not because he wanted to... but because he was forced to. Most of us have difficulty relinquishing control, but there is a day for that to happen. Moses didn't try to keep their loyalty; he shifted it all onto Joshua's shoulders. **HOLY GROUND:** Holy shepherds need to realize that the flock didn't belong to them in the first place. God placed it within their care and will move it on to other capable hands when the time is right. This isn't the easy way... but it is the right way.

Jehovah Raah, The flock is Yours. Thank you for allowing me to be a shepherd until You raise up another one to fill my sandals. I ask Your direction and guidance for the one who follows in my footsteps. Amen.

➤ ## Day 296: READ LAW TO EVERYONE
PASSAGE: **Deuteronomy 31:9-13**
VERSE: **Deuteronomy 31:12**

Assemble the people, the men and the women and children and the alien who is in your town, so that they may hear and learn and fear the LORD your God, and be careful to observe all the words of this law.

Because we have Christian television and radio, printed books, magazines and bound Bibles in every shape, size and color imaginable, the modern church has no reason to be Biblically illiterate. That would lead me to believe the only reason is laziness on our part—because God has surely done His part to get the Word to us. How would the God of Israel get His words and laws before His people? How would He insure that those walking into the Promised Land and all who came after would have the knowledge of what was required of them to walk in accordance with His commands? Every seven years at the day of remission of debts during the Feast of Tabernacles, as the people gathered in their nation to appear before God at the temple, the Law of Moses was to be read to everyone. That would mean new children born between the last reading and the next would hear it. Memorization was their only way of passing the law onto their children and writing it upon their own hearts. With everyone hearing it read completely every seven years, no one had an excuse for breaking it. Are you feeling more grateful for the Bible on your table or bookshelf?

COMMON GROUND: Look at this story from 2 Kings 22. *Hilkiah the high priest said to Shaphan the scribe, "I have found the book of the law in the house of the LORD." Shaphan the scribe came to the king and brought back word to the king and said... "Hilkiah the priest has given me a book." And Shaphan read it in the presence of the king. When the king heard the words of the book of the law, he tore his clothes. Then the king commanded Hilkiah, "Go, inquire of the LORD for me and the people and all Judah concerning the words of this book that has been found, for great is the wrath of the LORD that burns against us, because our fathers have not listened to the words of this book, to do according to all that is written concerning us."* **HOLY GROUND:** Josiah, the young King of Judah, was struck with grief when he realized the sin which plagued Judah was because of the lack of the reading of the Law. It had been seventy years since the people heard the Mosaic Law read. That means seventy years of each man doing what he thought was right. God help us in America. Surely His anger burns against us.

Father God, Families used to read the Bible together, discuss it and live by it. We used to pray together—and it bound us together.

We once talked of You openly in the public forum. Today we have
relegated You and Your Holy Word to a dusty bookshelf,
a pew on Sunday, and a hurried "Thank You for the Corn Flakes."
And we wonder why our nation is in peril? Amen.

➤ Day 297: GOD'S *SHEKINAH* GLORY
PASSAGE: **Deuteronomy 31:14-18**
VERSE: **Deuteronomy 31:15**

The LORD appeared in the tent in a pillar of cloud,
and the pillar of cloud stood at the doorway of the tent.

God said to Moses, *"Behold, the time for you to die is near; call Joshua, and present yourselves at the tent of meeting, that I may commission him."* So Moses and Joshua went and presented themselves at the tent of meeting. The LORD appeared in the tent in a pillar of cloud, and the pillar of cloud stood at the doorway of the tent. What a bittersweet moment for both men and the God they served. Moses looked at Joshua, knowing all his discipleship would soon have to be enough—for he would no longer be there to guide Joshua. Joshua looked fearfully at Moses, wondering how he would ever fill those aged, wise and obedient sandals. God looked at both of them, the one He chose from among the Midianite flocks and the one who chose to trust in Him when the others let fear dictate their destinies. God's *Shekinah* glory encompassed them as He spoke, *"Behold, you are about to lie down with your fathers... this people will arise and play the harlot with the strange gods of the land, into the midst of which they are going, and will forsake Me and break My covenant which I have made with them... My anger will be kindled against them in that day, and I will forsake them and hide My face from them, and they will be consumed... so that they will say in that day, 'Is it not because our God is not among us that these evils have come upon us?' But I will surely hide My face in that day because of all the evil which they will do."*

COMMON GROUND: Have you ever watched an elderly saint leave this world as they were ushered into the next one where the reward for faithful service awaited them? Now you understand the bittersweet tears on Joshua's heart. **HOLY GROUND:** Moses' work was nearly finished. He was tired... but the parting would not be easy. How grateful he and Joshua both must have been for all the hours they had spent together preparing Joshua to assume this new role.

LORD, Let the Shekinah Glory of God come upon Your house again. It has been gone far, far too long. Amen.

➤ Day 298: BOOK OF THE LAW BESIDE THE ARK
PASSAGE: Deuteronomy 31:24-29
VERSE: Deuteronomy 31:26

Take this book of the law and place it beside the Ark of the Covenant of the LORD your God, that it may remain there as a witness against you.

Painstakingly and accurately Moses looks over the complete book of Mosaic Law. This is not to be confused with the stone tablets of the Ten Commandments which are secured within the Ark of the Covenant. Once he was certain it was complete, he called the Levites who were in charge of moving the ark and told them to take the book and place it beside the ark as a *witness against Israel.* What did he mean by that choice of words? He knew Israel would sin, but they would do so in their own free will and not because they didn't have access to the moral guideposts they should follow. *"For I know your rebellion and your stubbornness; behold, while I am still alive with you today, you have been rebellious against the LORD; how much more, then, after my death? For I know that after my death you will act corruptly and turn from the way which I have commanded you; and evil will befall you in the latter days, for you will do that which is evil in the sight of the LORD, provoking Him to anger with the work of your hands."* Moses knew the painful truth that no matter how hard he had worked to serve these people, if they were so evil while he was alive... how very much worse they would become once he was gone. I feel sorry for Joshua...

COMMON GROUND: Think about this. Each human has the image of God stamped on him. That doesn't mean we look like Him, but rather that He is a spirit and we are to worship Him in spirit. We have an inherent sense of right and wrong. God knew the flesh would be susceptible to failure, which is why He gave us the Law. Why, if we have His inherent nature and His moral requirements, do we fall so far short of His glory? **HOLY GROUND:** We have dumbed down moral truths and replaced them with emotional blather, thinking we are being 'more inclusive'. If Moses' sin kept him from the Promised Land, how do we think our unconfessed sin will allow us into heaven?

My Adonai, I can imagine Moses reading each word and maybe explaining to Joshua what they meant. He was leaving no room for error. Moses was soon to be gone, but the law of God would remain forever... not losing one jot or tittle... forever! Amen.

➤ Day 299: MOSES' SONG
PASSAGE: **Deuteronomy 32:1-43**
VERSE: **Deuteronomy 32:1**

Give ear, O heavens, and let me speak;
and let the earth hear the words of my mouth.

Instead of cowering in defeat or pouting in frustration, Moses began to sing a song of glory and praise before God, his successor Joshua and the entire gathered congregation. Does praise come easily for you? Does gratitude fluently pour forth from your lips?

Maybe the reason it doesn't is because we haven't yet learned that all we have depends on His provision. Maybe we are still feeling too self-sufficient and sure of our own abilities. Fortunately for Moses, his ministry took place in the middle of nowhere with him having to totally rely on God to provide everything he needed. No wonder his praise poured out. He had watched the plagues attack Egypt—while the Hebrew in Goshen were immune. He had watched the Red Sea part for his people to pass over on dry ground—while it poured back in on the enemy army and drowned them. He had watched the manna fall, the quail fall, the water pour forth and the clothing not wear out. He had stood in the Presence of God on Mt. Sinai, heard His voice, and had Him hide him in the cleft of the rock! Who wouldn't be grateful? Who wouldn't praise? *For I proclaim the name of the LORD; ascribe greatness to our God! The Rock! His work is perfect, for all His ways are just; a God of faithfulness and without injustice, righteous and upright is He.*

COMMON GROUND: Have you forgotten where your victories come from? Where your food and shelter come from? Where your gifts and abilities come from? Where your ministry comes from? If you are finding it hard to praise... start with your next breath... without Him you wouldn't take it. **HOLY GROUND:** Psalm 103 is a good place to start... *Bless the LORD, O my soul, and all that is within me, bless His holy name. Bless the LORD, O my soul, and forget none of His benefits; Who pardons all your iniquities, Who heals all your diseases; Who redeems your life from the pit, Who crowns you with lovingkindness and compassion.*

Jesus, Bless the LORD, all you His hosts, You who serve Him, doing His will. Bless the LORD, all you works of His, in all places of His dominion; bless the LORD, O my soul! Amen.

➤ Day **300**: MOSES' EPITAPH
PASSAGE: **Deuteronomy 34:1-12**
VERSE: **Deuteronomy 34:5**

So Moses the servant of the LORD died there in the land of Moab,
according to the word of the LORD.

*N*ow Moses went up from the plains of Moab to Mount Nebo...
*which is opposite Jericho, and the LORD showed him all the
land, Gilead as far as Dan, and all Naphtali and the land of Ephraim
and Manasseh, and all the land of Judah as far as the western sea...
Then the LORD said to him, "This is the land which I swore to
Abraham, Isaac, and Jacob, saying, 'I will give it to your descendants'; I have let you see it with your eyes, but you shall not go over
there." So Moses the servant of the LORD died there in the land of
Moab, according to the word of the LORD. He buried him in the
valley in the land of Moab... but no man knows his burial place to
this day. **Although Moses was one hundred and twenty years old
when he died, his eye was not dim, nor his vigor abated.** So the
sons of Israel wept for Moses in the plains of Moab thirty days; then
the days of weeping and mourning for Moses came to an end. Now
**Joshua the son of Nun was filled with the spirit of wisdom, for
Moses had laid his hands on him**; and the sons of Israel listened to
him and did as the LORD had commanded Moses. Since that time
**no prophet has risen in Israel like Moses, whom the LORD knew
face to face,** for all the signs and wonders which the LORD sent him
to perform in the land of Egypt against Pharaoh, all his servants,
and all his land, and **for all the mighty power and for all the great
terror** which **Moses performed in the sight of all Israel**.*

COMMON GROUND: I felt the Scripture needed no help from
my feeble fingers. There is nothing I can add to perfection. Moses
wrote his epitaph every day he lived. What would someone write
about you—if, let's say, it was based on how you lived your life
yesterday? We need to live each day as Moses did, as if it could
be our last. Moses was finally resting from all his labors. **HOLY
GROUND:** I had a tear-fest when I finished this entry. Somehow,

knowing I am nearing the end of this book, I am relieved yet sad. Handing it over to the publisher and then to you is like handing you my third-born child. We are officially through four of our five-book journey. We are heading into the Promised Land. We are going to face mighty enemies, scale high walls and take our rightful place... as Holy Warriors. Are you ready?

Holy Spirit, Moses' legacy of integrity, compassion, obedience and humility would all be things I would like written on my grave stone. This has been a long journey... strengthen me for the last leg of it. Amen.

➤ Day 301: CALL TO ACTION
PASSAGE: Joshua 1:1-2
VERSE: Joshua 1:2

Moses My servant is dead; now therefore arise, cross this Jordan, you and all this people, to the land which I am giving to them, to the sons of Israel.

This is the day Joshua had waited for... or was it? Moses was dead, God was telling him it was time to cross the river and take the land, and the Hebrew nation was looking expectantly to him for guidance and direction. Joshua had been groomed for the day, but being groomed was easier than putting that grooming to the test. The sheer responsibility had to weigh heavy on his aging shoulders. Everyone was depending on him... can you feel his burden? Look ahead hundreds of years to the New Testament and think about how Peter, James, John, Andrew and Matthew felt as they watched Jesus ascend to His heavenly throne. Fear, anxiety, insecurity, self-doubt, and that awesome burden to fill big, big shoes had to have nearly overwhelmed them. Joshua, like the Apostles, was up to the task, but that wouldn't be revealed until the master was gone. Now the direction had to come from God alone—no middle man—so discernment and wisdom were the taskmasters. "*...arise, cross this Jordan, you* *and all this people, to the land which I am giving to them, to the sons of Israel."* The simple command to *arise*, if obeyed, would initiate a whole new journey. God knew Joshua… and Peter, James and John were ready… they merely needed to *arise*.

COMMON GROUND: The call of God on the lives of His children is not uncommon; their obedience to the call is. Human nature is usually content with the status quo—no change, no added effort and no new frontiers to explore. How have you—or will you—handle the call to *arise* and walk into a new journey—*A Transforming Journey* with God as your Tour Guide? **HOLY GROUND:** Are you afraid or insecure about what God might call you to do? He will never take you where He will not be there with you, or where He has not prepared for you to go. Holy people develop a trust in their Creator which supersedes all fleshly doubts and fears.

Father God, Arise is a call I have ignored. I have been content with things just as they are. Now I see it is time for me to step up, step out and step into this transformation. Hold me. Amen.

➤ Day 302: BE STRONG!
PASSAGE: Joshua 1:3-6
VERSE: Joshua 1:6

Be strong and courageous, for you shall give this people posses-sion of the land which I swore to their fathers to give them.

Yesterday we talked about heeding God's call to action. Would it be easier to arise if you knew for certain that God was going to bring success and victory where He was sending you? God wasn't finished speaking to Joshua. Look at the promises in these next few verses. *Every **place on which the sole of your foot treads, I have given it to you**… From the wilderness and this Lebanon, even as far as the great river, the river Euphrates, all the land of the Hittites, and **as far as the Great Sea toward the setting of the sun will be*** *your territory. No man will be able to stand before you all the days of your life. Just as I have been with Moses, I will be with you; I will not fail you or forsake you. Be strong and courageous, for you shall give this people possession of the land which I swore to their fathers to give them. Only be strong and very courageous; be careful to do according to all the law which Moses My servant commanded you; do not turn from it to the right or to the left, so that you may have success wherever you go.* Jesus left His disciples with a similar command: *"Go into all the world and preach the gospel to all creation."* He wouldn't give them the command if the mission was not possible. He wouldn't give you a command to teach, preach, and work in the mission field or any other area of ministry if He didn't first equip you to do that to which He calls you.

COMMON GROUND: Think back over the entries you have been reading for the last ten months. Did any of them strike a nerve or stir your heart? Did you feel God trying to get your attention? I would encourage you to reread them and listen for the *still small voice* of the Holy Spirit. Ask God what He is calling you to do. **HOLY GROUND:** Look again at the promises He gave to Joshua... new territory, no stronger enemies, His constant presence, possession of thus unclaimed land and success wherever his foot stepped. What an awesome God we serve!

*LORD, I am seeking Your guidance. Please reveal
Your perfect will for my life. I know everyone isn't called
to pastor and teach, but all of us are called to serve in the
kingdom. Where shall I serve? Amen.*

➤ Day 303: MEDITATE ON MY LAW
PASSAGE: Joshua 1:7-9
VERSE: Joshua 1:8

This book of the law shall not depart from your mouth, but you shall meditate on it day and night, so that you may be careful to do according to all that is written in it; for then you will make your way prosperous, and then you will have success.

Read again that last phrase in the verse above. The Mosaic Law, kept on the hearts of the Hebrew people, would—if obeyed— bring them prosperity and success. How could God make such a brash statement? The simple truth is that obedience to God's ways, always serves to bless the one who *chooses* to obey. Notice I said *chooses* (as opposed to *is forced to* obey). When God created man in His image He was creating a spirit-driven being which could *choose* to obey or disobey the calls God put on his heart. He didn't fashion mindless robots forced into a life of obedience. He designed His highest creation to fellowship with Him, to love Him and to *choose* Him above all other viable choices. How would they know what was required of them? The written Word of God. Notice the people were to *meditate on it day and night, not turn from it to the right or to the left* and not let it depart from their mouth. They were to study it, follow it completely, and speak of its powerful truths to their children and the strangers in their midst. If you know about the New Testament accounts of Jesus' life, you will remember how He used Scripture to rebuke the temptations of Satan in the wilderness. He *chose* to learn the Scriptures in order to have them within His heart when they were necessary for His survival. The same is true for us.

COMMON GROUND: Have you gotten the impression from these devotionals that you need to be studying the Bible and writing its words on the walls of your heart? If so, I have done my job. If not, I have more work to do. A wise Christian woman once told me, "Some day we might not have the Bible in our hands, so we'd better have it hidden in our hearts." I have never forgotten those words of wisdom. **HOLY GROUND:** Applying Scriptural truth to your life is your *choice*. Each day fewer people read the Bible than the day before. We have abandoned its moral foundation and lost the hunger for its promises. *God will not be mocked.* His commands are as sure today as they were in the days of Joshua... *This book of the law shall not depart from your mouth.*

My Adonai, Sanctify me in truth—and Your Word is truth. Give me a burning hunger and an unquenched passion for Your Holy Word. Help me to choose today to walk according to it. Amen.

➤ Day 304: THREE DAYS FROM NOW
PASSAGE: **Joshua 1:10-11**
VERSE: **Joshua 1:11b**

Prepare provisions for yourselves, for within three days you are to cross this Jordan, to go in to possess the land which the LORD your God is giving you, to possess it.

Here are the words the wandering tribes of Israel had been waiting for. Three days—just three more days before they would cross the Jordan River and step onto the soil of the Promised Land. God had brought them to this place. He had provided for their every need. He had given them strong and dedicated leaders. He would direct their paths and shower them with blessings for obedience. They had a lot of work to do—they had to prepare food, pack their belongings and pray. Wait a minute—prayer isn't even mentioned in this passage. It should have been. A corporate time of prayer would have been great affirmation that their safety on the journey depended entirely on the protection and direction of their God. Unified prayer and praise for God's past faithfulness would shore up their foundation of faith. If we look ahead to the upper room where the disciples of Jesus were gathered after His ascension with orders to wait there *'for the promise of the Father,'* we will find them praying together. (Acts 1:5-6) They were seeking His guidance and asking His will be revealed to them. Corporate prayer and seeking together for the direction and provision of God is essential for us to keep within His plans and to remind us of His constant presence. That truth was the same in Joshua's day, in the days of the early Christian church, and is still true today.

COMMON GROUND: How is your prayer life? If it isn't what you know it needs to be, you can begin today to develop the art of conversation with God. Prayer is dialogue, which simply means we need to speak and listen—and both parts are necessary for a dialogue to take place. If we are doing all the talking, that is a monologue. **HOLY GROUND:** Before the Hebrews crossed the Jordan they needed prayer. Before you walk through the doors God is going to open before you, you need to pray. Holy people ask, seek, knock, and then listen, hear and obey.

Jesus, Teach me how to be silent in my prayer time so I can hear Your voice and direction. The 'promise of the Father' is the Holy Spirit who will guide and help me in this application. Teach my ears to discern His teaching from all other teachings. Amen.

➤ Day 305: WE WILL FIGHT!
PASSAGE: Joshua 1:12-16
VERSE: Joshua 1:15

...until the LORD gives your brothers rest, as He gives you, and they also possess the land which the LORD your God is giving them. Then you shall return to your own land, and possess that which Moses the servant of the LORD gave you beyond the Jordan toward the sunrise.

The tribes of Reuben and Gad, along with half the tribe of Manasseh, were promised by Moses that they could settle on the eastern side of the Jordan River where the land was fertile for their large cattle herds. That promise was given to them in agreement that they would cross the river and fight alongside the other tribes for the land which would belong to them at God's direction. The leaders from Reuben, Gad and East Manasseh agreed to leave their wives and children in the already conquered land east of the Jordan as incentive to get in, fight the enemies, take the land for their brothers and get back to their families, flocks and herds. When Joshua spoke to the tribal heads they reconfirmed the commitment with these words. *"All that you have commanded us we will do, and wherever you send us we will go."* The leaders knew their families would be vulnerable to enemy attack without the men present to guard them, but they were trusting in God's promised hedge around their land, animals, tents and people. Faith grown over the years through God's constant provision and care would carry them through the battles ahead until they could return to their own land of promise.

COMMON GROUND: Part of the reason so few step up to God's call is that most of us are afraid to leave the comfortable place we currently reside. Imagine the call of God requiring you to change your location, leave a secure job, or be away from your family. The real question is this—do you trust God? Is your faith in the 'hip-service' stage or the 'lip-service' stage? **HOLY GROUND:** Reuben, Gad and East Manasseh were willing to cross the Jordan because they had a proven history of God's faithfulness to fall back on. If you have the same history—thank God. If you don't, begin today to watch for His reliability in your life situations.

Holy Spirit, I am nearer the hip-service stage than before I began this arduous journey. I am less prone to walk on common ground and more willing to step onto holy ground. I am trusting more, worrying less, and watching Your loving hand. Amen.

► Day **306**: WE WILL OBEY JOSHUA
PASSAGE: **Joshua 1:17-18**
VERSE: **Joshua 1:17**

Just as we obeyed Moses in all things, so we will obey you; only may the LORD your God be with you as He was with Moses.

I don't know if I would be thrilled with the promise above! If Joshua would be obeyed like Moses was obeyed—watch out Joshua! I am joking seriously here. The people had whined, complained, sinned and tried to have Moses stoned to death! Now they are promising total obedience to Joshua, the son of Nun—and he is supposed to feel reassured? Oh, here is the reassuring verse, *"Anyone who rebels against your command and does not obey your words in all that you command him, shall be put to death; only be strong and courageous."* That's better! If they rebel, grumble, whine or complain—just put them to death! I am already getting a headache on Joshua's behalf. Why would anyone want to be a leader? Who would put himself in the position to take this kind of abuse? Only one called of God for this specific purpose. I think Jesus must have felt the same way when Judas was robbing the money bag, Peter was comparing himself to the other Apostles, Thomas doubted, and His own brothers thought He was insane. Only someone committed to obeying the full will of God would agree to this sort of mission... to love the unlovable and lead the unleadable.

COMMON GROUND: Are you in a position of leadership within your church, your family, or at your chosen profession? It can be the most thankless job in the world, but someone has to do it. Have you felt the ingratitude of others, listened to their nasty barbs, or been accused falsely for something you didn't do? Maybe you are the barb thrower instead of the recipient... does this give you a spirit check? **HOLY GROUND:** Each of us must be either a leader or a follower. Neither job is easy. Remember that it is easy to complain about the leader when you are the follower. It is equally easy to complain about the followers when you are the leader. Holy people close their mouths in both situations.

Father God, Seal my lips. Teach me how to lead as You would have me lead, follow as You would have me follow, and look to You for strength, no matter which position I am in. Amen.

➤ Day 307: HIDING AT RAHAB'S PLACE
PASSAGE: Joshua 2:1-5
VERSE: Joshua 2:4

But the woman had taken the two men and hidden them,
and she said, "Yes, the men came to me, but I did not
know where they were from."

We first met Joshua when he and Caleb, along with ten other spies, were sent to spy on Canaan and report back to Moses what they saw there. Remember, Joshua and Caleb alone brought back good reports and encouraged their brothers to go in and take the land. Forty years later Joshua sends out two men to spy on the walled city of Jericho. The king of Jericho was informed of the infiltrators—last seen entering the home of Rahab the Harlot. He sent messengers to Rahab telling her to hand over the spies. She sent word that she did receive visitors earlier, but they had left through the city gate at dark and she had no idea where they were. She encouraged the king's men to *pursue them quickly,* in order to overtake them before they got too far away. Rahab was risking her life to protect men who were enemies of her people—why would she do that? Why would God direct the feet of the spies to the house of a known harlot? Was it all a part of His Master plan? I think so!

COMMON GROUND: Before I began to serve Christ in 1996 I was a vulgar, sexually impure, prideful and self-absorbed sinner. I am still a work-in-progress, but God has wrought an amazing work in my life. Rahab too was transformed by the renewing of her mind and her belief in the God of the Hebrews (as we will see tomorrow). No one is beyond the scope and ability of God—no one. Watch who you deem worthless in God's kingdom—He created Rahab—and me—for a purpose. **HOLY GROUND:** People judged Rahab for doing what she needed to do in order to survive. She knew nothing else. The bondage of her flesh held her captive and her reputation earned her the title of harlot. Rahab was a child of God and He had already begun His redemptive work in her.

LORD, It was no accident that the spies went to Rahab's house, was it? Your perfect plan was unfolding in unimaginable ways—as it always does. Thank You that even Rahab could be used for good. Amen.

➤ Day **308**: WE FEAR YOUR GOD
PASSAGE: **Joshua 2:6-11**
VERSE: **Joshua 2:9**

I know that the LORD has given you the land, and that the terror of you has fallen on us, and that all the inhabitants of the land have melted away before you.

Today we learn why Rahab, a former prostitute from Jericho, would go out of her way to hide Hebrew spies and risk her life by lying to her own king. *For we have heard how the LORD dried up the water of the Red Sea before you when you came out of Egypt, and what you did to the two kings of the Amorites who were beyond the Jordan... whom you utterly destroyed. When we heard it, our hearts melted and no courage remained in any man any longer because of you; for the LORD your God, He is God in heaven above and on earth beneath.* Rahab had heard of the wonders of God in freeing His people from Egyptian bondage, in defeating mighty enemies, and in fighting for His chosen nation. She heard with spiritual ears, as well as physical ears, and what she heard made her believe in the God of all creation. The Hebrew God was now her God and she would serve Him, no matter the cost—even her own life. Rahab jumped with both feet into serving God. She hid the men from the king's messengers. She provided a place for them to sleep. Rahab's past didn't matter, but her future was in God's hands and she was willing, like Moses, to say, *"Here I am, send me."*

COMMON GROUND: On February 14, 1996, I was given a new start. My past was past, my present was fresh, and my future was set before God to write the book of my life His way. Rahab learned the power of the Hebrew God and knew she too could have a new start to her life if she sought to serve Him. Other than the names, our stories are very similar. Do you know any Rahabs—any lost souls trapped in their sin? Tell them what you are learning; give them a glimpse of the hope you have found in the arms of God. **HOLY GROUND:** God brings change into our lives when we begin to see with spiritual eyes, hear with spiritual ears and think with spiritual minds. How are you doing in that area? Does the world still control your eyes, ears and mind? Tell God. Tell Him what you want. Tell Him what controls you... and ask Him for Rahab-like change.

My Adonai, There are still days when my flesh and my mind belong to the world—and to the prince of this world. I hate those days. I want to serve You every day—without fail. Make me righteous, Jehovah Tsidkenu—my Righteous God. Amen.

➤ Day 309: PEACE PACT
PASSAGE: **Joshua 2:12-16**
VERSE: **Joshua 2:14**

So the men said to her, "Our life for yours if you do not tell this business of ours; and it shall come about when the LORD gives us the land that we will deal kindly and faithfully with you."

The next morning, before the spies left to return to Joshua, Rahab asked them to make a covenant with her. *"Now therefore, please swear to me by the LORD, since I have dealt kindly with you, that you also will deal kindly with my father's household, and give me a pledge of truth, and spare my father and my mother and my brothers and my sisters, with all who belong to them, and deliver our lives from death."* The request was sincere and heartfelt. Rahab had risked her life to help the Hebrews get information about Jericho and she was now asking that her family be spared from the attack soon to come upon her city. Rahab was merely asking for the same treatment she had given... you know, *Do unto others as you would have them do unto you.* Her request was honored when these covenant words were spoken by the spies, *"Our life for yours if you do not tell this business of ours; and it shall come about when the LORD gives us the land that we will deal kindly and faithfully with you."* If Rahab remained silent and told no one of their visit, then one day when Jericho fell she would have provided a safety net for her entire family. What a selfless and godly woman—a reformed woman who was once a harlot.

COMMON GROUND: The spies could have used Rahab for protection and then turned her over to her king as a traitor. They could have left her with no promise. Why didn't those things happen? God wasn't finished with Rahab yet. Trust was building between the two parties to this agreement. How are you at trusting others at their word? **HOLY GROUND:** Some of us have a very difficult time trusting others—often because of past hurts, lies and betrayals. Rahab could have looked at these men like the other men she had known in her life. Something told her they were different. They were godly men—and their spirits and hers were focused on serving the same God. Holy people should be able to discern between worldly people and godly people—and ally with the latter.

Jesus, Help me know whom to trust. No man can be like You, LORD, and I know man will always let me down... like in the past, but I also know there are trustworthy believers in whom I can confide and share my heart. Show me, LORD. Amen.

► Day 310: RAHAB'S RESPONSIBILITY
PASSAGE: Joshua 2:17-21
VERSE: Joshua 2:18

...unless, when we come into the land, you tie this cord of scarlet thread in the window through which you let us down, and gather to yourself into the house your father and your mother and your brothers and all your father's household.

The Hebrew spies agreed to Rahab's request for protection of her life and that of her family. Certain terms were established which shifted the responsibility back into her hands. Rahab was to gather all her family members into her house and keep them there until the attack on Jericho began. *When we come into the land, you tie this cord of scarlet thread in the window through which you let us down, and gather to yourself into the house your father and your mother and your brothers and all your father's household.* The command seemed simple enough to obey... gather the family, lock them in her house, dangle the red cord out the same window which the spies used to escape over the wall and wait... and wait... and wait. Rahab had no idea how long it would take the spies to report to Joshua. The people had to cross the Jordan River and prepare for battle. Rahab didn't know how long it would take, but she knew she couldn't risk not being prepared when the battle ensued. Rahab obediently gathered her family and somehow convinced them to remain inside her home, watching for the Hebrew army from the city wall of Jericho. Hurry Rahab... and wait—trust—listen—watch—and pray.

COMMON GROUND: You know what waiting is like, don't you? Have you ever had to wait for someone who is perpetually late? I have no patience for that; and I wonder how much patience I would have had if I were Rahab. We all know when a family is together in close quarters that they can get on one another's nerves. Hurry and wait. What is your patience quotient? Are you willing to wait for God's perfect timing... or are you advising Him how to work in yours? **HOLY GROUND:** I am one of the least patient people I know. No tolerance in traffic, no peace in waiting for others, no sanity when things don't begin on time. Hurry up and wait drives me nuts—how about you? If patience is a virtue, I am missing that one. God is working in me to bring me to a patient place during this journey. Does He need to work on you a little too?

Holy Spirit, When I think of Abraham, Moses, Job and King David, I realize You choose some people because they are patient. It makes me realize there are things I am not chosen for because of my impatient attitude. Change me—and hurry! Amen.

➤ Day 311: GOD HAS GIVEN US JERICHO!
PASSAGE: Joshua 2:22-24
VERSE: Joshua 2:24

They said to Joshua, "Surely the LORD has given all the land into our hands; moreover, all the inhabitants of the land have melted away before us."

After hiding for three days to cool their trail before any pursuers, the spies hurried back to Joshua to report what had happened. After telling him of Rahab's protecting them and the covenant they had made with her, they told their new leader: *"...the LORD has given all the land into our hands; moreover, all the inhabitants of the land have melted away before us."* The excitement must have pulsed through Joshua's veins as he realized the long deferred hope of his heart was about to come true. What a different spy report this was—allies in the enemy city, protection and covering by God, and paralyzing fear among the nations because of His past faithfulness to the Hebrew people. Joshua wasn't foolish enough to think the battle would be easy, but he was wise enough to know who the Battle Leader was. Joshua was in this place—at this time—for this success—because of his past exhibition of faith in His God... *Jehovah Sabaoth*—The LORD of Hosts, The God of Mighty Armies... the God who would give Israel the land promised so long ago to his father Abraham—another man who had been willing to leave everything in search of the will of *Adonai* God.

COMMON GROUND: Are you like me? Do you like to fight easy battles—ones with no opponent and no chance of getting hurt? Or, are you an adventurer who loves a challenge? God used Moses and Joshua because they were battle-ready. It is so common to only walk where victory is obvious, but the rare child of God will willingly walk into the unknown... trusting. **HOLY GROUND:** He can only use willing vessels, because God will never force us into service. When we don't willingly offer ourselves, someone else steps up—and after the battle receives the blessings. Joshua is about to receive his just reward.

Father God, Bravery has never been my strong point... actually, I am a bit of a chicken! You already know that, but You still want to use me. How amazing! Here I am... send me (I think)! Amen.

➤ Day 312: FOLLOW THAT ARK!
PASSAGE: Joshua 3:1-4
VERSE: Joshua 3:3b

When you see the ark of the covenant of the LORD your God with the Levitical priests carrying it, then you shall set out from your place and go after it.

If you remember earlier entries about the ark of God, you will recall that it was placed in the tabernacle behind a special veil (or curtain) and represented the very presence of God among the Hebrew people. Inside the ark would be the stone tablets with the God-written Ten Commandments, a jar of manna, the bread of Heaven, and Aaron's staff that was used to initiate miracles before Pharaoh, the King of Egypt. The ark was covered by the mercy seat with guarding angels protecting it. One day each year the high priest would enter the Holy of Holies and sprinkle blood upon the corners of the ark to make atonement for his own sins and the sins of Israel. As we pick up our story of the movement of the Hebrew nation into the occupied land of Canaan, the ark was about to be moved. The people were to follow the ark approximately 3500 feet behind it. No one other than those God had ordained to move His holy furnishings were to venture near it. They were to follow it as God directed — never losing sight of His presence, for their wandering feet were about to walk on paths they had never walked on before. This surely would not have been the time to lose sight of God.

COMMON GROUND: How would you like to know that no matter where you walked God was with you? Would you venture out into new territories more? Would you dare to step from the common of today into the holy of forever? Where do your insecurities lay—

in past failure, a broken heart, abandonment? **HOLY GROUND:** God has promised to never leave us or forsake us. How can we be assured of that truth? The Holy Spirit lives within our hearts and testifies of God to our spirit man. Are you communicating with the Spirit? Are you walking with Him every minute? Those who have received salvation through Jesus Christ are indwelt by the very Spirit of God… and are never, ever truly alone.

LORD, I need to understand better the workings of the Holy Spirit so I can better discern Your leadings from those of my own flesh. I willingly open myself to this teaching and look forward to the newness in my life. Amen.

➤ Day 313: I WILL MAGNIFY YOU
PASSAGE: Joshua 3:5-7
VERSE: Joshua 3:7

Now the LORD said to Joshua, "This day I will begin to exalt you in the sight of all Israel, that they may know that just as I have been with Moses, I will be with you."

Joshua issued the command and the Levites lifted up the ark and began to carry it. The people had been cleansed and were ready to step into their future home—a home full of promise and hope. God spoke to Joshua some words for his ears alone. *"This day I will begin to exalt you in the sight of all Israel, that they may know that just as I have been with Moses, I will be with you."* Isn't God totally awesome? Talk about reassurance before you take the first step from common to holy! "I am going to work wonders through you and in doing so EVERYONE in Israel will know that I am with you, just as I was with Moses before you. There will be no denying My choosing you to lead My children home." Joshua must have felt like he was twelve feet tall! What a promise! What a source of encouragement! What a gift for someone who had remained dedicated and faithful! Has God ever whispered in your ear? During the writing of this book the Enemy has stepped up his attacks on me. Obviously, he doesn't want you to read it. My email has been hijacked by someone in Nigeria who is asking my contacts to send money. My video camera went kaput and I worked for two weeks with a new one and was unable to use the files it produced. Our store is so dead you could bowl between the displays. Yet, I hear Him whisper in my ear, *"Be still and know that I am God."*

COMMON GROUND: In order for God to whisper in your ear, you will have to have enough silence around you to hear the whisper. He will not shout over the television or radio and He will not close the pages of the novel you are reading and force His Word into your hands. He will not smack you upside the head with a baseball bat. He whispers in the stillness of your spirit. Are you listening? **HOLY GROUND:** Joshua heard the sweetest promise in the world when he listened for God's affirmation of his call. In order for that to happen, Joshua needed to be listening instead of talking. Ouch, that hurt!

My Adonai, I long to hear Your words of encouragement and life. I long to see Your face, feel Your touch and smell Your fragrance. I need that so desperately... Please hear my cry. Amen.

➤ Day 314: STAND AND WATCH!
PASSAGE: Joshua 3:8-11
VERSE: Joshua 3:8

You shall, moreover, command the priests who are carrying the Ark of the Covenant, saying, "When you come to the edge of the waters of the Jordan, you shall stand still in the Jordan."

God was still whispering... "Tell the priests carrying the ark to walk into the water of the Jordan River and stop. Tell them to stand there. I want all of Israel to know exactly who I am and what I am about to do on their behalf. I *will* dispossess from before you the

Canaanites, the Hittites, the Hivites, the Perizzites, the Girgashites, the Amorites, and the Jebusites. I *will* move those who worship idols and foreign gods. I *will* give you their land. I *will* walk with you. For now, simply stand still and watch Me work." *Stand still!* Are You crazy, God? These people are ready to push forward. They have wandered forty years and desperately want to walk into the land of Your promise. They are pushing forward... and You want me to tell them to stand still? *Stand still* is kind of like *be still*... and both are commands we hate to hear. I know from personal experience that when I *stand still* and watch God work I am always amazed. When I *be still* He always speaks. The Hebrew people weren't really that different than we are; they just had different demands. They had lands to conquer—we have bills to pay. They had children to feed—we have careers to build. They had a river to cross—we have emails to answer. When will we learn that in His timing all things are done perfectly?

COMMON GROUND: Can you think of a time when God clearly wanted you to stand still and wait for His perfect timing? Did you obey or rush forward in your own power? How did it turn out? If you failed in the plan, you are plagued with a disease common to man—Impatience. **HOLY GROUND:** Try this: Wherever you are, close your eyes, take a deep breath, and whisper the Name of Jesus. Repeat that Name as you ask Him for peace. Ask Him to give you patience. Ask Him to help you stand still before Him. Ask Him to gently place His hand on your shoulder and direct your paths. Practice this same thing each time you are tempted to keep pressing forward in your own strength.

Jesus, I am standing still. Show me what is next. Amen.

➤ Day 315: WALKING ON DRY LAND
PASSAGE: Joshua 3:12-17
VERSE: Joshua 3:13

It shall come about when the soles of the feet of the priests who carry the ark of the LORD, the LORD of all the earth, rest in the waters of the Jordan, the waters of the Jordan will be cut off, and the waters which are flowing down from above will stand in one heap.

As the people stood still to watch and the priests stood in the Jordan holding the ark above the water, God told Joshua the waters flowing into the Jordan from the northern city of Adam would stop flowing and pile up. The waters flowing to the south would flow away and in their place dry ground would appear... holy ground... like that which appeared in the midst of the Red Sea as Moses delivered the people from Egyptian bondage. How could that be? The river was high and fast—this was harvest season when the waters of the Jordan overflow their banks. How could this happen? Yet, much to Joshua's amazement... that is exactly what happened. As the priests held the ark—the very Presence of God among His people—the ground immediately dried up, leaving a highway in the middle of the riverbed. The people crossed until they were standing on land near the city of Jericho. Finally, finally... they were standing in the Promised Land. Oh, glory to God who made a way where there seemed to be no way! He removed the water obstacle, dried up the mud, and made the ground sure and safe for the multitude of the Hebrew nation to pass over. Has He made a way for you when there was no possible way... a way that led you from common ground to holy ground?

COMMON GROUND: You know what I am going to ask you this time. Has God opened impossibly locked doors, knocked down high impenetrable walls, or removed powerful enemies from your path? You may not have seen the Jordan waters dry up, but maybe you had a windfall of money at a much needed time, a word of encouragement when you were ready to give up, or a job window opened when another closed. Are you staring at the closed door and failing to see the open window next to it? **HOLY GROUND:** Boy, I needed this entry. As I look at what appear to be closed doors, I must remember the ones He has opened for me innumerable times in the past. My God is faithful to me—and I must not forget. The Hebrew people had just witnessed another impossible miracle of God. You would think they would be forever changed by it, but they will fail again… in just a short time.

Holy Spirit, I know a faithful God will always make a way through the struggles and obstacles of my life. I know, but I will need to be reminded… and often. After all, I am but flesh and blood. Amen.

➤ Day **316**: BUILD A MEMORIAL
PASSAGE: **Joshua 4:1-9, 20-23**
VERSE: **Joshua 4:6**

Let this be a sign among you, so that when your children ask later, saying, "What do these stones mean to you?"

After the people were safely established on the west side of the Jordan, God instructed Joshua to have one representative from each of the twelve tribes go back into the riverbed to find a large boulder. He was to carry it back to dry land on the west side of the Jordan. The boulders would be used to build a memorial—a monument to help them remember the faithfulness of God in parting the waters. Having each tribe participate was a show of solidarity. Tough days lay ahead and an eventual separation between the tribes when Reuben, Gad and East Manasseh would recross the river to their homeland. The memorial also served another purpose—likely the greater purpose. In the future, after this generation had passed, a new generation who had not witnessed the miracle would ask what the memorial was for. Wise ancestors should have passed the story of God's provision down so their questions would be answered: "Let me tell you about the God of Israel. One day your ancestors were in bondage in a foreign land. They cried out to God… He heard their cry... He delivered them from their captors... He parted the Red Sea... He sent the manna... He let them wander in their sin... He retired Moses and promoted Joshua... He later parted the Jordan... He ushered our people into the land He promised to our father Abraham generations before... He is an amazing God."

COMMON GROUND: God didn't want the monument built so the people could worship it. When you go to the cemetery to visit the grave of a loved one, you don't worship the gravestone. It is a reminder of the part that person played in your life. This monument was the same thing... God played an awesome part in delivering the people to the Promised Land. He did not want them to forget... and He knew that in our human weakness we would do just that. **HOLY GROUND:** How often we set up memorials to our own successes and worship them, forgetting who the Father of all our successes is. As you near the end of this journey, don't forget to look back at the milestone markers... the little monuments dedicated to changes He has been making in your life. Without them, you will forget.

Father God, I remember the day You showed me about stepping out of my comfort zone and reminded me I would have to leave the well-traveled path to have an encounter with You. I haven't forgotten—yet. Keep reminding me. Amen.

➤ Day 317: BRING THE ARK INTO THE LAND
PASSAGE: Joshua 4:10-14
VERSE: Joshua 4:11

...and when all the people had finished crossing, the ark of the LORD and the priests crossed before the people.

Imagine the awe of the people as they watched the priests carry the ark from the middle of the river up onto dry land. God truly was in their presence. I would have to think some fell on their knees in gratitude and adoration for His provision on the journey. If they didn't, they should have! The masses parted as the ark was safely carried through their midst by the Levites. Leading the way in an army of 40,000 armed soldiers were the tribes who would make their home on the other side of the river after the battles were fought. There in the desert plains of Jericho the people looked at the ark and then turned their gaze toward Joshua. God had kept His promise. Joshua had been exalted in the presence of the people. They could see the strength and purpose of God written all over him. Joshua (Yeshua) brought his brethren into the Promised Land. He is an Old Testament picture of Jesus (Yeshua), who will usher believers into their forever Promised Land where they will rule and reign forever. Joshua would soon fight physical battles in order to give the land to his people. Jesus, hundreds of years later, would fight spiritual battles against the forces of evil to do the same. Joshua was a strong leader and a mighty warrior. Jesus was the same. Joshua delivered people from aimless wandering in the wilderness. Jesus did the same—for me and hopefully by now—for you too.

COMMON GROUND: Do you know Jesus intimately and fully? Is He the center of your being—the first beat of your heart? Joshua could do what his physical abilities would allow, but Jesus fulfilled a purpose so much greater. He saved His lost, wandering children from wandering without purpose. He redeemed them from their sins. Have you accepted His gift of redemption? (See back of this book for the plan of salvation for your personal use or for use in evangelism). **HOLY GROUND:** Joshua's people would have been delivered, but they were not yet redeemed in their hearts. If they were, they wouldn't have continued in their sin. How does that statement sit with you? Is there sin yet to be removed for holiness to spring forth?

LORD, Redeem me. Free me. Renew me. Save me. Amen.

➤ Day 318: ALL WILL SEE OUR GOD
PASSAGE: Joshua 4:19-24
VERSE: Joshua 4:24

...that all the peoples of the earth may know that the hand of the LORD is mighty, so that you may fear the LORD your God forever.

The twelve stones were placed together near Gilgal as God commanded. The solemn process of placing them in a formation which nature couldn't match would ensure that for generations to come the unique stone monument would stand out from the other stones scattered on the land. These stones were smooth—washed clean by years and years of flowing river water. Their corners would likely be softened, not by cuts made by human hands, but by God's testing and proving with the washing of the running water. Joshua told the people they were there as a witness to future members of the nation of Israel, but they were also there so *all the peoples of the earth may know that the hand of the LORD is mighty, so that you may fear the LORD your God forever.* As long as Israel stood proud and strong—like the rock monument—they would shine among the nations of the world and their God would be revered above all other gods. Back to the cleaned and polished rocks... are you feeling like this journey has smoothed some rough edges, softened some past bumps and bruises, and worked to cleanse you from within? That is the goal, you know. Hundreds of hours didn't go into this manuscript for you to come away unaffected.

COMMON GROUND: On January 1, 2009, God spoke the words, *"From Common Ground to Holy Ground this year, Vicki."* I had no idea what that meant, but wrote it down on the pad next to my Bible study chair and began to pray about it. The next week I began teaching these five books of Scripture to my Seekers class and on television programming in our community. Little did I know the journey was mine as well as everyone else's to make. **HOLY GROUND:** Lots of rough edges needed to be rounded off. Some dirty spots needed to be scrubbed clean. Hopefully, when others look at me today they will see the wonder of God. In my flesh I am nothing... and I want future generations and nonbelievers alike to see the work He has done in me as they read this book. His refining me is a monument to His love, just like the monument at Gilgal.

My Adonai, What a journey this is! I had no idea how much work I needed. I sort of thought I had it pretty well 'together' in my faith walk. You continue to show me new areas for growth.
Thank You. Amen.

➤ Day 319: MARKED FOR GOD'S KINGDOM
PASSAGE: Joshua 5:1-8
VERSE: Joshua 5:4

This is the reason why Joshua circumcised them: all the people who came out of Egypt who were males, all the men of war, died in the wilderness along the way after they came out of Egypt.

The enemy nations surrounding the Jordan River area had heard of God's miracle with the river and all the other miracles He had performed. They were in fear of Israel. After all, Israel had a supernatural force fighting for them that no other nation had. Why did the Hebrew God answer prayers when their gods seemed impotent to help them at all? Just when the celebration was about to begin amid Joshua's flock God sent a new command, but not one I'm sure they wanted to hear! *"Make for yourself flint knives and circumcise again the sons of Israel the second time."* What was God thinking? They had walls to scale and enemies to defeat. How could a freshly circumcised army do that? God knew exactly what He was doing. It was time for the covenant to be renewed. *For all the people who came out (of Egypt) were circumcised, but all the people who were born in the wilderness... had not been circumcised. For the sons of Israel walked forty years in the wilderness, until all the nation perished because they did not listen to the voice of the LORD.* The mark of God on the males of the Hebrew nation was circumcision;

they could not go any farther into the land until the men were once again marked with His seal.

COMMON GROUND: God placed His mark upon His children to distinguish them from all the others in the world. Think of it this way: a wedding band doesn't make you married, but it serves as a means to let others know you are covenanted to your spouse. In the wilderness the people didn't need the mark because they were on common ground, but now they were moving into the Promised Land. **HOLY GROUND:** Are you marked by God for His kingdom? The mark is an outward sign (as in circumcision), but can also be an outward change of behavior and attitude. Before we can go into battle for God—and before we can walk fully into the land of His promise—we must be marked as belonging to Him.

Jesus, Mark my words, thoughts, attitudes and actions with Your stamp of approval. Man's mark means nothing, but Your mark makes me separate unto you. Mark me, LORD. Amen.

➤ Day 320: MANNA NO MORE
PASSAGE: Joshua 5:9-12
VERSE: Joshua 5:12

The manna ceased on the day after they had eaten some of the produce of the land, so that the sons of Israel no longer had manna, but they ate some of the yield of the land of Canaan during that year.

For the first time, the Jewish people celebrated the Passover feast on the fourteenth day of the first month in the land God promised their ancestors. They ate of the bounty the land provided. That day at Gilgal the manna, which had fed them for forty years in the wilderness, stopped falling from heaven upon their camp. Imagine that first morning when the people went out, as they had for years, to gather that which would sustain their families for that day... only to find no manna covering the ground. Reality set in. Either God was going to provide for their needs in a new way, or He was abandoning them after this long difficult journey. They realized He had provided Passover food for them, not by manna and not by the work of their hands. He provided what they needed at the hands of their enemies! Only God could have the foresight to know what they would need, when they would need it, and even have others do the work ahead of time! The manna stopped because God had an amazing new plan. After all, they were now in the *land of milk and honey...* and grain!

COMMON GROUND: God was doing what He spoke through David years later in Psalm 23. *You prepare a table before me in the presence of my enemies.* On land belonging to the Canaanites and from food planted by their Canaanite enemies, God was preparing the table for fellowship with His children. They were being sealed and fed on common ground—but common only for a while. **HOLY GROUND:** God was providing for all the basic needs of Israel in amazing ways. If He has done the same thing in your life, will you commit to complete dedication and obedience to Him? Holy people are Christ-marked and manna-fed. They forever belong to Him.

Holy Spirit, Your provision is amazing and Your ways are almost unimaginable to my small mind. Prepare me a table in the presence of my enemies—so that all will know my God. Amen.

➤ Day 321: GOD'S ARMY
PASSAGE: Joshua 5:13-15
VERSE: Joshua 5:14

He said, "No; rather I indeed come now as captain of the host of the LORD." And Joshua fell on his face to the earth, and bowed down, and said to him, "What has my LORD to say to his servant?"

Joshua was looking at Jericho, possibly trying to figure out a plan of attack on what looked like an impregnable walled fortress. Maybe he was praying for direction—because we are told *he lifted up his eyes and looked*—and before him stood a man with a sword in his hand. Joshua, the general of the Hebrew army, stood and approached the armed man. *"Are you for us or for our adversaries?"* For all Joshua knew, this man might be the first in a series of waves of enemy fighters coming to stop the advancement of Israel before it ever began. *"I indeed come now as captain of the host of the LORD."* Talk about manna from heaven! This was manna to Joshua's ears and balm to his heart. God was sending a protective army to fight alongside the Hebrew army. He hadn't forgotten them and hadn't abandoned them! On his face before the *captain of the host* (and I believe a pre-birth appearance of Jesus Christ), Joshua asked what word God sent for him. Imagine his overwhelming gratitude at the words which flowed from this warrior's mouth. *"Remove your sandals from your feet, for the place where you are standing is holy."* Joshua removed his sandals and, like his mentor Moses before him, stood for the first time on holy ground. The common ground of God's enemies was now anything but common... and Joshua knew in his heart that every battle ahead was covered by the hand of his God.

COMMON GROUND: If you could look around you right now and see the spiritual forces God has surrounded you with and could know that they would go before you into any battle—would you feel more inclined to walk out in faith? The message of the captain was to assure Joshua of his promotion from common life into holy life. Are you hearing the same message? It is yours... **HOLY GROUND:** This is a big step in your journey. Are you going to take the step from where the world walks to where the LORD walks? Great adventure lies ahead... after your sandals are removed... and the Captain of your army is firmly entrenched in His rightful place of leadership.

Father God, The sandals are off and the ground beneath my feet is warm as I walk into Your presence and welcome Your command over my life. Amen.

➤ Day 322: GOD'S WARFARE
PASSAGE: Joshua 6:1-3
VERSE: Joshua 6:3

You shall march around the city, all the men of war circling the city once. You shall do so for six days.

Students of the Bible know that God's ways and commands for His children are nearly always contrary to our human inclination. In today's entry we see a clear picture of that truth. Jericho is walled up, sealed from the outside with no one coming in and no one going out. Their watchmen have seen the massive Hebrew nation on the plains outside its walls. Joshua and his army were looking at that fortress and wondering exactly how God was going to give them the victory He had promised. Should they go underground through hidden tunnels and trenches? Should they build tall ladders to scale the walls under cover of darkness? Should they use catapults to fling huge rocks against the stone walls? Should they *march around the city... the men of war circling the city once... for six days*. What? Who came up with that hair-brained scheme? How will that serve the purpose of bringing Jericho to defeat? *The LORD said to Joshua, "See, I have given Jericho into your hand, with its king and the valiant warriors."* Like numerous other men of God throughout the pages of the Bible, Joshua must make a decision to obey God or to walk into the unknown in his own power.

COMMON GROUND: *Trust in the LORD with all your heart and do not lean on your own understanding. In all your ways acknowledge Him, and He will make your paths straight. Do not be wise in your own eyes; fear the LORD and turn away from evil.* **HOLY GROUND:** Big promise, big God. Whose wisdom are you leaning on—His or yours? He will not direct your paths if you are not listening to His direction.

LORD, Even when Your ways seem foolish in my eyes, I will trust in Your eventual outcome being the best for my life. After all, You are Jehovah Raah—the LORD my Shepherd. Amen.

➤ Day 323: THE WALL SHALL FALL
PASSAGE: Joshua 6:4-5
VERSE: Joshua 6:5

It shall be that when they make a long blast with the ram's horn, and when you hear the sound of the trumpet, all the people shall shout with a great shout; and the wall of the city will fall down flat, and the people will go up every man straight ahead.

While Joshua was still evaluating God's first method of warfare, He continued to reveal the rest of the strategy. *"...seven priests shall carry seven trumpets of rams' horns before the ark; then on the seventh day you shall march around the city seven times, and the priests shall blow the trumpets."* Joshua must have thought, "Oh yeah, that's better God! You want me to bring the Ark of the Covenant and the priests into the battle too? I know the ark represents Your presence among us, but we would be risking damage or capture of it. Let me get this straight. The army is to march six days in silence around Jericho with the priests carrying the ark? On day seven they do the same thing, except they circle seven times? And... You say they should wait for the trumpet blast... and then the shouts of all the people at the same exact time will make the fortified walls fall? Lord, are You and I looking at the same battle, LORD? We will look like absolute fools! We will be the laughing stock of all the nations around this place. But wait... You have parted seas and rivers for us and You have dropped quail and manna from Heaven. You have kept our sandals and clothes from wearing out for over forty years. You have been faithful in every way. Okay, God... We will step out in faith and do it Your way."

COMMON GROUND: Those who do not know our God, or those who actually reject Him as 'fantasy in the minds of weak individuals who need a crutch', will never understand His direction of our lives. Numerous people told Dan and me we were crazy to open His House and that no one would buy my books. People in my own family are waiting for me to take control of my life back and stop allowing God to direct my paths. Are you willing to be a 'fool' for Christ?

405

HOLY GROUND: Joshua may have doubted the rationality of the commands, but he couldn't deny that God had never failed Israel yet. Joshua had to be willing to ignore what others thought and to answer to the Audience of One in the heavens. Holy people know that earthly people have no ability to save them... thus the heavenly Audience is the only one they play to please.

My Adonai, As LORD of my life, You are the Audience I answer to.
You are the One I seek to please. Yours is the only "Bravo"
I need to hear at the end of my journey. Amen.

➤ Day 324: BE STILL
PASSAGE: **Joshua 6:6-14**
VERSE: **Joshua 6:10**

But Joshua commanded the people, saying, "You shall not shout nor let your voice be heard nor let a word proceed out of your mouth, until the day I tell you, 'Shout!' Then you shall shout!"

Joshua had come to grips with blind obedience in his heart. Now he had to convince the army and populace to follow his lead. Knowing Israel's history that was easier said than done. Remember how they tried to stone Moses and Aaron when they didn't like their leadership? Joshua told them the plan and waited to hear their doubts and grumbling. Finally, everyone was in agreement and the first day of marching commenced. How eerie it must have been for the guards on top of Jericho's walls when the people remained completely silent—no singing, no talking, no marching cadence, no celebrating. Talk about throwing the enemy off kilter! They were either laughing at the silent army with the Ark of the Covenant leading the way, or they were discomfited by the strange silence... with only the sound of their feet moving upon holy ground. Six days this happened and the enemy must have thought it would go on forever. Maybe they began to let their guard down—relax and simply watch Israel in their foolish quest. Whatever the attitude was in Jericho, the more amazing attitude was the obedience of the Hebrew people to be silent for such a long period of time... silent and patient... waiting... waiting... waiting for the ram's horn shofar to sound.

COMMON GROUND: Maybe this story is from where the saying, 'silence is golden' originated. I love silence, and am writing this entry in silence. No television blaring with blather, no phone conversations, no husband talking to me, no sound but a distant train whistle... and the silence is indeed golden. God was preparing both Israel and Jericho for the battle. Israel was being prepared for victory and Jericho for defeat. **HOLY GROUND:** If the sound of silence is God preparing you for victory, are you happy with stillness? We talked recently about listening for Him. Today, I encourage you to seek Him, search for Him, mine through the noise and stuff of this world to pursue Him and His holy silence. You will receive in accordance to what you offer to Him.

Jesus, My soul waits in silence for God only;
from Him is my salvation. Amen.

➤ Day 325: BLOW THAT TRUMPET!
PASSAGE: Joshua 6:15-16
VERSE: Joshua 6:16

At the seventh time, when the priests blew the trumpets, Joshua said to the people, "Shout! For the LORD has given you the city."

Day seven dawned bright in the plains outside the walls of the Canaanite city of Jericho. The Levites hoisted the heavy ark with its gold-covered poles onto their shoulders. The army was lined up in marching formation and there was a palpable sense of expectancy in the air. The watchmen of Jericho had been lulled into a sense of complacency by the inane actions of the Hebrew army. "Here they go again with that same silent march around the city... what kind of foolish practice is this? Wait... something is different today...

they are going around a second time... a third... fourth... fifth... sixth..." As the ark completed its seventh march around the wall, a sudden blast of the trumpet shofar filled the air and the people began a deafening shout. The walls began to shake from the sheer volume of their cries and suddenly the impenetrable fortress walls of Jericho began to fall. The impossible had happened! *Jehovah Sabaoth*, the LORD of Hosts, had turned what seemed to be idiotic warfare practices into sudden victory! He didn't use blitzkrieg (lightning warfare) or catapults; He used silence and authority. He used obedience and discipline. He used fallible men and women. He used His obedient army to bring down the enemy fortress.

COMMON GROUND: Food for thought: when God tells you to 'shout' about His victories in your life, do you 'shout'? When He tells you to share Christ with others, do you? When you read, *Sing to Him, sing praises to Him; Speak of all His wonders,* do you do that? There is a time for silence and a time for shouting. Are you shouting when He says it is time? **HOLY GROUND:** If the rock-hard walls of Jericho could not stand strong in the face of the shout of God's people, why would we think the rock-hard walls around the hearts of our unbelieving friends and family members will not fall the same way if we shout of the glory of our LORD? Open your mouth and start 'SHOUTING'!

Holy Spirit, Show me when to be silent. Then, show me when it is 'Shouting Time' so Your glory can reign. Amen.

➤ Day 326: DON'T TAKE PERSONAL SPOIL
PASSAGE: Joshua 6:17-19
VERSE: Joshua 6:18

But as for you, only keep yourselves from the things under the ban, so that you do not covet them and take some of the things under the ban, and make the camp of Israel accursed and bring trouble on it.

Joshua told the people the LORD had given them the city, but he also cautioned them that the covenant with Rahab still stood. *"...only Rahab the harlot and all who are with her in the house shall live, because she hid the messengers whom we sent."* A man's word is only as good as his ability to keep it... and Joshua's word was good. He also cautioned the people *"...keep yourselves **from** the things under the ban, so that you **do not covet them** and take some of the things under the ban, and make the camp of Israel accursed and bring trouble on it. But all the silver and gold and articles of bronze and iron are holy to the LORD; they shall go into the treasury of the LORD."* The *ban* referred to here was the command for spoil which God gave to the army, telling them whether they were to take battle spoil for themselves, gather it for the temple treasury, or destroy it altogether. In this case, the gold, silver, bronze and iron were to be gathered for the temple. It was cursed, and anyone disobeying by taking it for personal gain would bring that curse upon the Hebrew camp. God was setting strict limits for the army because He knew what could happen in the heat and excitement of battle when adrenaline was pumping and men had access to abundant riches. In those moments the soldiers might forget who gave them the victory and begin to think the wall fell and the enemy fell because of their own great power. God was keeping a tight rein—as any good Shepherd should—on His unruly charges.

COMMON GROUND: How common it is to pray for God's hand, have Him guide us to sure victory, and then take all the credit upon our own shoulders. Oh, sometimes we give Him a little nod... like this: "I prayed for God to help me get out of debt. I received a check for $9,278 dollars. I paid off my credit card balances. I bought the new refrigerator we needed. I am so lucky that check came. I must be living right!" How does the check Provider feel? **HOLY GROUND:** God doesn't need your accolades—He needs your eyes to be open to where all victories, gifts and abilities come from. Are you giving Him credit for being *Jehovah Jireh*—Your Provider God?

Father God, I pray in faith; You respond in love; but I sometimes fail to acknowledge Your provision. That equals taking the 'spoil' for my glory and not Yours. I am sorry, LORD. Amen.

➤ Day 327: TAKING JERICHO!
PASSAGE: **Joshua 6:20-21**
VERSE: **Joshua 6:20**

So the people shouted, and priests blew the trumpets; and when the people heard the sound of the trumpet, the people shouted with a great shout and the wall fell down flat, so that the people went up into the city, every man straight ahead, and they took the city.

With the protective wall down, Jericho was vulnerable to the Israeli nation. Those not injured or killed when the walls collapsed were slain when the people took the city. The spoil was gathered and the precious metals would later be purified by fire and added to the treasury of the House of God. Everything else was burned. All life was destroyed, per God's command. Why would a loving God give that command? Why would He command the eradication of a race or a nationality of people? I am not God and cannot explain for His ways, but I trust Him. We do find glimpses in the book of Genesis. Jericho was a major city in the land of Canaan. If we look in Genesis 9, we find a curse being pronounced upon Canaan and his heirs because of blatant sin. Canaan was cast out of the presence of his brothers and became an enemy nation to Israel. The enmity was sure enough that Jacob, the father of the twelve tribes of Israel, had to have a wife brought from far away so he would not blend the Israelite race with the Canaanites. God knew that Israel in Joshua's day could easily fall prey to the same compromises, so He was striving to keep the Jewish bloodline pure.

COMMON GROUND: As I said, I will not try to explain God's ways, but I pray you can see His heart. He takes faithfulness very seriously. Canaan chose sin. Canaan chose to worship other gods. Canaan became an enemy of God. Do you understand God's admonition for believers not to be married (yoked) unequally with unbelievers? Compromise always leads to destruction. **HOLY GROUND:** Holy people may not always understand Bible stories when they are taken out of the context of the Bible as a whole. God's decisions and choices are most often a result of a previous event or series of events... and the suffering is the resulting consequence for sin or moral failure. We must make the decision that we will trust Him and His character when we look at His record of provision.

LORD, I don't have to know everything. What you show me is enough. When I open my eyes in heaven and the blinders are removed, I will understand everything. Until then, I trust. Amen.

➤ Day 328: COVENANT KEPT
PASSAGE: Joshua 6:22-26
VERSE: Joshua 6:23

So the young men who were spies went in and brought out Rahab and her father and her mother and her brothers and all she had; they also brought out all her relatives and placed them outside the camp of Israel.

Rahab and her family were spared! She had put the scarlet cord in the window overlooking Jericho's outer wall. She had gathered her loved ones near. She had stayed inside and waited for God's work to be finished. Rahab could have been frustrated at the delay while Joshua's army marched around the perimeter of the city day after day after day. Instead, she watched with faith-filled eyes for the glory of the Hebrew God to be revealed. She was not to be disappointed. In the midst of the defeat of Jericho, Rahab and her family were safely escorted out of the city and placed near the camp of the Israelite nation. Imagine the looks exchanged between those two factions! Hebrew people, not knowing all the details, were likely wondering why this one Canaanite woman and her family were spared. Rahab and her family were looking at the massive nation before them and wondering how they would ever fit in among them. She need not have worried. I spoke in an earlier Rahab entry about her being used as part of God's Master plan. Look with me at this Scripture taken from the New Testament Gospel of Matthew: *The record of the genealogy of Jesus the Messiah, the son of David,* *the son of Abraham: Abraham was the father of Isaac, Isaac the father of Jacob... Salmon was the father of Boaz by **Rahab**, Boaz was the father of Obed by Ruth, and Obed the father of Jesse. Jesse was the father of David the king... Jacob was the father of Joseph the husband of Mary, by whom Jesus was born, who is called the Messiah.* God's unmistakable plan included allowing a former harlot named Rahab prominently to be listed in the genealogy of our LORD and Savior, Jesus Christ. Rahab's legacy in our lives is the promise that God can use anyone He chooses to accomplish what He chooses to accomplish! Good news for you and me!

COMMON GROUND: The Gospel of Jesus Christ is that God sent His Son to the earth to eliminate the sin barrier between the Creator and Creation. Sin separates us from God, but the shed blood of Jesus Christ erases that sin stain when we believe with our whole heart that He is our Redeemer—fully man, yet fully Divine. Rahab turned from her life of sin and began a new walk with the God of all Creation. **HOLY GROUND:** I've asked before and I'll ask again... know any Rahabs? No one—as you can see from this lesson—is beyond the redemptive work of Christ. If Rahab was named in the lineage of the Messiah, who are we to say someone is beyond hope?

My Adonai, Only You could write this story. In my limited imagination I would never use Rahab in that lineage. How awed I am by Your ways... amazing, unbelievable and infinite. Amen.

➤ Day 329: DON'T REBUILD THAT CITY
PASSAGE: Joshua 6:26-27
VERSE: Joshua 6:26

Then Joshua made them take an oath at that time, saying, "Cursed before the LORD is the man who rises up and builds this city Jericho; with the loss of his firstborn he shall lay its foundation, and with the loss of his youngest son he shall set up its gates."

Once Jericho was captured and burned, as God commanded, and Rahab and her family were safely outside the ruins, Joshua made a proclamation before the nation. No man was to rebuild the city of Jericho... ever. *"Cursed before the LORD is the man who rises up and builds this city Jericho; with the loss of his firstborn he shall lay its foundation, and with the loss of his youngest son he shall set up its gates."* The evil was so prevalent within the walled city God commanded it never be resurrected from its ruins. The people swore an oath to never be part of that reconstruction. Have you ever heard these words: *That which has been is that which will be, and that which has been done is that which will be done. So there is nothing new under the sun.* (Ecclesiastes 1:9) History and evil do have a way of repeating themselves, and we see this if we look ahead approximately five-hundred years to the days of evil King Ahab. *In his days Hiel the Bethelite built Jericho; he laid its foundations with the loss of Abiram his firstborn, and set up its gates with the loss of his youngest son Segub, according to the word of the LORD, which He spoke by Joshua the son of Nun.* (1 Kings 16:34) See the prophecy in today's key verse? It was fulfilled perfectly in Ahab's days.

COMMON GROUND: As I pondered the application for this entry I was reminded about resurrecting the past, once we are released from it by Christ's grace. The lure of past sinful lifestyles will have its pull on us until we truly find rest in the arms of our Messiah. The enemy will not stop tempting, so we must become strong enough to rebuke his schemes. **HOLY GROUND:** Jericho was rebuilt at great cost to Hiel. We resurrect our sins and fall back into them at that same cost. Guard your heart to withstand evil. Holy people press onward toward a goal... not backward toward past cesspools.

Jesus, Resurrection of my past is not what I want for my life.
You redeemed me from that, so why would I want to go back there?
I do know, however, that the Enemy will not stop making
it look attractive and tempting. Amen.

➤ Day 330: SIN'S DEFEAT
PASSAGE: Joshua 7:1-5
VERSE: Joshua 7:5

*The men of Ai struck down about thirty-six of their men, and
pursued them from the gate as far as Shebarim and struck them
down on the descent, so the hearts of the people melted
and became as water.*

When do you think a person—or nation—is most vulnerable to
defeat? Most people would assume the answer to be at a low
point or after a great failure. The truth is that we are most vulnerable
when we come off a great victory—when we feel invincible and
immune to defeat. Joshua's army was high from Jericho's fall when
he sent a party to spy out Ai, a small city east of Beth-el. They came
back and said, *"Do not let all the people go up; only about two or
three thousand men need go up to Ai... for they are few."* Joshua
took their word for it, sent three-thousand into the battle and they
were chased away with thirty-six Hebrew soldiers killed. *The hearts
of the people melted and became as water.* How could they bring
down the walls of mighty Jericho and turn around and face defeat at
the hands of tiny Ai? Look with me at verse one of this chapter. *But
the sons of Israel **acted unfaithfully** in regard to the things under
the ban, for **Achan**, the son of Carmi, the son of Zabdi, the son
of Zerah, from the tribe of Judah, **took some of the things under
the ban**, therefore **the anger of the LORD burned** against the sons
of Israel.* Achan blatantly ignored God's command... and unknow-
ingly, his fellow soldiers walked into defeat and death.

COMMON GROUND: When are you most vulnerable to the lures
of the enemy of your soul? It is altogether common for us to thrive
on success—to get high on victory—and to think the win came at
our own hands. Think about this when you are down and defeated.
You are not walking in Holy Spirit power—and are thus no threat to
the Enemy. Victory brings self-assurance and pride... and both are
tools to lead us to a fall. **HOLY GROUND:** One man's sin brought

defeat on God's mighty army... what a superb victory Achan's sin gave to Satan.

Holy Spirit, I must learn to resist pride after a success.
I do not want to give any victory to the Enemy who will strive
to keep me on common ground. Amen.

➤ Day 331: WHY GOD?
PASSAGE: **Joshua 7:6-12**
VERSE: **Joshua 7:7**

Joshua said, "Alas, O LORD GOD, why did You ever bring
this people over the Jordan, only to deliver us into the hand
of the Amorites, to destroy us? If only we had been willing
to dwell beyond the Jordan!"

Joshua was devastated by the Ai defeat and the deaths of the men in his charge. What could have happened? He turned to God for his answers. *Joshua tore his clothes and fell to the earth on his face before the ark of the LORD until the evening, both he and the elders of Israel; and they put dust on their heads. Joshua said, "Alas, O LORD GOD, why did You ever bring this people over the Jordan, only to deliver us into the hand of the Amorites, to destroy us? If only we had been willing to dwell beyond the Jordan!"* Joshua wasn't aware of the sin Achan had brought into the camp and reacted the way most of us would: He blamed God and challenged why He brought them across the Jordan. He knew that news of the Hebrew defeat would spread throughout the nations surrounding Canaan, strengthening his enemies and giving them incentive to attack his people. His time before the ark—seeking answers from God—was rewarded. *So the LORD said to Joshua, "Rise up! Why is it that you have fallen on your face? **Israel has sinned**, and they have also transgressed My covenant which I commanded them. And they have even **taken some of the things under the ban** and have both stolen and deceived. Moreover, they have also **put them among*** *their own things. Therefore the sons of **Israel cannot stand before their enemies;** they turn their backs before their enemies, for **they have become accursed. I will not be with you** anymore **unless you destroy the things under the ban from your midst."***

COMMON GROUND: The painful truth is that we bring much of our suffering upon ourselves by blatant disobedience to the commands of God. We cheapen marriage and condone adultery—and our kids pay the price. We lie, cheat and steal, and our nation is a cesspool. We worship a god of our own creation, and then wonder how we have gone so far astray. **HOLY GROUND:** Joshua wasn't aware of Achan's sin, but he was seeing the consequence of it. God said Israel was on its own—no hedge of protection—until the evil was removed. Hard word. Wake up call to America and the contemporary church… we are on our own.

Father God, You will not fight for those who blatantly disregard or disobey Your commands, and I am seeing this in our nation and in our churches. Compromise destroys purity and cannot be condoned. Amen.

➤ Day 332: THERE IS SIN IN THE CAMP
PASSAGE: Joshua 7:13-15
VERSE: Joshua 7:13

…Consecrate yourselves for tomorrow, for thus the LORD, the God of Israel, has said, "There are things under the ban in your midst, O Israel. You cannot stand before your enemies until you have removed the things under the ban from your midst."

Joshua knew the reason for the defeat, but needed to find the source of the sin which was plaguing his nation. Someone had defiled the camp—but whom? God answered that question too. *"In the morning then you shall come near by your tribes. And it shall be that the tribe which the LORD takes by lot shall come near by families, and the family which the LORD takes shall come near by households, and the household which the LORD takes shall come near man by man. It shall be that the one who is taken with the things under the ban shall be burned with fire, he and all that belongs to him, because he has transgressed the covenant of the LORD, and because he has committed a disgraceful thing in Israel."* Joshua would need every bit of wisdom and discernment he could find. The tribes would be paraded before him and he was to discern God's prompting in telling him which one the sin had come from. Next, the families of that tribe would be presented... and Joshua needed to choose the offending family. After that, the households came... and from those households he would need to determine which one fostered the army defeat. Finally, the men of that household would stand before their leader and the man who had broken God's command by taking from the spoil would be revealed.

COMMON GROUND: Imagine being there in the Hebrew camp and watching the tribes, families, households and men paraded before Joshua. It would be fascinating if you had nothing to hide, but imagine if you were from Achan's tribe when it was chosen. Think about the terror of knowing your sin was about to be revealed. Isn't it easier to obey in the first place than face that hour of dread? **HOLY GROUND:** In order for us to walk in holiness, we are going to have to resist the lust of our flesh. Each of us will answer for our thoughts, words and deeds when we face Jesus, because... *every tongue will confess that Jesus Christ is LORD, to the glory of God the Father.* That *'every'* includes the righteous and the unrighteous... in which category will you be?

LORD, The truth is that some will bow in regret and shame—just like Achan. What a heavy thought it is to imagine standing before the Judge and hearing our sins proclaimed—the obvious ones and the hidden ones too. Amen.

➤ Day 333: SINNER EXPOSED
PASSAGE: Joshua 7:16-26
VERSE: Joshua 7:20-21

So Achan answered Joshua and said, "Truly, I have sinned against the LORD, the God of Israel, and this is what I did: when I saw among the spoil a beautiful mantle from Shinar and two hundred shekels of silver and a bar of gold fifty shekels in weight, then I coveted them and took them; and behold, they are concealed in the earth inside my tent..."

The next morning dawned bright over Israel, but not on the house of Achan where judgment was about to take place. The tribes were brought forward and Judah was chosen. Next the Zerahite family was chosen, and then the household of Zabdi. We have no idea if anyone else in his family knew of Achan's sin and cannot imagine the heaviness in his family's hearts as their household was chosen. Picture them looking at one another in distrust, trying to surmise who the lawbreaker was. Finally, Achan was singled out by the God who knows all things done in darkness, as well as in light. *Then Joshua said to Achan, "My son, I implore you, give glory to the LORD, the God of Israel, and give praise to Him; and tell me now what you have done. Do not hide it from me." So Achan answered Joshua and said, "Truly, I have sinned against the LORD, the God of Israel, and this is what I did: when I saw among the spoil a beautiful mantle from Shinar and two hundred shekels of silver and a bar of gold fifty shekels in weight, then I coveted them and took them; and behold, they are concealed in the earth inside my tent with the silver underneath it."* Achan and his entire household died because of his sin against God. Sin could not be allowed to live in the camp of God.

COMMON GROUND: Joshua didn't tell Achan to confess because it would remove his sin. The confession was a profession before the gathered nation that indeed God had pinpointed the sinner from among all the people—once and for all proving His divine authority. **HOLY GROUND:** Always remember this truth though...

even confessed sin has consequences. Confession does not remove the consequences of a committed sin. Achan's evil was exposed, judged and punished. We may not like the deadly consequence, but unchecked sin would surely have destroyed Israel's hedge of protection.

My Adonai, Help me to look at things through rational eyes and not emotional ones. Achan's sin was a blatant spit in the face of his God. He believed the laws pertained to everyone but him. Such decisions always bring consequences. Amen.

➤ Day 334: BATTLE GOD'S WAY
PASSAGE: Joshua 8:1-12
VERSE: Joshua 8:7

And you shall rise from your ambush and take possession of the city, for the LORD your God will deliver it into your hand.

Now that the sin had been removed from the Hebrew camp, God told Joshua to go back into battle against Ai with the entire army, for He had delivered Ai into Joshua's hands. *(Note: Joshua relied on the spy report instead of God's direction when he attacked Ai the first time. If he had sought God's permission, the sin of Achan might have been revealed before thirty-six men died in battle.)* This time they were to take the spoil and cattle for themselves. Joshua deployed 30,000 men under cover of darkness to set ambush behind Ai. He and the rest of the army would advance head-on and pretend to run when Ai pursued them—leaving their city unprotected. The rear ambush team would then enter the city and take it as they did Jericho. The battle was about to take place, with God plotting the plan of attack. Joshua learned a hard lesson during the earlier defeat. He would never again enter a battle without consulting God for direction. Sometimes the hardest lessons to learn are the ones teaching us to lean on God—trusting Him to lead us into sweet victory and not bittersweet defeat.

COMMON GROUND: God's plan for a full army force divided in half and attacking Ai from two sides makes a lot of sense to us as we look back in perfect 20/20 hindsight. Have you learned a Joshua-like lesson by trying to go into battles on your own? Can you use that same hindsight and understand your defeats more clearly? If so, that should encourage you... common is as common does... but you aren't walking among the common any longer. **HOLY GROUND:** Learning to lean completely on Him for everything means letting God help in picking our friends and marriage partners. It means listening to His wisdom on finances, partnerships and parenting. We need God's discernment with us for wisdom in every area of our lives. Holy people do not want to be out of His will for one minute... thus they never go it alone.

Jesus, You want to be involved in every part of my life. LORD, that will take some work on my part—so begin Your good work in me. I never want to be outside of Your perfect will. Amen.

➤ Day 335: GOD'S WAY WORKS
PASSAGE: Joshua 8:13-29
VERSE: Joshua 8:18

Then the LORD said to Joshua, "Stretch out the javelin that is in your hand toward Ai, for I will give it into your hand." So Joshua stretched out the javelin that was in his hand toward the city.

When the morning sun revealed the army of Israel set against Ai for the second time, the men of Ai armed themselves, called up their reinforcements and abandoned the city behind them. They attacked Israel, who turned and fled in apparent defeat. God's plan was working perfectly. *The LORD said to Joshua, "Stretch out the javelin that is in your hand toward Ai, for I will give it into your hand."* Joshua stretched the javelin and the rear ambush team moved into Ai, gathered the spoil and set the city afire. When the soldiers of Ai spotted the smoke rising from their city, they turned back toward home, only to find the ambush team now moving toward them. Caught between the two halves of Israel's army, the people were destroyed. Joshua fought the battle as God commanded and victory was theirs. The spoil was taken and divided among the warriors and Ai was razed, never to be built again. God's people were slowly taking the land of God's promise.

COMMON GROUND: Did you know that many of the battle plans described within the pages of the Bible are still used by modern military installations today? Did you know that for century's shipbuilders have used the proportions God defined for Noah's ark? God's word is complete—for all men and for all time. You may not be a military buff, but you cannot help but be impressed with how God worked in the life of Israel. **HOLY GROUND:** People will tell you the Bible is outdated and doesn't apply in the 21st Century. They are wrong. During this writing I sent the first five entries to a high school friend I haven't seen in nearly thirty-five years. I had him read them and give me feedback... and he was amazed at how applicable the historical accounts are in his life today. The Bible is somewhat like the Constitution—perfect and timeless—flawless documents emphasizing freedom and liberty.

Holy Spirit, Your way the first time is always better than my way first and Your way second. Fewer pieces to pick up later. Amen.

➤ Day 336: OFFER HIM THANKS
PASSAGE: **Joshua 8:30-31**
VERSE: **Joshua 8:31**

...just as Moses the servant of the LORD had commanded the sons of Israel, as it is written in the book of the law of Moses, an altar of uncut stones on which no man had wielded an iron tool; and they offered burnt offerings on it to the LORD, and sacrificed peace offerings.

In the midst of the battles for the land God promised Israel we find quite a remarkable event in these verses. Everything else—training, equipping the army, strategy sessions—was put on hold while Joshua and the nation of Israel stopped and worshipped their God. In the religions of the nations around Canaan, the focus for worship was stone or wooden idols. The people could carry them with them and worship as their particular rituals required. Israel could pray, but real worship took place in a communal place like the tabernacle... and later in the temple in Jerusalem. Joshua wasn't foolish enough to believe his great military ability brought victory over Ai; and it was time to pay tribute to the real Strategist. He built an altar of uncut stones and offered burnt offerings and peace offerings upon it. The uncut stones were perfect in their plain and natural simplicity... the way God wants our worship to be. Even though Israel had enemies on every side, they paused and worshipped. And most likely, God kept the enemies away because of the nation's faithfulness. The altar was on Mt. Ebal. They worshipped on Ebal and gave God all the glory for the victory... and all the victories yet to come.

COMMON GROUND: Uncut by iron, unchanged by human hands, perfect in their form and plainness... does that describe you? God isn't looking for beautifully manicured nails, the latest hair style and designer clothing. He isn't concerned with what car you drive, how big your house is, or how many degrees follow your signature on a piece of paper. **HOLY GROUND:** I am not saying we shouldn't get our hair done nor have a nice house. I am saying that God wants you in all your plainness. He wants you unencumbered and spotless. He wants you bare and pure before Him. The other things are mere pretenses to impress others... He is not impressed. After all, He is the God of all creation.

*Father God, How wonderful it is that You like me just as
You fashioned me to be. You look heart-ward, not flesh-ward,
and see me as I was meant to be. That is really very reassuring
to this flawed clay pot. Amen.*

➤ Day 337: READ ALL OF THE LAW
PASSAGE: Joshua 8:32-35
VERSE: Joshua 8:35

There was not a word of all that Moses had commanded
which Joshua did not read before all the assembly of Israel
with the women and the little ones and the strangers
who were living among them.

Once the altar and the offerings were completed, Joshua took stones and wrote the Law of Moses on them as Israel watched. With the ark before him and the priests observing his careful rendering, Joshua wrote... and wrote... and wrote. The congregation was divided in two, with half before Mount Gerizim and half before Mount Ebal—exactly as Moses had commanded. After the writing was completed Joshua stood and *read all the words of the law, the blessing and the curse, according to all that is written in the book of the law. There was not a word of all that Moses had commanded which Joshua did not read before all the assembly of Israel with the women and the little ones and the strangers who were living among them.* Notice these truths: Joshua their leader read the law to them; he read every single word in the presence of men, women and children; and he skipped nothing, even though part of what he read was blessings for obedience and part was curses for disobedience. I have a real question for you to ponder. A new movement within the Christian church called 'The Emergent Church' is happying up and dumbing down the message of the Gospel of Jesus Christ. Those who are part of the movement rely on emotional experiences rather than sound Biblical teaching. There is no accountability and no definition of sin within the church, its programs or its curriculum. My question is—why would anyone need a Savior if he is without sin? Without the hard truths of what sin is—and a conviction in the heart of the sinner—no life will be changed by the Gospel of Jesus Christ. The people following these leaders are being blindly led to their destruction.

COMMON GROUND: Joshua didn't teach only the happy parts of the Mosaic Law. He wasn't the least bit concerned whether the people liked what they were hearing or not. He was more worried about their souls and the moral condition of this new nation as they prepared to enter this land. **HOLY GROUND:** When you hear about people who are part of the 'Emergent Church', it is your responsibility to learn about the movement and alert them to the full Gospel message, which boils down to Sinners Redeemed from Sin by the Blood of Christ. One of their key ploys is to get people to believe there is no absolute truth. Once we believe that, our own sins are then acceptable.

> *LORD, Our world is being led astray because we have turned away from the moral foundations of Scripture. I must learn not to underestimate the smooth tactics of the Enemy who is seeking to lead believers astray. Your Word is truth—that means all of Your Word. Amen.*

➤ Day 338: ALLIED ENEMIES
PASSAGE: Joshua 9:1-7
VERSE: Joshua 9:2

> *...that they gathered themselves together with one accord to fight with Joshua and with Israel.*

As word spread throughout the surrounding area of Jericho, the nations began to fear for their own safety, due to Israel's defeat of Jericho and Ai. When *the Hittite and the Amorite, the Canaanite, the Perizzite, the Hivite and the Jebusite, heard of it, that they gathered themselves together with one accord to fight with Joshua and with Israel.* When the Gibeonites heard what was happening *they also acted craftily and set out as envoys, and took worn-out sacks on their donkeys, and wineskins worn-out and torn and mended, and worn-out and patched sandals on their feet, and worn-out clothes on themselves; and all the bread of their provision was dry and had become crumbled.* They went to Joshua and asked him to make a covenant (a peace treaty) with them. Joshua, seeing their worn out clothes and wineskins, believed their word that they were from a *far country* and listened to them. Let me ask you a question at this point. How good are you at discerning between good and evil, right and wrong, and true and false prophets? Godly discernment is a wisdom in your spirit—an acute ability to understand on a level deeper than what your eyes actually see. Joshua trusted his eyes and the physical condition of the men before him. He should have used his discerning spiritual eyes instead of only his physical eyes.

COMMON GROUND: The Emergent Church movement I talked about in the last entry is emotion-driven and encourages people to live their lives in the emotional realm rather than in the spiritually discerning realm of God's truths. Naturally, no one wants to be told he is a sinner—he would rather see what looks back at him from the flesh mirror over his bathroom sink. The problem is that God will judge based on the mirror of His directives—His Holy Word. **HOLY GROUND:** Joshua trusted what his eyes saw, instead of asking God to reveal truth to his heart. At that point he was probably looking for anyone who would be a friend to Israel. The problem was... his physical eyes did not reveal the *false prophets* standing before him.

My Adonai, My physical eyes have led me astray before.
Let my eyes and my heart discern Your truths in EVERY
situation I encounter. The traps are many, and only the wise
will avoid the pitfalls of the Enemy. Amen.

➤ Day 339: PEACE TREATY
PASSAGE: **Joshua 9:8-15**
VERSE: **Joshua 9:15**

Joshua made peace with them and made a covenant with them,
to let them live; and the leaders of the congregation
swore an oath to them.

Joshua did have the presence of mind to ask the Gibeonite men who they were and where they had traveled from. Still, he was not discerning when it came to their story: *"Your servants have come from a very far country because of the fame of the LORD your God; for we have heard the report of Him and all that He did in Egypt... so our elders and all the inhabitants of our country spoke to us, saying, 'Take provisions in your hand for the journey, and go to meet them and say to them, "We are your servants; now then, make a covenant with us."'" This our bread was warm when we took it for our provisions... it is dry and has become crumbled. These wineskins which we filled were new, and behold, they are torn; and these our clothes and our sandals are worn out because of the very long journey."* Joshua listened to their words, looked with his physical eyes, and was moved by their words concerning their hunger to learn more about his God. *The men of Israel took some of their provisions, and did not ask for the counsel of the LORD. Joshua made peace with them and made a covenant with them, to let them live; and the leaders of the congregation swore an oath to them.*

COMMON GROUND: Joshua allied his nation with strangers who talked a good story... in spite of God's commands to make no alliances with the enemy nations around Canaan. Notice that the leaders *did not ask for the counsel of the LORD* before they *made a covenant* with virtual strangers and sealed the deal when they *swore an oath to them.* **HOLY GROUND:** Beware! Watch yourself! Be alert! Use the discerning power of the Holy Spirit! If you don't do all those things, you will fall for anything and it will lead you astray. You must learn to weigh all things against the Scriptures in order to keep your feet upon holy ground.

Jesus, Stop me if I even begin to fall for the lies of the Enemy. How subtle, how crafty and deceitful are his ways. Amen.

➤ Day **340**: WORD GIVEN-WORD KEPT
PASSAGE: **Joshua 9:16-27**
VERSE: **Joshua 9:19**

But all the leaders said to the whole congregation,
"We have sworn to them by the LORD, the God of Israel,
and now we cannot touch them."

Three days later the Gibeonite deception was revealed to the Hebrew leaders. When Israel neared the Gibeonite cities they did not destroy them—because they had made a non-aggression treaty with the imposters. The people were furious with Joshua and the elders for putting them in this difficult position contrary to the commands of their God. *"We have sworn to them by the LORD, the God of Israel, and now we cannot touch them. This we will do to them, even let them live, so that wrath will not be upon us for the oath which we swore to them."* If Joshua had attacked the city after he had sworn in God's name not to do so, his people would have seen that his word wasn't worth much. Israel was bound by the rash oath of Joshua to keep peace with the Gibeonite people. To appease his own congregation, Joshua made them *hewers of wood and drawers of water for the whole congregation,* and servants of Israel in exchange for their lives. After he had appeased his own people, Joshua asked the Gibeonite men why they had deceived him. Their response showed the simple truth that they were more intent on self-preservation than honesty. They were afraid of the Hebrew God and the defeat they had seen of mighty Jericho. The Gibeonites would rather be slaves to Israel than be defeated like the Amorite kings, the army of Jericho and the people of Ai.

COMMON GROUND: Joshua's compromise was despised by the Hebrew people, but the real sorrow had to be in his own heart. Don't think for a moment that Joshua didn't recognize his failure as he tried to fill Moses' sandals. He was assuredly more worried about losing God's favor than of losing the people's affection. **HOLY GROUND:** Have you made bad decisions and formed unholy alliances? Have you had to live with the consequences of those actions?

Ask God for resolution and restoration. After that, get yourself so grounded in Him that nothing can lead you astray, trip you up, or capture you in a snare. God forgives you; forgive yourself and move forward into a new commitment to serve Him fully.

Holy Spirit, I have made moves contrary to Your will... some in ignorance... some in blatant disobedience. This story hits right at my heart. Thank You for resolution and restoration. Amen.

➤ Day 341: WORD SPREADS
PASSAGE: Joshua 10:1-11
VERSE: Joshua 10:1-2

Now it came about when Adoni-zedek king of Jerusalem heard that Joshua had captured Ai, and had utterly destroyed it... and that the inhabitants of Gibeon had made peace with Israel and were within their land, that he feared greatly, because Gibeon was a great city, like one of the royal cities, and because it was greater than Ai, and all its men were mighty.

When word spread that Gibeon was allied and had made peace with Israel, the kings in the surrounding nations were even more afraid. Israel with their mighty God was frightening enough, but couple that with Gibeon, a great and strong city, and disaster loomed before the nations. Adoni-zedek, the king of Jerusalem, gathered other kings with him to attack Gibeon and at least remove that flank of Israel's power. Gibeon sent word to Joshua, *"Do not abandon your servants; come up to us quickly and save us and help us, for all the kings of the Amorites that live in the hill country have assembled against us."* Joshua sought God's direction and was assured, *"Do not fear them, for I have given them into your hands; not one of them shall stand before you."* Joshua's army came upon the enemy under cover of darkness and God sent confusion and panic among the Amorite armies. They fled before the onslaught of Israel as God dropped huge hailstones upon them from the heavens.

Israel had victory and God was continuing to go before them into their battles.

COMMON GROUND: God had promised Israel in Exodus 23 to give them Canaan over a period of time. *"I will not drive them out before you in a single year, that the land may not become desolate and the beasts of the field become too numerous for you. I will drive them out before you little by little, until you become fruitful and take possession of the land."* If Joshua and the people were content to take the land in increments, they would remain in God's will and gain the inheritance in His perfect timing. **HOLY GROUND:** God was giving the land to Israel bit by bit so they could go in, settle one area, regroup, and then prepare for the next shofar signal to move onward. Are you content to have Him move you—or do you take the ball into your own hands and try to gain everything in your own time?

Father God, You never promised us everything—just everything we need. You never promised us full understanding—just enough wisdom for each day as it comes. You never said the battles would be non-existent—just never fought alone. Amen.

► ## Day 342: NEED MORE DAYLIGHT
PASSAGE: Joshua 10:12-14
VERSE: Joshua 10:13

So the sun stood still, and the moon stopped, until the nation avenged themselves of their enemies. Is it not written in the book of Jashar? And the sun stopped in the middle of the sky and did not hasten to go down for about a whole day.

As Israel and Gibeon fought the Amorite armies and God sent the hailstones, the daylight hours were dwindling. The battle was nearly won and Joshua prayed an unusual prayer to the LORD. *"O sun, stand still at Gibeon, and O moon in the valley of Aijalon."*

How foolish a request that would have seemed to anyone who heard it prayed from the general's lips? Stop the advancing sun—and hold back the rising of the moon—is Joshua losing his mind due to his body's overwhelming exhaustion? Must be his God didn't think the request foolish... because *the sun stood still, and the moon stopped, until the nation avenged themselves of their enemies.* Imagine the fatigue of the Amorite armies as the daylight hours marched on, Joshua's army marched and fought on, and God's amazing faithfulness to His Hebrew children was miraculously evident as they pressed onward toward eventual control of the Promised Land! *There was no day like that before it or after it, when the LORD listened to the voice of a man; for the LORD fought for Israel.* Are you facing a formidable enemy? You serve a *supernatural God.* He will take His *super*, put it with your *natural*, and make the *supernatural* happen!

COMMON GROUND: I haven't had God change the daylight hours for me, but I have had Him supernaturally provide money when it was desperately needed and heal friends I held up before Him in prayer. He is the Great Physician and also my Provider. He provided the finances and means to open His House, write three books and continue in my ministry. All those things were supernaturally done. Where have 'your natural and His super' worked together in your life? **HOLY GROUND:** You need to realize at this point that your walk with Christ is a supernatural event. Nothing—nothing—in your (or my) flesh hungers after righteousness. Nothing in your flesh longs to relinquish control to the God of all Creation. Nothing in you—except the Spirit of God—brings you to perfect salvation in Christ. See? He has already done supernatural work in your life. Praise Him!

LORD, I praise You for taking me from being controlled by my flesh to being controlled by Your Spirit. I am so glad to serve the supernatural God above all gods... and His Son, my Messiah, Jesus Christ. May I never forget Your miraculous interventions in my life. Amen.

➤ Day 343: CHECKPOINT #4
PASSAGE: **Revelation 2**
VERSE: **Revelation 2:7**

"He who has an ear, let him hear what the Spirit says to the churches. To him who overcomes, I will grant to eat of the tree of life which is in the Paradise of God."

While God is defeating the enemies of Israel, let's jump today and tomorrow into Revelation—the last book of the New Testament, so you may measure your progress in this journey. In John's vision he was given messages from Jesus for seven Messianic churches in Asia, telling the churches what they were doing right, doing wrong, and what they needed to do to correct shortcomings. Let's weigh our own progress against these serious evaluations. To the **Church at Ephesus**: *"I have this against you, that you have left your first love."* Are you as passionate about Christ as you were on the day you received His grace, welcomed His pardon for your sins and made a profession to walk with Him? If not: *"...remember from where you have fallen, and repent and do the deeds you did at first; or else I am coming to you and will remove your* (church) *out of its place..."* To the **Church at Pergamum**: *"I know... you dwell where Satan's throne is... and you hold fast My name... But I have a few things against you, because you have there some who hold the teaching of Balaam... to eat things sacrificed to idols and to commit acts of immorality."* Are you worshipping where false doctrines are being proclaimed from the pulpit? Are you sanctioning sin in the camp? If so: *"Repent; or else I am coming to you quickly, and I will make war against them with the sword of My mouth."* He will war against the false prophets and you may get caught in the crosshairs if you are among them. To the **Church at Thyatira**: *"You tolerate the woman Jezebel... and she... leads My bond-servants astray so that they commit acts of immorality... I gave her time... and she does not want to repent of her immorality... I will throw her on a bed of sickness, and those who commit adultery with her into great tribulation..."* Are you allowing a spirit of tolerance, political correctness or false peace to keep you silent about practices contrary to Scripture? If so: *"...repent of her deeds... hold fast until I come."* False prophets will be judged, but so will those who follow them. Spiritual adultery will not be tolerated any more than physical adultery.

COMMON GROUND: Please do not ignore these very necessary assessments. I would recommend you read chapters two and three of Revelation. Most churches have ignored this teaching. Why? Because they are afraid to tackle the truths of Revelation where change is required, holiness is commanded and judgments are defined. **HOLY GROUND:** The apathetic church is not ready for these truths, but you are no longer part of the apathetic church, are you?

My Adonai, If I have turned from You, my first love, followed false doctrines or allowed pseudo-peace to silence me... open my heart to see my errors and my mouth to speak against them. This is the true call to holiness. Amen.

➤ Day 344: CHECKPOINT #5
PASSAGE: **Revelation 3**
VERSE: **Revelation 3:5**

"He who overcomes will thus be clothed in white garments; and I will not erase his name from the book of life, and I will confess his name before My Father and before His angels."

Let's continue in our personal spiritual assessments in this 5th Checkpoint. If you need to reread yesterday's entry before moving into this one, do so. This is important application from the Bible for your spiritual walk. To the **Church at Sardis:** *"I know your deeds, that you have a name that you are alive, but you are dead."* Are you deceiving yourself into thinking you are alive in Christ—when in actuality you are dead inside? Be honest here. Are you thriving and alive in your faith walk—and are you producing faith fruit? If not: *"Wake up, and strengthen the things that remain, which were about to die... remember what you have received and* *heard; and keep it... if you do not wake up, I will come like a thief, and you will not know at what hour I will come to you.*" To the **Church at Laodicea**: "*I know your deeds, that you are neither cold nor hot; I wish that you were cold or hot... because you are lukewarm, and neither hot nor cold, I will spit you out of My mouth... you say, 'I am rich, and... have need of nothing,' and you do not know that you are wretched and miserable and poor and blind and naked...*" Are you on fire for Jesus? Tepid, lukewarm faith is no more pleasing to Him than room temperature chili is to you on a cold winter's day. He gave His all for you—what are you giving back? If you are lukewarm: "*...buy from Me gold refined by fire so that you may become rich, and white garments so that you may clothe yourself... and eye salve to anoint your eyes so that you may see. Those whom I love, I reprove and discipline; therefore be zealous and repent.*" The last two **Churches** of **Philadelphia** and **Smyrna** were found to be doing right in the eyes of the LORD. Both were persevering and obeying the Gospel message. To them was this promise: "*Behold, I stand at the door and knock; if anyone hears My voice and opens the door, I will come in to him and will dine with him, and he with Me. He who overcomes, I will grant to him to sit down with Me on My throne...*"

COMMON GROUND: Are you either dead or lukewarm? Are you striving every day to passionately serve Christ? Are you giving Him 100% of your commitment? Is He first in your life? Do you need eye-ointment like the church at Laodicea—you know, to open your eyes for more spiritual awareness? **HOLY GROUND:** Let us all strive together to be found like the Churches at Philadelphia and Smyrna—perseverant and obedient at His coming. Apply these spiritual bandages to your wounds and let the healing and renewed commitment begin.

Jesus, I am overwhelmed with how much still needs to be changed in my life. I had no idea. LORD, take my hand and walk with me on this never-ending journey into completeness and holiness. Amen.

➤ Day 345: MUCH WORK TO DO
PASSAGE: Joshua 13:1-8
VERSE: Joshua 13:1

Now Joshua was old and advanced in years when the LORD said to him, "You are old and advanced in years, and very much of the land remains to be possessed."

Back from our Checkpoint detour to the battle at hand. Chapters eleven and twelve of Joshua show God's amazing hand in gaining the land of Canaan for the Hebrew nation. Beginning in this chapter we see the land begin to be apportioned to the tribes of Israel. Joshua was getting old, but God assured him it was not yet retirement time, for there was much work to do. Before the lands were even taken by Joshua's army, God wanted them assigned. *"All the inhabitants of the hill country from Lebanon... I will drive them out from before the sons of Israel; only allot it to Israel for an inheritance as I have commanded you... apportion this land for an inheritance to the nine tribes and the half-tribe of Manasseh."* God was watching the people and sensed their fatigue and saw they were losing their will to fight constant battles. He knew if the army took a piece of land already assigned to a tribe—they would have the added incentive of knowing they were fighting for their own home-land. Remember that *the other half-tribe, the Reubenites and the Gadites received their inheritance which Moses gave them beyond the Jordan to the east, just as Moses the servant of the LORD gave to them.* The eastern tribes had been away from their families and their land for a long time; God was moving His people to action. Sometimes we too get satisfied with status quo—things as they have always been—because less effort is required if we are not taking new ground.

COMMON GROUND: Joshua was tired. The army was tired. The nation was tired. The enemies were tired. God gave them an incentive to press on... He told Joshua to show them the actual land they would inherit when the conquests were complete. Are you tired? Do you feel like you are hurrying to get nowhere... beating your head against the proverbial wall? Don't quit now—you are almost to the end of this year's long journey out of the common and into the holy! **HOLY GROUND:** Don't give up. Effort is always required if you want the blessings of God. Israel was tired, but the Promised Land awaited them. You may be tired, but God is watching to see how you have done on this journey. What is He seeing when He watches you... half-hearted effort... or relentless progress?

Holy Spirit, I press on toward the goal. Almost there! Amen.

➤ Day 346: ISRAEL'S INHERITANCE
PASSAGE: Joshua 13:9-32
VERSE: Joshua 13:15

So Moses gave an inheritance to the tribe of the sons of Reuben according to their families.

Once the land west of the Jordan River was completely taken by the armies of Israel, it would be time for the tribes to divide and disperse to their assigned lands. Israel and Israel alone holds deed (through Scriptural records) to the lands Joshua assigned in this chapter. God raised this nation as His own and assigned the physical strip of land on the Mediterranean Sea to belong to them. When we began this story, Moses was being called upon to deliver the Hebrew slaves from Egyptian bondage. Prior to that bondage the sons of Jacob (Israel) had lived in Canaan... the land promised to Abraham hundreds of years before. The land always belonged to Israel—it was created to house Israel. Let's look ahead to current history. Throughout history Israel was exiled repeatedly from her homeland because of blatant disregard for God's commands. Each time though, He left a remnant of His children in the nation to keep His promises to Abraham and later King David. In May 1948, Israel became an independent state after she was recognized by the United Nations as a country in its own right within the Middle East. During her exile the Palestinians 'squatted on her lands' and took control of part of her capital city, Jerusalem. Upon it being granted independence, Israel was attacked by a number of Arab nations. Israel would have ceased to exist, had she not fought back against those attacks. The battles continue today as Israel fights for full ownership of the land we see assigned in Joshua 13.

COMMON GROUND: I know this is difficult to understand if you are not familiar with Israel and her history. Please stick with me. News reports have numerous references to this Middle East battle and the fight over Jerusalem. You now know more about the history of Israel than most of the people in the world. **HOLY GROUND:** God's command for Israel to keep and never sell that land means she cannot give any portion to another nation. Those who are trying to get her to give up part of it for 'peace' are deceivers. Israel will never have true peace—until she knows the Prince of Peace.

Father God, I pray for the true Peace of Jerusalem... in the day when she finally realizes who Jesus is and accepts Him as the Messiah she has waited for. Amen.

➤ Day 347: JOSEPH'S SONS INHERIT HIS SHARE
PASSAGE: Joshua 14:1-5
VERSE: Joshua 14:4

For the sons of Joseph were two tribes, Manasseh and Ephraim, and they did not give a portion to the Levites in the land, except cities to live in, with their pasture lands for their livestock and for their property.

It is time for another brief history lesson as we look at the land division process in Canaan. You will recall that we started out with twelve sons of Jacob (whose name was changed to Israel). If you are watching closely, you have seen that the sons of Levi did not inherit land portions as did the other tribes—yet we read land was assigned to *the nine tribes and the half-tribe... (and to) the two tribes and the half-tribe beyond the Jordan...* Unless my small brain has ceased to function, that still adds up to twelve tribes. How can that be? Joseph, one of Israel's sons, was despised by his brothers and sold by them into slavery—eventually ending up in Egypt. Separated from his family for decades, Joseph worked hard and remained faithful to the God of his father, garnering the support of Pharaoh. He actually (talk about God's amazing ways) ended up second in command over all the nation of Egypt. While there he had two sons, Ephraim and Manasseh. Later, the famine which brought the Hebrews into bondage in Egypt also brought Joseph's brothers seeking grain from the only nation who had it—Egypt. Joseph and his brothers were reunited; his father Jacob traveled to Egypt and Pharaoh provided land for them in Goshen. When the blessings were given out to the sons of Jacob, he gave Joseph's portion to his sons. In the Promised Land those sons each inherited a share, with Manasseh choosing to live partly on the east side of the Jordan and partly on the west.

COMMON GROUND: Even though Joseph wasn't raised among his brothers, he was one of Jacob's heirs. His father showed him favor by doubling his portion, giving one portion to Ephraim (Joseph's portion) and one to Manasseh (Levi's portion). Joseph didn't have to fight for revenge—he forgave his brothers instead. God still had the last word and achieved His ultimate purpose. **HOLY GROUND:** The thirst for revenge or clearing your name is often overwhelming. I have felt both and don't like myself when I feel either one. Joseph trusted the God who preserved him, blessed him and protected him to clear his name before his brothers. God did just that and they ended up telling him they were wrong. Joseph told them that what they had meant as harm—God ultimately used for good—their good!

LORD, When I feel the need to avenge or clear my good name, may I handle that emotion just as Joseph did—with class, dignity, and complete faith that You will clear my reputation—because I belong to You and You alone. Amen.

➤ Day 348: CALEB: STILL STRONG
PASSAGE: Joshua 14:6-14
VERSE: Joshua 14:11

"I am still as strong today as I was in the day Moses sent me;
as my strength was then, so my strength is now,
for war and for going out and coming in."

Remember Caleb? When the original twelve spies explored Canaan only two wanted to pursue taking the land for Israel: Joshua, now the leader of the Hebrew population, and Caleb— whom we haven't heard from in a while. It is time to hear from Caleb again. *"You know the word which the LORD spoke to Moses... concerning you and me in Kadesh-barnea. I was forty years old when Moses the servant of the LORD sent me... to spy out the land, and I brought word back to him as it was in my heart. Nevertheless my brethren who went up with me made the heart of the people melt with fear; but I followed the LORD my God fully. So Moses swore on that day, saying, 'Surely the land on which your foot has trodden will be an inheritance to you and to your children forever, because you have followed the LORD my God fully.' Now behold, the LORD has let me live, just as He spoke, these forty-five years, from the time that the LORD spoke this word to Moses, when Israel walked in the wilderness; and now behold, I am eighty-five years old today."* Caleb was eighty-five years old and had waited forty-five years for that promise to come true! (That man defines having the patience of a saint!) He had watched Israel reject God, had seen Moses give every ounce of his effort to deliver them—the same Moses who was kept from entering the Promised Land because of Israel's sins—and had seen God's over-whelming faithfulness to His people. Caleb was ready. He was still strong and he was claiming that which was rightfully his—because it was a promise from God!

COMMON GROUND: Do you have the same good measure of patience as Caleb? I sure don't! I want it—want it all—and want it now! Caleb held on to the promise of God that one day he and his heirs would have a portion of the land. All of us need to take a lesson from our friend Caleb. We all need a dose of his 'stick-to-it-iveness' and faith. **HOLY GROUND:** The Bible is full of promises for the believer to claim as God's truth. *I have been young and now I am old, yet I have not seen the righteous forsaken or his descendants begging bread.* (Psalm 37:25) *No weapon that is formed against you will prosper...* (Isaiah 54:17) *...seek first His kingdom and His righteousness, and all these things will be added to you.* (Matthew 6:33) Are you claiming these truths and others like them?

My Adonai, Caleb could have given up when the promise wasn't immediately fulfilled, but he stayed strong, committed and faithful. After he did that, You kept Your promise and he was greatly rewarded. Give me a Caleb-like heart. Amen.

➤ Day 349: SPURRED TO ACTION
PASSAGE: Joshua 18:1-8
VERSE: Joshua 18:4

Provide for yourselves three men from each tribe that I may send them, and that they may arise and walk through the land and write a description of it according to their inheritance; then they shall return to me.

Sometimes we just need a bit of a burr under our saddle to get us to move! You would think that once the enemies of Israel were gone from Canaan that the tribes would have been anxious to get to their assigned lands and begin to build cities for their families. No, they were actually quite happy in their tent city at Shiloh with peace on every side. Joshua placed the burr: *"How long will you put off entering to take possession of the land which the LORD, the God of your fathers, has given you? Provide for yourselves three men from each tribe that I may send them, and that they may arise and walk through the land and write a description of it according to their inheritance; then they shall return to me."* Joshua was doing his best to be a good leader—and he knew the power of apathy. He sent these teams of men from the tribes to scout out Canaan, to draw landmark maps and bring the information back to him. Joshua would disperse the land by drawing lots. Judah had claimed land in the south of Israel and Joseph's sons had theirs in the north. The rest was to be divided into seven parcels. The methods seem quite primitive to us, but the maps and landmarks they drew up would be the defining lines for the perpetual ownership of the land of Israel by her twelve tribes. Now... if Joshua could just get them to move, once the lots were drawn!

COMMON GROUND: Are you a go-getter or a stay-putter? Think about the Hebrews. They were fed off the provision of the land. They were clothed with clothing that never wore out. They were sheltered—in tents which lasted for more than forty years... and they were safe. God defeated their enemies on every side. Who would want to move? Maybe God should have put burrs in their bedrolls! **HOLY GROUND:** Holy people must finish that which they start. They must look and see what needs doing, and then do it. In the workplace they must be the best workers, and in the marketplace the best vendors. In their communities they must be the trusted leaders. How else will they avoid apathy and commonness?

Jesus, The malaise of apathy is crippling and the comfort of safe can be paralyzing. LORD, light that fire, place that burr, or smack me upside the head if necessary to get me to move. Amen.

➤ Day 350: CITIES OF REFUGE
PASSAGE: Joshua 20:1-6
VERSE: Joshua 20:4

He shall flee to one of these cities, and shall stand at the entrance of the gate of the city and state his case in the hearing of the elders of that city; and they shall take him into the city to them and give him a place, so that he may dwell among them.

We talked about cities of refuge in earlier entries, but it is important for us to look at them again as they are being designated from the tribal lands. Remember, the purpose of these cities was to provide a safe haven—a refuge, if you will—for the man who killed someone without premeditation or plotting. The offender would flee to the city of refuge, proclaim his story to the elders and be admitted there for protection from one who would seek to avenge the death of the man who was slain. The city was to protect him until a trial could be held to determine his guilt or innocence. If it was determined that he didn't kill in premeditation, he would live there until the death of the high priest—and then return to the home of his birth. Cities of refuge were on both sides of the Jordan River and were dispersed throughout the land, so that the one fleeing could gain safety without a long and difficult journey. They were on hills so they could be seen from a far distance and were all appointed from the cities which were given by the tribes to the Levites. That made the Levites the servants of God—the judges over the people of the nation. To you these may not seem to be of great importance, but I can assure you that the man who committed manslaughter found them abundantly welcoming.

COMMON GROUND: Where is your refuge—your safe place? When do you run there? Why do you run there and what are you running from? Jesus Christ is our refuge, our strength, our hiding place, our shelter... are you running to Him for safety? **HOLY GROUND:** No matter what you have done and where you have been, when you approach Him with a sincerely repentant heart, He will open His outstretched arms and welcome you in. He will dry your tears, hear your confessions and forgive your sins.

Holy Spirit, You are my refuge from the storms of this life.
How I praise God that I know You. Amen.

➤ Day 351: GOD KEPT EVERY PROMISE
PASSAGE: Joshua 21:43-45
VERSE: Joshua 21:45

Not one of the good promises which the LORD had made
to the house of Israel failed; all came to pass.

Israel was finally home. The promise God made to Abraham hundreds of years before had been fulfilled. Each tribe had its own portion of land assigned... some on the east side of the Jordan and some on the west. As Joshua looked at the land and praised his God who delivered it to this flawed nation, he realized that every single promise of God was kept—both good and bad. Moses was their deliverer who led them from Egyptian bondage. Pharaoh's heart was hardened and his people watched the mighty hand of the Hebrew God. God's children were isolated from the horror of the plagues, were given the spoil of the wealthy Egyptians, and were covered by the blood of an innocent lamb which protected them from the death plague. When Israel's back was to the Red Sea, God made a path where there had been no way before. In the wilderness the people ate manna—the food of the angels which fell from heaven. God led them by a cloud and a pillar of fire. He also gave them laws—ones they quickly agreed to and then cast aside for the lusts of their flesh. Adonai kept every promise—He fought for them, delivered mighty enemies into their hands and gave them battle plans. He ushered them into the land He had ordained for them from the beginning of time. God was so faithful—and all Joshua could do was praise Him.

COMMON GROUND: How could people who had witnessed all I just listed above turn from their God and serve stone idols? How could they forsake Him for the lust of foreign women? How could they shame the legacy of Moses and Joshua after all they had done on the nation's behalf? I don't know the answers—only that we are very quick to do the same thing in our lives today. **HOLY GROUND:** You have been on a year-long journey. I assume that you, like me, have had high points and low moments. Now is the time to thank Him for the changes He has wrought in your life. As your author—in the process of being pruned, I surely thank Him for the work He is doing in my heart.

Father God, You are faithful—always faithful—even when I am not. Father God, help me to be as faithful to You as You have been to me... I love You, El Shaddai. Amen.

➤ Day 352: DIVIDED BY NATURAL BARRIERS
PASSAGE: Joshua 22:1-9
VERSE: Joshua 22:4

And now the LORD your God has given rest to your brothers, as He spoke to them; therefore turn now and go to your tents, to the land of your possession, which Moses the servant of the LORD gave you beyond the Jordan.

After months of battles and watching their tribal brethren receive their land allotments, Reuben, Gad and East Manasseh heard words from Joshua's mouth that must have been music to their ears. *"You have kept all that Moses the servant of the LORD commanded you, and have listened to my voice in all that I commanded you... And now the LORD your God has given rest to your brothers, as He spoke to them; therefore turn now and go to your tents, to the land of your possession, which Moses the servant of the LORD gave you beyond the Jordan."* The eastern tribes had kept their promise to fight the enemies of their brothers and to help them take the land. Now—finally—they would go home. They could build their houses, harvest or plant crops, love their families and build their cities. Knowing that things would never again be the same—because the natural barrier of the Jordan River would separate them from the rest of the tribes—Joshua spoke these words of caution: *"...be very careful to observe the commandment and the law which Moses... commanded you... love the LORD your God... walk in all His ways... keep His commandments... hold fast to Him... serve Him with all your heart and with all your soul."* After he blessed them, Joshua sent Reuben, Gad and Manasseh home to their families.

COMMON GROUND: Have you ever had friends or close family members move away... and after the tears were shed you began to move on with your life as surely as they did in their new home? Soon days turn into weeks, and then months, without hearing from one another. Physical distance has a cooling effect on relationships. That was the gut fear of Joshua as he watched the tribes depart. Would their families grow up without knowing one another? **HOLY GROUND:** We should work and strive to keep family ties and friendships strong in spite of the miles separating us. That goes doubly true for Christian brothers and sisters. Miles can never erase the common faith you share. Relationships are always worth the effort required to feed them and keep them alive. Call someone you have lost touch with—renew that precious heart connection.

LORD, It is easy to forget and to watch time slip so quickly away. If I am not working on maintaining relationships—I am saying they are of no value to me. You are the Author of love and friendship and You showed us how to be a friend. Amen.

➤ Day 353: TRIBAL DIVISION?
PASSAGE: Joshua 22:7-20
VERSE: Joshua 22:16

Thus says the whole congregation of the LORD, "What is this unfaithful act which you have committed against the God of Israel, turning away from following the LORD this day, by building yourselves an altar, to rebel against the LORD...?"

Jumping to conclusions is always dangerous, but in the case of this story in today's entry it could divide Israel permanently and

444

forever. When the three tribes who were going to the other side of the Jordan came to the water, they stopped and built an altar there. Word traveled back to Joshua that they had built the altar on the shore of the river and that the western tribes were preparing to go out to battle against their brothers. Ahead of the army went Phineas the priest and ten tribal chiefs to confront them. *"What is this unfaithful act which you have committed against the God of Israel, turning away from following the LORD this day, by building yourselves an altar, to rebel against the LORD...? If you rebel against the LORD today, He will be angry with the whole congregation of Israel tomorrow."* The priest reminded them of how Achan's sin brought defeat on the entire nation and pleaded with them not to do the same thing by building an altar apart from the altar in the tabernacle. Phineas continued by telling them if the land they chose was somehow unclean, they needed to gather their families, flocks and herds and come to dwell among their brothers.

COMMON GROUND: Upon hearing of the altar the eastern tribes had erected on western land, the other tribes were immediately ready for war—against their own brothers. They assumed the worst. Don't we do the same when the gossip swirls and the rumor mill churns? Just thought I would point that out. **HOLY GROUND:** 'Trust and verify' is a great rule of thumb. Words spoken in anger cannot be taken back—and how hard it would be if the words were never justified in the first place.

> *My Adonai, I am quick to jump and assume. I know I have made snap judgments before and was proven wrong. May Your Spirit guide my tongue and temper. Amen.*

➤ Day 354: LEST WE FORGET
PASSAGE: Joshua 22:21-34
VERSE: Joshua 22:24

But truly we have done this out of concern, for a reason... In time to come your sons may say to our sons, "What have you to do with the LORD, the God of Israel?"

The reply of the eastern tribes silenced all their accusers. *"The Mighty One... He knows, and may Israel itself know. If it was in rebellion, or if in an unfaithful act against the LORD do not save us this day! If it was in rebellion... to turn away from following the LORD, or if to offer a burnt offering... may the LORD Himself require it... we have done this out of concern... saying, 'In time to come your sons may say to our sons, "What have you to do with the LORD, the God of Israel? For the LORD has made the Jordan a border between us and you... you have no portion in the LORD." So your sons may make our sons stop fearing the LORD ...we said, 'Let us build an altar... it shall be a witness between us and you and between our generations after us that we are to perform the service of the LORD before Him...'"* What a gut buster statement that was! The nine and one-half tribes were about to attack their Hebrew brothers because of what they assumed was a blatant nose-thumbing toward them. Instead, their act was one of love and faith... faith that even though time and distance would separate them, their common faith and heritage would be the glue that held them together. Their concern was that one day the tribes on the west would forbid their sons from coming to worship with them in the house of God. The altar wasn't for offerings... it was a memorial reminder that their brothers lived just beyond the river.

COMMON GROUND: Instead of a war, the confrontation at the edge of the Jordan brought a recommitment between the sons of Jacob. The memorial would be a constant reminder that across the river their brothers were worshipping the same God as they were. A tragedy was averted by simply asking one question... "Why are you doing what you are doing?" The question was followed by being still and listening for an answer instead of jumping to a conclusion. **HOLY GROUND:** We need to learn to ask simple questions in order to avoid hatred, animosity and lost relationships. Just ask the question. Holy people are fair people and wouldn't want to have to answer for jumping to wrong conclusions.

Jesus, What a powerful lesson this one was on not making assumptions. I hear Your teaching loud and clear, LORD. Amen.

➤ Day 355: CLEAVE TO YOUR GOD
PASSAGE: Joshua 23:1-10
VERSE: Joshua 23:8

...cling to the LORD your God, as you have done to this day.

Joshua gave this address and cautioned the nation he loved to keep their focus on God and walk in His commands. The result would be a long and healthy life in their new land. *"Be very firm... to keep and do all that is written in the book of the law of Moses, so that you may not turn aside from it to the right hand or to the left, so that you will not associate with these nations, these which remain among you, or mention the name of their gods, or make anyone swear by them, or serve them, or bow down to them."* Joshua was under no mistaken impression that Israel was immune to sin. Remember... he was Moses' right-hand man for over forty years! Notice the caution to not turn to either side—but to instead keep their eyes firmly on their God as they proceeded forward. *"But you are to cling to the LORD your God... For the LORD has driven out great and strong nations from before you... no man has stood before you to this day. One of your men puts to flight a thousand, for the LORD your God is He who fights for you, just as He promised you."* Joshua reminded them to cling to their God and to never forget that their victories were His victories and their successes were His successes.

COMMON GROUND: Let's look at the commands in this very important passage. *Be firm. Keep the Law. Do not turn aside. Do not serve other gods. Cling to the LORD. Fight for He fights with you.* Good checklist—how are you doing? If you think I have spent far too much time on obedience and faithfulness to God in this book, then you need to do a deep spiritual-evaluation. We get tired of that which strikes a conviction cord in our heart. Why do you think God spent so much time on this subject—He knows our hearts. **HOLY GROUND:** As I near the end of this journey I find myself thinking deeper, looking closer at my own spiritual-mirror reflection, and wondering how much more pruning will be necessary until I am where I need to be. As a believer seeking holiness, I press on toward that goal. My prayer is that this is your personal goal too.

Holy Spirit, Mold me, shape me, trim me and purify me. Amen.

➤ Day 356: NO INTERMARRIAGE
PASSAGE: Joshua 23:11-13
VERSE: Joshua 23:12

For if you ever go back and cling to the rest of these nations,
these which remain among you, and intermarry with them,
so that you associate with them and they with you...

In Joshua's closing remarks to the nation of Israel, he felt the need to remind them again of one of God's most repeated (and most ignored) commands. *"...if you ever go back and cling to the rest of these nations, these which remain among you, and intermarry with them, so that you associate with them and they with you, know with certainty that the LORD your God will not continue to drive these nations out from before you; but they will be a snare and a trap to you, and a whip on your sides and thorns in your eyes, until you perish from off this good land which the LORD your God has given you."* Let me pull some key words into one concise and very specific statement. *If you... cling to these nations... God will not drive these nations out before you... they will be a snare... and thorns in your eyes... until you perish from off this land.* Do you see any exceptions or room for compromise in that statement? No. God doesn't leave leeway because He knows the temptation they entertain each day will become the sin which ensnares them for all their tomorrows. Reread what I just wrote. The temptation we entertain (bow to, agree to, tolerate or drift toward) will be the sin which ensnares us (puts us in bondage, destroys our freedom) for our tomorrows. Enough said.

COMMON GROUND: Compromise—especially within God's moral commands—will lead us back into bondage. That goes for the modern church which is bowing to inclusiveness, ecumenism, ear-tickling messages and political correctness. We must keep ourselves set apart—holy unto the LORD. Are you flirting with sin—walking too close to the forbidden fruit tree and thinking you are immune? **HOLY GROUND:** Are you influencing the world, or is the world influencing you? Are you making a difference for Christ within your sphere of influence, or are you being influenced by others in that sphere? You know what is right and what is required... holy feet on holy pathways.

Father God, There are still temptations I am susceptible to. I will not fool myself into thinking I can walk close to the forbidden fruit tree and not fall into sin. I am helpless without You. Amen.

➤ Day 357: I AM GOING SOON
PASSAGE: Joshua 23:14-16
VERSE: Joshua 23:14

Now behold, today I am going the way of all the earth, and you know in all your hearts and in all your souls that not one word of all the good words which the LORD your God spoke concerning you has failed; all have been fulfilled for you, not one of them has failed.

Joshua was on a roll... he gave them the good news first: *"... all the good words which the LORD your God spoke concerning you... have been fulfilled for you, not one of them has failed."* He reminded them of God's past faithfulness and provision. He had been the strongest leader he could be. He had filled the big sandals of his mentor Moses. He had warned and cautioned his charges of the dire consequences of their sins. Now for the bad news: *"It shall come about that **just as all the good words** which the LORD your God spoke to you have come upon you, **so the LORD will bring upon you all the threats... When you transgress the covenant of the LORD your God... then the anger of the LORD will burn against you..."*** You may be thinking Joshua could have ended his reign on a more positive note—he could have just told them the happy blessings... and left off the heavy curses. If he had done that he would simply be another false prophet. *For the time will come when they will not endure sound doctrine; but wanting to have their ears tickled, they will accumulate for themselves teachers in accordance to their own desires...*(2 Timothy 4:3) Joshua answered to God alone, and not to the desire of the people to have their *ears tickled.*

COMMON GROUND: I know a kind and wonderful pastor who was recently released from the church he shepherded because it was decided by the congregation that in order to grow they needed a *'younger, more Seeker-friendly'* pastor. This man's holiness teaching would be too harsh on the delicate ears of the coming flock. That is fluff and that is a tool of Satan to pull the wool over the eyes of the modern church. **HOLY GROUND:** We need the hard teachings of Scripture. We need the *No Compromise* message—the *Change is Required* message, and the *Sinner Saved by Grace* message. We need strong 'Joshuas' to stand up, speak truth, and stop this movement away from holiness. We need you to demand solid Biblical truth from those who preach and teach in your church. Some of you might think I am being legalistic or demanding works in order to receive grace. That is not my message. My message is because of sin, we need grace... and that grace needs to change us from the inside out. Just telling people Jesus will make their lives better is not going to work change in their lives... and is quite contrary to the holy Word of God. *Whoever then annuls one of the least of these* *commandments, and teaches others to do the same, shall be called least in the kingdom of heaven; but whoever keeps and teaches them, he shall be called great in the kingdom of heaven. For I say to you that unless your righteousness surpasses that of the scribes and Pharisees, you will not enter the kingdom of heaven.* (Matthew 5:19-20) He demands this teaching, not me. We need you to apply what you have learned in this devotional.

LORD, Keep me from apathy. Give me boldness. May I seek to please You and You alone, my Audience of One. Amen.

➤ Day 358: PROMISE TO ABRAHAM
PASSAGE: Joshua 24:1-6
VERSE: Joshua 24:3

"Then I took your father Abraham from beyond the River, and led him through all the land of Canaan, and multiplied his descendants and gave him Isaac."

Joshua paused to remind Israel of where their magnificent nation could find its origins. Abraham—the one called the Father of the Hebrew nation—was born in Ur of the Chaldees, a part of the land of Babylon. God called Abraham out of there and promised him a land and a nation which would grow to be as numerous as the dust of the earth. Abraham could have doubted, for he had not even one heir. Instead, he believed God's promise and took off from the common ground of Babylon to the promised ground of some unknown plot of land. When he arrived in Canaan God told him that this was the land prepared for him and commanded him to walk its length and width. That land is the modern day land of Israel. Every promise God made to Abraham came true. The childless father was now the patriarch of millions of Jews who finally were at rest in that land of promise. Why did Joshua take the time to retell the story of Abraham to the people who now stood on Israel's soil? It reinforced what he had told them before—God keeps His promises... in His way and in His timing. Every man listening had a common heritage in Abraham. Every man there was called to take this journey from common ground to holy ground... and they would make the ground holy by compliance and obedience to God's commands.

COMMON GROUND: You may live in the most unholy city in the world, but you are still called to holiness. You may be surrounded by the most ungodly sinners on the face of the earth, but you are still called to holiness. You may think there is no hope because Satan has ruined any good that remains in our society, but you are still called to holiness. We see a great picture of this in Isaiah chapter 6: *Then I said, "Woe is me, for I am ruined! Because **I am a man of unclean lips**, and **I live among a people of unclean lips**; for my eyes have seen the King, the LORD of hosts." Then one of the seraphim flew to me with a burning coal in his hand, which he had taken from the altar with tongs. He touched my mouth with it and said, "Behold, this has touched your lips; and **your iniquity is taken away and your sin is forgiven**."* The searing cleansing of the blood of Jesus has set you apart for God just as the burning coal did for Isaiah. **HOLY GROUND:** *"You shall be My own possession... and you shall be to Me a kingdom of priests and a holy nation."* No excuses given—because none will be received.

My Adonai, Create in me a pure heart, make me holy, set me apart, show me how to be a royal priesthood, make me peculiar and make me Yours today, tomorrow and forever. Amen.

➤ Day 359: CHECKPOINT #6
PASSAGE: **Jeremiah 29:11-13**
VERSE: **Jeremiah 29:11**

"For I know the plans that I have for you," declares the LORD, "plans for welfare and not for calamity to give you a future and a hope."

We are at the point in our journey where I feel the urging to ask you if you trust God completely to direct your paths and walk you on right roadways. Do you believe beyond a shadow of a doubt that God loves you, that Jesus died for you, and that He alone is God in the entire world? Do you relinquish your control into His capable hands and lay your desires down to do what He commands? Have you heard Him speak to you during our time together this year? Are you calling out to Him for clarity, discernment, and a clear sense of His presence? *"Then you will call upon Me and come and pray to Me, and I will listen to you. You will seek Me and find Me when you search for Me with all your heart."* Is your whole heart in this quest for holiness, or are you merely reading these devotions to get through the book? I am burdened as I write this entry, for I fear some of you might scan the questions without answering them. Please don't do that, for at this very time you are reading the questions He is laying on my heart to ask you. He is calling you to a higher place... a place you haven't visited before. He wants you to take up residence there, to continue to seek after Him, to develop your prayer life and to fellowship with Him every minute of every day you have left on the earth. He is calling out to you... are you answering that call? If so, I have done my job.

COMMON GROUND: As you finish this book, please do not substitute what is good for what is great. Don't put church service (which is good) in place of personal study (which is great). Don't put singing in the choir (which is good) in place of developing a deeper prayer life (which is great). Don't put being called a Christian (which is good) in place of walking the Gospel message wherever you go (which is great). **HOLY GROUND:** A higher calling means we always seek to do that which is great; knowing if we do... all the other things will be given to us. *Seek first His kingdom and His righteousness, and all these things will be added to you.*

Watch out, LORD. I am on fire and ready to step up, step out, speak up and be Your hands and feet. Shadow me with Your Spirit, empower me with Your might and take me where You wish. Amen.

➤ Day **360**: LAND YOU DIDN'T PREPARE
PASSAGE: **Joshua 24:11-13**
VERSE: **Joshua 24:13**

"I gave you a land on which you had not labored, and cities which you had not built, and you have lived in them; you are eating of vineyards and olive groves which you did not plant."

Here is a great truth which should keep you from feeling pride in the fact that you are going to walk on holy ground. Countless numbers of men and women have gone before you, stepped up to the call of Christ, served Him no matter the cost, and left this earth with their indelible mark cast upon it. They have carried the Gospel message to the mission fields at the risk of their own lives. They have preached, taught Sunday school, cooked for potlucks, visited the shut-ins, and have sung in worship choirs. They have worn their knees out praying for the lost, praying for their fellow believers, and praying for this nation. Isn't it wonderful to know that you have this great cloud of witnesses who have gone before you and paved the way? Thank the unknown faces who transcribed the history, prophesy and epistles of the Bible, so that you might hold it in your hand today. Be grateful for the path they laid, the foundation they built it upon, and their uncompromising backbone. Just as Israel would now live in cities they did not build, take nourishment from land they did not tame, and walk on paths they did not clear... so you will do. Those who went before will stand with you one day and hear the words they waited so long to hear, *"Well done, good and faithful slave. You were faithful with a few things, I will put you in charge of many things; enter into the joy of your master."* (Matthew 25:23)

COMMON GROUND: The road ahead may look daunting and all uphill. Don't lose heart; you are not alone. Remember how high the walls of Jericho were, but they crumbled at a joyous shout of praise from the people of God. **HOLY GROUND:** Shout His praises! You are nearing the end of maybe one of the longest years of growth you will ever face. You are being refined and redefined! Are you seeing the changes? How exciting!

Holy Spirit, Keep me humble—Keep me strong. Amen.

➤ Day **361**: CHOOSE THIS DAY
PASSAGE: **Joshua 24:14-15**
VERSE: **Joshua 24:15**

"...choose for yourselves today whom you will serve: whether the gods which your fathers served which were beyond the River, or the gods of the Amorites in whose land you are living; but as for me and my house, we will serve the LORD."

L ife is full of choices, and some of those choices will have long-term impact on our lives. Joshua knew this better than anyone. He chose to believe in God's power when the rest of his nation believed the fears of the other spies. He chose to walk beside and behind Moses, being groomed for a job he thought might never come. He chose to listen to God when the directions seemed almost impossible. He chose to walk out of the common and into the holy. I am not unlike Joshua. I chose to heed the call of the Holy Spirit after thirty-seven years of walking my own way. I chose to commit my life into His hands and His service when others told me I was crazy. I chose to study diligently every day from the Scriptures—so that I would be ready to write as He directs. I chose to be obedient to the visions He has laid out before me. I chose to pray for you as I wrote these last entries. Now the choice is yours. The choice to serve God without condition is not an easy one. Joshua knew that. Moses knew that. Noah knew that. Abraham knew that. I know that. Still, the choice must be made. *No servant can serve two masters; for either he will hate the one and love the other, or else he will be devoted to one and despise the other You cannot serve God and wealth.* Jesus talked about serving the God of money in Matthew 6; but the god can be pride, selfishness, drugs, alcohol, material possessions, careers, pornography, or anything else you choose to put before Him.

COMMON GROUND: The word 'choose' is a verb. It requires action. Making a choice doesn't happen by osmosis—you cannot walk on holy ground because your mother was a Christian or you went to Sunday school when you were a child. The choice is yours—common or holy—which will it be? **HOLY GROUND:** If you choose holy, effort is required. Holiness has a price. Are you willing to pay that price? Your salvation cost Jesus everything. Aren't you glad He was willing to pay the price?

Father God, Choosing to serve You means no longer serving myself and this world. That is a big requirement. Help me. Amen.

➤ Day 362: WE CHOOSE HIM
PASSAGE: Joshua 24:16-18
VERSE: Joshua 24:16

The people answered and said, "Far be it from us that we should forsake the LORD to serve other gods..."

In the moment of their emotion and in the face of losing their beloved leader Joshua, the people said all the right words. *"Far be it from us that we should forsake the LORD to serve other gods; for the LORD our God is He who brought us and our fathers up out of the land of Egypt, from the house of bondage... The LORD drove out from before us all the peoples, even the Amorites who lived in the land. We also will serve the LORD, for He is our God."* That sounded like a pretty serious commitment to serve God. Israel remembered He delivered them from bondage and fought for them against enemies. They almost dismissed the very thought that they could ever be led off the holy ground path again. They were confident... but their resolve would be short-lived. Look ahead with me into the next book of the Old Testament at this verse. *All that gener-*

ation also were gathered to their fathers; and there arose another generation after them who did not know the LORD, nor yet the work which He had done for Israel. (Judges 2:10) Just one generation later, when the miracle of God's rescue of the people from Egypt was no longer talked about, the people forgot Him. What a tragedy! Here is a hard truth: Many people (I have read statistics of up to 90%) who convert to Christianity will fall away. How does that happen? Because they are not taught. They are not discipled and disciplined in Scripture. They do not have a firm foundation to build their faith on... and the things of life draw them away. Some things never change.

COMMON GROUND: If you have made a commitment to serve the LORD with all your heart, your soul and your mind, the Devil will increase his efforts to trip you up. It is called spiritual warfare. The committed believer is a threat to evil. Temptations will come your way—and some will seem quite harmless. Watch yourself! **HOLY GROUND:** Please read Ephesians 6:10-17. You must be equipped and ready for the battles that lie ahead. *"...taking up the shield of faith with which you will be able to extinguish all the flaming arrows of the evil one."*

LORD, Keep me from uncommitted commitments and breakable promises. Be my armor and my shield, O'LORD. Amen.

➤ Day 363: YOU WILL ANGER HIM
PASSAGE: **Joshua 24:19-27**
VERSE: **Joshua 24:19-20**

Then Joshua said to the people, "You will not be able to serve the LORD, for He is a holy God. He is a jealous God; He will not forgive your transgression or your sins. If you forsake the LORD and serve foreign gods, then He will turn and do you harm and consume you after He has done good to you."

I find it interesting that Joshua openly told the people they would not be able to serve God because He is jealous (*El Qanna*) and holy (*Jehovah Tsidkenu*). Three times He challenged their promised obedience; and three times they insisted they would serve Him alone. Joshua told them to *put away the foreign gods which are in your midst* and to incline their hearts toward God. Why did they still have idols in their midst? *Joshua wrote these words in the book of the law of God; and he took a large stone and set it up there under the oak that was by the sanctuary of the LORD. Joshua said to all the people, "Behold, this stone shall be for a witness against us, for it has heard all the words of the LORD which He spoke to us; thus it shall be for a witness against you, so that you do not deny your God."* Joshua used a simple rock as a challenge to the people. The rock heard him warn them that God would not tolerate compromise. It also heard them profess their commitment and obedience to Him. How would a dull, heavy, hard rock serve as a witness against the adulterous hearts of the people? Maybe Joshua wrote their promise on it—thus making the rock 'speak out' as a witness against them. All that mattered is that the rock heard the promise... and when they looked at it, it would serve as a reminder of their covenant with their God.

COMMON GROUND: Let me play Joshua for a moment. I am saying to you, "Your faith commitment will not be easy to keep. You will stumble over it many, many times. It will challenge you when you are tempted. You will fail. When you do, pick yourself up, dust yourself off, confess the failure to the Rock of your salvation and move onward toward the holiness goal." **HOLY GROUND:** No man is perfect. No man is holy. We are all cracked pots with clay feet. The real truth is that we are held to a standard higher than the rest of the world... and with the help of the Holy Spirit; we will one day face an end to all our striving. Until then, we must press on.

My Adonai, Even when my knees are scraped from the falls,
I will stand up and press onward toward the goal of my glorifica-
tion in Your kingdom and finally... rest. Amen.

➤ Day 364: JOSHUA AT REST
PASSAGE: Joshua 24:28-33
VERSE: Joshua 24:29

It came about after these things that Joshua the son of Nun, the servant of the LORD, died, being one hundred and ten years old.

Joshua was at rest. No more struggles—no more battles. He would stand before his God and say, "Mission Accomplished! They are in their land. I have poured every ounce of my energy into this nation. I have taught them, cautioned them, challenged them and rebuked them. Now they are on their own, LORD, until You raise up a new leader. They will need that leadership for they are weak-willed and easily led astray. I have done my best and You know that. I am so glad to finally be coming home." It almost seems unfair that Joshua would not live long in the land of his inheritance—like all his work was for nothing—but Joshua would not agree with you. All his work hinged on one word of faith he and Caleb spoke way back when the spies returned from their mission into Canaan. *"If the LORD is pleased with us, then He will bring us into this land and give it to us, a land which flows with milk and honey. Only do not rebel against the LORD; and do not fear the people of the land, for they will be our prey. Their protection has been removed from them, and the LORD is with us; do not fear them."* Those words set Joshua's course and determined his eternal destiny. Joshua, like Moses, is a picture of a true servant of the LORD. He is an Old Testament picture for us of Jesus (Yeshua, a form of Joshua) who will one day escort His children from this world to the Promised Land that awaits them.

COMMON GROUND: Joshua worked hard to serve a thankless congregation. He didn't hear their praises or their gratitude. He likely heard more complaining than kindness. That's okay. He didn't live for the accolades of man. Remember, Joshua—like you and me—worked to please only an Audience of One. **HOLY GROUND:** Work as if everything you do is for the glory of God. In the end it is what Jesus says about you that matters in the light of eternity.

Jesus, All to Jesus, I surrender; All to Him I freely give;
I will ever love and trust Him, In His presence daily live.
I surrender all. I surrender all. Amen.

► Day 365: CHECKPOINT #7
PASSAGE: 1 Timothy 1:12-14
VERSE: 1 Timothy 1:13

"...even though I was formerly a blasphemer and a persecutor
and a violent aggressor... I was shown mercy because
I acted ignorantly in unbelief..."

In our final Checkpoint, I want to show you the Scripture I claim as my own. It describes who I was, what changed, and who I am now. These verses are why I will not shut up about the Good News Gospel message. *I thank Christ Jesus our LORD, who has strengthened me, because He considered me faithful, putting me into service...* I know beyond a shadow of a doubt that Christ chose me out of my selfish, flesh-controlled life prior to 1995. He strengthened me to face the hurdles my newfound faith would come against; and for some reason He put me into service writing books, teaching the Bible and speaking His name in the public forum. *...even though I was formerly a blasphemer and a persecutor and a violent aggressor. Yet I was shown mercy because I acted ignorantly in unbelief...* I was a blasphemer who used His name as a swear word to punctuate nearly every sentence I spoke. I made fun of those who had a deep and abiding faith. I was blatantly rude to those who tried to share the truth of Christ with me. I was shown mercy—because He knew I was ignorant—I didn't know any better. Sin was my life. *...and the grace of our LORD was more than abundant, with the faith and love which are found in Christ Jesus.* Out of the mess and mire of my life He showed me grace—unearned, unmerited favor—and unconditional love, the thing I had looked for my entire life. I just wanted someone to love me for who I was... it wasn't a man. The One I longed for loves on a very different level—for He loves from the heart. That One is Jesus Christ who redeemed me on February 14, 1996, when I cried out to Him for a new start.

COMMON GROUND: I shared this with you because you need to know that the journey through these pages has impacted my life in every way. I am not a paragon of virtue. I am just like you. I am always looking for meaning and purpose and hope and unconditional love. **HOLY GROUND:** I never want to forget where I came from... because it is part of who I am today. Holy people don't erase their past—they merely press on to a brighter eternity.

Jesus, Thank You for my Redemption. Thank You for the Cross. Thank You for choosing me. I am completely humbled. Amen.

➤ Day 366: FINAL THOUGHTS
PASSAGE: Revelation 22:1-2
VERSE: Revelation 22:1-2

Then he showed me a river of the water of life, clear as crystal, coming from the throne of God and of the Lamb, in the middle of its street. On either side of the river was the tree of life, bearing twelve kinds of fruit, yielding its fruit every month; and the leaves of the tree were for the healing of the nations.

This has been some journey, hasn't it? You know so much more than you knew on Day One—because you have applied yourself and kept with the teaching. I am so proud of you and the changes God has wrought in your hearts through these entries. Let me share a picture God gave me about one week before I was done writing. As I talked to my grandson Tyler I told him I felt like a rock thrown into a raging river as I lived out this fourteenth year in my faith walk. You see, a rock that has always lain in the riverbed is smooth and rounded; the rough edges are worn away by the constant washing of the flowing waters over its surface. I am not a river rock. I am a hard ground rock with rough edges and sharp points. Once I was thrown into the river of this journey from common to holy, the Holy Spirit began to rough me up a little, round some of my sharp edges off and smooth out things like pride, a biting tongue and self-reliance. When I resisted, He rubbed harder and the battle continued. I sort of liked the rock I used to be—I looked really good on the outside, said all the right words, and could reveal everyone else's flaws. I had most people fooled... but I could not fool Jesus. He could see the hypocrisy—thus more water flowed over me and little particles of river sand scrubbed at my heart. Today I am far from perfect—but I am also far from whom I once was. I have been humbled. I am working on my sharp tongue. I am finding out that my self-reliance is merely a cover-up for insecurity. I wouldn't change the river washing for anything... because it was done in love for my ultimate benefit and to achieve His ultimate purpose.

COMMON GROUND: Have you felt any of that scrubbing during this journey? Don't ignore it—let Him have His way in your life. Let Him sand away your rough edges and shine up the good that's already beginning in your heart. You will be better able to serve Him if you are willing to be tossed into the river. **HOLY GROUND:** *Wash me thoroughly from my iniquity... cleanse me from my sin... and I shall be clean; Wash me, and I shall be whiter than snow.*

Father God, This is not the end of our journey together. I will allow the work of the Holy Spirit to continue in my heart. I am Yours forever. Thank You for choosing me and loving me enough to cleanse me. Amen.

What Readers are saying about:

For Such a Time as This...
By Vicki Renee Bryant

Brilliant! Vicki has a special gift from God to be able to put scripture into a practical use for everyday life. Her truthfulness about her testimony and her walk with God since she became a Christian is an inspiration to everyone who has had the opportunity to hear her speak or to read her books. *For Such a Time as This...* and A*bout Face!* are inspirational, sometimes humorous, the hard 'truth' and hard to put down.... I can't wait to read her next book!

Bonnie S., Owosso, MI

For Such A Time As This... speaks to my soul about God's amazing love, forgiveness, and grace as I face life's daily challenges, defeats, and triumphs. Vicki Bryant frames the messages in a way that is easy to understand and apply to my life, helping me to deepen my relationship with the LORD as I travel on this journey of faith.

Chris K., Warren, Michigan

Hats off to *For Such a Time as This...* by Vicki Bryant - This is a wonderfully written book. Ms. Bryant has a wonderful way of taking the Scripture and making it very easy to understand, whether you read and study the Bible everyday or you are new to being a Christian. Thank you Ms. Bryant for writing such a wonderful devotional that has such inspiration.

Margaret S., Owosso, Michigan

JUST A QUICK NOTE THIS MORNING TO THANK YOU AGAIN FOR YOUR WONDERFUL BOOK. I HAD A LADY FROM MY CHURCH FOR SUPPER LAST NIGHT AND I SHOWED HER YOUR BOOK AND I READ HER GAIL'S STORY. SHE ENJOYED IT AND MAY BE INTERESTED IN GETTING A BOOK. I DO STILL ENJOY YOUR BOOK. GOD BLESS.

ALMA S., ROCHESTER, NY

Writing a book is a daunting task, especially if you desire that the words you write will help to transform a person's life. *For Such A Time as This...* is a book meant to transform. Vicki takes the Word of God and uses her life story to show that the Bible is relevant today. She shares life's ups and downs to show how God has transformed her life and how He can do the same for you. She is clear that following God is not always easy, but it is worth it. I applaud her first journey in writing. God's inspiration is definitely evident.

Deeann B., Owosso, Michigan

For Such a Time as This... is an enjoyable daily devotional book. ...looking forward to Vicki's next book.

Michele W., Austin, TX

I was in your store last Saturday looking for a devotional book to give to my sister-in-law for her birthday. The gal at the store showed me your book and I bought it. I looked it over and decided I had to keep it for myself, so I did. I'm so glad I did, as I have been blessed by it every time I read it. I decided to play catch-up, so I started reading from January 1st.

Katie S., Owosso, Michigan

This devotional is written on a level anyone can understand, even if they are not a Biblical scholar. As Christians, we seek a deeper walk in our spiritual lives; this daily devotional encourages that on every page. Do you know someone who is seeking the LORD but doesn't know where to begin? Presented here are clear Biblical principles, as well as the interspersing of personal experiences from the heart of the author. Vicki Renee Bryant shares her own spiritual journey with the reader. It would be a great Christmas present to remind those you love 365 days a year of your interest in their spiritual growth.

Rachel G., Corunna, Michigan

For Such a Time As This... is the perfect devotional for anyone who wants to have a daily encounter with God.

Marta R., Durand, Michigan

My heart-felt thanks to you, Vicki, for the book *For Such a Time as This...* I appreciate the time you took to write this wonderful, inspiring devotional. While reading it I found myself in prayer many times, making sure I was walking in Gods perfect will. Thanks for not sugar coating the hard times we walk in sometimes, but inspiring us to take hold of the Word of God and believe it. The God of all will walk with us and lead us into all His righteous ways. He gives us all things pertaining to life and Godliness according to His knowledge. You encourage me to put the Word first. I have told several people that I think it is very well done and may be the best 'devotional' I have ever read.

LaWanda H., Portland, TX

For Christmas my parents got me the devotional book you wrote. I've tried to keep up with reading it daily since I've gotten it, although I haven't always managed to stay with it. But lately I've been doing devotionals more on a daily basis again, with your book and another one I got a few weeks ago. Today I had a really great chat with God about my devotional time and really making it personal between us, not just a time to read more about God and then keep going with my day. I just wanted to thank you for this book, and your faith is a great inspiration for how I want mine to develop.

Molly M., Owosso, Michigan

For me, *For Such a Time as This...* is a daily encourager. I read of Vicki's personal experiences and can't help but see how God has changed her heart to be become one like His. Through her journal entries we learn how to receive His love by knowing Him through 'His Word' and the gift of forgiveness in His Son, Jesus.

Marie B., Sterling Heights, Michigan

For Such a Time as This... Relevant messages that apply to life today! Thought provoking messages that stretch your faith.

Cynthia F., Owosso, Michigan

(The following section on Salvation is taken from previously published *For Such a Time as This...*)

God's
Plan of Salvation

☦

Dear Reader,

Throughout this book you have heard me refer to Salvation—the reality that we are Sinners and the Redemptive work of Jesus Christ on Calvary's Cross. Some of you may have never formally given your heart to Jesus in the process of Admitting that you are a Sinner, Acknowledging your personal faith in Jesus Christ, the Son of God, and praying a simple prayer asking Jesus to come into your heart and give you a new start.

These pages are also effective witnessing tools for you to use as you share the Good News of the Gospel to those God puts in your paths. Feel free to copy them and share them. We aren't all called to preach or teach, but we are all called to 'Go and Share' the Gospel message. That message can never change a heart until the heart is broken over the sin it has walked in. Each of us needs to come to the end of self—before we can step into the beginning of Christ's Lordship.

If you have questions, please email me for help with committing to Christ or sharing the Good News with others. I believe strongly enough in these four pages to have used them in both previous books and to add them to this one too. God bless you as you pore over each word and allow His Spirit to speak to yours. Worship Him, Trust Him, and Glorify in His Name above all Names.

From a Sinner Saved by God's Grace,
~Vicki~

(Originally published in *For Such a Time as This...*)

STEP ONE
<u>Salvation: Why We Need It</u>

For God so loved the world, that He gave His only begotten
Son, that whoever believes in Him shall not perish, but
have eternal life. (John 3:16)

Whether you are already a Christian, saved by the power of Jesus, or a seeker longing to find what the term salvation means, these lessons are written to bring you into a deeper walk with Jesus Christ. Why is being born again necessary? Jesus addressed this question in John 3:3-7. Nicodemus, a Jewish leader, came to Christ under cover of darkness for teaching. Nicodemus asked what the new birth meant.

> *Jesus answered and said to him, "Truly, truly, I say to you,*
> *unless one is born again he cannot see the kingdom of God."*
> *Nicodemus said to Him, "How can a man be born when he is*
> *old? He cannot enter a second time into his mother's womb*
> *and be born, can he?" Jesus answered, "Truly, truly, I say*
> *to you, unless one is born of water and the Spirit he cannot*
> *enter into the kingdom of God. That which is born of the flesh*
> *is flesh, and that which is born of the Spirit is spirit. Do not*
> *be amazed that I said to you, 'You must be born again.'"*

If you did not fully hear what Jesus was saying, read those words again. Jesus is emphatic about the fact that the rebirth experience is essential to entering the Kingdom of Heaven. This one passage refutes the world's teachings that everyone will go to Heaven, or that a loving God would not send good people to hell. God sends no one to hell (eternal separation from Him), but we must choose where we will spend eternity. We must be born again—not as in our first birth (water birth) into the world, but into our spiritual birth into God's world.

APPLICATION: What you are reading may be absolutely life-changing as to the direction you will walk in the future. Let me ask you a few questions. Do you live to serve yourself and your own needs? Have you ever truly asked Jesus to come into your heart and direct your paths? Do you feel empty, purposeless, or spiritually hungry? Be honest with yourself; you may fool others, but God knows your heart. Are you ready to renew your commitment to Christ and to begin anew with Him in charge of your life? Stop now and pray for the Holy Spirit to open your eyes to His truths.

Holy Spirit, I hunger for a purpose and meaning, which my life lacks. I live for myself... and feel dead inside. Open my ears, eyes, and mind to receive the truths You will reveal to my spirit in these lessons. Amen.

STEP TWO
Salvation: Admission of Sin

...for all have sinned and fall short of the glory of God...
(Romans 3:23)

Now, let us look at the first of the ABC's of salvation in Christ: A=Admit you are a sinner, B=Believe who Christ is and the power He has to change you and C=Confess your sins and confess His Name. One of the first sermons I ever heard nearly caused me to leave the church. The Pastor said that all people in the pews were sinners and needed the salvation of Christ. Who did he think he was, calling me a sinner? I didn't steal openly, hate my parents or kill others, so I was a good person. When compared to Ted Bundy and Jeffrey Dahmer... I was an angel! I began to read the Bible and realized that the Ten Commandments were a series of life guideposts. I began to understand what sin is and the effect it has in our lives. Sin is anything contrary to God's perfect will. All sin separates us from God.

Yes, my gossiping and lying are just as despicable in His eyes as were the murders committed by the men I mentioned above. God is holy and cannot be part of any evil. Sin is born with us. If you doubt the inherent sin nature of man, give two toddlers one toy to play with! We have placed human standards on which sin is the worst, but let me say again... all sin separates us from God. What can bring sinners back into right standing with a holy God? Is there hope for sinners to not sin? Will we always be separated from Him? There is hope. *Even so consider yourselves to be dead to sin, but alive to God in Christ Jesus... For sin shall not be master over you, for you are not under law but under grace.* (Romans 6:11&14) There is hope through a personal relationship with Jesus Christ!

APPLICATION: Are you having a hard time absorbing the truth that you are a sinner? That truth is contrary to everything we hold dear. We never want to admit we are lacking in any aspect of our lives. Truth sometimes hurts; if you are hurting because of this passage, the Holy Spirit is showing you the things which need to be revealed in order for you to come into a saving knowledge of Jesus Christ. Go ahead, admit you are a sinner; once you do, reconstructive surgery on your spiritual life can begin.

Holy Spirit, it hurts me to confess that yes, I am a sinner. I always thought I was 'good enough' to get to Heaven on my own merit. Reveal all of my sins to me... I hold nothing back. Amen.

STEP THREE
Salvation: Believe in Christ

But God demonstrates His own love toward us, in that while we were yet sinners, Christ died for us. (Romans 5:8)

You are moving toward a heart-changing, life-changing new understanding of the emptiness you feel in your life. Now join with me as we look at the 'B' portion of the plan of salvation. B=Believe in who Christ is and the power He has to change you. You have learned that we are all sinners. Let me teach you about my Jesus. God created man to walk in intimacy and fellowship with Him. There were no life expectancy charts in the days of creation...

man was to live eternally with God. When sin entered the Garden of Eden, all of that changed. Sin brought death; and death brought eternal separation from God. He needed a solution to reconcile His children to Him.

Throughout the Old Testament God's prophets talked about a 'Messiah', a 'Redeemer' who would be used to cleanse man from his sin. This Redeemer had to be perfect and sinless, a spotless lamb. He could not be born of the union of a woman and a man, for that union produced the sin-filled children of the evil world. God sent His Holy Spirit upon a virgin girl named Mary. Her son was born in humble circumstances and was revealed first to the shepherds. He was the Shepherd who would lead us, the blemished flock, back to God. Jesus lived thirty-three years, taught, healed the sick, challenged the concept of religion versus relationship, cast out demons, and loved everyone.

He did exactly what His Father sent Him to do. Jesus was falsely accused, tried and crucified. He hung on a sinner's cross between Heaven and earth, and as 1 Peter 2:24 reads ...*and He Himself bore our sins in His body on the Cross, so that we might die to sin and live to righteousness; for by His wounds you were healed.* Three days later Jesus was raised from the dead, appeared to hundreds of people in His resurrected body, and then went to sit at the right hand of God. This is a picture of our resurrection to eternal life.

APPLICATION: Jesus died on that sinner's cross to give us eternal life. That sacrifice must be acknowledged as part of the plan for our salvation. Do you believe what is written here? It is all taught directly from the pages of the Bible. If you had been the only person on earth, He would have done the same... just for you. That is Love—the kind we have never known. If you are feeling empty and purposeless, it is because you need that Love.

Holy Spirit, now I have a better picture of exactly who Jesus was and what His purpose on earth was. He was sent here to save me! He was sent here to save everyone who will call upon His Name. Praises only to God! Amen.

STEP FOUR
<u>Salvation: Confession</u>

...if you confess with your mouth Jesus as LORD, and
believe in your heart that God raised Him from the dead,
you will be saved; for with the heart a person believes,
resulting in righteousness, and with the mouth he
confesses, resulting in salvation.
(Romans 10:9-10)

This is the last entry in our ABC's of Salvation teachings. You have heard why salvation is necessary, the truth of the inherent sin nature of man, and the Scriptural basis for who Christ is. I do not pretend to be an expert in theology, but I am an expert in the difference Christ can make in a life. I walked for thirty-eight years my way. I have walked for twelve years His way...and there is no comparison. My prayer is that a burning passion has been ignited in your heart from these passages. You may want to stop now, pray for the power of the Holy Spirit, and reread the three previous entries.

Don't rush this step. A commitment to Christ should always be a life-changing decision. The final step to new birth in Christ is to C=Confess your sins and confess (or profess) His Name. Most people think confession means only to speak out what you have done wrong. We also confess our belief in something. This entry's Scripture verse tells us that we must confess with our mouth that Jesus is LORD. Do you believe who He is? Are you willing to allow Him to be LORD in your life? If you aren't willing to do that, He cannot make life changes in you. Do you believe in His resurrection? He is waiting for you to call out to Him. Here is a sample prayer for you to use as you take these steps to salvation in Christ:

Jesus, I am a sinner. I have tried to do things my way and to
live my life by my own standards. I confess those sins and ask
You to take them away from me. I believe You are God's Son
sent from Heaven to redeem a lost world. I believe You died
for me and were resurrected into eternal life. Your resur-
rection is my resurrection. Today I receive my salvation, my

'new birth.' I receive Your Spirit into my spirit that I may walk in newness of life. Amen.

<u>APPLICATION</u>: If you prayed this prayer for the first time—and meant it, you are part of the family of God! Go tell someone about your decision. That will make it very real in your life. Speak to God in prayer... simple conversation. Get yourself into The Bible and begin to walk a new life!

Holy Spirit, I have made this confession of faith. Please help me to be strong in the face of temptation to return to my old ways. Help me to understand the Bible and the things of God. Amen.

CLOSING WORDS ON SALVATION

The most important decision of my life came on February 14, 1996. That Valentine's Day I gave my heart to Jesus Christ. When I prayed the words you just read, He took up residence in my heart and changed my life... forever. I am glad that God inspired me to put these salvation entries in this book. From personal experience, I know that many people have no idea what being 'saved' means—and many of those people belong to our churches. The lack of real heart-changing conversions is partly the fault of passionless teaching and an increasingly apathetic church. My prayer is that this *Transforming Journey* has changed that for you.

What Readers are saying regarding:

About Face!
By Vicki Renee Bryant

Surely God has inspired Vicki Renee Bryant to write the pages in between the covers of *ABOUT FACE!* Every Christian should read the Bible first and this book second. Vicki takes you through the steps of salvation, explains what it means to live for our LORD and Savior, and then addresses popular trends that deceive Christians today. Whether we are a new Christian or a seasoned believer, we all need to deepen our commitment to Jesus Christ. Vicki lovingly and non-judgmentally instructs us through to a victorious Christian life.

Jessie O., Brodhead, Kentucky

In *About Face!* Vicki Bryant awakened me to the fact that I was lukewarm in my relationship with the LORD. I had to turn <u>about face</u>, surrender to Him and allow Him to work in me <u>continually</u>. Vicki doesn't 'tickle your ears' with feel-good words. She makes you take a serious look at where you are in your faithful following of God.

Chris K., Warren, Michigan

Hard hitting, timely masterpiece. A must read for those who are serious about their relationship with Jesus Christ.

Deborah K., Owosso, Michigan

I have read both of Vicki Bryant's books, *ABOUT FACE!* and *FOR SUCH A TIME AS THIS... ABOUT FACE!* was especially insightful, timely and dead-on Scripturally for me at the precise time that I read it. It is strong doctrinally and is useful to any who want to find an anchor in an ever-changing Christian culture. I highly recommend both books with *FOR SUCH A TIME AS THIS...* as a devotional that has incredible timeliness to everyday life. Mrs. Bryant is a courageous woman who has sensed God's hand upon her to write under divine anointing.

Roger Van Donkelaar, Robinson, IL
Robinson Free Methodist Church

I have edited/formatted this book chapter by chapter as the author has completed each one, so I'm privileged to be the first to read it. Vicki has excellent insight into why professing Christians (the Church) are ineffective in our world as witnesses for Jesus, due to 'sitting on the fence' between good and evil, and she TELLS IT LIKE IT IS in *About Face!* She names sin and complacency for what they are in the modern day Church, but also gives direction for the eradication of both. She is straightforward in her stand that 'change is required' if believers are to live a victorious life in Christ. Whether you already know Jesus Christ as your Savior, or whether you are seeking to know Him as your Savior, I strongly recommend that you read *About Face!*

Esther D., Owosso, Michigan

We all need to hear the truth and get the most out of our relationship with God, and *About Face!* is the book which will set you on a path that will change your life forever.

Marta R., Durand, Michigan

I find Vicki's writing comparable to looking in the mirror. What do you see? If it is not Christ... more grooming is needed.

Hospice Chaplain, Beverly A., Owosso, Michigan

Vicki Bryant's book *About Face!* reminds me of my obligation as a Christian to step up and take a stand against world view morals that seem to ramble that anything is good and ok with God as long as it is done in the name of peace and love. Vicki warns us of this distorted view and points us to Scripture that tells otherwise. Hooray for Vicki to bring us back to God's basic truth!

Marie B., Sterling Heights, Michigan

Whether you are looking for a retreat speaker,
a workshop presentation or a keynote address,
Vicki Bryant brings her own unique style
and testimony to your venue.

Vicki Bryant is passionate about her faith, her witness and teaching others the joy of daily time in God's Word. Her daily devotional, *For Such a Time as This...* was released in August of 2007. The book is a result of an early morning vision on January 27, 2007. Her second book, *About Face!* was officially released in February, 2009 and is a book with basic foundational teachings on Scripture, Salvation and the Change Required for a full walk with Jesus Christ. Vicki's goal here was not to tickle ears but to teach the hard truths of subjects like the weakening Politically Correct church, Sin in the Camp, New Age Influences in the Pews, Why Believers Need the Bible's Teachings and Spiritual Warfare's Manifestations.

Vicki has a unique testimony, and didn't begin her walk with Christ until she was thirty-eight years old. With a past she is less than proud of; Vicki could hide her shame and tell no one of the difficulties she has faced. Instead, she strives to share her personal testimony from darkness into God's grace and light with others who need to know that new beginnings are absolutely possible. Are you looking for a speaker who brings humor, compassion, teaching and her own personal testimony?

Contact Vicki to discuss your upcoming event at (989) 723-8977 or via email at hishouse2006@yahoo.com